Portrait of a Young Painter

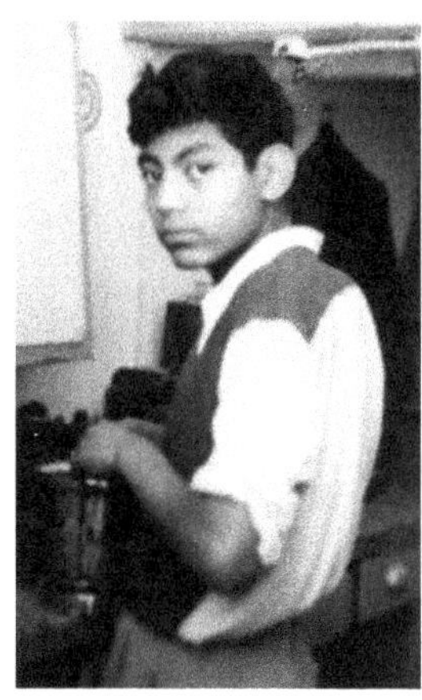

Portrait of a Young Painter

Pepe Zúñiga and Mexico City's Rebel Generation

Mary Kay Vaughan

Duke University Press
Durham and London
2015

Designed by Chris Crochetière
Typeset in Minion and Meta type by BW&A Books, Inc.

Library of Congress Cataloging-in-Publication Data
Vaughan, Mary K., 1942–
Portrait of a young painter : Pepe Zúñiga and Mexico City's rebel generation / Mary Kay Vaughan.
pages cm
Includes bibliographical references and index.
ISBN 978-0-8223-5765-0 (hardcover : alk. paper)
ISBN 978-0-8223-5781-0 (pbk. : alk. paper)
ISBN 978-0-8223-7612-5 (e-book)
1. Zúñiga, José, 1937– 2. Painters—Mexico—Biography.
3. Art—Political aspects—Mexico. I. Title.
ND259.Z787V38 2014
759.972—dc23
[B]
2014030835

Unless otherwise noted, all photographs in this book are from the personal collection of José "Pepe" Zúñiga and are used by permission.

Title page photograph: Pepe in 1952.
Cover art: Pepe Zúñiga, *Autoretrato*, 1968. Photograph: Juan Miranda Salgado.

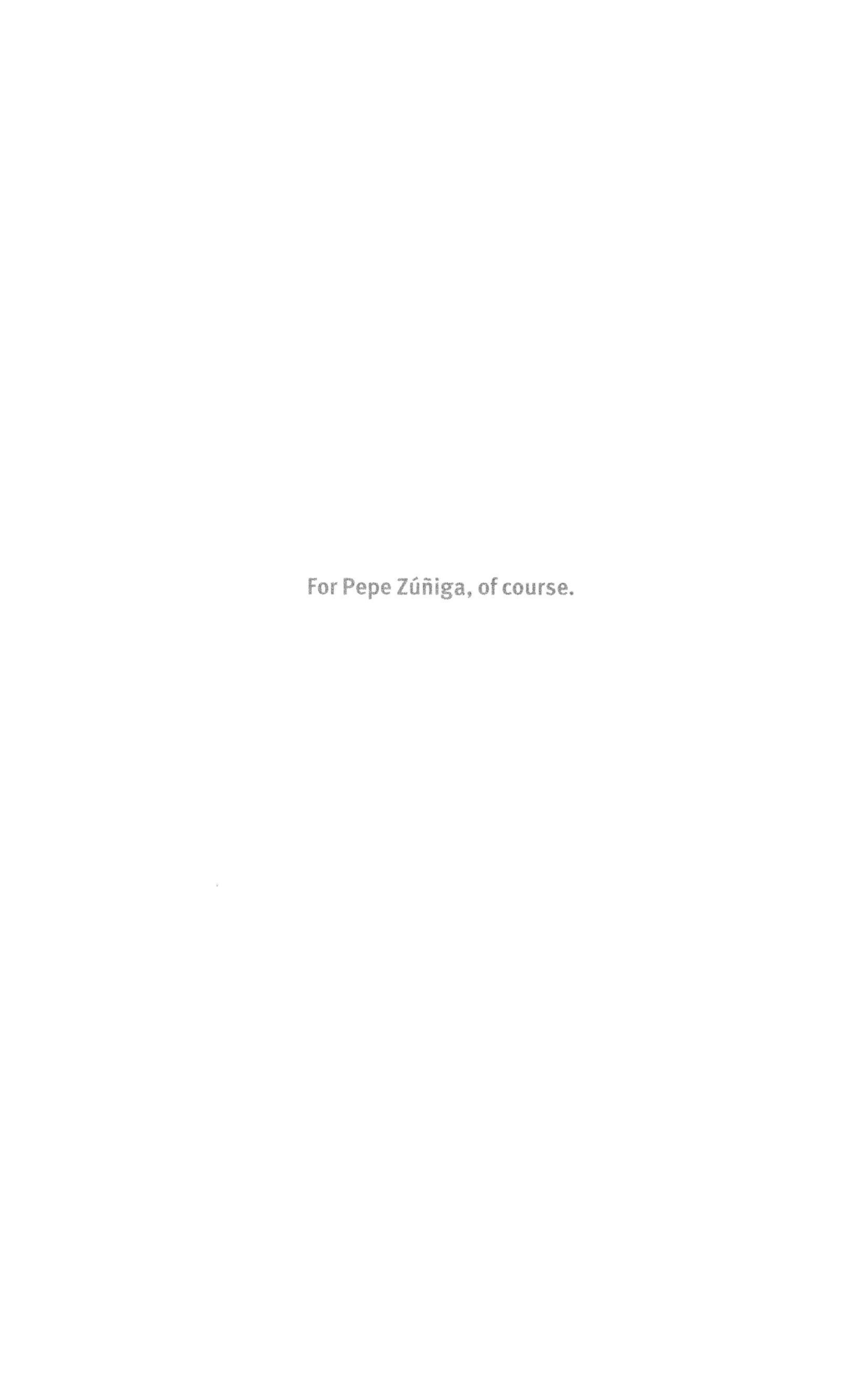

For Pepe Zúñiga, of course.

Contents

Acknowledgments

In May 1970, when the United States bombed Cambodia, students at the University of Wisconsin went wild with angry frustration. At a huge meeting on the terrace of the student union, dozens proposed different measures we might take after years of fruitless protest. One *compañera* rose to her feet and announced that the students of Northwestern University had announced their secession from the Union and declared their campus a free republic. That night at home, I asked myself, "How could this be? Was there no good, no hope in human history?" An idea came to me, very small in relation to the problem but vital to me. I recalled a life-giving historical movement I had studied. That was the crusade for education and art launched from Mexico City by José Vasconcelos in 1921 in the aftermath of the Mexican Revolution. I decided to write my dissertation on that movement. I was naive, of course. Vasconcelos's crusade was as full of contradictions as any other historical event. But it was constructive, not violent, and there began my personal quest to understand the puzzle of Mexican culture. As I have moved from Mexico City, where I studied the educational and arts policies of the 1920s, to Puebla and Sonora, where I sought to understand the implementation of educational policy as a negotiated community experience in the 1930s, back to the capital to explore the learning experience of an individual who participated in the youth rebellions of the 1960s, I have discovered ever new layers of multitextured, historically sedimented cultures that differ from region to region across classes and ethnicities and that move within different time frames. Almost always what I have learned flies in the face of what I had assumed and has required reassessment. In the course of my journey, I have met magnificent people who have helped me understand. Especially, I have had extraordinary guides and mentors in four intimate friends: Carlos Schaffer Vázquez, Epifanio López, Marco Antonio Velázquez, and before his death in 1998, Sergio de la Peña. My debt to them runs very deep.

In this project, which has lasted over ten years, I am immeasurably indebted to José "Pepe" Zúñiga, who opened his educational odyssey to me. As his story is the subject of the book, let me simply say here how exhilarating it was to learn that we shared many experiences, as likely did thousands in different parts of the globe who challenged the social, political, and artistic order in the 1960s. He took me through the legendary Colonia Guerrero, where he introduced me to childhood friends and acquaintances and to his places of memory. I learned so much from his brothers Jesús (Chucho) and Efrén and his cousins Nicolás, Susana, and Marta. Pepe took me to art exhibits and to the homes and studios of his friends from youth, distinguished painters Guillermo Ceniceros, Esther González, Juan Castaneda, Elba Garma, and Elizabeth del Castillo Velasco, the celebrated caricaturist Rogelio Naranjo, and the equally celebrated scenographer Felida Medina. I was fortunate as well to meet muralist Daniel Manrique, engraver Carlos García, and painter Pedro Banda before their deaths. I had the pleasure of interviewing the widows of Pepe's mentors, painter Benito Messeguer and journalist, art critic, and historian Antonio Rodríguez. We visited Alicia Ursuastegui, Benito's wife, in her home and his former studio in San Gerónimo. María Antoinette Fernández Moreno de Rodríguez and her son, Cuauhtémoc Rodríguez, came to Pepe's apartment in the Colonia Guerrero to talk about Don Antonio's radical political beginnings in Portugal and his professional life in Mexico City.

Evenings spent with Guillermo Ceniceros and Esther González in their home and studio in the Colonia Roma were much more than interviews: they were a communion of memories, sentiments, and opinions remarkably shared yet so enriching because of their singularities, all deepened by singing the songs of the Chilean Unidad Popular, by good wine, and by Esther's superb cooking. On several occasions, I had the pleasure of getting to know Manrique and his *compañera* and wife, Brisa Avila López. What stands out to me most in one of our encounters in Pepe's studio was his and Daniel's detailed explanation of *lucha libre* as an art form—and Brisa's insistence that it was violent. In his home in the Colonia Condesa, journalist and ecologist Ivan Restrepo provided us with a detailed history of the arrival and reception of Afro-Cuban music in Mexico City in the 1940s and 1950s, to which Pepe as a fan had much to contribute. He knew all the groups and their instruments. Ivan and I found other experiences in common for we had both been involved in international agrarian reform politics in the 1960s, he out of the Instituto Politécnico Nacional in Mexico City and I as a graduate assistant at the Land Tenure Center in Madison.

On long car rides to Oaxaca, Pepe and I discussed the radio programs he had heard, the music he loved, and the films he had seen as a child and youth. In my home in Tlalixtac, we watched countless movies and listened to many songs that conjured up his memories (and mine) and provoked extended dialogues. On occasion, Pepe's brothers Chucho and Efrén and their cousin Nicolás joined us in Oaxaca. We engaged in discussions about what did and did not happen, delighting in recalling the nitty-gritty sexuality of daily life and the moments both of rollicking humor, music, and dance and of deep wounding and sadness. We cried a lot. We walked through the streets of Carmen Alto, where these boys had been born and spent their first years; we visited Carmen Alto church, relatives, their primary school, their tiny home in a sprawling *vecindad*. We watched the procession in honor of the Virgin de la Soledad in the atrium of her church. Chucho taught me to sing "Oh María, madre mía, Oh Consuelo del mortal, amparadme y guiadme a la patria celestial."

Perhaps for a research project that has been so much fun, I should hesitate to thank the foundations that made it possible through their grants. I certainly hope their investment will be judged worthwhile by the reception of the book. So my thanks to the National Endowment for the Humanities, the Fulbright Foundation, the John Simon Guggenheim Foundation, and the History Department of the University of Maryland for having made the study possible. My deepest thanks as well to Pepe Zúñiga for having given so much and having been so patient in awaiting the book's publication.

I am grateful to Francie Chassen López, Pablo Piccato, Ivan Restrepo, and Barbara Weinstein for having read the entire manuscript and offered indispensable critiques. Commenting on parts of the manuscript and providing equally useful feedback were Ariadna Acevedo, Milada Bazant, Leandro Benmergui, Ann Blum, Gabriela Cano, Guillermo Ceniceros, María Teresa Fernández, William French, Javier García Diego, Paula Halperín, Aaron Lacayo, Clara Lida, Soledad Loaeza, Paula López Caballero, Ed McCaughan, Susana Quintanilla, Anne Rubenstein, Daniela Spenser, Alvaro Vásquez Mantecón, Pam Voekel, and Agustín Zarzosa. I want to express my thanks as well to Milada Bazant, William Beezley, Leticia Briseño and Francisco José Ruiz Cervantes, William French and Ann Blum, Clara Lida, Candelaria Ochoa, Jocelyn Olcott and John French, Abisai Pérez Zamarripa, Rogelio Ruis Ríos, Daniela Spenser, and the organizing collective of the Tepoztlán Institute in Transnational History for having invited me to present my work at the Colegio Mexiquense, the Oaxaca Seminar in Modern Mexican History, the Coloquia Internacional "Género, Cultura y Desarrollo" at the Universidad Autónoma Benito Juárez of Oaxaca, the Seminario de Historia Social at the Colegio de México, the Centro de Estudios de Género at the Universidad de Guadalajara, the Duke Labor History Conference, the Instituto de Estudios Históricos of the Universidad Autónoma de Baja California-Tijuana, the history program at the Benemérito Universidad Autónoma de Puebla, the conference *Biografía? Para Qué?* at the Centro de Investigaciones y Estudios Superiores en Antropología Social (CIESAS), and the Tepoztlán Institute of Transnational History. The two biography conferences at the Colegio Mexiquense and CIESAS grew out of our innovative group of historical biographers formed in 2011: we are Lourdes Alvarado, Milada Bazant, Francie Chassen López, Susana Quintanilla, Daniela Spenser, Ana María Suárez, and myself.

Thanks as well to my University of Maryland Latin Americanist colleagues: Barbara Weinstein (now at NYU), Daryle Williams, Karin Rosemblatt, David Sartorius, and Alejandro Cañeque. My discussions with U.S. historians James Gilbert and Saverio Giovacchini were invaluable. The then graduate students Ricardo López, Paula Halperin, Leandro Benmergui, Pablo Acuahuitl, and Shane Dillingham helped in the elaboration of the study, transcribing, translating, researching, and commenting, as did current graduate student Joshua Walker. Susanne Eineigel, Shari Orisich, and Reid Gustafson have written dissertations about Mexico City culture and youth in the twentieth century that have informed my study in unexpected, much appreciated ways.

My gratitude to Gilbert Joseph, Alan Knight, and Florencia Mallon for their consistent support of my work. While many doubted, we have broken new ground. When I started out, education was the black sheep of the historical profession. Now many historians see its importance to politics and societal and subjective formation. To the late Carlos Monsiváis I owe the germination of Pepe's biography as well as so much cultural insight that has guided me.

Many people have helped move this book into production: Mario Brena, who translated it so that Pepe could read and approve it; Tracy Goode, who chased down missing citations; photographers Carlos Cruz, Alejandro Echeverría, and Juan Miranda; and Gisela Fosado, Susan Albury, Willa Armstrong, Amy Buchanan, and Lorien Olive at Duke University Press. Above all, my debt is to Valerie Millholland, Duke's Latin American editor. Valerie had faith in me. She got to know Pepe at dinner parties in Mexico City and photo shoots of Epifanio López's cooking, which fascinates her. In this year of her retirement, I thank her on behalf of so many of us who have had the privilege of publishing with her, as it has always been a deeply personal experience. I thank her too on behalf of Latin American historians, for under her leadership Duke University Press has moved our field forward in rich, provocative, and enduring ways.

Introduction Portrait of a Young Painter

Pepe Zúñiga in Mexico City, 1943–1972

I first met Pepe José Zúñiga in 2001. Friends introduced me to him as a distinguished painter with a fascinating background—from childhood he had lived in the Colonia Guerrero, a popular barrio in central Mexico City of legendary fame for its music and dance, its nightlife, its color, its violence and violations. For many, the Colonia Guerrero was a nostalgic site, a reminder of popular artistic effervescence, of romantic intimacy, and of gritty solidarity from the 1930s into the 1950s. To live there still, as Pepe does, was proof of the strength of his roots in this barrio of tenements (*vecindades*) that had housed so many migrants pouring into Mexico City in those decades. He cut a commanding figure with his thick shock of white hair. He exuded an air of achievement and confidence: he was certainly comfortable in his skin.

My friends told me he had been director of the La Esmeralda, the school of painting and sculpture established by Diego Rivera, Frida Kahlo, and Antonio M. Ruíz in 1943 as a popular, more flexible alternative to the Academia de San Carlos. He told me of the wonderful years he had spent in Paris in the 1970s on a French government scholarship and in the 1980s completing his master's thesis at the École des Artes Decoratifs. I went to his exhibits and visited his studio in the vecindad on Soto Street—walking up two flights of uneven cement stairs, dodging hanging laundry and barking dogs. Painted canvases, piles of books and albums and old LP records covered his studio's tables and the creaking floor of faded wood. On the walls hung paintings, photos of French cathedrals, James Dean,

Elizabeth Taylor, family members, and himself with friends, lovers, and the famous—the painter Rufino Tamayo and art critic Antonio Rodríguez. The smog-filtered sunlight flooded through a large window with its view of the dusty gray leaves of trees that lined the sidewalk below. Pepe's paintings immediately captivated me—I saw them as musical pieces of undulating sensuous human forms in carefully crafted composition and color. He painted an aesthetics of sexuality—not a brutal sexuality but an affectionate one. Not one that objectified women. Rather, he painted a refined rhythm of tender, gender-neutral, erotic pleasure.

As we talked, I recognized he had a photographic memory befitting a painter. He could remember the shots, scenes, plots, and stars of every movie he had seen. He had a refined ear as well—not surprising for a man who began his career as a radio technician specializing in high fidelity and stereo sound. He remembered every song, classical composition, and much radio programming he had heard as a child. Of course, many Mexican children remember the playful songs of the cricket Cri-Cri, but those of the risqué popular singer María Luisa Landín? Only Carlos Monsiváis seemed to know more than Pepe, and it was after an evening with Carlos, reminiscing about and singing the songs of the U.S. Hit Parade they had heard on the radio in the 1950s, that Pepe asked me to write his biography. "I have a lot to say," he told me. He knew that I was searching at the time for a group of individuals, veterans of the Mexico City student movement of 1968, who would share their stories with me. Although Pepe was slightly older than most '68ers (he was born in 1937 and was no longer a student in 1968), I knew from our discussions that he had participated in the broader youth rebellion of which the 1968 protests formed a part. I decided he would be an ideal partner in my project—the more so because of his openness and willingness to discuss his emotional history. Generally considered private by Mexican men, emotional experience was precisely what I wanted to probe.

As a historian of education, I sought to understand learning experiences of a generation of Mexico City youth, particularly represented in higher education, that rebelled in the 1960s against social and political authoritarianism, hierarchies, convention, and repression. I expanded a narrow definition of education to include multiple learning sites: the family, schools, neighborhood, church, movies, radio, theater, sports, work, leisure activities, professional, social, and political associations. As the Mexican youth movement had much in common with other rebellions in Berlin, Paris, Turin, New York, Madison, Tokyo, and elsewhere, I took as a guide Norbert Elias's foundational story of the 1960s, his essay in *The*

Germans.[1] Elias suggested that rebellious middle-class and working-class youth coming of age in the 1960s shared certain experiences that influenced the contagious protest that swept the globe in 1968. Born into a world marked by war and scarcity, they moved into one of unprecedented prosperity, consumption, and mobility facilitated by market and technological development and the protection of the welfare state. Their basic needs for food, security, and protection satisfied, they could become concerned with personal meaning. Their parents, argued Elias, were more liberal and permissive with their children than their grandparents. The children shared a prolonged period of formal schooling through which they bonded in a youth culture, assisted by the proliferating mass media that catered to their angst, their exploding libidos, and their ability to spend a little money. In the postwar, Cold War context, their education was highly ideological: it promised democracy, freedom, peace, racial equality, and well-being. They moved into expanded sites of higher education with great personal, social, and political expectations. They chafed at the repressive structures that contained them, clashed with their values, and dashed their hopes.

If these were key shared factors across borders, what distinguished particular national, local, and personal experiences? What was at stake in this broad social movement was subjectivity—the cognitive, active, feeling, experiencing self. I already knew that a critical, freedom-seeking, libidinous subjectivity flourished in the Mexican youth movement. We know it from literature, testimonials and autobiography, studies of music and art movements, from analysis of gender openings and conflicts within a still very patriarchal, heteronormative society. We know it from participants' historical reflections and from accounts and analysis of transformative social relations in the festive street democracy that reigned in the summer of 1968.[2]

To this dialogue, biography can bring insight into the socializing, educational experiences that produced the subjectivities of this generation. Unlike traditional biography, new biography is less interested in a person for his or her unique contribution to history or the arts and more interested in how an individual life reflects and illuminates historical processes. New biography pushes back against cultural history's tendency to inscribe onto the individual a set of social discourses and representations already embedded in society. It probes the principle that individuals are situated "within but not imprisoned in social structures and discursive regimes."[3] What defines human beings for phenomenologist Maurice Merleau-Ponty is "the capacity of going beyond created structures in order to create others."[4] Drawing on Merleau-Ponty, Michel de Certeau, Anthony Giddens, and Andreas Reckwitz, Gabrielle Spiegel has suggested a neophenomenological approach "founded on the re-evaluation of the individual as historical subject . . . a belief in individual perception as the agent's own structure of knowledge about and action in the world—a perception mediated and perhaps constrained but not wholly controlled by the cultural scaffolding or conceptual schemes within which it takes place."[5]

We are talking about subjectivity as a condition of subjection, that is, being subjected to the power of prevailing institutions, messages, and specific events, and the individual capacity to appropriate messages and experiences intellectually, affectively, physically.[6] Biography allows us to see how individuals negotiate educational encounters. Individuals are not simply written upon by external texts: they become authors of their own text as they move through multiple experiences, bringing their accumulation of prior experiences to their interpretation of new ones.[7] Scholars usually examine a single institution (cinema, the school, the juvenile court) and deduce its messages from analysis of formal texts or programs. Few venture into the complicated field of reception, and even fewer explore how the individual appropriates and combines messages from multiple institutions, reflects, and acts upon them. Biography can bring to light a surprising heterogeneity of discourses (dominant, residual, marginal, and spatially circumscribed) that an individual encounters; the complicated ways in which he/she combines them to constitute subjectivity; and the conditions through which new, often subversive discourses emerge to become dominant, to join the polyphony, or to be relegated to the margins. Through intimate, detailed focus on one individual, biography gives us insight into the sociocultural conflicts that gnaw at established structures and conventions and can produce enormous creativity and historical change, even when that change is tempered by the strength of existing structures and conventions.[8] Of course, examination of one individual life can never achieve a level of generalization. Yet this approach to biography as educational process tackles a gamut of institutions and events that affected (in different combinations, levels of exposure, and intensity) a sector of society scholars have deemed significant for historical analysis—in this case, a generation of youth that in their decade of rebellion played a critical role in Mexico's movement toward a more democratic and pluralist politics in public and private life, in art, culture, and affairs of state.

I use this introduction to point out both the general and the specific in Pepe Zúñiga's growing-up and coming-of-age experience. First, I describe how we constructed this story. I begin by noting a discourse of self that Pepe and I likely share with many who came of age in the 1960s. How formative for us was a notion of some special intrinsic creativity we strove to realize through a combination of self-discipline, rational learning, and libidinal intensity. Pepe and I come from different countries. We are of distinct social background and gender. Yet we broadly share an affective-intellectual framework and experience. By listening to Pepe's story, I became more aware of how shaped we were by post–World War II notions of child and personality development that formed part of modernization theory and politics and how moved we were by the idea of the artistic self, promoted by the movies and neohumanism in higher education. The movies and neohumanism are much more connected in this period than scholars have noted because we are so accustomed to dividing elite from popular culture.

Pepe's memory is the major source for constructing his biography. Memory is part of one's subjectivity. It is clearly an extraction from experience.[9] I am referring here to conscious memory as an intellectualization and selection of experience. Such memory is as necessary for the constitution and day-to-day continuity of the human being as it is subject to revision, forgetting, amplification, embellishment, as well as adjustment to any particular audience. Obviously, it is not about what exactly happened—neither the historian nor the subject can entirely re-create what was once experienced. But that does not negate memory's value as a historical source. Every historical source, whether an archival document or oral reminiscence, is an interpretation of what "really" happened and becomes more so in the hands of the historian. My purpose in writing this book is not to submit Pepe's memory to discourse analysis, as Daniel James brilliantly did in his story of Doña María, the Peronist militant.[10] Rather, I explore his memory as a source for understanding his participation in historical processes and his negotiation of contradictory discourses he encountered in distinct educating sites. As he was so generous in sharing his experiences with me, I respect as well his silences and his desire not to move into print certain intimacies of his life. They do not detract from the richness of his educational narrative.

His narrative is itself an intertwining of socioeconomic process with learned discourses for interpreting that process. Pepe tells the story of a poor boy brought in 1943 from Oaxaca by his mother, a seamstress, to join his father, a tailor, in a vecindad at 17 Lerdo Street in Mexico City's Colonia Guerrero. The poor boy was determined to *superar* (overcome) his poverty, to develop his talent and skills—or, better said, his creative potential, a sacralized idea and quest he absorbed from Hollywood movies, his primary school experience, and his education at La Esmeralda painting school. His mother and father helped him, as did particular members of the extended family, benefactors, friends, and teachers and the distinguished painters and art critics he met through his experience at La Esmeralda. Pepe embellished this narrative of upward mobility with stories of marvelous encounters with the movies and radio, with popular and classical music, with the mambo, *danzón*, *lucha libre* wrestlers, James Dean, Chavela Vargas, and Celia Cruz, with sexually charged practical jokes played at family gatherings, with discourses on hygiene, with sometimes unbearable tension and exploding conflict between his parents and within the extended family, and with bitter experiences of betrayal, fraud, and cruelty in the public world of work. As he tells his story of "moving up," he weaves together residual, dominant, and emergent discourses. He appropriated messages and cultural goods which helped him to express opposition to certain values and conduct that he associated with his parents and a social environment he found to be repressive and constraining. He sought "freedom to be himself," a discourse of the late 1950s and the 1960s that was at once humanist and libidinous. In seeking his unique creative path, he also longed to "communicate" openly and freely, to express himself affectively, sexually, and in painting, to find "tenderness" and to be "tender."

As I was interested in exploring his encounter with educational sites, I used secondary materials (art, education, music, urban, sports histories, essays on popular culture, biographies of his artist friends) and primary sources (song lyrics and melodies, movies and theater productions, school textbooks, books and magazines, and newspaper reviews of his exhibits and of the spectacles he saw). An avid collector, Pepe supplied many photographs, books, catalogs, press clippings, postcards, and other memorabilia that sparked more memories and more dialogue between us, enriching and sometimes reshaping the story. Sharing these materials with him sometimes as much as sixty years after he had first experienced them amplified and sharpened recall, although such recall was necessarily marked by subsequent events and perhaps by the narrative he himself was constructing.

Filling out the story required lateral interviewing, that is, talks with surviving members of Pepe's family, with friends and neighbors from his childhood, and with distinguished artists, intellectuals, and the widows of his mentors at La Esmeralda painting school in the tumultuous 1960s.

Particularly critical for understanding his childhood were interviews with Pepe's brothers Jesús (Chucho) and Efrén. Efrén's growing-up experience was significantly different from that of his older brothers. Born in 1946, he grew up at a time when both the family and the urban society had a bit more wealth and opportunity to share. He was the only one to go to secondary, preparatory school, and the university. Unlike Pepe, he was a direct participant rather than a sympathetic onlooker in the student rebellion of 1968. By contrast, although born four years apart, Chucho (b. 1933) and Pepe (b. 1937) shared their childhood in Oaxaca, their migration to the city, and years of scarcity, struggle, and exploration in the metropolis. Pepe introduced Chucho to me as his "childhood protector" who knew "more about the family." Indeed, Chucho's narrative—earthy, unpretentious, apparently unscripted, full of his own wounds and pleasures—proved an important complement to Pepe's. As he did not plot his story as one of "moving up," Chucho's testimony served to illuminate the sometimes sanitized character of Pepe's. In the text, I register the difference in opinion between the two brothers about events and personalities when these discrepancies surged in the interviews.

We walked as well through the neighborhood. We spoke with residents who remembered things Pepe had forgotten or never known. At the huge vecindad at Lerdo 20, razed after the 1986 earthquake and now rebuilt, we chatted with Elvia "La Boogie" Martínez Figueroa, who provided rich details about the dances Pepe had enjoyed there as a child and adolescent and about the many vendors who had sold from their shops or their homes on Lerdo Street. We visited Manuel Buendía's carpentry shop he had passed every day on his way to school and reminisced with his son Juan, the current owner. We sat in the pews of the church of Santa María la Redonda Pepe had attended as a boy. We visited the Plaza Garibaldi, where family members had enjoyed so much entertainment—not just the still ubiquitous mariachi singers but the mambo of Dámaso Pérez Prado, the boleros of María Luisa Landín, the "exotic" dancing of Tongolele, and the political parodies of the comic El Palillo. As we sat at a table in the Tenampa bar, we remembered the stories about José Alfredo Jiménez and Chavela Vargas singing tragic ballads as they drank into the dawn. We looked up to read a poem of composer Pepe Guizar inscribed in a wall mural. "We would see him walking to the Martínez de La Torre market. We went to the XEW studios across the Alameda to hear him sing. They called him El Pintor Musical. We used to laugh because he wrote very macho patriotic songs like *Guadalajara!* and *Como México no hay dos!*, and he was very gay."

If biography or life history can elucidate processes at work in society that are not so immediately perceived at the macro level, these can complicate, complement, or contradict prevailing narratives.[11] When Luis González y González published his now classic microhistory *Pueblo en Vilo* in 1968, his story of San José de Gracia broke the accepted narrative of the Mexican Revolution.[12] The village of San José moved to rhythms and rules distinct from the dominant story of the prerevolutionary period as one of exploitation, land expropriation, material suffering, and religious oppression. José Zúñiga's story—while lacking the explanatory power of an entire village's history—also tells of lives removed from the prevailing historical narrative of political repression, worker and campesino resistance, sprawling poverty and state neglect that has come to dominate our understanding of Mexican history between 1940 and 1968.[13] Even though Pepe's experiences take place just blocks away from the Buena Vista railroad yards where the period's most significant labor struggle unfolded in 1957–58 and although he lived near the Puente de Nonoalco, the poverty belt (*cinturón*) made famous by Luis Buñuel's film *Los olvidados* and the prints of the Taller de Gráfica Popular, his experiences register with neither. Pepe's story should not and cannot bear the burden of a reinterpretation of Mexico City history. He could have told other stories, I could have asked other questions, and thousands in his age cohort have other memories.

Yet the experiences he relates elucidate four processes which were to some degree shared by a significant sector of youth coming of age in the 1960s. These are 1) a post–World War II mobilization for child welfare and self-development transnational in scope and in Mexico fed by political stability, economic growth, and state investment; 2) the flourishing of entertainment (particularly the mass media) in the city's public sphere that shaped the subjectivity of children as well as adults; 3) the domestication of violent masculinity related to social policy and political change, shifting economic, social, and commercial structures, and the mass media; and 4) the formation of a critical public of youth in the 1960s that catalyzed the emergence of a more democratic public sphere of political discussion, artistic expression, and entertainment after 1970. That increasingly democratic public sphere shaped and has been shaped by the opening of the political and social regimes and by movements of markets and technologies. Current scholarly trends helped me to detect and flesh out these processes as I pursued the biography of a particular individual. They in turn provided a conceptual context for interpreting Pepe's story. While each has its own separate, discrete bibliography,

Pepe's story threads them together and illuminates them in ways that macro approaches cannot. As my goal in narrating Pepe's story is to free it from extensive analytical commentary, I here lay out my understanding of these processes.

The Mobilization for Children

I detect from Pepe's story a broad didactic mobilization orchestrated by the state and private institutions on behalf of children's welfare and development. We uncover this agenda (sometimes tightly, sometimes loosely shared among dominant actors) by looking at a multiplicity of institutions and efforts—radio programming, the movies, schools, churches, clinics, health campaigns, and hospitals, toy manufacturers and vendors, producers of special foods and health enhancers (from chocolate milk to cod liver oil), parks and playgrounds, museums, juvenile courts, sports facilities and promotion, and subsidized housing. Even when social policy focused on workers, it gave special consideration to their children. New housing projects, like the Conjunto Miguel Alemán, created spaces for play and sports, and the Instituto de Seguro Social provided health care for all members' children, legitimate and natural.[14]

When Eve Kosofsky Sedgwick and Adam Frank examine images of childhood in the transition from nineteenth- to twentieth-century British literature, they note the displacement of Dickens's destitute, abandoned children by Christopher Robin, the playful boy loved, cared for, watched over, and disciplined by his nanny and his mother.[15] In Mexican popular culture, the child as Christopher Robin became visible and audible to millions of children with access to radio through the songs of the cricket Cri-Cri, broadcast every weekend from 1934 over XEW, "La Voz de América Latina desde México." It is not that the image of the destitute, abandoned child disappeared in Mexico City from discourse, the media, or the streets but rather that the loved child who delights in the adventures of Cri-Cri's animals (akin to Christopher Robin's friends Winnie the Pooh, Tigger, and Eeyore) came to occupy a central, instructive position—a kind of discursive mandate, a rush of affect, and a claim to entitlement.[16]

We may explain the mobilization for children in several ways. A post–World War I focus on child welfare became evident in pan American congresses, League of Nations meetings, and in the educational, health, and social policies of Mexico's postrevolutionary governments from 1920.[17] As Elena Jackson Albarran persuasively shows, the federal government's drive for education, intensified by the church-state struggle, privileged the child as the product of the revolution.[18] During World War II and in its immediate aftermath, the project linked to a reinvigorated transnational campaign for children's rights, articulated by the United Nations.[19] With greater technical and financial capacity, the PRI state (referring to the Partido Revolucionario Institucional) after 1940 could flesh out particular social and cultural programs to complement its embrace of a Fordist model of industrialization. This model, embellished in these years by theories of modernization and development (personal as well as social and economic), depended upon the nurturing of healthy, productive, disciplined workers and their consuming families. One can argue that the programs were insufficient and benefited only a portion of the population. But in Mexico City, with its concentration of public and private resources, critical beneficiaries of the mobilization came from broad sectors of an urban society burgeoning with migrants and animated by social peace and the promise of economic opportunity.

Most educators, including parents, sought to nurture the development of a modern subject, clean, healthy, self-disciplined, responsible in work and family life, and an enthusiastic participant in the nation's march toward progress. However, the interinstitutional matrix of socialization encouraged children to play, to imagine, and to take initiative. It prompted them to cultivate their minds, hearts, senses, and bodies, to consume increasingly available market goods, to think critically, and to seek greater affection and freedom. In other words, as Elias wrote, it allowed children and youth to focus on themselves. How widespread this sensibility was over a cross section of Mexico City youth in the 1960s we do not yet know. Current evidence for it is in the protests of youth—mostly associated with postsecondary education—who rebelled against authoritarianism, convention, and violence and in favor of greater personal and political freedom, governmental transparency, and social responsibility. While dissident youth often identified with previous struggles for collective rights of groups privileged by the Mexican revolutionary process and postrevolutionary state (organized workers, campesinos, teachers, and other government employees), rebel youth of the 1960s spoke for the common good in defense of the rights of all citizens: they called for the opening of the autocratic system of the PRI.

Several factors influenced Pepe's participation in this mobilization. If the first was location in Mexico City's center, where resources were many, location was not determinate, as we know from Oscar Lewis's study of the children of Jesús Sánchez, residents of the barrio of Tepito, adjacent to the Colonia Guerrero. Lewis saw the Sánchez children as victims of an emotionally absent father and a succession of erstwhile, inattentive stepmothers.[20] In Lewis's reading, the children drifted into a culture of violence and violation, of social and moral poverty, accessible to them in Tepito. Critical for Pepe were his migrant parents' enthusiasm and energy to struggle—in the midst of material scarcity and unsteady income—for survival and a better life. To do so, they often utilized "traditional" means for enabling "modernity"—as, for example, their extensive deployment of Oaxaca networks of family and friends to access goods, work, workers, educational opportunities, and legal assistance. In a city with little public trust, the protection and facility afforded by such networks cannot be overestimated. They were committed, vigilant parents concerned with their children's education and health. They also gave them freedom to move in a city they did not regard as particularly dangerous. They came from a provincial city that gave them tools for negotiating the metropolis. The Zúñiga family experience demonstrates the futility of reducing poverty to pathology, analyzing it exclusively in terms of monetary income, or homogenizing its social behavior across a particular physical space. One must consider the social, cultural, and affective capital with which families (of many different sorts) and individuals work and with which they engage the messages and opportunities offered by dominant institutions and processes.

Entertainment in Mexico City's Public Sphere

In the Zúñiga parents' marshaling of "traditional" means to enable "modernity," none was as spectacularly important to Pepe as his father's enthusiastic engagement of entertainment in Mexico City's public sphere. Oaxaca's public world of religious celebration, sacred and profane—the processions with their giant puppets, wind bands, and ornately clothed saints reverently carried on their pedestals, the churches' sumptuous, gold-painted altars wrapped in clouds of incense and adorned with thickets of flowers in honor of the Virgin, the Christmas posadas with their solemn pilgrimage followed by "*la hora romántica*" of song, *ponche*, and chocolate—all of these hailed the senses of sight, hearing, and smell in seductive synchronization. If they engaged body and soul in devotion, they had always engaged them in more earthly pleasures as well—increasingly in the twentieth century, in intimate romantic song and body-liberating dance. Pepe's mother, Lupe Delgado de Zúñiga, sang in church and at the horas románticas. After sacred devotion and ritual masses, his father, José

Zúñiga Sr., sponsored dances of the tango, the shimmy, and the Charleston, with music he had heard in the movies brought to life by his musician friends. In Mexico City, José Zúñiga Sr. practiced his faith in prayer at home and energetically embraced the public world of entertainment. Just a short walk from the apartment on Lerdo Street were XEW radio station, dozens of movie theaters, the lucha libre arena, boxing and bull rings, nightclubs, and burlesque and musical theaters.

Students of the public sphere in Mexico City in this period generally look at its explicitly political dimension and define it as a space for rational discussion generated by the print media. In doing so, they follow its classical theorist, Jürgen Habermas. They stress censorship in the print media. Although they may include street demonstrations as part of the political public sphere, have begun to uncover more critical press opinion in the 1950s and 1960s, and point to a diversity of publics, they have not looked at the nonprint mass media or entertainment as part of the public sphere.[21]

Habermas argued that in the bourgeois public sphere of the eighteenth and early nineteenth centuries, entertainment or what he called cultural production and commodification (literature, art, theater, and music) forged—among bourgeois men—subjectivities appropriate to rational participation in the public sphere's political realm.[22] Although he did not elaborate, such formation would refer to conduct, sentiment, sensibility, clothing, bodily habits, comportment, and the like. Seeing twentieth-century developments as destructive of rational, independent political debate, Habermas particularly singled out the mass media, a new stage of cultural commodification. Controlled by monopolies, censored, and commercialized, the media reached a public broader than the bourgeoisie but served to privatize sentiment and reason in order to promote consumption and political quiescence. The media, he argued, created disdain for and apathy toward public institutions and political life.[23]

His treatise, first published in 1962, has much in common with other pessimistic, totalizing academic critiques of those years.[24] He understood modern capitalist society and its welfare state as an interlocking network of corporate bureaucracies—the state, entrepreneurs, unions, political parties, and the mass media—that allegedly made citizens' rational intervention difficult or impossible. Subsequently, scholars, including Habermas, have pushed back against such theories of impenetrable structures and narrow interpretations of the media.[25] Indeed, in many places, television, radio, film, and the recording industry publicized the youth protests of the 1960s in ways that provoked widespread political debate and enabled discussion about, permeation of, and reaction against new discourses, behaviors, and rights.

Miriam Hansen and Jason Lovigilio, among others, have argued that mass media technologies (principally photography, cinema, radio, and recorded music) provoked sensorial, affective revolutions and enabled the creation of new, inclusive communities—national, local, and transnational.[26] The media fostered bonds of empathy and mutual recognition that razed barriers and formed the basis for political and social discussion. Further, by making private life public, they created or broadcast discourses, practices, and feelings for navigating processes of modernization—migration, urbanization, mobility, changing patterns and places of work, family life, courting and romance, fashion, consumption, and gender roles.[27] Most media from the 1930s into the 1950s were censored and didactic. They were so in pathological (consider Nazi Germany in the 1930s and early 1940s) or constructive ways, as I argue for Mexico. Despite their didactic moralizing, they necessarily contained transgressive dimensions. As Pepe's story illustrates, they presented immensely appealing sinful characters (e.g., the beautiful prostitute with the heart of gold), impure sentiments and desires relished by thousands (e.g., Agustín Lara's music), and narratives that deliberately complicated and contradicted dominant moral paradigms (e.g., *rhumberas* films).

As many illuminating works on Mexico City have argued, the media mimicked existing conduct and feeling while opening to audiences new ways of behaving and viewing themselves and each other.[28] In other words, from the 1920s into the 1950s, the media participated in the creation of publics and subjects and, indeed, a shared notion of the city they lived in.[29] In many of his writings, Carlos Monsiváis, the extraordinary analyst of the city's entertainment world, suggested the emergence of a public that was vibrant, active, increasingly conscious of itself and its engagement with urban life, yet politically disengaged and compatible with authoritarian rule. In this thesis, he might seem to have been in agreement with Habermas. Yet in the interest of his global argument, he necessarily overlooked the complexity of individual members of this public, as we shall see in the case of José Zúñiga Sr. and his wife, Lupe. And clearly he was not writing about their son Pepe or other children who grew up with this media only to rebel against the authoritarian regime. Pepe's story shows how the mass media, its messages, and technologies suggest the formation of a more critical and demanding subjectivity and a new notion of rights—quite the opposite of what Habermas predicted and more in tune with Elias's notion of a qualitative space for personal development and communication in the immediate postwar period.

As detailed in chapter 4, José Zúñiga Sr. introduced his family to many sites of entertainment. For Pepe, the most fun were the lucha libre matches, but the most memorable formative messages came from the radio, recorded and broadcast music, and the movies. His father purchased a Philco radio that played all day and into the night in the apartment that served both for family life and his workshop. Radio programming—soap operas (*radionovelas*), advice programs, and romantic music—promoted affectionately bonded and respectfully ordered families, as well as nonviolent amorous intimacy within and outside of marriage. Children's programming, particularly the songs of Cri-Cri, opened a world of fantasy, humor, and musical pleasure to the Zúñiga boys. Cri-Cri celebrated the old values of *civisimo*—work, respect, order, discipline, self-control, and liberty—that their parents taught them but in a modern paradigm of productivity that insisted upon study and cleanliness but also affection, imagination, initiative, aesthetic beauty, movement, and freedom. Cri-Cri echoed but turned the paradigm of the primary school into something more enchanting, rhythmic, and playful. Both promoted the notion of a child's right to care, love, health, personal development, and consumption. While both Cri-Cri's songs and primary school textbooks encouraged a certain privatization of sentiment within the family and among friends, the primary school, like much radio programming and Mexican Golden Age cinema, also sowed bonds of empathy among Mexicans with the potential to mitigate discrimination, abuse, and violence in social relations. Because the songs of Cri-Cri and the school programs were messages Pepe shared with thousands of other children, I devote space to examining their content in chapters 2 and 3.

These children went to the movies. As detailed in chapter 4, José Zúñiga Sr. introduced Pepe to film. From his father, Pepe grasped and internalized the Hollywood genre of success—the individual struggling to break out of poverty, confronting a world of change and challenge, not simply to have a more comfortable material life but to "become someone"—to develop one's special "talent" or "gift." Every Sunday at the movie matinee and without his father, Pepe joined a critical public of children taking in, commenting upon, and judging with their feet, cries, sighs, whistles, sniffles, and singing seemingly endless films from Mexico, Hollywood, Latin America, and Europe. Moviegoing was a distinctly international and cosmopolitan experience. Movies were increasingly made for children or for their viewing and spoke to them of their rights to self-expression, affection, and protection. We here meet such characters as Flash Gordon, model of modern virility, deploying the most advanced space technology to liberate the people of the planet Mongo from the tyranny of the emperor Ming, and Snow White, the beautiful little girl rescued by a band of kindly dwarfs from her wicked stepmother and delivered into the arms of a handsome prince. The gender dichotomy of male agency and female passivity was present but increasingly complicated. Snow White's story moved little boys like Pepe. Pepe's friends Elva Garma and Elizabeth del Castillo loved Flash Gordon, Superman, cowboy and war films. Elva recalls how she thought she could be Superman and fly right off the street![30]

What each child sees in a film or hears in a song and learns from it varies. Variation may have a lot to do with what adults allow them to see, what is available to be seen, what else is going on in their lives, and what other educational experiences engage them. Pepe's childhood formation took place in a variegated milieu of old and new educating sites. One imagines his milieu to have been a more heterogeneous mixture of the officially proper and officially risqué than that of middle-class children growing up on the city's expanding residential south side. Pepe's was certainly an environment distinct in its urban openness and diversity from the family homes with gardens and gates depicted in primary school textbooks.

Every Sunday morning before running off to the matinee, Pepe attended mass at the church of Santa María la Redonda, constructed in 1524. If his school and doctors' offices were around the corner from Santa María, the Momia nightclub faced the church. Across the street, the mariachi bands trumpeted and gay vendors sold tacos in Garibaldi Plaza, where the Teatro Margot featured Pérez Prado's mambo, condemned from the pulpit by the priest at Santa María la Redonda. Near the church as well were the *carpas*, the tent theaters full of off-color humor and political criticism, where the comedian Cantinflas got his start before becoming one of the biggest stars of Pepe's childhood. Nearby too were the prostitutes of the Calle Chueco. For Pepe and his cousin Nicolás, watching the prostitutes and the gay vendors was like going to the movies. But if these boys wished, they could climb to the rooftop of their vecindad and watch a movie being filmed in the tenement next door. More frequently Pepe and Nicolás crossed the Alameda Park to attend the live radio broadcasts at XEW studios, where they heard Pepe Guizar sing of *México bravo*, took in Agustín Lara's latest bolero dedicated to a lady of the night, and heard the mystery show *Nick Carter, Detective*. On one occasion, they saw Pedro Infante dressed up as a traffic cop to advertise his latest film, *ATM*.[31]

While many children of Pepe's age on Lerdo Street joined the lines waiting to enter the XEW studios and never missed a Sunday matinee, they likely differed in the messages they took away and the experiences they had with child-development institutions. They were not likely to be as steeped in such institutions as middle-class children living on the south side. They were for the most part of very humble background. Their parents came from the countryside, provincial cities, or generations of urban residence and worked at different things in distinct places—as independent artisans, factory workers, low-level government employees, technicians in the entertainment industry, and practitioners of *mil usos*, a lower social category of work that implied both the absence of an *oficio* (learned skill) and impermanence and was often associated with men's fondness for the bottle and their wives' need to cope with such fondness. In any case, as much as children bonded through play, mischief, sports, the movies, radio, or dance, new messages of child development together with old ones encouraged them to distinguish among themselves: between those who were clean and kempt and those who were slovenly, between those who wore store-bought clothes and those obliged to wear pants their mothers stitched, between those who got metal skates and those who had to borrow them, between those who went regularly to school and those who played hooky, between those teenage boys who pursued a skilled trade and those condemned to the work of mil usos, between children who continued on to secondary school and those who went to work after completing primary school, between those with light skin and those with darker skin, between girls focused on getting married and those who enjoyed or were coerced into more casual, often commercial sexual relations. For instance, on the block lived Lucha "La Loca," a beautiful, naive girl who reminded the children on Lerdo Street of Silvana Mangano, whom they had seen in the Italian neorealist film *Bitter Rice*. "La Loca" loved gringos and particularly their dollars. She solicited in the Alameda Park. More than once, she walked into the clinic of Dr. Luis Valiente Plascencia. After he delivered her baby, she walked out without the infant. Whatever child-development messages she had received, neither she nor her parents had likely taken them very seriously.

The Domestication of Violent Masculinity

Clearly then, the mobilization for child welfare took place within a variegated milieu, and any single child's exposure to it or parts of it depended upon specific circumstances and experiences, as did the child's internalization of its messages. One of the particular trends within this mobilization that we detect through listening to Pepe's story is the domestication of violent masculinity, the softening of masculine hardness, and the feminization of male sensibility. This I believe we can link to the Mexican student movement of 1968, for if the movement had a particular program, it was not to end the war in Vietnam, to realize a Cuban Revolution in Mexico, or to transform higher education. It was originally a movement against violence—state, police, and military violence against Mexican citizens. What animated many of its participants and grew through the experience was a joy in love. Novels, testimonials, memoirs, and theater productions expressed this sentiment significantly more than the plastic arts, where Pepe chose to express it.[32] I do not discount private acts of violence in personal relationships or public violence in the political protests of 1968 or the violence of armed groups that came out of 1968 convinced of Che Guevara's notion of foco-based revolution. But in 1968, Pepe joined throngs of young people who lined up and crowded the aisles to see the student-produced play *El cementerio de los automóviles*, in which Che Guevara symbolized love. Che was perhaps the first revolutionary hero after Christ to do so, and in the play Che is likened to Christ.

In three generations of Zúñiga men, we see a change in the *armas que portan* (the weapons they bear). Pepe's grandfather, José Zúñiga Heredia, born around 1880, carried a knife, the arm of choice for men of the popular sectors prior to the Mexican Revolution.[33] He used it for shoemaking, one of his several trades. He also drew it to defend his honor. He had the proud reputation of having killed at least one man in his barrio in Oaxaca. By no means did he invest his honor in defending the family he created: he left his wife and five children without support and went to Orizaba to form another family and engage in other amorous escapades. His son José Zúñiga Pérez (b. 1914), Pepe's father, chose as his arm a pair of scissors with which he made elegant suits for fashionable men and women in the city of Mexico. These scissors and a silver thimble cherished by his sons helped him to sustain his family. His son Pepe took as his weapon a brush with which he created paintings that expressed affectionate, tender, sexual intimacy within a framework of gender neutrality. As an adolescent, Chucho chose as his arms a pair of boxing gloves, because, like many, he believed that organized sports disciplined masculine violence. Eventually Chucho inherited his father's scissors and worked as a tailor. Their brother Efrén took up a pencil and slide rule to work as an architect.

Although today Mexican society appears enveloped in violence stemming from the drug trade and its persecution by the state, the transition in arms over three generations of Zúñiga men is no aberration. It was a social project. We can identify the processes that facilitated it. From the late nineteenth century, Mexican psychologists, employers, military officers, sociologists, novelists, hygienists, doctors, social workers, educators, journalists, Catholic activists, and sundry public intellectuals expressed concern about what they viewed as a lower-class masculinity, prone to social, political, and familial violence, irresponsibility, alcoholism, and sexually transmitted disease.[34] If in the Porfiriato, criminologists viewed this "condition" as a product of biological degeneracy and a sordid environment of poverty best isolated from decent society, the postrevolutionary state focused concerted social policy on reform and integration, health and education.[35] From the late 1930s, when a good part of the world was entering an intense and devastating period of war, Mexico began a prolonged period of demilitarization, social peace, and economic growth. In 1946, the PRI abolished its military sector. Overt and violent social conflict decreased. Such conflict had positioned organized workers for considerable material improvement. After 1940, possibilities for legal, protected employment grew, particularly in cities.

The economic model of Fordism rested on family formation and the male worker's garnering of a wage to support that family.[36] Mexico took part in .a broad trend of rising marriage rates in large Latin American countries with welfare states.[37] Criticism mounted against male domestic violence, long considered an acceptable practice.[38] Adoption, as Ann Blum has shown, increasingly focused on affective family formation rather than the use of adopted children for labor.[39] Sociophysical conditions of daily life improved for many in Mexico City so as to facilitate family life. Although the Zúñigas occupied a very small apartment in a vecindad, their access to running water, a toilet, drainage, a kitchen, and garbage collection contrasted starkly with the almost complete absence of services that made private life difficult in the popular barrios during the Porfiriato.[40] They benefited as well from the rent control law passed by the government in 1942.

Consumption, generally identified in the literature with women, engaged men as well and trended toward sentimental domestication and family responsibility. It linked to personal presentation (lotions, soaps, shampoos, clothing, hats, shoes) and to prestige (the purchase of a radio, later a TV, still later a car—and of items used by their wives such as a refrigerator or a stove). It linked particularly to entertainment. Although it suggested family responsibility, it did not necessarily demand fidelity. As Ageeth Sluis has argued, the new "modernist male subject," shaped by the beauty, health, and entertainment industries, maintained his long-standing right to "step out."[41]

As noted, for men as well as women, radio programs stressed sentiments of love, affection, and responsibility, and, in advice programs, rational resolution of disputes. School textbooks dropped their presentation of destitute children rescued by charitable rich men for representations of those diligently cared for by father and mother, who never resorted to physical punishment. Children were to learn nonviolent, affectionate parenting in their care of pets. Formally, the school banned corporal punishment. Even if Mexican film entertained with violent criminals, cowboys, and revolutionaries, the premier icons—Jorge Negrete and Pedro Infante—captured a masculinity in transition from the 1940s into the 1950s. Jorge Negrete personified authoritarian, aristocratic male privilege and bravado. He was a charming conquistador; not a family man but rather an elegant, singing Hispanic horseman ensconced in the disappeared world of the hacienda. Pedro Infante was an ordinary guy, a muscle-bound worker and athlete. For all the rural roles he played, he was quintessentially urban. He seduced many women, but he loved them tenderly and showed special care and affection toward children.[42] He was, for all his occasional outbursts of temper, a soft, vulnerable romantic and a good dad. José Zúñiga Sr. loved Negrete and thought Infante a punk. Pepe liked Pedro Infante and learned all his songs.

In the 1950s and early 1960s, Oscar Lewis articulated new trends in psychology and personality development in his focus on Jesús Sánchez's emotional abuse of his children. Octavio Paz, in *Laberinto de la soledad* (1950), psychologized the Mexican man as enclosed in deep insecurity, prone to uncontrollable drunken eruptions of violence, and not mature enough to embrace a universal humanism. Psychologist Erich Fromm, who made his home in Cuernavaca, confirmed a patriarchal paradigm in his *Art of Loving*, published in 1956: the mother owed unconditional love, while the father was to guide the child into the ways of the world. However, he called for a more emotionally open and mature masculinity.[43] These intellectuals gave voice to an ongoing, multifaceted, moral and social project.

The same critique came through in the films Pepe Zúñiga watched as an adolescent in the 1950s while he trained and worked as a radio technician. The Hollywood bildungsroman shifted from the rags-to-riches stories that had animated Jose Zúñiga Sr. to youths caught up in affective turbulence, struggling to express their inner feelings and sense of justice, pitted against male adults and fathers who were closed, cold, corrupt, often violent, and emotionally clueless. The characters played by James Dean in *Rebel without a Cause* and *East of Eden*, by Marlon Brando in *On the Waterfront*, and by John Kerr in *Tea and Sympathy* resolved their conflicts in tender—if precarious and fleeting—solidarity with deeply sympathetic women and sometimes with one another. Indeed, *ternura* (tenderness), the word Gustavo Sainz chooses for the emotional awakening and subduing of his wild delinquent hero *Compadre Lobo*, seems an emerging sentiment among Mexico City youth from the late 1950s.[44]

Tenderness could move in many directions—companionate marriage or partnerships, spontaneous love affairs, homosexual intimacy, platonic friendships, literary or artistic creativity. Tenderness does not necessarily spell the end of patriarchy: most of its expression stayed within this frame well into the 1970s. Rather, tenderness speaks to a certain feminization of male sensibility which punctuates Pepe's story. By linking tenderness to female sensibility, I do not wish to essentialize femininity but rather call attention to the images, symbols, and discourses of the time that played with the Enlightenment dichotomy between male rationality and female sentiment. From the late nineteenth century and particularly from the initial years of postrevolutionary government, the elite preoccupation with violent and dissolute masculinity had its counterpart in assigning responsibility and affective care to the mother.[45] Whether we are listening to a song from Cri-Cri, watching Sara García in *Cuando los niños se van* or Bambi's mother in the movies, or beholding in a Mexican mural or official sculpture the essential mother—full-bodied, nursing a baby, protecting her children, washing clothes, making tortillas—the spectator learns that the mother was the source of care and tenderness toward now cherished children, a tenderness intended to permeate male as well as female children.

The ideal twentieth-century Mexican mother was more than tender. She was also responsible for her family's well-being and her children's health, education, discipline, and future, duties assigned to her by and shared with a somewhat "feminized" state (consider its nurturing, curing, and educating dimensions). In this endeavor, she assumed some tasks historically assigned to men. Although such active motherhood has deep historical roots in Mexico, mid-twentieth-century discourse and practice reified and amplified it. A social type emerged in popular culture in these years. La Borola, heroine of the *Familia Burrón* comic series; *La Bartola*, of Chava Flores's song; and *La Patita*, of Gabilondo Soler's Cri-Cri were all energetic promoters and protectors of their families and, in the case of La Bartola and La Patita, were hampered by irresponsible husbands.

As noted in chapters 5 and 6, Pepe's mother, Lupe Zúñiga, was ferociously responsible. It was she who struggled in the public world of commerce to make ends meet. It was she who stitched the children's clothes, made good meals out of little, found the children doctors, dentists, and barbers, and fed them nasty cod liver oil. She assumed responsibility for their formal education and job training. Supremely responsible, she was not very tender. Her violent streak will immediately strike the reader. Her children accepted it as part of her service in defense of their education, her family, and herself, for in Pepe's opinion, his father and his father's female relatives abused her.

Pepe was more critical of his father's violence. Pepe's father was the direct source and object of the boy's love. It was José Zúñiga Sr. who taught Pepe how to see the movies. Although he had only three years of formal schooling, José Zúñiga Sr. was a connoisseur of cinema, a maestro and student of exquisite sensibility and perception. Particularly because he had grown up with silent film, he understood the camera's affective deployment to highlight the aesthetic or athletic plasticity, the emotion, the subtle sexuality of the human body and face. It was his perception of cinema that informed his impressive, seductive self-presentation and his son's artistic sensibility. Cinema, treated by U.S. film studies scholars as the genre of female sentiment, formed and affected both Pepe and his father. And in moments of deep despondence outside of cinema, it was often Pepe's father who consoled him.

But his father could also be hard and distant, occasionally abusive and violent toward his wife and children, financially and morally irresponsible, and passive in the face of the aggression his mother and sisters showed toward Lupe. He also insisted in a traditional manner that his son follow him into the tailor's trade, a position Pepe rejected with his mother's support. Multiple messages appropriated from school, the movies, radio programs, and daily life informed the son's critique of his father. In it, Pepe identified with his mother and with the abused women and children he had seen in the movies. Against what he perceived to be negative elements in his father's character, he rebelled as a teenager and a young man—identifying, as did many of his friends, with the iconic

James Dean, the misunderstood, emotionally deprived adolescent rebel in search of love, recognition, and his own voice.

From a Critical Public of Youth to a More Democratic Public Sphere

Shortly after he embraced James Dean and purchased readily available Dean paraphernalia—a red sweater and a red vest (he could not afford the jacket)—Pepe signed up for an evening class in drawing at the Esmeralda painting school on San Fernando Street in the Colonia Guerrero. It was the mission of his teacher, the painter Benito Messeguer, to encourage the artist in each of his students—mostly young men of modest background who worked in the day. He had them read the biographies of famous painters who had painstakingly struggled to discover and express their inner soul. In recent years, Pepe had drawn the portraits of James Dean and Marlon Brando, of Elizabeth Taylor and Grace Kelly. Now in night class, Messeguer took note of his portrait of the Esmeralda model Timoteo. In its expressive power, Messeguer told him, the painting reminded him of José Clemente Orozco, about whom Pepe Zúñiga knew very little.

Pepe continued working as a radio technician, taking night classes until the milieu completely absorbed him and he entered the degree-granting day program. Through the Esmeralda, Pepe joined and participated in a new critical public of youth in Mexico City, a diverse group mostly concentrated in postsecondary education that began to take shape at the end of the 1950s. We now know a great deal about this movement. We generally learn about one of its several dimensions—in politics, art, literature and poetry, music, theater, or hippy-inspired counterculture. In different degrees, these overlapped in the lives of participants. The movement is usually defined as middle class. The term is vague and underestimates the presence of hundreds who had joined the middle class in these years of economic growth or gained access to it through higher education. It excludes participants from the popular sectors—among them, the militant students of the vocational schools and many rock musicians.[46] Overall, this public was predominantly male with a significant, growing female presence that raised gender questions at the level of practice and everyday life but not yet at the level of politics, theory, or analytical reflection.[47] Reaching back to the late 1950s and spilling into the 1970s, the new public included minigenerations. Pepe belonged to the early wave raised on radio and the movies. Those just a few years younger had watched more television. Pepe was out of school and struggling to establish his career as a painter when students took to the streets in 1968. Many of the youth who undertook radical activity in politics and the arts in the 1970s were barely in preparatory school in 1968.

Further, the movement was not sui generis. Its critique developed in dialogue with extensive consumption of national and transnational cultural goods and information and with more seasoned adult mentors. It likely would not have reached the drama and political impact it achieved had it not been fed by a very public quarrel within the ruling PRI, as ex-president Lázaro Cárdenas formed the Movimiento de Liberación Nacional in support of the Cuban Revolution and the party's powerful conservative faction recoiled. The tension fed the communicative and political opening, its effervescence, and its repression.

What does Pepe Zúñiga's experience tell us about this critical public information? His story, related in chapters 7, 8, and 9, tells less about the political actions of 1968 and more about a prior period of neohumanism—a transnationally shared humanism that permeated the classrooms, workshops, corridors, campuses, theaters, and galleries associated with the vastly expanded sphere of higher education in Mexico City—particularly the art schools and the national university. It was a critical humanism, full of existential angst in a world threatened by nuclear war, perplexed by capitalist materialism and growing technocratization (much as Habermas presented it in 1962). It was a humanism equally disillusioned by Stalinism in the socialist world and alarmed by colonial violence being perpetrated against people of color in search of their liberation. It was full of sociopolitical criticism, whether it was to subvert the stultifying censorship of entertainment imposed by Uruchurtu, the mayor of Mexico City, to marvel at the Cuban Revolution as a new possibility for the redemption of the oppressed, to fault the Mexican government for revolutionary promises unfulfilled, or to insist on pushing the limits of press censorship. It was rebellious—in painting, José Luis Cuevas, Juan Soriano, Mathias Goeritz, Lilia Carillo, and Manuel Felguérez from the early 1950s led the Ruptura, declaring war against the Mexican school of social realist painting.[48] Pepe's teachers at La Esmeralda, a redoubt of the Mexican school, encouraged individual expression as did new theater and literary movements. In psychic matters, Alejandro Jodorowsky's Teatro Pánico staged shattering therapy sessions in schools and cafés to engage young spectators in what they did not want to see for the sake of their own liberation from society's constraints and distortions.[49] It was spiritual—moved by Bach's masses, the new vernacular Misa Criolla from Argentina and Missa Luba from the Congo, and Paolini's film *The Gospel according to St. Matthew.* The music of the Beatles captured its libidinal exuberance, its exhilarating embrace of freedom and experimentation and sense of generational uniqueness, for the Beatles were a totally new sound.

It was a cosmopolitan world, as Carlos Monsiváis eloquently described it. For Monsiváis, its epicenter was the new campus of the National University on the far south side of the city.[50] In the 1930s the university had held out in favor of freedom of thought against pressure from the government and the labor leader Vicente Lombardo Toledano to submit to a singular social-political agenda. In the 1960s that independence bore fruit. The new campus, with its modernist architecture and wide open spaces, became a place for critical thought, international exchange, and vanguards of all sorts. It was a site from which came the new word (magazines like *La Revista de la Universidad de Mexico*); new sounds (stereo sound recordings of classical music and jazz broadcast over Radio Universidad); new visions (art exhibits, cine clubs, and experimental theater). We explore these through Pepe's experience in the city's center, where theaters debuted the works of young playwrights and directors Hector Azar, Juan Ibañez, and Julio Castillo with stunningly expressive student actors and haunting scenography. Pepe took in the new cinema—Fellini, Pasolini, Bergman—at downtown movie houses or the cine club of the Instituto Politécnico Nacional closer to his neighborhood. He was certainly not alone here. The major art schools, La Esmeralda and the Academia de San Carlos, were located in the center, and here the young painters, sculptors, and graphic artists wove an intoxicating milieu of creativity, questioning, and revelry.

As much as it was a moment of cosmopolitan awakening, it was also an experience of learning more about Mexico. Exposés of Mexican poverty, injustice, and official corruption proliferated. In 1962 Carlos Fuentes published *The Death of Artemio Cruz*, reinterpreting the Mexican Revolution not as a movement of liberation accomplished by a benevolent state but through the life of an excessively corrupt official who enriched himself at the expense of society. In 1964 Fondo de Cultura Económica published the Spanish edition of Oscar Lewis's *Children of Sanchez*. His shockingly detailed exposure of urban poverty in the barrio of Tepito elicited enormous public response and sold out immediately.[51] In 1965, UNAM professor Pablo González Casanova published his iconic critique *Democracy in Mexico*. Rodolfo Stavenhagen's key essays on sociology and underdevelopment appeared in *El Día* in June 1965. Fernando Benítez began to publish his culturally affirmative and politically denunciatory series *Los indios de México*.[52] In 1962 Benítez, always a daring journalist, brought his *México en la Cultura*, the repressed cultural supplement of the newspaper *Novedades*, to *Siempre!*, the decade's most enduring magazine of plural political and cultural opinion.[53] In 1961, in the aftermath of protests against the U.S.-backed invasion of Cuba, the government permitted the publication of the more radical magazine *Política*. It enjoyed an avid readership until it shut down in 1967, in part because the government paper monopoly would not supply it.

Journalist and art historian Antonio Rodríguez published articles in *Siempre!* detailing the disastrous results of agrarian reform in the henequen industry in Yucatán. Introduced to Pepe by Benito Messeguer, Rodríguez became a mentor. He gave Pepe his articles and his books and secured him exhibiting opportunities. Rodríguez was one of several distinguished figures connecting Pepe to a broader world of art, history, and politics and one of many older professors, artists, and intellectuals delighted to share their politics, art, literature, and music with open and eager youth. Together they constituted the new critical public. In the effervescence of the period, hierarchies held and dissolved at the same time in a creative exuberance that profoundly marked the subjectivity of youth. Pepe, in particular, found in this communicative network of peers and mentors a trust and confidence that had often eluded him in the world of work. In this network, he learned new languages, altering his sense of self and his possibilities.

Long ashamed of his dark Oaxacan skin and enamored of modern urban ways, Pepe learned the value of pre-Colombian civilization (aesthetic and grand) and contemporary indigenous culture (artistic, culturally "authentic," unjustly neglected) through the high modernist language of his mentors and teachers—Antonio Rodríguez, Benito Messeguer, sculptor Francisco Zúñiga, and painter Raul Anguiano. In 1964 he joined Anguiano's team, one of many made up of scores of young artists led by established painters and sculptors executing murals, walls, maps, and archaeological replicas for the new Museum of Anthropology. For all, it was a profound learning experience creating a new dimension of self-identity, linking their youthful energy and search for artistic freedom with an overwhelming diversity of Mesoamerican aesthetic expression about which they had known little or nothing. Intellectuals have treated the museum's construction and design critically—in part, because state repression of the 1968 protests came on the heels of its opening in 1964 and made it vulnerable to scathing critiques of cultural expropriation and popular manipulation.[54] But for the young artists who worked to bring it to life, the many artists and scholars who would use it as a source for their work, and thousands upon thousands of its visitors, it was much more than the monument of an authoritarian state.

The young painters at the Museo de Antropología created there a space linked to others (cafés, theaters, galleries, *pánicos*, private studios, and their professors' homes and apartments) to foster critical dialogue and cultural experimentation. This new extended space constructed itself in varying degrees against society and against the state, in part because its critique led it into opposition and in part because the government and some sectors of society reacted against it.[55] As Pepe remembers, students were badly seen and likely to be picked up by the police on any pretext. At the unconventional fashions (long hair and beards for men, miniskirts for women, peasant garb and sandals) and behavior (new dances, marijuana smoking, new romantic activity, insolence toward authority), the government, the press, fellow citizens, and many parents recoiled. After all, they had provided these children with every advantage to become healthy, productive, compliant adults. Pepe's father could not figure out why he wanted to become an artist, associated as that profession was with irresponsibility, poverty, drunkenness, and homosexuality. Pepe could resist his father's opposition because his own critical public affirmed his choice. State anxiety produced police raids and repression that in turn fueled youth's defiance, experimentation, and solidarity.

But the understandable critique of state repression tended to minimize the degree to which the government had made the rebellion possible through its social and cultural policies and its own internal conflicts. It had constructed the expanded educational system that was virtually tuition free. Between 1942 and 1965, enrollments at UNAM and the Instituto Politécnico Nacional had quadrupled, from 27,059 students to 115,523.[56] Its funds had built or refurbished the theaters where young directors and actors staged experimental works for other students admitted at discount rates. It had subsidized the publication of new literature. In its art galleries and competitions, Pepe Zúñiga and his friends—boys and some girls from modest backgrounds with no social, political, or cultural connections except those forged with their professors—got their first opportunities to exhibit.

Youth also expressed a certain disdain toward capitalism, technology, and markets. Pepe read and took to heart the treatise of Herbert Read, *Cartas a un joven pintor*, in which the English critic defined the artist as a solitary genius struggling to find "a new land," discovering new symbols to express his emotions, and "widening the space of coherent consciousness in a world in which the majority of our civilization [are] alienated beings, slaves of the machine, robots in a demolished land, deprived of the joy of creation."[57] Pepe's professors, who held teaching jobs in public institutions and public works contracts, suggested to their students that to produce art for commercial purposes was contaminating and corrupt. They seemed not to consider their own dependence on a state they criticized as corrupt. Further, perhaps because young people in higher education and their mentors made a distinction between high-brow and low-brow consumption, they seemed reluctant to recognize how much they participated in material consumption—particularly in the exploding market for transnationally shared cultural goods in the form of books, magazines, music, and film developed through new market-based communications technologies—stereo and FM sound, the LP record, the transistor radio, the paperback book, the television, and the jet plane.[58] Along with youth, an expanded middle and upper class enlarged the market for cultural goods and helped to explain the new art galleries and exhibiting opportunities that opened for Pepe and his friends. In fact, in the 1960s, state largesse, new prosperity, and proliferating markets pegged to innovative and deepening sensorial technologies catalyzed the social movements that challenged political, social, and aesthetic authority.

As this book treats the education of a young painter, its narrative ends in 1972 with Pepe's departure for Paris on a French government scholarship. Yet the major argument of this biography, that of a freedom-seeking subjectivity animating Pepe and the youth movement of the 1960s, remains abstract unless we examine its impact on the subsequent period. The student protests of 1968 and the broader critical public of the 1960s spoke for the common good (not a special corporate group within society) and demanded a fundamental change in authoritarian, repressive, corrupt politics at the level of the state, society, and private life. They did not immediately nor did they fully achieve these goals. Nonetheless, they catalyzed the expansion, liberalization, and diversification of political, social, and cultural opinion in the public sphere that worked in tandem with the opening of the political system and social relations after 1970. Not fully liberated from the behaviors and conventions they decried, the rebels of the 1960s nonetheless contributed to a transformation that has necessarily engaged subsequent generations and a much broader Mexico City public. Propelling it have been major events: the collapse of the Fordist import-substitution development model in 1982 and the introduction of neoliberal economics and politics; the earthquake of 1985, which devastated the central city; the AIDS epidemic of the 1980s and 1990s; the victory of the Partido Revolucionario Democrático over the PRI in Federal

District elections in 1997; and the defeat of the PRI at the national level in 2000. From the 1990s full-blown globalization and a communications revolution, similar to but very different from the revolutions of the 1960s, have further transformed the public sphere.

In effect, the classically Habermasian bourgeois public sphere conducive to critical exchange and rational debate that has come to operate in Mexico City owes much to the 1960s movement. It is a far more inclusive, democratic, and diverse sphere than that described by Habermas for the eighteenth and nineteenth centuries. It includes the mass media and ironically grew out of the media Habermas so deplored in 1962 for their alleged privatization of sentiment and curtailment of interest in public life and politics. Further, the public sphere opened with permission, guidance, and funding from the PRI state whose rule it critiqued and undermined. Today, the vigorous state-society dialogue sustained in Mexico City's public sphere translates into citizen participation and policy that capitalizes upon globalization's positive dimensions and helps to mitigate some of its harsher aspects. If it is a city of greater economic inequality, it is one of diverse publics, conscious of their right to speak, object, and propose.

In the final chapter of the book, we explore Pepe Zúñiga's mature painting, that of his friends, and his age cohort as part of Mexico City's public sphere in the 1980s and 1990s. We explore how art has reflected and contributed to changing social relations, state-society relations, and the recognition of basic individual rights within a state of law. We do so with particular focus on Pepe's representations of the body as the repository for affection, sexuality, rational reflection, and solidarity. We look at his paintings, their content and composition, their reception, and their place of exhibition to understand how intimate subjectivity has linked to changes in the public sphere and politics in Mexico City.

1. Lupe's Voice

Today the city of Oaxaca is a magical place for the visitor. It is a polished jewel of aesthetics, old and new, with its splendid colonial churches and contemporary art galleries. Calling the public to fiesta, dancing giants lead parades of horns and drums, women in native dress balancing baskets of fruit and candies on their heads, and boys blasting firecrackers. Cafés open onto the shaded *zócalo*, the central plaza where couples perform the graceful *danzón* to the music of wind bands and marimbas. In the 1930s it was a small town wracked by earthquakes, epidemic disease, and class and racial divisions. Its aristocracy might claim a noble Zapotec heritage but took pride in its white skin and its control over native communities. Religion papered over social distinctions as life revolved around Catholic celebration, recently fortified by the modernizing campaigns of priests and women religious.[1]

In the prosperous years of the Porfiriato (1876–1910), the city center had taken on a Parisian veneer—the transformation of its plazas into gardens, the placement of wrought-iron benches on the zócalo, the introduction of art nouveau touches to the refurbished cathedral. But Oaxaca remained a preindustrial town of artisan producers supplied by indigenous farmers and pastors from surrounding villages in the central valley and high sierras. The weavers and candy makers lived in the barrio of Xochimilco, where the click-clack of the looms can still be heard like the clopping of horses on cobblestone. Tanners and leather workers lived in Jalatlaco, shawl (*rebozo*) and hatmakers in Los Principes, the pork butch-

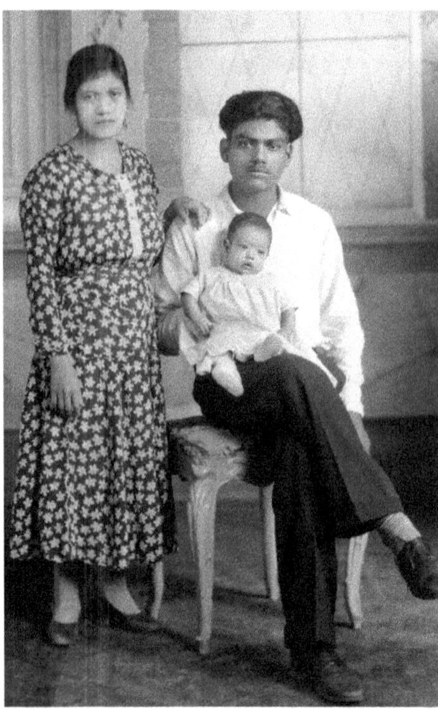

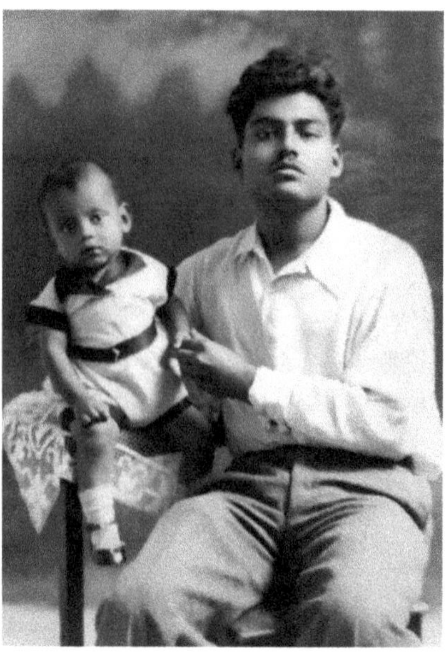

(*left*) Figure 1.1. Lupe, José, and Chuco. Black-and-white photograph, 1934.
(*right*) Figure 1.2. José and Pepe. Black-and-white photograph, 1938.

ers in Coyula. Each had their *gremio* (guild), and each gremio had its saints and feast days replete with masses, parades, and partying. Through the culture of devotion ran a deep undercurrent of pleasure and of violence, fed by alcohol, rancor, raw sexuality, and the exercise of power.[2]

Here in 1933, José Zúñiga Pérez and Guadalupe Delgado Olivera married. He was a nineteen-year-old tailor. She was a seamstress of twenty-four. They had known each other since childhood, for they had lived on the same block of Cosijopi Street in the barrio of Carmen Alto. They danced together as youths—to the new rhythms of the foxtrot, tango, and shimmy—at the parties José organized with his tailor friends. Shortly after they married, Guadalupe gave birth to Jesús. They called him Chucho. Very soon, she had another baby they named José. He was white. With affection, almost adoration, they called him "El Guero," the light-skinned one. He had a marvelous sense of rhythm, always prancing around on his unsteady baby legs, even as he was dying of dysentery. Lupe was pregnant with another child when they buried him. In 1937, she gave birth to a dark-skinned infant. They named him José after the departed angel and after his father. They called him Pepe.

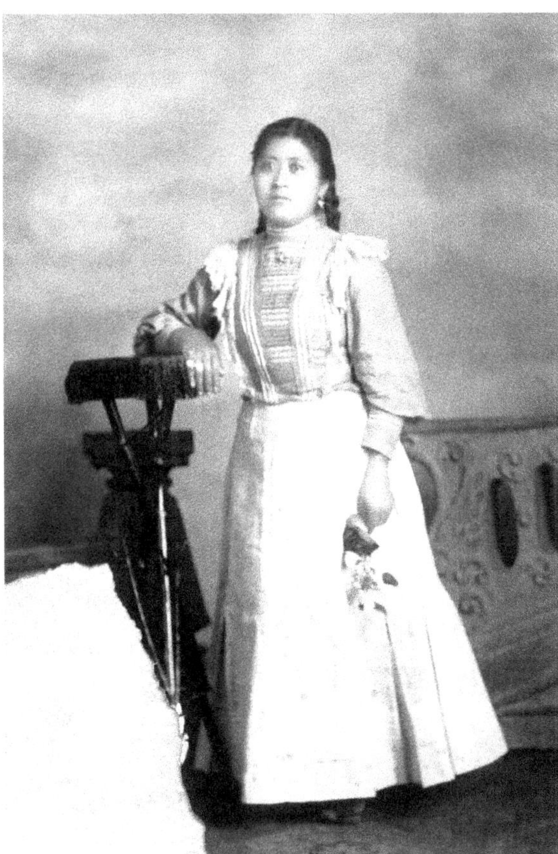

Figure 1.3. Clotilde Ortiz Mendoza. Sepia photograph, ca. 1922.

In the photographs, Lupe and José posed with Chucho, and José later had his picture taken with Pepe. "Photography was all the rage. Oaxaca had many studios," Pepe reflected years later. "My father loved to have his picture taken. Not my mother. We will not see many photographs of my mother."

A short while later, José Zúñiga Pérez left for Mexico City to create a new life for himself and his family. He left Lupe to care for the children in a small apartment in a big *vecindad* owned by Don Amado Alcázar, on Porfirio Díaz Street in Carmen Alto. Lupe worked in a factory producing mica for the Allied war effort. At home in the afternoon and evenings, she sewed dresses for clients and napkins for the Leyva weaving clan, to which she was related. She and the children lived with Arcadia Mendoza and Clotilde Ortiz Mendoza. Clotilde and Lupe's deceased father, Man-

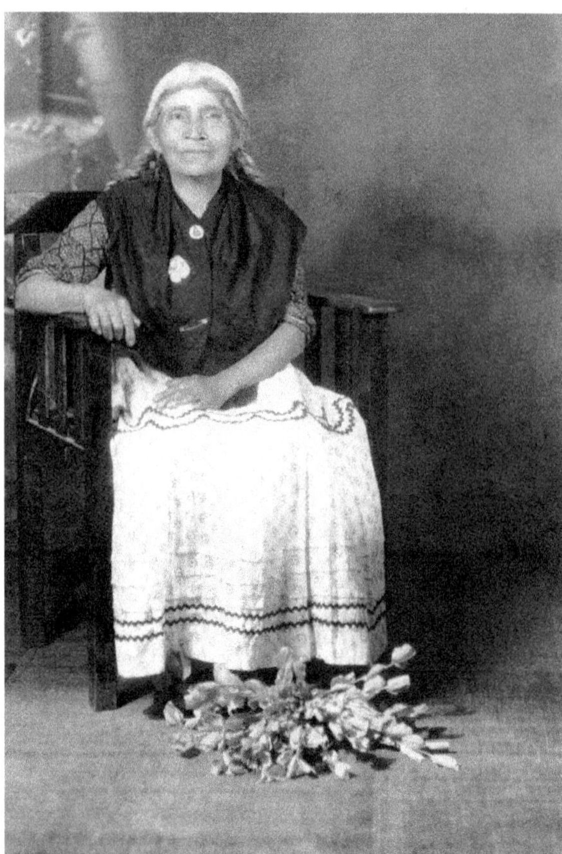

Figure 1.4. Arcadia Mendoza. Black-and-white photograph, ca. 1935.

uel, were brother and sister. They were Arcadia's natural children, fathered by different men. Mother and daughter eked out a living preparing chocolate in the patio. They covered their bodies in rebozos, skirts, and aprons. They braided their hair. In these pictures, Clotilde's likely taken in the early 1920s when she was young, we note the bouquet of artificial flowers that hid Tía Arcadia's bare feet.

The first memories of Pepe and Chucho are of their mother's voice. She sang solo in the cathedral and in the choir at Carmen Alto church. Her boys can still hear her clear, rich soprano timbre breaking the silence of the sacred vaults. She sang as well in the churches of Santo Domingo, Guadalupe, San José, and the Virgin de la Soledad. She knew Latin and how to read notes. She learned all the litanies and prayers and was frequently called upon to recite them at wakes, funerals, and, of course, the Christmas posadas.

How she had learned the sacred texts is not clear. Her mother, Pastora, had died when she was young. Her father, Manuel, was a brute of a man given to drink and fornication (he is said to have died drunk over a woman's body). Likely, his half-sister, the devout Clotilde, had played a role. Raised in a convent, she left as a young woman to care for Lupe and Lupe's brother, Manuel Jr., upon their mother's death. She went to mass every day, and in their small quarters she maintained an elaborate altar from floor to ceiling for the virgins of Guadalupe, Juquila, La Soledad, and Las Carmenes. On holy days she adorned the altar with flowers and illuminated the virgin mothers with candles. She rigorously oversaw the religious training of Chucho. She took him to catechism classes and to mass every Sunday. At home, in the afternoon they prayed the rosary. During Holy Week, at the Church of San José or the Virgin de la Soledad, she obliged him to get down on his knees and pray the rosary at all twelve stations depicting the anguish of Christ's crucifixion. She pinched him to keep him awake. "*Andale, hijo,*" she nudged him, "*Aquí está el Señor!*"[3] She kept strict watch during that sacred week: no one could go out except to church. At three o'clock on Good Friday afternoon, when Christ died, they all fell to their knees and prayed.[4]

Alone at her sewing machine, Lupe sang the romantic songs of the day—"Verdad amarga," composed by Consuelo Velázquez, and "Jurame," written by María Grever, and María Luisa Landín's interpretations of "Que te vaya bien" and "Amor perdido." She had learned them from listening to Don Amado Alcázar's radio and at the dances her husband, José, had organized. She learned them also during *la hora romántica* of the posadas. She sang them there accompanied on guitar by the young Manuel Santaella while the children ate *dulces* (candies) and drank chocolate. These were songs of great feeling, of love lost and betrayed, of deception and aching solitude. They were reminiscent of the deep melancholy of Oaxaca's nineteenth-century waltzes—"La Sandunga," "La Llorona," and "Dios Nunca Muere"—but without their mystical solemnity. They went at a faster clip, sung to lively percussion and melodious brass. One of Lupe's favorites was "Que te vaya bien," sung by María Luisa Landín:

> I don't care if you love someone and scorn me.
> I don't care if you leave me crying for your love.
> You're free to love in life and I don't blame you
> If your heart cannot love me as I love you.
> I know it's in vain to ask you to return,
> Because I know you always deceived me declaring your love,

And I don't want to fool you or hurt your life,
I am sincere and know how to forgive you without bitterness,
Stay happy on your path! Stay well, stay well![5]

As Lupe sang them at her sewing machine, she cried, pausing at times to wipe her eyes. Much later in his life, Pepe called these "*canciones de arrastradas*"—songs in which the woman begs the *macho* to command, to drag her by her hair across the floor. "'Hit me,' they say," he reminisced. "And they don't just speak of submission. They declare that power is at another level, not in them. They are songs of misery and the *arrabal*."[6] Yet as María Luisa Landín reminded her public, "Anyone can lose in love, a man as well as a woman." Men and women composed and interpreted these songs. Mellow and poetic, they lightened the devastation of betrayal and abandonment to capture the poignancy of feeling. In fact, Pepe loves them. They bring tears to his eyes. "Mama sang and cried because she had a sexual and affective longing for my father." Not only was he physically absent, she felt his emotional distance as well. Even if his father was dark skinned and she white, reflected Pepe, it was he who was handsome. She was plain, marked by the smallpox she had suffered as a child. She knew how popular he was among both men and women. She thought, recalled her son Chucho, he had had at least two lovers in Oaxaca after they had married, and she could only imagine what he was doing in Mexico City.[7]

According to Chucho, she sang from pure grief. It was his grief as well. Behind Lupe's sadness was a sordid story that she would later tell him.[8] She had fallen in love with the handsome, charismatic José, but he had seduced her in an act of vengeance ordered by his mother. José was the only son and youngest child of Petrona Pérez, abandoned by José Zúñiga Heredia, a tall, commanding *galán*, who had left her with five children.[9] He enjoyed many women and moved to Orizaba, Veracruz, where he created another family. Petrona supported her children by taking in laundry, ironing, and making firecrackers, always in demand for the endless rounds of religious celebrations in Oaxaca. We see her in the photograph taken in 1921 with her daughter María, then pregnant, and her barefoot son José. She posed as if reading a book to cover her eye blinded by smallpox. She could not read.

She doted on her son and depended on him. When he reached the age of twelve, she took him to apprentice with a tailor: "Turn this meat into bones," she said. "By this," her grandson Pepe recalled, "she meant to say 'Work this kid to death so he learns something.'" When he was nineteen, according to Chucho's story, Petrona asked him to avenge the family's

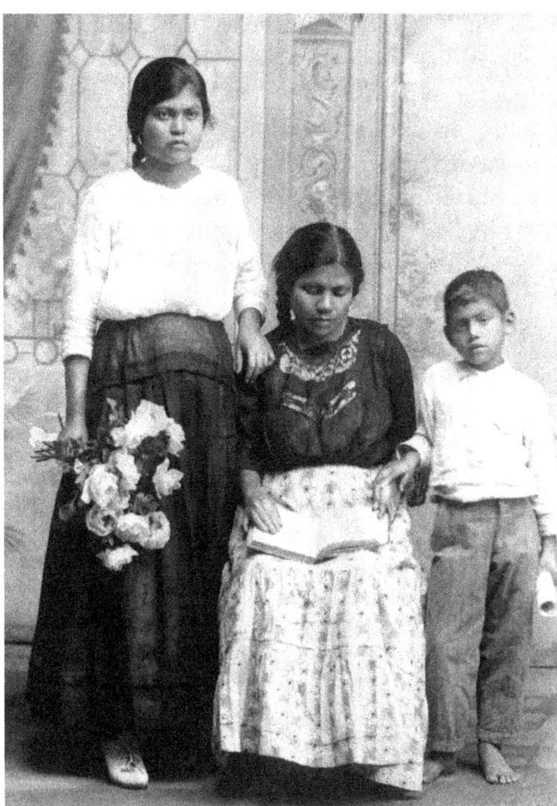

Figure 1.5. María, Petrona, and José. Sepia photograph, 1921.

honor. She believed that Manuel Delgado, Lupe's father, had violated her eldest daughter, Filomena. Filomena died giving birth to the child of this encounter, likely from the consequences of a deliberate abortion. For this tragedy, Petrona intended to make the Delgado family pay. She asked her son to deflower Lupe. He obliged.

When Lupe learned she was pregnant, she sought out José. He shrugged his shoulders. What did he have to do with it? And if he did, he wasn't going to do anything about it. If she was really pregnant, she should get an abortion. Furious, Lupe took the scissors from her apron and held them to José's throat: "You do your duty or we'll just see what happens." José Zúñiga complied. He married her. He did not love her, but he married her. He married her despite the fierce opposition of his mother and his sisters. They did not believe she was pregnant, and if she was, likely it was not José's child but maybe Manuel Santaella's—that fellow who accompanied her singing during the posadas. If she was pregnant, she should get an abortion. Yet José Zúñiga defied them and married Lupe. No one is sure why. Perhaps he married because he knew from his own experience how sad it was for a child to be without a father. Maybe the movies influenced him or friends around him who were marrying under such circumstances. Perhaps, as Chucho ponders, he took counsel from his employer, Don Victorino, who made clothes for the wealthiest people in Oaxaca. Tío Lino, as Chucho called him, was an important figure in Oaxaca's Catholic social movement begun by Bishop Gillow some decades before. Whether or not he encouraged his employees to join the Catholic workers' circles, he saw to it that his tailors attended mass and religious celebrations. He encouraged them to lead honorable lives according to the sacraments, one of which was matrimony.

So José Zúñiga married Lupe, but now he was gone. He had left her open to the torment of his mother's family, some of whom lived in Don Amado's big house and the others around the corner. Only José's sister María was kind: she gave her breast to the baby Chucho when Lupe could not. Her defenses were so low she had contracted scarlet fever. But the others and in particular the mother, Petrona, and her daughter Rosa's child Susana spread hurtful gossip. Chucho was not José's child, they said—he was born of some other of Lupe's sins. Worse than simply rejecting Chucho, they taunted him, and they harassed Lupe. Susana, who sang with Lupe at the posadas, wrote to José in Mexico City that Lupe would leave the parties with men and not return until dawn. For too many years, José would harbor suspicions of Lupe until he finally learned the stories had been untrue.

Lupe had little support to fall back upon. Her parents were dead, and the aunts Clotilde and Arcadia were strictly devout and not prepared for the kind of struggle the Zúñiga women waged. Lupe's brother Manuel made things worse. Lupe's dying mother had given her and Clotilde a *manda* to take care of the boy—a mission to fulfill for God and the Virgin.[10] They took care of him, but they had been unable or unwilling to discipline him. Although the Leyva family had taught him to weave, Manuel had grown into a surly, irresponsible youth, given to drink. He idled away hours in cantinas playing cards and listening to the jukebox. Like his peers, he was handy and quick with a knife. Then came the tragedy, one afternoon in 1941. Chucho remembers it was during the celebrations of the Day of the Dead, because Tía Clotilde had adorned the altar of saintly images with marigolds, chocolate, plates of mole, bread of the dead, sugarcane preserves, and stuffed chili peppers. Pepe does not remember, but Chucho recalls vividly.[11] He was playing marbles outside when his Tío Manuel ran screaming into the house. He was covered with blood. He told them he had been drinking in a cantina when some friends disconnected the jukebox because they did not like the song he had put on. Three times he reconnected it, and they turned it off. They told him if he reconnected it, there would be consequences. He reconnected it. As he sat alone at his table drinking mezcal, one of the boys plunged a knife through his arm into the wooden tabletop. Manuel dislodged the knife and ran screaming the two blocks to the vecindad. After the aunts cleaned his wound, he returned to the bar where he found his adversaries, now joined by his close friend Santaella, who accompanied Lupe in the horas románticas. The young men were all laughing about their deed. Not to be shamed, Manuel Delgado returned to the jukebox and put on the same song. They kept laughing. Manuel took out his knife and hurled it. It pierced his friend Santaella. The boys and the bartender left him to die. Manuel ran to the apartment, threw his knife behind Tía Clotilde's altar, and fled.

When Lupe returned from work, she learned Manuel was hiding with the Leyva family in the adjacent barrio of Xochimilco. The Santaella family pressed charges. The police came with a warrant for Manuel's arrest. Lupe disguised herself in campesino clothing and headed for the Leyva house. She paid a mule skinner to take her and Manuel some miles out to the Etla hills. She stayed with him there. She did not return for the posadas. In her absence, Chucho had to take care of his little brother Pepe and his elderly aunts. Once Lupe returned, she took the boys to visit Manuel in his hiding place in San Sebastian Etla. Chucho remembers that when they saw him, he was practicing his skills hurling his dagger into a cactus plant. Lupe helped Manuel cross into Veracruz.

The event gave the Zúñiga family more material to throw at Lupe. Then something worse happened. In front of the house, four-year-old Pepe called out "ugly" to a little girl who was passing by. The girl came up and slapped him. Jumping to his brother's defense, Chucho picked up a clay jug and threw it at the girl. It hit her forehead and blood streamed down her face. Her parents arrived at the house to lodge a complaint. Clotilde told Lupe when she came back from work. Lupe was livid. Chucho had a temper and a fighting spirit. Lupe had told him before that if he fought again she would burn his hands "so you don't turn out to be a murderer like my brother." Enraged, Lupe called for him. "Chucho, come," she said, "What do you have in your hands? Open them!" Lupe took Clotilde's red-hot pincers from the fire and branded them into Chucho's hand. "So you won't go doing these kinds of things!" she yelled. He yelped with pain.

Pepe hid under the bed. Lupe stood there mortified. What had she done? She immediately embraced Chucho and begged his pardon. "But you know, you know," she cried, "how many problems I have without your father, with my work!" The Zúñiga sisters immediately went to the police and tried to press charges against Lupe, but no witnesses came forward.[12]

Chucho was left with a gaping wound that scarred his hand for life. But he had to forgive his mother, for he was her support. With her, he suffered the attacks of the Zúñiga women. He listened to her woes. He helped her with her work. She suffered from hemorrhoids so badly that sometimes she could not sit at her sewing machine. Chucho pumped the pedals for her as she stood guiding the needle and the cloth. She was terribly modest and did this only at night. She was so sad, her teeth hurt. She put alcohol in her coffee to kill the pain. And her children listened to her sing María Grever's "Jurame":

> Everyone says it is not true that I love you
> Because they've never seen me in love.
> I swear to you I don't understand why you enchant me.
> When I am near you and you are happy,
> I don't want you to remember anybody else,
> I am jealous even in the thought of your
> Remembering somebody else.
> Swear to me that even after much time passes,
> You won't forget the moment I met you,
> Look at me because there is nothing deeper
> Or greater in this world than the love I give you.
> Kiss me with a kiss of love
> As no one has kissed me since the day I was born,
> Love me, love me like crazy
> And then you will know the bitterness I am suffering for you.[13]

"Why are you crying, Mama?" the children asked. "Because I want to talk to your papa," she answered, "I want to tell him that I'm alone, that I miss him so much, and that I want us to be with him." She talked a lot about him. In the boys' eyes, he assumed the stature of a noble god. "The enormous love she had for him," she transmitted to them, Pepe recalled. "She hugged and kissed us. She stroked my hair." Pepe was more fortunate than Chucho. He did not assume responsibility for her pain as Chucho did, and he had inherited the love felt for the little white angel who had died. She gave him a photograph of his father. "I cherished it. I put the picture under my pillow and I dreamed about him. On little pieces of paper, I scribbled letters to him and stuffed them under the tablecloth imagining it was a mail box."

One day, Lupe took Pepe to Mexico City to visit his father. The train conductor charged her for his ticket. He said Pepe was a "big child," not an infant, and she would have to pay. She was not expecting that. She left him alone for a bit on the seat that smelled of wood and sweat. From a distance, he could hear her singing, begging for money to pay for the ticket. Remembering the moment many years later, he cried. It was not humiliating, he said, it was about poverty. "Not the poverty of being unable to pay for the ticket but the spiritual poverty of her abandonment, her sacrifices, and her lack of love."

His sadness disappeared when his father came to meet them at the station. He was so handsome in his Tardan hat, his coffee-colored suit, his tie, and his two-toned shoes. During the visit, they went to the shrine of the Virgin of Guadalupe at La Villa. They posed there, father, mother, and son with José's nephew Gilberto Colón, the son of his sister María. Colón wore a hat to hide his head: the police had shaved it when they jailed him on a robbery charge. José Zúñiga, in fact, looks gaunt and sickly in the photograph. He was suffering from a venereal disease. He was taking a cure. The disease would leave him deaf in an ear, nearly blind in an eye, and suffering from glaucoma. Little Pepe would not have noticed. He was enchanted and returned to tell his brother that his father owned a store near the Lecumberri prison. His father had taken him there; he did not own it but the idea filled the boys with pride and hope.

All around, Chucho suffered more in his early childhood than Pepe. Pepe did not have to bear his mother's cross nor submit to Tía Clotilde's rigid religious education. He does not remember much about the violence still engraved in Chucho's mind and hand. He does not remember his father throwing a piece of wood at Lupe during an argument nor Lupe's pelting the house of a woman she suspected of being her husband's girlfriend. Chucho remembers her yelling: "I am the real wife of José Zúñiga!"[14] Nor does Pepe remember how Luis Ramírez, the partner of his Tía María, demanded his dinner while his stepson Gilberto Colón was eating. He was so drunk and insistent, Gilberto got up and punched him, and they fell brawling to the floor. Nor does Pepe remember when an older boy tried to violate him in Don Amado's latrine. Chucho recalls because he was Pepe's protector.

Instead Pepe remembers how his cousins Marta and Carmen looked like pretty little brides in the white dresses they wore for their first com-

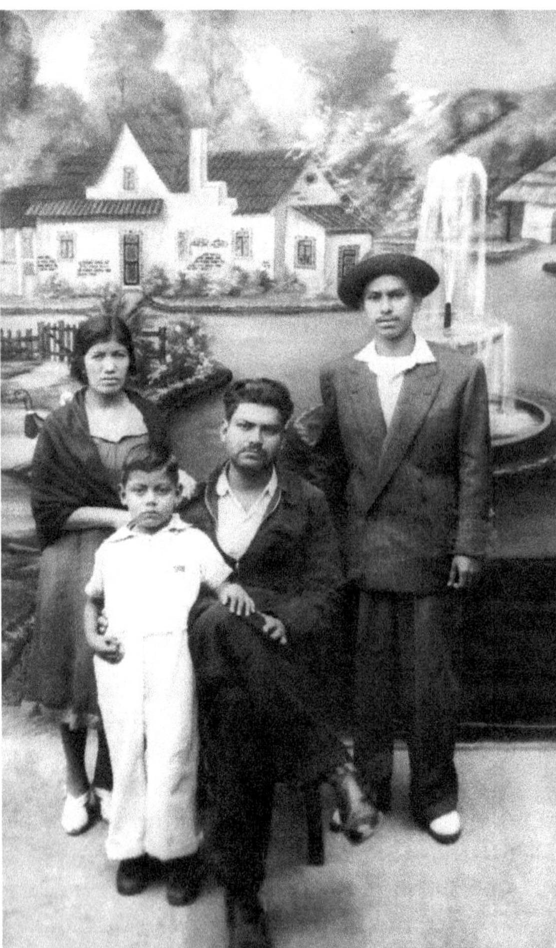

Figure 1.6. Lupe, Pepe, José, and Gilberto Colón. Black-and-white photograph, 1941.

munion and how tasty was the breakfast afterward of tamales and chocolate. He remembers the church of Carmen Alto. He remembers the beautiful Virgin, the magnificent organ, and the sound of his mother's voice. In the atrium, he followed the birds that made their nests in the walls. He remembers the summer festival at the church in honor of the Virgin del Carmen. "There were food stands where we ate corn *molotes* filled with potatoes and sausage and delicious fruit-flavored gelatins. We rode the mechanical rides: the carousel, the Ferris wheel, the little cars that bounced around." In the evenings, the atrium filled with processions of rebozo-covered señoras, children, and men who doffed their hats in respect for the Virgin they carried out of the church. With their candles glowing in the night, they marched around the atrium to the music of the wind bands. "At the end of the evening came the best part," Pepe recalls, "The castles burned with their multicolored wheels twirling round and round and up and down as the fireworks exploded in the dark."

The fair also had a tent (*carpa*) where the children watched freak shows. Their favorite was the serpent woman. She had the body of a slithering boa constrictor and the head of a woman. The children asked her, "Can you eat?" "Yes," she replied, "I eat everything." Asked by the master of ceremonies how she had gotten the body of the snake, she ruefully confessed, "Because I behaved badly with my parents, they put a curse on me and my body turned into a snake." "And what do you advise the little children so that they will not have a body like yours?" he asked. "That they obey their parents, refrain from naughty language, and study hard in school." The children listened carefully.

In the courtyard of the church, Pepe recalls the wonderful Día de la Samaritana, when during Lent in the high heat of March, the beautiful señoras in their *china poblana* costumes served cool waters of watermelon, cantaloupe, tuna, cactus fruit, and rice milk from glass jugs decorated with green bamboo and tiny colored flags.[15] Rose petals floated on top, lending a perfumed scent to the water the señoras ladled with *jicaro* gourds. Their gift symbolized the water given by the Samaritan to the thirsty Christ in the desert. In the spring as well, Pepe remembers the day in the federal Escuela Tipo Benito Juárez when the teachers let the children climb the mango tree in the patio and shake down and gather up all the fruit they could. There in kindergarten he first experimented formally with art. He marveled at the pretty scenes he created with a nail he etched into unbaked clay. He carved butterflies, birds, houses, wells, and clouds. The teacher baked them into little plates, cups, and saucers and sent them home with the children. Lupe accumulated a collection.

The Zúñiga children lived close to the ground with few material comforts. They went barefoot and dressed in simple clothes Lupe sewed from her leftover *manta* (cloth). Pepe remembers that the children they met at the posadas where Lupe sang were much better dressed. The brothers bathed every three days in rainwater in a tub in the patio warmed by the sun. There was one toilet with two big holes for the many people who lived in Don Amado's vecindad. Lupe was keenly aware of the problem of disease. She herself had suffered from smallpox and scarlet fever. Her first little José had died of dysentery, and her sister-in-law, Petrona's daughter, María, was dying of tuberculosis in her apartment at the back of the vecindad. Pepe remembers an epidemic of *sarna* in the school—a skin infection that swept over the children's bodies. So Lupe did her best to maintain hygiene: she complemented the patio washings with regular visits to the public baths, where she scrubbed the boys with sulfur. Pepe remembers watching cascades of suds falling from the women's naked bodies.

Lupe fed them what she could and gave them gelatin laced with alcohol to rid them of bacteria. "Mama would take us on Saturday to the central market," Pepe recalled, "where we drank the fruit-flavored waters at Tía Casilda's famous stand. She also bought us rice pudding in the market. We loved these treats." At the back of the patio in the kitchen area of Don Amado's house, the boys watched Tías Clotilde and Arcadia grind chocolate. They waited to poke their fingers into the rich oily mass sweetened with sugar, cinnamon, and egg yolk. They delighted in eating the tortillas prepared by a señora in the street by the house. She filled them with the big insects known as *chicatanas* that came with the summer rains. The tortillas were tasty with salt and full of protein.

The children's play and their delights came from their imaginative use of their surroundings and the practices and objects of everyday life. From her sewing scraps, Lupe made Pepe an enormous doll with long rag braids. He carried her over his shoulder and rode her like a horse. He pulled her with a string along the floor imagining she was a car. He hung her from a tree and attacked her with a slingshot. He called her "Tunca" because after the rough treatment he gave her, she lost a leg. Finally she got so full of ticks, the adults cremated her. Absent Tunca, he and Chucho and their cousin Nicolás, the dying María's son, made their own toys. When the rains came, they delighted in exploring the hundreds of beetles that littered the streets, some dead, some crawling, some dying. They played with the grasshoppers and captured the june bugs with their beautiful blue and green wings. Attaching a string to one of their legs, they would twirl them in the air; the more june bugs one could fly, the more admired the child. With the husk of *carrizo* stalks and pieces of cardboard, they fashioned propellers that turned in the wind as they raced them.[16] They played with Lupe's chickens too. She made them responsible for feeding them and collecting the eggs, to the point of asking them to put their fingers inside the hens to see if an egg was coming. They invented their own games with them—often to no good end. Chucho peed on the hens only to have the rooster angrily peck his penis. When Pepe got in the way of two fornicating chickens and cupped the rooster's semen in his hand, his mother boxed him and told him not to do it again. The brothers love to remember things like that.

As the weather got hot, their Tío Manuel, before he fled the city, took them to the pools and swimming holes, where they splashed around nude with other men and boys. One was on the steep hill behind the house, and it was here in the summer that the white lilies, the *azucena* flowers, bloomed and bathed the brush in a cloud of sweet scent. "We played with the grasshoppers there and I picked flowers for Mama. We knew from the scent of the azucenas that the Lunes de Cero was coming. That was the day for the celebration of the Gueleguetza, when groups come from the eight regions of the state to dance. We heard the music, but we never went."

One of their favorite spectacles and play sites was the garbage dump down the street. It stunk but was a treasure house full of strangeness and horror. Once, they encountered a boa, a huge enormous snake. It was dead, and from a cut in its stomach oozed what seemed like dozens of frogs the serpent had been unable to digest. They stared and stared and said to themselves, "Oh, dear, they have killed the serpent lady." But they could not find her head. On another occasion, they came across a dead body. They drew close and saw a gaping hole in the man's cheek made by a knife wound—a hole so big they saw all his teeth from above his jaw. His sombrero lay at the side of his decomposing body. Later, his mother told Pepe an uncle had come by and taken the hat. The police came after him thinking he had killed the man.

But the best spectacle from Pepe's point of view was the movie *The Thief of Bagdad*. Lupe took him to see the film one afternoon when he was five. "I had never seen the sea, I had never seen a ship, not even in a picture. I had certainly never seen a princess or a garden full of flowering vines and gurgling fountains. Now they were in front of me in rich Technicolor. I couldn't believe the wooden toy horse that flew through the air, but most of all I was thrilled by the giant genie who popped out of a bottle. This genie prepared food out of thin air. He rescued the prince and princess from a cave and flew them to safety on his magic carpet. What wonderful things! At home, I made a carpet from my mother's sewing scraps. I put it over me and ran around the house pretending I was flying. With a candle I projected light onto the wall and captured my own shadow in flight with the carpet. I had produced a movie."

One fall day in 1943, Lupe received a letter from her husband in Mexico City. He told her to gather up the children. They were moving to the capital.

2. Enchanting City / Magical Radio

In December 1943, Pepe Zúñiga, six years old, and his brother Chucho, ten, arrived at the San Lázaro train station in Mexico City. They came clutching their mother's hand. Then they let go. Chucho remembers the tall buildings, the giant tower with the huge billboard advertising the food company Clemente Jacques. Oaxaca had no building more than two stories tall. He remembers the noise and speed of the cars in the wide, paved streets. Pepe ate his first tangerine and a clear soup totally different from anything he had tasted.

Their father took them across town on a bus to the Colonia Guerrero, a barrio crowded with immigrants and longtime residents of modest means. He settled them into a small apartment in the *vecindad* at 17 Lerdo Street. Pepe remembers it as a quiet block of vecindades and apartment buildings. These were large stone structures, some with tall windows facing the street, their decorative stone- and ironwork, sometimes with art nouveau touches, reminiscent of the colonia's early years as a more upscale neighborhood before Mexico's 1910 Revolution. Since the revolution, the colonia's population had doubled and with it, the fractioning of the buildings' interiors.[1] In 1943, behind the facades were many small, dark living quarters connected by stairs and, in the case of the vecindades, an interior patio. Pedro Moreno Street bordered the block to the south and to the north, Magnolia Street, where the buses clanged and snorted on their way north to the shrine of the Virgin of Guadalupe, east to the Zócalo, and west to Chapultepec Park. No longer did horses ply the streets—just an occasional burro brought by his owner to produce "leche de burro." Burro's milk was said to cure bad backs and help pregnant women. Young ladies coveted it to smooth their skin.[2]

Pepe remembers the Tendajón El Lirio across from the vecindad that sold many things and the *lecheria* around the corner on Magnolia, where his mother lined up to get milk, La Lecheria de los Bebes, where she bought gelatins as delicious as those in Oaxaca. He remembers the lady in the vecindad at Lerdo 23 who made and sold the corn-based gruel, *atole*. In the first difficult years, Lupe served her boys much more atole than milk. He remembers the public baths with a strange Purhepecha name, Ziruauen, between the huge vecindad at Lerdo 20 and the corner of Magnolia. He recalls the restaurant Teocalli, on Pedro Moreno Street, owned by Oaxaqueños whom the family befriended. There were two *pulquerías* on the corners, El Rancho Grande and La Cariñosa, whose owners exploded Judases during Holy Week. The Zúñiga children learned quickly that only the very poor and those from the countryside frequented the pulquerías.

Young children remember what touches them directly. Pepe's brother Chucho and Elvia, their friend who lived in Lerdo 20, were older and remember more.[3] They recall that many people worked out of their homes—electricians, shoe repairers, food preparers, carpenters, furriers, wigmakers as well as hatmakers, tailors, and seamstresses like José and Lupe. Many of these provided goods and services for nearby downtown stores, for entertainers, and for the neighborhood. The daughters of the owner of the Tendajón made wedding dresses for local brides. The furrier serviced downtown stores while his daughters dressed neighborhood women's hair and mended their stockings. Others worked outside the colonía: the boys' friend Joaquín's father worked for the Singer Sewing Machine Company, another man in the vecindad worked at El Popo Tire Company, Elvia's father was a chauffeur for the Secretaría de Educación Pública, and the boys' Tío Efrén was a writer in government offices. It was a cosmopolitan neighborhood: the furrier was Russian, a Japanese family owned the butcher shop next to the Tendajón, the midwife Teresita "La Japonesa" lived on the corner of Magnolia and Lerdo and split her time between delivering babies and betting at the racetrack. Many worked in the entertainment industry: a movie projectionist, the boxer "El Papelero" Sánchez, and Ramón Berumé, the famous boxing referee, lived in Lerdo 20. Marcelo, sidekick to the comic movie star Tin Tan, visited his girlfriend there. The boxer Pituca Pérez, who played in Pedro Infante's film *Pepe el Toro*, also had a girlfriend in Lerdo 20. Delia Magaña, who played the comic drunk "La Tostada" in the movie *Nosotros los Pobres*, had a house on the corner of Lerdo and Magnolia. The boxer "Kid Azteca" had a place on Pedro Moreno Street. In his shop at the corner of Magnolia and Soto, a block away from Lerdo, Julio Chávez, the famed gay tailor, sewed dresses for the stars. On nearby Moctezuma Street lived the popular Cuban musician Consejo Valiente, known as Acerina because of his dark skin. It was his son, a doctor, who delivered the babies of Lucha "La Loca" at his clinic on another block of Lerdo Street.

In Lerdo 17, José had rented for the family two small windowless rooms, one of which served as his workshop and for Guadalupe's sewing. It was also living room and dining room. The other room was for sleeping. Outside, a small patio contained a stone sink, an old toilet that flushed with a chain, and a little kitchen where Lupe cooked over a grate she heated with wood. José's sister Antonia and her *compañero* Tio Efrén lived in another apartment in Lerdo 17. They had come from Oaxaca some years before and found lodgings for José in the vecindad. Soon José called for his mother, Petrona, who brought Nicolás and Teresa, orphans of her daughter María who had died of tuberculosis in Oaxaca. José's other sister, Rosa, came with her daughters Susana, Carmen, and Marta and moved into a nearby vecindad. Lupe's family arrived as well. Tía Arcadia had died, but Tía Clotilde came with the fugitive brother Manuel. They moved into Lerdo 17. Having gathered the feuding clans, José and Lupe could not have created a better stage for intense melodrama, but for the children they opened a world of wonder, a paradise for the imagination, and a different yardstick by which to measure life.

When they moved into the vecindad in 1943, it was almost Christmas and time for the posadas. They had none of the religious sobriety that marked the celebration in Oaxaca. In the vecindad, the posadas were an excuse to have a party. Pepe had never seen a piñata, and suddenly there were many children competing to break it apart and scrambling over each other to gather the candies, nuts, and fruit. He remembers the fireworks and streamers of cutout colored paper (*papel china*) and lanterns and candles that lit up the night. Teenagers and adults enjoyed music and dancing. Adults contracted the musicians and brought out the liquor. For children the posadas were an opportunity for raucous fun, naughtiness, and physical exuberance—particularly for Pepe and his cousin Nicolás who became fast buddies in adventures and misdemeanors. They delighted in tilting their candles to burn the hair of the little girls in front of them in the pilgrims' procession. They came to relish these and other fiestas year after year, occasion after occasion. During Independence Day celebrations in September, as the Marcha de Zacatecas blared all day from record players, the boys set off firecrackers in the streets until the whole neighborhood reeked of gunpowder and clouded with smoke. They climbed up to the *azotea* (rooftop) and hurled them into the patio below. The pistol shots, ubiquitous on Independence Day in the 1920s, were gone now; firecrackers remained and belonged to the domain of children.

Shortly after they arrived, Pepe and Nico almost died when a car crashed into them on the busy street of Pedro Moreno. It threw a bloodied Nico several meters onto a market stall and pinned Pepe under the car. Lupe came running down the street to gather them up. They had never had to watch out for cars in Oaxaca. After the accident, they became more careful with traffic. Much of the time they played with children in the patios of the vecindades. They learned the games of statues, hide-and-seek, donkey, Vibora del Mar (London Bridge is the Anglo-Saxon version), and La Roña, a game reflective of the contemporary fear of contagious diseases as children scampered about to avoid being tapped by one suffering from a deadly illness. They played with tops—wooden ones made for them by the neighborhood carpenter, Manuel Buendía, or colorful metal ones that sang as they twirled. These substituted for the beetles they had flown through the air in Oaxaca. They no longer tortured insects nor teased chickens, although Pepe acquired a pet hen he named Milenosca after a Russian dancer and the family a dog they called Sultán.

The wonder and horror they had found in the *carpas* and garbage dump in Carmen Alto they now encountered in the ubiquitous entertainment industry. In the puppet shows they staged in the vecindad, they told stories they had heard over the radio, seen in the movies, read about in school, or watched in the *lucha libre* matches. For maximum fright and suspense they did more than listen to the radio show *Nick Carter, Master Detective*; they walked across the Alameda to the XEW radio station to watch the program live. Packed with excited people, mostly children waiting to be scared, the studio fell silent as the boys fixed their eyes on the huge microphone, listened to the shots produced by exploding gunpowder, and shivered in the suspense created by the sound of opening locks and banging doors. There were at least ten movie theaters within walking distance of the vecindad and they got to know them all. (We shall later visit these and the movies that inspired Pepe's imagination, toymaking, and theatrical productions.) Many films were made right there in the Colonia Guerrero—those of the *arrabal* (slum) and *carbaretera* (nightclub) genre that thrived on scenes in the vecindades. Children and adults flocked to movie sets in hopes of a getting a part: parts as extras were highly coveted.[4]

From the azotea they could also watch the filming of a movie in the surrounding vecindades. If this space served primarily for mothers to launder clothes, it was also a space of mischief, wonder, adventure, and escape for children. Here little boys and girls pulled down their panties and explored their hidden treasures and were mortified when caught in the act by an adult. The azotea also served Pepe and Nicolás as a safe place to clean up after sullying clothes, shoes, and faces in some escapade. If they could get themselves in order, they might avoid a whipping.

And explore the city they did! They seldom ventured to the northern end of the Colonia Guerrero area around the railroad yards, a neighborhood less serviced by the city and denser in pulquerias, cantinas, and brothels. They were told they might get assaulted there. Instead they took the short walk south to the Alameda. From there, they headed east along the downtown shopping corridors to the great central plaza of the Zócalo, home to the huge, sinking cathedral, government headquarters in the Palacio Nacional, and the giant pawnshop of Monte de Piedad. Or they headed west to the Monumento de la Revolución and careened down its surrounding cement slopes on homemade skateboards. There Nicolás performed in a mask he had made like that of the wrestler Suguisito he admired at the lucha libre matches.[5]

They ran frequently south across the Alameda to XEW studios not just to see the mystery shows of Nick Carter, Detective, and the Crazy Monk but especially to hear Agustín Lara, the greatest composer of the day. He had his own program, *La Hora Azul*. The crowded studio hushed when the "singing poet," seated at his white grand piano adorned with a bouquet of fresh gladiolas, touched the keys in subtle crescendo and crooned:

I owe to the moon the enchantment of your fantasy
And to your glance my pain and melancholy.
I want to sing you my trivial song, Señora Temptation,
You with frivolous look and delicious lips hungry for a kiss.[6]

From their infancy in Oaxaca, the boys had enjoyed a precocious exposure to the earthy side of life—of sex, romantic desire, and violence. For many middle-class children, the boleros of Agustín Lara or María Luisa Landín were out of bounds—let alone other wonders the Zúñiga boys explored. They would head northeast from home across Garibaldi Plaza to the Calle Chueca, otherwise known as the Calle Organo or the

Calle Panama, where the prostitutes beckoned from their doorways.[7] At the Garibaldi Plaza, they watched the homosexuals who owned the food stands. What a curious spectacle!—these men who painted their eyelashes and brows with mascara and talked to each other in the feminine, "Oye tu, María," they would say to a Mario. The boys thrived as well on morbid urban legends. When they were ten, the media began to report on the crimes of the serial killer Gregorio Cárdenas, alias El Goyo, who murdered prostitutes and buried their corpses in a lot in Tacubaya. This monster lived right near them at the corner of Violeta and Soto just two blocks away! The police finally caught him, but while he was on the loose, Lupe went every day to school to pick up the boys, because it was rumored that he or others might be robbing children from school. Parents used such dangers to elicit good behavior much as the serpent lady had done in the carpas of Oaxaca: "If you don't behave, the kidnapper might get you," they would say.

Despite the tensions plaguing their own relationship and their interaction with their in-laws, José and Guadalupe Zúñiga united in the care and education of their children. They allowed the children considerable freedom but maintained vigilance and provided direction from the home where they both worked. They punished what they believed to be wrongdoing and inculcated discipline—particularly in their sons Chucho and Pepe, for Nicolás was ultimately his grandmother's ward. José and Lupe instilled a fundamental code of morality that the boys called *civismo*, or rules of civility and moral conduct I had first encountered in school textbooks used in Puebla at the end of the colonial period and the beginning of independence.[8] They sought to instill dignity in their children through the practice of principles of respect and honor, work, duty, and justice; to use the *Usted* form, to defer to adults, to give one's seat or hand to the elderly; to respect the streets by not throwing garbage or behaving rudely, to be clean and kempt. Lupe and José looked after the children's religious education: they had to attend mass every Sunday morning or they could not go to the movie matinee. Although neither José nor Guadalupe had finished primary school, they sought it for their children and withheld their meager *domingo* (Sunday allowance) and permission to go to the movies if they had not completed their homework.

These lessons and so many more the children also learned from the radio. José purchased the big Philco box that played constantly in the apartment and became the center of family life and learning. Subject to censorship, banned from discussing politics or religion, obliged to broadcast scores of Mexican music, radio programming was as didactic as it was entertaining. Even the advertisements intended to educate and "morally improve" body, mind, and behavior. At the most basic level, the radio's advertisements for soaps, creams, cleansers, toothpaste, and laundry detergents confirmed and strengthened the family's concerns for healthy survival in tight quarters with limited facilities. Hygiene became a near obsession for the boys. When Pepe and Chucho today describe family members, they comment on their personal hygiene. The boys bathed in a tub on the patio with water Lupe heated on her grate. With their parents, they visited the nearby Baños Teresa, public baths with a sauna. Like "modern men" of his day, José Zúñiga used scented lotions. He had impeccable teeth, brushed them after he ate, and insisted that the children do the same. His notions of hygiene responded in part to the model of beauty he had drawn from the movies and the bout of syphilis he had suffered in the city before the family's arrival. "My father," recalled Pepe, "was very clean, but his sister, my Tía Antonia, was very dirty. She was a natural beauty, but she seldom bathed. She smelled of rancid perfume soaked in dirt and sweat. She spit into her hand and threw the saliva to the floor. She even peed in the street! Nicolás was my best friend, but he was dirty, too. The Abuela Petrona let him run around ragged and soiled. One day when my mother gave him a bath, the skin of his legs peeled off with cakes of dirt."

From the radio, the family learned history. One *radionovela* told the story of Emperor Maximiliano and the Empress Carlota, and another that of the nineteenth-century Mexican patriot Benito Juárez, who opposed them. The radio gave them their first exposure to literature—the stories of Guy de Maupassant and Alexander Dumas's *Count of Monte Cristo*—and to classical music and art. Elgar's *Pomp and Circumstance* introduced *Maximiliano and Carlota*. A Chopin nocturne accompanied *Single Women and Divorcées*, a series of real-life love stories. A Bach cantata played for the *Mysteries of the Crazy Monk*, and Dvořák's New World Symphony for *The Police Always on the Watch* and for its parody of police malfeasance, *The Police Doing Nothing*.[9] Commercial sponsors of radio shows sold their products by linking sales to educational cards or box tops like the matchboxes Clásicos that featured the great works of Western art. These included, along with Michelangelo and Titian, Mexican artists Diego Rivera and José Clemente Orozco, as well as the pyramids of Teotihuacán and Chichen Itza. The children collected them and pasted them into a scrapbook marketed for this purpose. On a matchbox rather than in a museum or government building, the future painter Pepe

Zúñiga first saw the works of Rivera and Orozco, although he did not pay much attention to them.

The boys laughed with programs like *The Hour of Doctor IQ*, with his trick questions, and Cuca, the telephone operator, with her silly responses to callers' silly inquiries. "Is it going to rain today?" the caller would ask. "No, it's not raining here," Cuca would answer, "but it's raining in Africa." They delighted in programs of terror and suspense like *Nick Carter* and the *Crazy Monk*. The children's favorite program was Cri-Cri, the cricket created by Gabilondo Soler, who from 1934 sang to Mexican children every Saturday afternoon over XEW radio. In these songs, Cri-Cri celebrated old values of civismo—work, respect, order, discipline, self-control—in a modern paradigm of productivity that encouraged study and cleanliness but also affection, imagination, initiative, and movement.[10]

Cri-Cri's paradigm was modern, but his notions of liberty and work had very old artisan roots, familiar to the Zúñigas. He did not promote the artisans' closed gremial traditions that informed the corporativist formation of Mexico's postrevolutionary state. He did not encourage the religiosity that permeated the artisan guilds of Oaxaca: religion was out of bounds for the radio. He did not condone the hard living—the alcohol, womanizing, and violence—that sometimes marked the behavior of a perfectly fine shoemaker or tailor in Oaxaca. Rather, Cri-Cri was very clean in every sense of the word. What he promoted from the artisans' tradition was their notion of individual freedom, their pride in their craft, and their sense of solidarity in work.

Cri-Cri sang to the rhythms of songs and dances popular on the radio and in the movies—the *danzón*, the foxtrot, the rumba, the tango, the bolero. He created a sanitized world of animals, insects, fairies, kings, sultans, and princesses. Extracted from the dirt and smells of the barnyard, mother pig made sure her three little piglets were squeaky clean, dressed warmly in their pajamas, and tucked into bed with her many kisses. One morning they cried because the sun had not come up and they could not go to school. They asked their mother for a candle to light their way. In "Walking to School," the animals paraded to class—the mouse with his glasses, the peacock grasping his notebook, the dog biting an eraser, five well-bathed kittens, the lion, the monkeys and even a shark because "in books we always learn to live better." The tortoise brought up the rear and wrote a note to Santa Claus asking for a pair of skates so that he could be punctual.[11]

Cri-Cri gently criticized social hierarchies when they generated uncharitable behavior. He sang of a rich little girl who refused to share her candy with a poor little boy. He sang of a boy who complained of the servant because she served his milk very cold or very hot; he called her "a nuisance."[12] In his songs, Cri-Cri rejected the disdain for manual labor typical of the upper class and many in the middle class. Cri-Cri's animals were always making something—the rabbits massaging the dough to prepare a feast of delicious-smelling golden bread, or Micifuz, the carpenter cat, building a staircase to the stars. If Cri-Cri celebrated artisans like Pepe's father, he also honored those who performed a public service—the puppy dog who delivered the mail, the mice who formed the fire squadron in their metal jackets aboard their shiny engine shrieking with bells and sirens.[13]

Cri-Cri would never have created a children's public had his messages been uniquely productivist and disciplining. Rather, his characters turned school into fun and work into fiesta. They inhabited a world of nature that celebrated the magic and beauty of life: when the butterfly emerges from the rose, her brilliant silver winglets fluttering in the sun, all the animals of the forest strike up their instruments in a symphony of celebration.[14] True to official Mexican approaches to modernity—particularly those of the Secretaría de Educación Pública—Cri-Cri fostered initiative and achievement but never competition. Life was not a race but a concert of many artists playing different instruments in a fiesta of solidarity and cooperation.

Cri-Cri shared with children his wonder at nature, a world the Zúñiga boys had experienced more in Oaxaca than in the city. He sang of the changing seasons, the water that makes the daisy stand straight and beautiful, the flowers that splashed the meadow into a carpet of colors and prompted the forest to explode in song, the birds' morning concert outside the child's window, the breeze from the mountains that turned the sugarcane into singing flutes of gold, the moon that lit the forest and made the lake shimmer and glisten, beckoning the elves to dance, the crickets to sing, and the little calf to come to drink.[15] It was a world to adore and not to destroy. Children accompanied two beetles as they stumbled down the path of the garden, both crippled but determined to reach a place in the sun; Cri-Cri told them to respect these creatures and their right to the sun.[16] Cri-Cri's sensitivity was pre-ecological, the gestation of a word that would emerge when children of the 1940s grew to adulthood.

Cri-Cri awakened the imagination of children like Pepe in effulgent, multisensorial, exuberant ways. Through verse and music, he created a visual imaginary. He provoked all the bodily senses: the capacity to see the way the little stream of water expanded and contracted with the rain and the sun or the musty, dingy corner where the old doll had been tossed like Pepe's beloved Tunca, to relish the aroma of the soup the elves made from daises, carnations, and hibiscus or the bread the rabbits prepared, to hear the water gurgling in the brook or the cricket's violin, to taste the Rey Bombon's castle of quince and almond pastes, to kick up one's heels and dance like Ché Araña. His songs delighted mind and tongue in their infinite rhyming wordplay. Cri-Cri sang of adventures familiar to Pepe, like riding on the train, its cottonlike smoke spewing from the engine, its whistles blaring, and its chug, chug, chug. "The songs reminded me," reflected Pepe, "of all the things I had seen from the train window when I came to Mexico City—the cows, the sheep, the bull, the cactus, the mountains—and the excitement I felt when the train passed through a tunnel and for a moment, the world turned black!"

Cri-Cri sang intensely of freedom. He mourned the life of the cuckoo bird condemned to emerge mechanically from the clock every hour, incapable of chirping of her own free will. He celebrated the shoes that, defying the cobbler, jumped out of their boxes and danced up a storm. But he condemned foolhardiness. So the cat Micifuz was forced to conclude. Sailing the sea in a shoe, he braved the waves and a hurricane as he searched for an island full of treasure. Then he discovered a bottle with a message inside. "Señor," read the note, "Don't be a fool. There is no greater treasure than studying." Heeding the advice, Micifuz returned to school, studied hard, and became a great doctor.[17]

Cri-Cri sang of children's rights to love and protection. He invested parental authority and responsibility principally in the mother. "Mama . . . la más divina" clothed, bathed, fed, and nursed her children and made sure they studied hard and behaved properly. Fathers were by and large distant, absent, and often irresponsible in Cri-Cri's world. The beloved duck Patita waddled her way to market to bargain for food to feed her hungry ducklings. She received little help from their "lazy, shameful" father, who likely joined Cri-Cri's spider Ché Araña in tangoing the night away at a club. The hen Doña Cocorica recognized her rooster's authority. She told her chicks his cry ordered the sun to rise in the morning. Yet it was she who took full responsibility for the children's safety and education.[18]

The reification of motherhood implied a feminization of sensibility to be absorbed by both male and female children, an antidote to brusque, distant, or even violent masculinity and to parental irresponsibility. It did not mark the end of patriarchy. Cri-Cri's mothers shared the socialization of children with a new set of mostly male professionals—doctors, dentists, school directors, all of whom became familiar to the Zúñiga boys. Cri-Cri recognized a diversity of artisanal and professional roles for men that were not available to women, whose primary task was to take care of the home and family. If they worked, it was to "make ends meet," as in the case of Lupe, who sewed when the family needed money; or when they had no choice, as in the case of Doña Inez, the concierge in Lerdo 17, who had no husband and supplemented her income running a newsstand on the corner; or Elvia's mother, who sold used clothes because she could never get hold of her husband's wages. She sent her children every payday to the Secretaría de Educación Pública to pin down their father before he left for the cantina, but he always managed to escape through another door.[19] Pepe knew a few women with professions: the midwife Teresita la Japonesa and his first schoolteachers, whom he adored when they, like Cri-Cri's mamas, combined affection with discipline. He knew young women in the Colonia Guerrero, like his cousin Carmen and Chucho's future wife, Josefina, who went to vocational school and became secretaries.

José Zúñiga Sr. was not an absent father, nor was he like Patita's lazy good-for-nothing mate. He worked at home and brought in money. But like Patita, Cocorica, and "la Madre Divina," Lupe performed in Mexico City as the caring, energetic mother about whom Cri-Cri sang. It was she who ensured daily subsistence by negotiating with local merchants, making friends with the neighbors, and nurturing her Oaxaca networks to access supplies and assistance. What she did to care for her family and ensure their healthy survival did not necessarily elicit appreciation—likely a common situation that Cri-Cri sought gently to correct with his praise for maternal care. The Zúñiga boys recoiled at the cod liver oil she fed them to keep them healthy. They feared the dentist's drill and the barber's scissors she obliged them to endure. Pepe cried and cried when she served his beloved hen Milenosca for dinner. The boys detested the pants she sewed for them. A ribbon of elastic held them together and at school, children would pull the elastic to make fun of them. The pants reminded Pepe of those of campesinos or the overalls that lowly Negroes wore in Hollywood movies. Every time he heard Cri-Cri's song of the El Tlacuache (the *ropavejero*), he thought of his mother giving this familiar street peddler what Pepe regarded as family valuables, like his grandfather's wide sombreros, in exchange for used pots and pans. Even Lupe was ashamed and told the family she had bought them in a store. Worse still were the trips Lupe obliged Pepe to take with her to the Monte de Piedad on the Zócalo, where she hocked scraps from José's tailoring or her own gold earrings, so prized by Oaxacan women. "To stand in the long line of people publicly declaring their poverty was painful." Pepe remembers, "I was ashamed to be there with people who could not live within their means." For Lupe it was a survival mechanism in a situation of scarcity. Cri-Cri praised the commitment of such active mothers. Children like Pepe got the message, but they also suffered discomfort and humiliation.

While the mother was clearly the critical parental figure in Cri-Cri's songs, he nurtured respect for elders, particularly grandmothers. From his own grandmother, Gabilondo Soler had learned many of the tales he turned into music. The Zúñiga boys particularly liked the song in which the child implored his grandmother to open her trunk to show him the sword of his grandfather the "colonel," the doll his mother had played with, her own dress that swished as she walked across the floor, the old book of stories he so wanted to hear.[20] "My grandmother Petrona's dress swished that way across the floor," Pepe remembered, "She was not a nice person. She was mean and unkempt. But we loved it when she told her stories of goblins and ghosts who wandered the streets and hills of Oaxaca. We loved it when she opened her chest full of yellowed photos, old metal irons, rosaries, coins, and worn-down *huaraches*." She wove a magical past the children could fantasize about in the noisy, sometimes brutal city. But like the Abuela Petrona and the aging Tía Clotilde, that past was also set in a fading notion of a yesterday of want, disease, religious rigidity, and sadness. The present was full of *alegria* and adventure. The future would be even better. These boys grew up seduced by change—the desire and the experience, the idea and the ideology.

"Cri-Cri awakened our imagination with his world of animals, nature, and the characters of our neighborhood," remembered Pepe, "He criticized bad customs and taught us conduct." The boys did not internalize all of his lessons. They delighted in Ché Araña as he danced the night away at a club. They ignored his lack of responsibility. They did not seem to mind their father's going out at night to the clubs; Chucho remarked years later, "After all, he was a man."[21] Cri-Cri intended children to admire the dream of the little pig who wanted to do nothing more than help his mother, but the boys fixed on the little pig who dreamed of getting a great big cake. They wanted a cake and they never got one. Cri-Cri's songs often filled them with desire and a sense of shame. Like the tortoise who asked Santa Claus for skates, they looked forward to every Día de los Reyes on January 6, expecting these prized gifts—but they never got them. Mostly they settled for clothes, a wooden top, or a rubber ball. Skates they had to borrow or accept as hand-me-downs from their friend Joaquín. In the new world of increasing consumption—a world Cri-Cri modestly, perhaps unconsciously constructed—used goods and home-made ones became a mark of shame, that powerful affect that denies us our dignity and leaves us painfully alone. Shame may goad us to violence, as it did Tío Manuel in the cantina, or it can goad us to construct, to change ourselves, in our desire to reestablish the recognition shame has denied us.[22] Pepe and Chucho never got skates, but they relished the possibility of self-improvement that elicited approval.

Cri-Cri's song of the *Negrito Sandía* caused Pepe hurt and shame. In Cri-Cri's world, adults reprimanded children who behaved badly, but the most egregiously punished for his atrocious behavior was the Negrito Sandía.[23] In this song composed to the rhythm of the Afro-Cuban danzón, the child had the face of an angel, but filthy language (*groserías*) spewed from his mouth in the form of snakes. His aunt whipped him and registered his naughtiness in a book reminiscent of the plantation overseer's. The watermelon (*sandía*) was a racist stereotype from the United States that Pepe had seen in the movies. These images wounded Pepe. He and his cousin Nicolás won the title of "los cenizos de catorce" from their neighbors. "Catorce" referred to the number of their apartment, and "los cenizos" to a combination of filth, garbage, naughtiness, and dark skin. The terms *negro, negrito*, used in the family, the patio, or the school, dogged Pepe as a child. Sometimes he recognized them as terms of affection, but sometimes they caused him deep shame. He recalls neighbors saying to his mother, "Pity you, Lupe. You are so white and you have such dark children."

Curiously, these terms addressed to Chucho did not bother him at all. Four years older than Pepe, Chucho was an adolescent when Afro-Caribbean (*afroantillana*) music invaded the Colonia Guerrero. The boys often saw the sensational Cuban drummer Acerina (Consejo Valiente) walking along the streets. In 1948, Pérez Prado arrived with the mambo. Together with singers Beny Moré and Celia Cruz of the Mulatas de Fuego and the Sonora Mantancera, Pérez Prado transformed the music scene, taking over the theaters, the movies, and the airwaves. "You could hear them," recalls Pepe, "over the jukeboxes in the corner stores, at exclusive clubs like El Patio and Capri and not so exclusive ones like El Burro, El Caracol, [and] La Momia, and over the loudspeakers at public pools like Las Termas, where I went with Nico and Joaquín to swim, in the dance halls like Salón México, La Smyrna, and Los Angeles, and the musical reviews in the theaters, even at the Instituto Politécnico Nacional, for which Pérez Prado composed a special mambo." The Teatro Margot made a celebrity of Pérez Prado. In its wildly popular mambo contests, every participant got five pesos and a sandwich whether they won or not.[24] Pepe did not go, but the music and dance enchanted Chucho. Still a minor at the age of fourteen and unable to get into the clubs, he unloaded instruments for the Cuban bands playing at the Salón Los Angeles at Lerdo 206. He talked the doorman into letting him into the club to watch them perform. He became so enamored of Afro-Caribbean music that he tried to give himself natty hair and remembered fondly a story he had been told—that as an infant, a *mulata* woman had given him her breast when his mother fell ill with scarlet fever.[25] Although Pepe saw all the *rhumbera* movies with the sexy Cuban dancers Ninon Sevilla, Maria Antonieta Pons, Rosa Carmina, and Amalia Aguilar and delighted in the music of Pérez Prado and Celia Cruz, he never became as invested as Chucho in the new craze, at least not to the point of wanting to nat his hair and celebrate his dark skin. As an adolescent he preferred to learn the exquisitely refined Mexican version of the originally Cuban danzón.

3. Pepe at School and with God, the Virgin, and the Saints

Pepe at School

Today when he passes Señor Buendía's carpentry shop on Magnolia Street, the sweet smell of cedar reminds Pepe of his walks to school with his mother. The Francisco González Bocanegra primary school was three blocks away on Riva Palacios Street. The new world of children in the classroom thrilled him. They were exclusively boys in his first years; coeducation had been suspended by the conservative administration in the Secretaría de Educación Pública. Pepe adored his first-grade teacher, Señorita Lucio. With her simple dress, clean nails, and neatly cropped hair, she was a model of *cariño* and intelligence and a mother to all the children who learned and bonded quickly. Once she came to the classroom crying, and the children all cried with her. He also liked his second-grade teacher, la Maestra Cabrera. These teachers were the children's heroes, their mothers. "I learned to read very fast," Pepe recalled, "I looked forward to going to school every morning. I even wished there were classes on Saturday—not Sunday because that was the day for mass, the matinee, and radio programs."

Pepe remembers the moral lessons of Cri-Cri more than he does those from his primary school textbooks, perhaps because Cri-Cri sang them in melodious, rhyming songs frequently repeated. Looking recently at a group of textbooks used in Mexico City schools in the mid-1940s, he noted that the textbooks preached similar virtues to those he learned

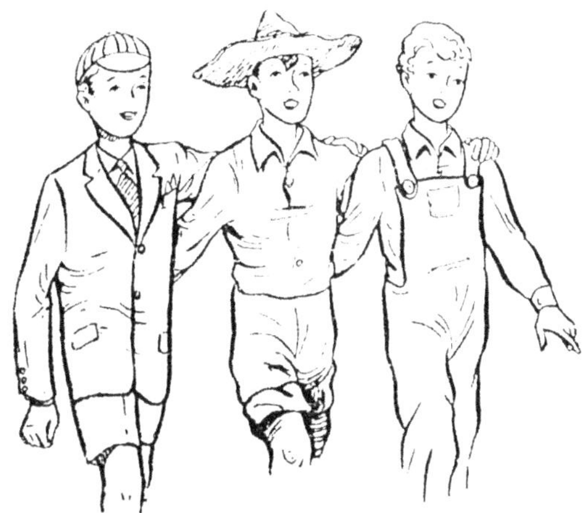

Figure 3.1. Illustration by Cesareo Sánchez, in Carmen Basurto, *Mi patria, Libro tercero de lectura* (Mexico City: Editorial El Material Didáctico de Prof. Carlos Rodriguez, n.d.), 212.

in his family, from Cri-Cri, and from the church: work, study, respect, prudence, punctuality, order, and savings; charity, tolerance, gratitude; and, of course, cleanliness. He noted the familiar vices of laziness, anger, avarice, envy, disrespect, and imprudence.[1] Perhaps the school gave special emphasis to certain values—work and application, cleanliness, health, and savings. It oriented virtuous behavior toward the nation and patriotism. Every Monday morning the children lined up for an elaborate ceremony in honor of the Mexican flag, replete with drums and bugles. Clad in white, they bellowed the national anthem and *O Santa Bandera!*

In those years, the Secretaría de Educación Publica approved a variety of textbooks for use in Mexico City schools. Although Pepe has no clear memory of them, they speak to the transition in attitudes, affect, technologies, and notions of citizenship that marked his childhood. They reflect the residual, dominant, and emerging sentiments he negotiated as a child and youth. Some, like those of Daniel Delgadillo and María Enriqueta Camarillo de Pereyra, had first been published at the beginning of the twentieth century. Others, like Guadalupe Cejudo's *Chiquillo*, Carmen Norma's *Juanito y Rosita*, and Carmen Basurto's *Mi patria* were more recent. Looking at these texts in order of their original publication, we note a movement in emphasis from scarcity and class distinction to mobilization for progress and prosperity to be achieved through the dedicated energy of Mexican children in defense of their nation.[2]

The mobilization required the unity of children across social classes, converted into soldiers in the struggle for progress. They would, as illustrated in figure 3.1, march in a "round of harmony," "children of the worker dressed in overalls, Indian children of the Sierra in their sandals and their manta," together with "rich children."[3] They joined a universal march as peace, technology, good government, and good will promised unity, health, and prosperity among the world's peoples, regardless of race or nationality.[4]

This upbeat, optimistic, universalist vision came out of the horrors of World War II and the corrective formation of the United Nations. The vision contrasted with that put forward by Daniel Delgadillo in *Saber leer*. In his text, a voyager encountered a big rock he could not move. He despaired that he would die for lack of food. Others came, tried, and despaired, until they realized that together they could move the rock. "The voyage is life, the rock is the misery one encounters on the way."[5] In the newer texts, the march continued, but "misery" lost out to fascinating challenges and expansive possibilities. In the Delgadillo reader, children flew kites. In the Basurto reader, they could imagine flying in an airplane to Buenos Aires or Istanbul or Indochina. Pepe imagined those airplanes. He saw them in the sky, gliding over Mexico City trailing advertisements for Pepsi-Cola. And he saw them in the movies—in the newsreels, the famous Mexican Squadron 201 that flew in the Philippines in World War II, and in the matinees, Flash Gordon's fantastic spaceship.

Like Cri-Cri, the textbooks celebrated the magic, bounty, and beauty of nature but with subtle differences over time. The older texts emphasized natural dangers (turbulent seas, storms, predatory animals).[6] Technology was not much more than a promise. Moreover, science might be mistaken. In Delgadillo's *Saber leer*, an old woman's donkey knew better than two eminent meteorologists that it would rain.[7] In the newer texts, nature not only provided (urban) children with an affective experience of physical exuberance, wonder, beauty, and caring (for animals, flowers, and trees), it produced sustenance linked to new technologies. As nature became more benign and romanticized, it also became more instrumental. Chickens and cows produced meat; trees provided fruit and wood to burn; water produced electricity and made the crops grow.[8] Trains and trucks brought the bounty to the city. In his text *Adelante*, Delgadillo was unsure of the advantages of the "dangerous" city over the "tranquil" countryside.[9] His ambiguity may have reflected his desire to reach a broad audience of children in countryside and city. However, text writer Basurto was certain that the city was the emporium of modernity and progress.[10] Outside Mexico City (other Mexican cities might be included), life was backward and blighted by poverty despite the countryside's role in providing the cities' sustenance. Textbooks pictured the humble shepherd boy tending his flock or the lone campesino waiting for the rain to cultivate his tiny milpa.[11] There were no rural communities and no mention of the land reform that had been carried out in the preceding decades. Indigenous peoples were represented as very poor, as folkloric, or as grand princes of a once great Mesoamerican civilization.[12]

Nor did the textbooks make mention of individual or collective rights in these years of conservative pushback against the militancy of workers and peasants and the redistributive reforms implemented in the 1920s and 1930s. Gone were the socialist texts of the 1930s that celebrated industrial laborers and agrarian reform beneficiaries in collective production. In the 1940s, the collective became the entire nation.[13] Individual freedom was to be exercised and won through the mobilization of all Mexican children, hand in hand, respecting each other in the struggle for a "new life" without exploitation, oppression, humiliation, or racism.[14] Defensive nationalism cradled this quest for individual liberty. "Think of the heroic men who fought so bravely so that no foreigner will rob you of liberty and the right to happiness," wrote Basurto.[15] Oh, how Pepe learned about the burning feet of the Aztec prince Cuauhtémoc as he resisted the torture of the invading Spanish! The *Niños Héroes* ("child heroes"), Pepe remembers, were every bit a "doctrine" in these years, particularly the young soldier Juan Escutia, who allegedly leaped to his death wrapped in the Mexican flag to save it from capture by the invading Americans in 1847. Later Pepe's brother Efrén, nine years his junior, would tell him that the stories of the *Niños Héroes*—particularly that of Juan Escutia—were all a big myth propagated by the government, but for Pepe and undoubtedly other children of his age they were instructive models.

The *Niños Héroes* and the children of mid-1940s were linked in a process of becoming—not only of the nation but, for contemporary children, of the individual, of life rather than death, of development rather than sacrifice, of peace rather than war. The texts exhorted the student to develop his or her individual talents and skills, to cultivate mind and body, not simply for national but for individual empowerment. Mobility would come from one's application, not so much from the generosity and charity highly placed individuals showed to the poor and unfortunate in the older textbooks. In Daniel Delgadillo's *Saber leer*, a magnanimous *hacendado* gave a piece of land to a humble Indian who had done him a favor. In the Basurto textbook, the hacendado left his land exclusively to his most thrifty, productive son.[16] Delgadillo in his textbooks showed sensitivity toward misfortune as the creator of poverty. Misfortune called for acts of charity toward the fruit vendor who had gone blind, the old person who had fallen sick, the abandoned elderly lady, the physically handicapped child.[17] The newer texts focused on individual effort and productivity; they rarely pictured the weak, disabled, or old.

The newer textbooks suggest a trending of the idea of charity toward cariño, a more private, intimate sentiment of endearment expressed and practiced within the context of the family and the school—between parents and children, between siblings, friends, and classmates, between children and their ubiquitous pets, between teachers and students. These educating sites taught and disciplined with cariño. Although the text featured families and homes from different social classes, the ideal mode of conduct was vested in the middle-class family.[18] It was a nuclear family consisting of parents and children, without grandparents, aunts, uncles, or cousins. Their home was "an oasis of love."[19] It was ample and uncrowded: children had their own bedrooms.[20] The house was set in a walled-off garden without a neighborhood, distinct from Pepe's life on Lerdo Street. As in Cri-Cri's songs, the mother was all sacrifice (*abnegación*) caring for home and children. "The future of the child is the work of the mother," declared a text.[21] The father wore a suit and tie and often carried a cane. The provider and protector of the family, he was authoritative and distant. Children did not sit on his lap as he relaxed from a hard day's work in his easy chair, but they did gratefully wait upon him. He was attentive to them. He gave them presents when they were good and took them to the circus to see the animals and the clowns, to Chapultepec Park to play, and to the pyramids at Teotihuacán to appreciate their history.

Looking at the textbook illustrations today, Pepe exclaimed, "They look French!" Even the children in the drawing of the march of progress shared the same Caucasian features, ignoring Mexico's racial diversity. These textbook children certainly looked different from Pepe and his classmates. (Figures 3.2–3.5 juxtapose Pepe's fourth-grade class picture with illustrations from different texts.) Yet Pepe does not recall the textbooks or the school program as having marked him with class or, more importantly for his own sensitivity, with racial anxieties. He recalls the sting of Cri-Cri's *Negrito Sandía* and racial slurs in the vecindad but nothing from the textbooks. Rather, he suffered from his classmates' teasing him for his homemade britches and his own shame and discomfort at having to wear the oversized shoes his father bought him so that they would last as he grew. "They were like miner's shoes and people called me 'Tribeline' after a character from Walt Disney who had huge shoes." But the social circumstances of children who teased him were similar to his.

If we look closely at the illustrations and the stories in the texts, this

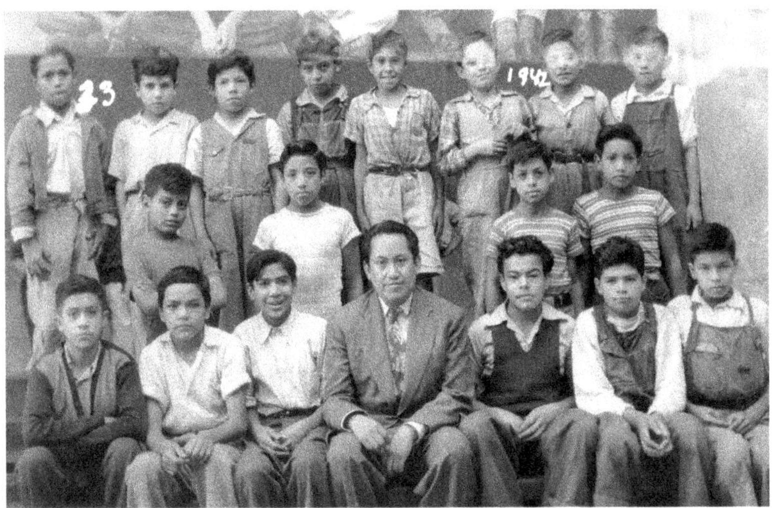

Figure 3.2. Pepe is at the far left in the second row. Black-and-white photograph, 1947.

ideal family appears like a device more for teaching habits, sentiments, and aspirations than an insensitive imposition on those less privileged. Its modest presentation seems deliberate. The furnishings are few, a dining table, a comfortable chair, a child's bed. The mother often wears an apron and, upon occasion, a rebozo. She sews, she prepares and serves the meals.[22] There is no servant. The children's toys are simple, many of them homemade or bought at a market stall: kites, balls, tops, dolls, marbles, a jump rope, a hobbyhorse that is a broomstick with a floppy head of cloth and straw.[23] Children might bathe in a metal tub in cold water, although Basurto's child had the luxury of a porcelain bathtub fed by warm water from a showerhead.[24] A few show more elaborate, store-bought toys: cameras, toy automobiles and trucks, and fancy dolls.[25] These became more common in the textbooks of the 1950s.

But if in texts in the 1940s children's consumption was modest, it had also become a right, an entitlement, an integral part of their development. Children were no longer naturally wayward creatures in need of discipline as they were in the older readers; they were instead to be nurtured and protected—only then would they become "*sanos, fuertes, alegres.*"[26] They had a right to dream of the gifts they wanted to receive on the Día de los Reyes and a right to the gifts if they had been well behaved.[27] They expected their parents to take them to the circus, festivals, and parks.[28] They expected their teachers to open the world for them. It was proper to play: through play they learned and developed their minds, senses, bodies, and

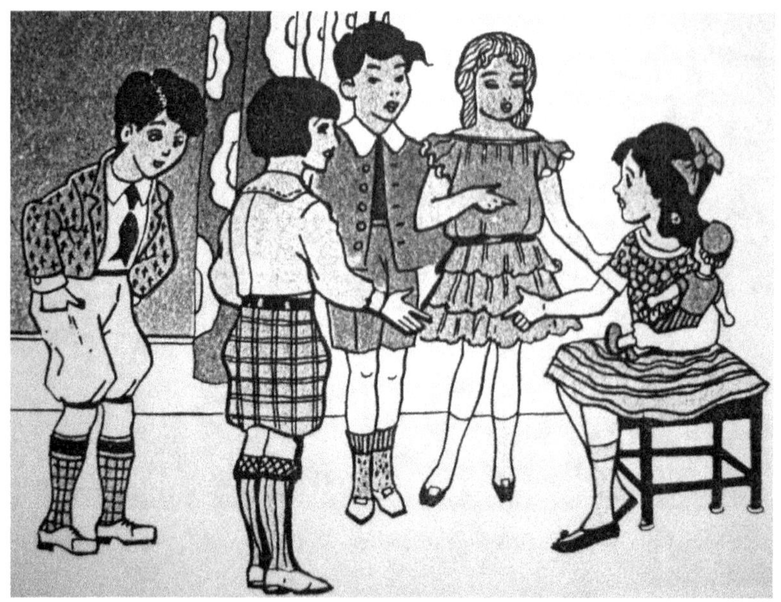

Figure 3.3. Chiquillo's friends. Illustrator unknown, in Guadalupe Cedujo, *Chiquillo, Libro de lectura oral para segundo año* (Mexico City: S. Turanzas del Valle, 1943), 37.

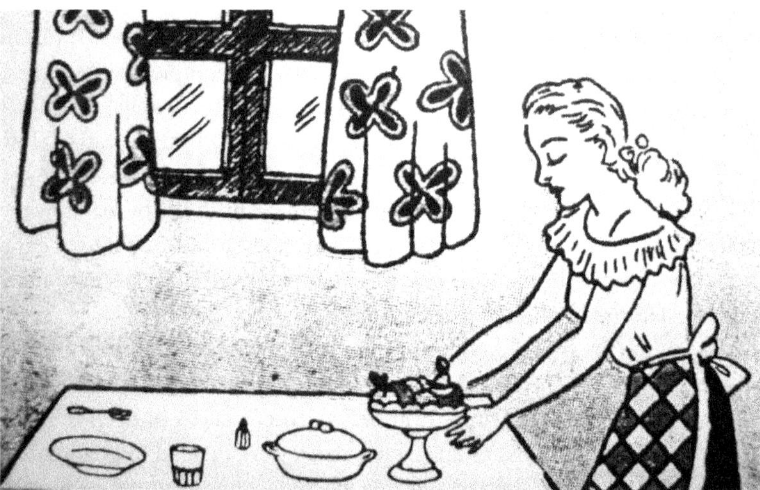

Figure 3.4. Mama of Rosito and Juanito. Illustrator unknown, from Carmen Norma, *Rosita y Juanito*, 9th ed. (Mexico City: Ediciones Aguilas, 1953), 12.

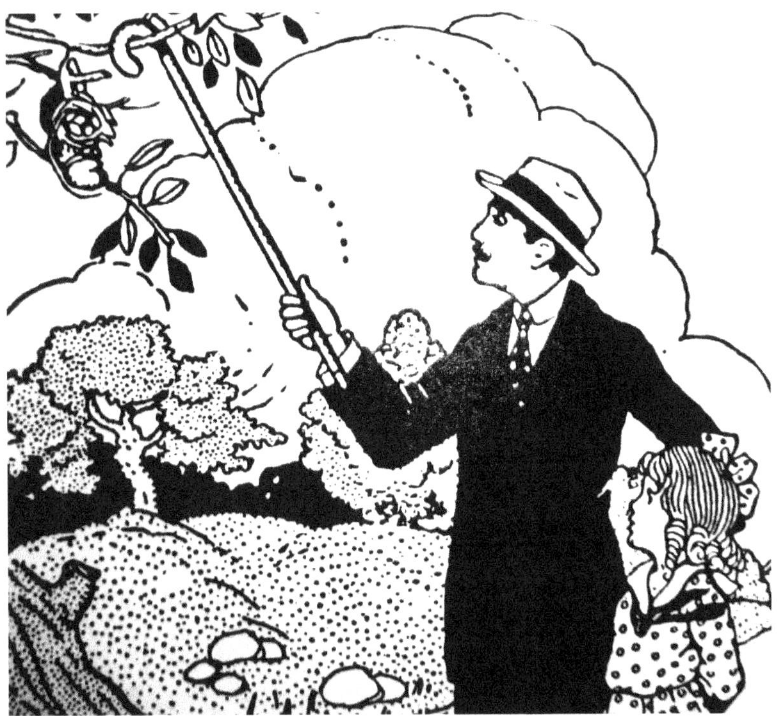

Figure 3.5. Illustrator unknown, in Daniel Delgadillo, *Poco a poco, Libro segundo*, 40th ed. (Mexico City: Herrero Hermanos, 1943).

values. Through the doctor, the dentist, the teacher, the mother, and their own efforts, their bodies grew healthy, strong, and beautiful.

The privatization of cariño in the texts was complemented by the projection of empathy outward to the nation and even the world. The newer texts identified children as part of a crusade for global peace and prosperity. As the child developed him- or herself, the newer texts stressed the facilitating role of the government, which provided infrastructure and opportunity: firemen and policemen guaranteed order and safety; the Red Cross, medical clinics, scientists combated contagious diseases, and sanitary officers promoted health; schools and museums furthered education. It depended upon the individual to rise to the occasion, to take advantage of new opportunities. Basurto so exhorted in her essay entitled "The Staircase":

> When you look at me, think of your life. I want you to see your life as a ladder. . . . ! You go up, stair by stair, with firm steps! Go

up with your ideas and your feelings! Absorb what you are taught, correct your defects, try to be more worthy and a little better every day. . . . Each year you will feel yourself taller because of your merits. When you are big, for having cared for your body, you will feel big as well for having climbed the staircase of life and you will find yourself at the height of goodness.[29]

For the striving child, the future opened wide: "Think about those today who are good professionals, industrialists, merchants, and excellent workers; to be successful later, they were active and studious from childhood."[30] That is, the future opened wide primarily for boys. They were the "soldiers" marching toward progress in the first illustration. They were the *Niños Héroes*. They were the appointed producers of history and goods. Girls continued to be essential background sentiment and household caretakers, but as girls received similar schooling to that of boys, they moved forward in these years, negotiating a difficult but potentially creative contradiction.

Pepe was fortunate not to have to grapple with this contradiction. What immediately enchanted him about school was akin to Basurto's staircase: the school's encouragement of individual application and performance. The mastery of skill depended on the development of good habits: punctuality, persistence, patience, and study. Listening to Cri-Cri awakened mind, body, and senses, but listening did not require their coordinated application. Neither did it produce the joy of personal achievement. Nor could his parents excite Pepe's desire to apply himself: "They made me sew shoulder pads and hem skirts. I hated it. I cried. At school, I would draw. I excelled at it. By drawing, I learned the capitals of the Mexican states and the insects and animals of nature. My teachers loved my work and my friends offered me candy and notebooks if I would do their drawings for them." He did their drawings with pleasure. He did not see it as subverting the rules but rather as part of the warm camaraderie among the students. He took great pride in the prize he won for his drawing of Benito Juárez as a shepherd boy. He submitted it to the contest held in conjunction with the festival honoring Juárez's birthday.

As for cultivating new habits, Pepe got himself a piggy bank and opened a savings account where he deposited some of the proceeds from his drawings, his *domingos* from his parents and his Tía Antonia, and what he earned emptying the neighbors' garbage. Although his father told him, "Man's best friend is a peso in the pocket," his father's practice fell short of his preaching. His parents did not use a bank, and it was their lack of savings, he judged, that forced his mother to go to the Monte de Piedad. With his savings account, Pepe intended to avoid the shame he felt in the long lines at the pawnshop. His cousin Nicolás mocked him. He called him Rico Mac Pato, after Donald Duck's avaricious uncle. Although his best friend, Nico was also Pepe's foil, the negative against which he measured his own development. Nico never saved a centavo. He lost the little he had gambling at cards. To cover his debts, he borrowed from his grandmother, Petrona. She charged interest.

Pepe's primary-school teachers were critical to his performance: the cariño and discipline of his first *maestras*, the discipline and radical exhortations to patriotic service of his later male teachers. By and large, Pepe's primary school had abandoned practices of corporal punishment. That is why the children were shocked speechless one day when their beloved first-grade teacher, Señorita Lucio, lost her temper. As she wrote on the blackboard, a child challenged her: "You forgot to put the dot on the *i*." "I am the teacher and you are not here to teach me," she retorted sharply. She ordered the child to pile furniture on a table, then she demanded he climb it. He fell of course. The school director immediately called her to his office, and as the children later learned, she almost lost her job. As a rule, teachers reprimanded mildly. They obliged the disorderly or careless student to write over and over on the blackboard or in his or her notebook "I ought not to behave badly." In more serious cases, the school authorities called in the parents. "Twice," Pepe recalls, "I got sent home in the first grade for not following the rules. The first time, the teacher shamed me in front of everyone for failing to come in white clothes for the flag celebration. She sent me home. I was in tears, and I got angry with my parents for not having sent me in the right clothes. They had forgotten it was Monday. My mother sent me back in white. Another time, the teacher sent me to the director's office because I did not have a notebook with double lines. He gave me a citation and sent me home to my parents. I arrived in tears again. 'They gave me this because of you. It's your fault,' I told them." Although a principle of *civismo* prohibited him from criticizing his parents, it competed with another—his desire to comply with the rules of a socializing institution respected by his parents. The school functioned as a site of potential and partial liberation from the regime of home.

In these years of growing demand and a scarcity of educational facilities and personnel, children often moved from school to school. Such shifts hurt Pepe's performance. The camaraderie he so loved between children and teachers broke down when he transferred in the third grade to the nearby Andrés del Río primary school. It was a much bigger school without the order he had grown to expect. The bathrooms were dirty and smelled. Children fought each other in the patio. He found his third-grade teacher vulgar and disgusting. She wore too much makeup, dyed her hair, and smoked. She seemed more interested in showing her low neckline and legs to the male teachers than in teaching. She left the class alone a lot. "We took to throwing papers," said Pepe, "robbing pencils, and fighting with one another. The teacher marked up my multiplication tables and I spent my time decorating her marks with colors and designs."

When he returned to Francisco González Bocanegra for the fourth grade, he had lost the discipline of study. He improved his arithmetic and began to paint in watercolors, but overall he performed poorly. In the fifth grade he transferred to the Belisario Domínguez school, a still larger establishment where the director blared orders to the students over a loudspeaker. By this time, he was failing and missing school—in large part because of calamities he suffered from misbehaving. In the fourth and fifth grades, many of Pepe's and Nico's adventures ended badly. One afternoon, as they played in front of the church of Santa María la Redonda, their dog, Sultán, jumped into a deep pool of water in a drainage project. The dog swam to the other side, and Nico dared Pepe to do the same. Pepe did not yet know how to swim. He jumped in on the dare. He would have drowned had a man not come along, pulled him out, and scolded him soundly. The same year, during the Independence Day celebrations, a wad of firecrackers blew up in Pepe's face. On another occasion, he climbed up on the rooftop and fell through the skylight of a neighboring building onto a party below. He seriously gashed his leg. On a family excursion to the Desierto de los Leones, his father told him not to play on the swings. He disobeyed. He fell off the swing and bloodied his face and legs.

At this point, José Zúñiga Sr. separated Pepe and Nico. Seizing authority from his unhappy mother, the Abuela Petrona, he sent Nico to a boarding school for wayward boys, the Internado San Juan Bosco, run by the Colegio Salesiano. It was not one of the state's several reform schools but likely one it used in its post-1940 collaboration with private (primarily Catholic) social assistance programs. Tío Efrén, who worked in the government corrections office at the time, secured Nico's place at the school. Nico returned every other weekend to visit. Pepe and Chucho watched him transform into what in their opinion was a model child. He wore nice, clean clothes. His hair was closely cropped. He had bathed. He was even clean behind the ears and under his nails. He had learned to eat with a fork, knife, and spoon when the family was still eating with tortillas. He showed the boys some clever games he had learned to play with a simple string. Pepe envied Nico and wanted to go to the Internado himself.

Pepe did not go to the Internado, but he did become more serious about school. He repeated the fifth grade at Belisario Domínguez. The second time around, he became the proud assistant to his teacher. In the fifth and sixth grades, he gladly submitted to the discipline of his Yucatecan male teachers, renowned in this period for their toughness and radical exhortations to patriotic service and, for Pepe, their excellent instruction in writing and penmanship. Although his sixth-grade teacher pinched the cheeks and pulled the ears of disobedient children, Pepe appreciated his authority. But when the school switched the teacher in the middle of the year, discipline collapsed. Of his own volition, Pepe repeated the sixth grade at night school. He did not like it that others his age seemed to know more than he did. He wanted to excel. He wanted to *superar.* He now felt he had the energy and discipline to do so on his own. Yet he did not qualify for secondary school, and his parents did not want him to continue. Like many other families in the Colonia Guerrero, they expected their son to go to work—to apprentice in a trade. As far as their father was concerned, Pepe and Chucho would become tailors.

Pepe with God, the Virgin, and the Saints

Every Sunday morning before the matinee, Pepe and Nico attended mass at the church of Santa María la Redonda three blocks from their house. They took their first communion there after preparing for it with a neighborhood catechist. The life-size figures of Jesus, San José, San Antonio, the Virgin of Guadalupe, and the Virgin de los Dolores must have impressed the children in their robes of silk and velvet, their gaze of infinite devotion and suffering. "Not suffering," said Pepe, looking at them today, "they are tranquil and at peace. How moving and tender is the figure of San José holding his son with a lily in his hand."

At Santa María la Redonda on Good Friday, Lupe often began her visit with Pepe and Chucho to the seven churches. Like those of Santa Veracruz and San Juan de Dios on the Alameda, all were centuries-old sanctuaries in the center of Mexico City. As they walked from church to church with their rosaries, they relived Christ's painful path: from betrayal, to the garden of Gethsemane, to his sentencing by the Romans, to the beatings and pillorying he suffered as he bore his cross along the road to Calvary. On Good Friday, purple cloth shrouded all the saints and relics in the churches. Only the Holy Sacrament gleamed solemnly on the altar, lit up with candles and adorned with flowers. The faithful knelt before it, contemplating the sacrifice Jesus made for humankind, expressing their gratitude, doing penance, and praying for pardon. Of course Pepe prayed too, although today he is not sure he completely understood what it was all about.

Santa María la Redonda, one of the oldest churches in Mexico, was built in the Aztec barrio of Tlaquechihuacán in 1524 by orders from the Franciscan friar Pedro de Gante. Pedro de Gante's Colegio de Santa Cruz de Tlaltelolco, just a short distance away, became a flourishing center of Nahua learning and artistic expression in the mid-sixteenth century. Santa María's indigenous structure of stone and *tezontle* (volcanic rock) cemented with lime plaster became more elaborate over time with the addition of a majestic baroque rotunda reigning over the altar, a side chapel dedicated to the Sacred Heart of Jesus, and a tower flanking the right side of the facade. Richly textured clothing, crowns, paintings, and silver memorabilia of miracles came to embellish the side altars during the height of baroque opulence in the seventeenth century. Then in 1769 began the long process of secularization, when the archbishop ordered the Franciscans to turn over the church to the secular clergy. Adjacent to Santa María la Redonda stood the Santa Paula Cemetery, a further step in secularization. Created as a burial ground for the victims of the 1779 smallpox epidemic, Santa Paula became an official cemetery when, for purposes of sanitation in 1789, the viceroy ordered the moving of tombs from church interiors to high ground distant from homes. Santa Paula became the resting place of notables: Don Manuel Romero de Terreros, benefactor of the Monte de Piedad, Leonora Vicario, heroine of the independence movement, two Mexican presidents, and several soldiers who defended Chapultepec Castle against the U.S. invaders. But the most notorious inhabitant was Santa Ana's leg. The self-styled hero of national independence and many times president of Mexico had lost the leg in a skirmish with invading French soldiers in Veracruz in 1838. He brought it to the capital in 1842 and had it buried with full military honors in Santa Paula. A few years later, angry crowds dug it up and paraded it through the street to protest Santa Ana's bid to become Mexico's emperor. In 1869 the government closed Santa Paula, transferred the remains to more distant cemeteries, and fractioned the land for the city's expansion. Largely out of nationalized church land and shrinking indigenous barrios, developers had created the Colonia Guerrero in the late nineteenth century.

By 1945, all that remained of Santa Paula were the ghost stories that circulated in the neighborhood, a small chapel, a gate, and a plaza where

Pepe and other children played *frontón* and football. It had become the playground for the Francisco González Bocanegra school. Secularization, earthquakes, population growth, and building booms had likewise shriveled Santa María la Redonda's land and splendor. Still a quiet sanctuary within, the church's plaza was unpaved and unadorned. On all sides, the forces of ludic exuberance and godless sobriety pressed in around it. Across the street, mariachi musicians roamed Garibaldi Plaza, where the gay men Pepe and Nico watched sold food from sidewalk stands and bars like the Tenampa filled with music and revelry into the dawn. Pérez Prado's orchestra launched the mambo craze there in 1949. In the apartments along the south side of the church lived mariachi musicians. On the church's southern flank, nightclubs churned with business, music, and the promise of sex—the Dragón Rojo, La Momia, and the Bombay. The Salón Los Angeles ballroom where Chucho helped out was a short distance away. The comedian Cantinflas got his start in the surrounding *carpas,* where the Zúñiga family went to watch the comic El Palillo parody the government's latest act of corruption and injustice (he was regularly jailed and regularly released). The Cine Isabel and Pepe's godless primary school backed right into the church. And safely close to God (or way too close to holiness) was the nearby Calle del Organo, otherwise known as the Calle Chueca and the Calle Panama, where prostitutes dodged police raids by filing out of their rooms with baskets, as if they were proper housewives on their way to market. They grabbed men on the street to accompany them as their husbands when they were really soliciting.[31]

The sacred and profane had always lived symbiotically side by side in Mexico. The profane entertainment accompanying many religious events made the sacred more seductive and more communal. The profane provoked excess and so inevitably a return to God and pleas for His pardon. But by 1945 in Mexico City, religion, like the church of Santa María la Redonda, was a necessary part of life but no longer its organizing principle. For the Zúñiga family, the particular integration between the sacred and the profane they had known in Oaxaca changed in Mexico City. Churches no longer called on Lupe to sing. In Oaxaca, people sought her out for her command of the prayers. In Mexico City, she prayed alone and every evening with her children—three Hail Marys and a *Padre Nuestro,* after which Pepe prayed alone. Upon the death of a family member, she guided their souls through nine days of prayers into the protective hands of God, but she prayed for family members, not a broader community.

In Oaxaca, José had belonged to the tailors' guild organized around a patron saint. He had taken advice from his employer, Tío Lino, who belonged to the Catholic social movement. In Mexico City, José had no guild. His religious and moral convictions became, like Lupe's, a private and familial affair. Like Lupe, he attended mass at Santa María la Redonda but by himself. He read the Bible, given to him by his sister Antonia's *compañero*, Efrén. He set up altars in the apartment to the Oaxacan Virgin de la Soledad and the Virgin de Juquila and illuminated them with colored lights. He prayed to them, but he also displayed a photograph of Clark Gable (Rhett Butler) kissing Vivien Leigh (Scarlett O'Hara) in *Gone with the Wind* and another of Tongolele, the first of Mexico City's "exotic dancers." This scantily clad artist who "smiled with her hips" performed at the nearby Teatro Follies Bergere. He went to see her often. It bothered José not the least that the Catholic Liga de la Decencia hysterically denounced her. He had initiated his love for pleasure in the movie theaters and dances in Oaxaca. He had no intention of repressing it in the rich paradise of entertainment in Mexico City. He was moderate in his extravagances, but he stepped out at night from time to time to visit the clubs, the bars, and the striptease at the Tívoli, where the male public called for "Hair! Hair!"[32]

Yet as much as the Catholic religion appeared to retreat in the face of secularization, its very fluidity across space meant that it continued to be a powerful force in the anonymous city. Immigrants came from all over Mexico to find self, family, and community in the religious institutions, symbols, and celebrations they had known so intimately at home. In the Colonia Guerrero, people practiced their faith in many places. At the entrance to every *vecindad*—or as in the case of Lerdo 17, at the back—stood an altar to the Virgin of Guadalupe. The neighbors collectively tended her. They brought her flowers, illuminated her with lights, and kept her garments clean and fresh. On December 12, her feast day, they pooled their money to invite a priest to celebrate mass. Families had altars in their homes, and artisans had them in their workshops. Individuals wore medals of Christ and the saints—Pepe treasured the medallion of San José he received from his Tía Antonia. Families and friends took frequent trips to the basilica to honor the Virgin of Guadalupe, to eat, and to have their pictures taken on a stuffed donkey or beside a portrait of the Virgin. The Zúñigas celebrated saint's days with family members. On the Día de los Muertos, they made an altar in the apartment adorned with the photographs of departed relatives and with marigolds, candles, and small offerings of bread, chocolate, and fruit. The aged Clotilde tended to the details of the altar as she had done in Oaxaca. On the patio, she prepared the chocolate on her *metate*, using the old wooden tablets she had brought with her to the city. From Oaxaca came the chocolate, the *mezcal*, *mole*, and tiny artisanal "padrecitos," representing priests. Lupe purchased them from her network of women who regularly supplied Oaxacan migrants with goods from home. But the Zúñigas did not attend mass on the Day of the Dead as they had in Oaxaca. If it had always been a family affair, it became more of one in Mexico City.

Neighbors created community in the eagerly anticipated posadas. As noted, the posadas took on new meaning: they were no longer those of Oaxaca, where the lugubrious litany of pilgrims ended with a brief *hora romántica*, a glass of punch for the adults, and hot chocolate for the children. They became events for consumption and sheer enjoyment. Just as the breaking of the *rosca*, the special sweet bread eaten on the Día de los Reyes, became less important than the clamor for toys on that day, so for children the posada meant piñatas. The school fostered this. Forbidden to discuss God, textbooks pictured the posadas and the Día de los Reyes as happy moments of consumption.[33] The merchants—whether in the market, the corner shops, or department stores, like the recently opened Sears Roebuck—never missed an opportunity to meet the demand for candies, nuts, fruits, and toys. The posadas and the Día de los Reyes became celebrations privileging children in ways they had not been before. "Santa Clos" began to make his appearance—not for the Zúñiga boys in Lerdo 17 but for the children in Lerdo 20. He came leading a donkey with fake reindeer horns on his head and a sack full of gifts parents had bought for their children. "Ho, ho, ho!" he would say ringing his jingle bells. "Here comes Santa Clos! Here comes Santa Clos!" Not for Elvia Martínez and her brothers and sisters. They were too poor. "We were really screwed. . . . It was a question of giving us food or giving us gifts. Pinche Santa Clos, Pinche Santa Clos, he never brought us anything."[34] Santa Clos, like the Christmas tree, interrupted the solemnity of the birth of Jesus: he contributed to children's growing habit of wanting and getting "things."

If in Oaxaca the posadas had been occasions for social networking and the affirmation of solidarity and trust among adults, that function intensified in the rude, anonymous world of the city. Everyone—or almost everyone, as there were exceptions among the recalcitrants and practitioners of other faiths—cooperated in buying the streams of *papel china*, lanterns, and candles for the procession and the Spanish moss they strung across the patio, in making the punch and the bread, in preparing tamales, in contracting the band or providing the records. Everyone knew the best posadas took place in Lerdo 20, where Elvia lived: that huge *vecindad* stretched an entire block from Lerdo west to Soto Street. Here, they broke open 24 piñatas on the 24th day of December, the first for the adults and then others for the children, full of peanuts, oranges, *techote*, and candies. Then they danced. Adults and youths showed off the steps they had learned at the ballrooms—the mambo, the swing, the cha-cha-cha, later rock 'n' roll. Those who did not know the dances learned them in this multigenerational ambience of delight and movement. Dancing was for everybody. For the Santa Clos–deprived Elvia, known as "La Boogie" for her exceptional talent, dancing was her path to happiness and fame. Close to midnight, the neighbors would gather and walk to the Basilica of the Virgin of Guadalupe for midnight mass. After mass, they climbed up the hill of Chiquihuite where they danced to the music of a violin until they fell asleep on their *petates*.[35]

Little wonder, Pepe could not take the priest seriously when from the pulpit of Santa María la Redonda he denounced the mambo as obscene. "Very soon the devil is coming here," the priest warned the faithful. "Reject him! Don't let him tempt you!" "He threatened anyone who took up this dance! Can you believe it! How stupid!" Pepe did not even know the priest's name, and he did not like him. He had disliked him since he took his First Communion. Because of his accidents and their misadventures, he and Nico missed several catechism classes and had to make them up. Claiming they were not sufficiently prepared, the priest excluded them from the ceremony on August 15, the day of the Virgin María's Assumption. The priest did not give them the blue jackets, white pants and shirts, and new shoes he gave to those who had finished their classes on time. Not the rosary, prayer book, and candle either. Nico and Pepe had to take their First Communion alone in simpler white pants and shirts. They wore tennis shoes. José took them to a photography studio to pose in front of an image of Christ (see figure 3.6). They were disappointed not to have received the new clothes and ashamed not to have been in the group picture.

Worse, Pepe remembers that prior to the communion, he had to confess to the priest. The priest placed his big hand on Pepe's thigh and asked if he had ever seen a girl's private parts. Of course he had, but he was not about to tell the priest. What really bothered him was the priest's hand on his thigh. It did not feel right. Such reports of priestly transgression abound in Mexico, and we cannot tell if it was a testimony of reverse guilt registered by a naughty little boy. Recalling the time, Pepe reflected about himself and Nicolás, "We were terrible, tremendous, extremely mischievous!" Still, the priest's behavior is clear and sharp in his memory.

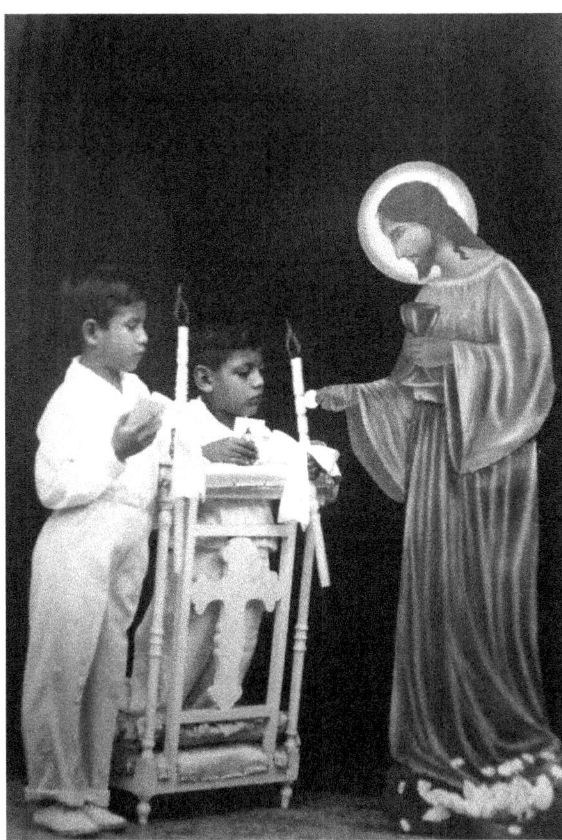

Figure 3.6. Nico and Pepe at their first communion. Black-and-white photograph, 1946.

All the more reason to nourish his own personal religious faith. It was a deep source of moral security and strength for him as he grew older. When in adolescence he began to earn money, his mother told him to go every Saturday morning to the church of San Juan de Díos, in front of the Alameda to deposit three coins on the altar to the Santísima Trinidad. He expressed his gratitude for his job when he deposited the coins in different receptacles signifying home, clothing, and sustenance. Years later, when his antireligious professors at the Esmeralda painting school told the students to get rid of their religious medals, Pepe, like his classmates, protested. Pepe obliged by putting his medal of San José into a box, but in his head he had not taken it off.

At the age of seventeen in 1954, Pepe went with his brother Chucho and Chucho's godfather, Martín Pacheco, to render homage to the Virgin of Juquila in the mountains of western Oaxaca. He went to fill a promise he had made to his cousin Alfonso. He adored Alfonso, who died at the age of twenty-seven of heart failure. When Alfonso knew that he had not much longer to live, he asked Pepe to honor a *manda* he had made to the Virgin of Juquila. He had suffered an accident when the bus he was driving went off the road and crashed into a ravine. Several people had died, but Alfonso believed that his petition to the Virgin had saved his life. The accident occurred on the road to Sola de Vega, the last stop for the buses carrying pilgrims to the shrine. Pepe, Chucho, and Martín arrived in Sola de Vega in the first days of December, just before the Virgin's festival on the eighth of the month. Pilgrims packed the buses and others arrived on foot. "It was late when we got there, about ten at night, and we immediately began to climb the mountain," Pepe recalls, "We were in a group of about twenty persons with a guide. We carried canes, sticks, and branches to help us because the terrain was so steep. When we got to the top, we started to descend straight down until we got to the bottom about four o'clock in the morning. I collapsed on the ground under a tree and slept. I could walk around Mexico City, but I was not used to this! Soon we were up again. We drank *atole*. People shared their tamales. Martín swallowed two raw eggs in mezcal. *!Que bárbaro!* Then it was back to climbing. Two days and two nights it took us to get there! Chucho made friends with a woman he met on the bus, a teacher. She went with us and slept with my brother. When we crossed the river Juchatengo, Chucho asked for a burro for the woman, and we all mounted it guided by mule skinners. We laughed because the mule skinners had taken off all their clothes to pull the donkeys through the water. Our joking irritated the teacher who called us all 'shameless.' What hypocrisy on her part after having slept with my brother! In the river, we saw native women bathing nude. How strange! We'd never seen women bathing in a river let alone with their breasts in the air! We came to a place called Chacagua, famous for the *caimanes* in the river there, and I remembered that Alfonso's bus was called Chacagua. Along the way, the guide told us the legends of the place. In the tree of La Preñada, he told us there were many tiny cradles of palm representing wishes to have children, to get pregnant, and that the children would be well cared for. He pointed to another pair of craggy rocks and told the story of a man and woman who had sex along the way and turned to stone for their sin." As pilgrims passed a similar marker on their way to the shrine at Chalma, romance along the road must have been something of a regular habit. Chucho and the teacher were living proof.

"When we came upon a deep ravine, the guide advised us to pass with great care and told us the story of a priest who, returning from a visit to the Virgin, repented his trip and told the arriving pilgrims not to bother to go on because she was such a small little thing and the church very insignificant. Exactly when he passed the ravine, by divine punishment he fell into it and died. We came upon another river with very fine sand glittering with gold dust. It reminded me of Humphrey Bogart in *Treasure of the Sierra Madre*. When we got to the top of the highest mountain, we could see the Pacific Ocean far in the distance. After two days and nights we got to the church. I remember there were lots of people, brass bands, and piles of canes people had left outside the shrine. I deposited my stick. Outside and inside the church, there were many black men protecting the Virgin. They jealously guarded the altar with their machetes, not letting anyone get near her. They must have had their reasons. Probably there had been robberies, but given the ferocious demeanor of the guards, one couldn't linger long in the church. I prayed and told the Virgin I was praying in honor of Alfonso and thanking her for saving his life in the accident. We got out quickly. There were no hotels as there are today. We slept on the ground. I don't know how we got back to Oaxaca or Mexico City for that matter. It had been a trip full of surprises. I am glad I went, but I never went back. Nowadays, buses take you all the way to the shrine."

4. My Father, My Teacher

In the photograph, José Zúñiga Pérez strides down a Mexico City sidewalk near the Zócalo. It is 1954. Filled out in middle age, he cuts a gallant figure in his fashionable cashmere suit this master tailor has sewn for himself (see figure 4.1). The Tardan hat and crocodile skin shoes he has purchased and treated with great care. He has modeled himself after those tall, dark, and handsome icons of film—Clark Gable, Errol Flynn, and Tyrone Power. He has watched how they move, gesture, smile, and seduce on screen. In his demeanor he exudes confidence. Erect and proud, he knows he is a participant in the creation of a new mass public in the teeming city.

In the 1920s, a bon vivant like José Zúñiga Sr. would have been derisively called a "fifi," an effeminate, frivolous man, because of his attention to appearance and his love for entertainment, but in the 1950s, with the increased strength of the media, the markets, and the leisure industry, he was simply fashionable.[1] Behind his public persona was a modern respect for the body. As noted, he brushed his teeth after he ate and bathed regularly. He took special care with his mustache and silkened his hair with the famous cream Glostora advertised on the radio and in the newspapers. "Glostora exalts the personality," ran the ad. "It reveals good taste and distinction."[2] He appreciated modern medicine, particularly after being cured of a nasty bout of syphilis. For him as for many, pleasure came to be linked—sometimes through bitter experiences—to new forms of discipline. Medicine and commerce, cinema, music, and radio pro-

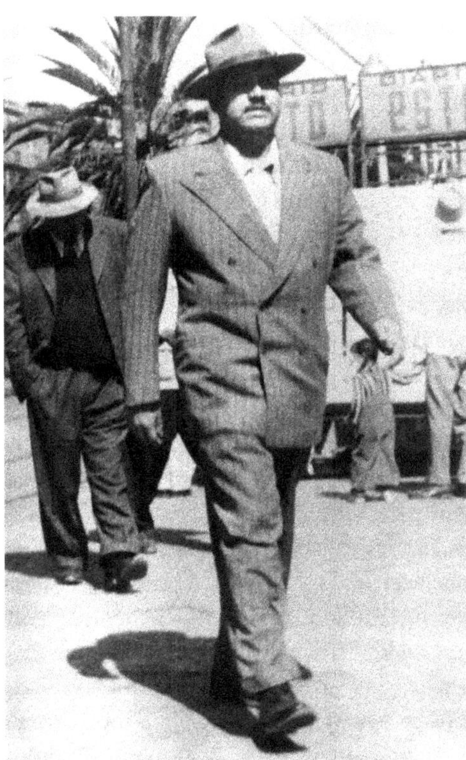

Figure 4.1. José Zúñiga Pérez. Black-and-white photograph, 1954.

grams promoted notions of health and beauty that melded into a general thrust toward a tempering of violent masculinity after decades of revolution and social turmoil. The romantic boleros he loved—of María Luisa Landín and Agustín Lara—consecrated feeling over physical conquest. The movies he watched suggested to him how much sexier was sexuality when artfully concealed and touched with affection, although one could sense—and José surely did—the violent sexuality that seethed within the characters played by Gable and Flynn.

Born in 1914, he had had a sad childhood—without a father, going barefoot and in tattered clothing, subject to a willful mother who apprenticed him at the age of twelve to a tailor. Later in life, he loved telling his sons how he and his friends had discovered the movies. As young boys, they had sacrificed the centavos they had for candy to buy the tickets, cheaply priced to attract a public. José sharpened his scant reading skills deciphering the subtitles of the silent films. More than the words, the images, effects, and action enthralled the children. They went to laugh, tremble, and scream. Fixed on the oft-repeated “chase” animated by live band music from the pit, they shouted instructions to the beleaguered hero, “Watch out! They’re gonna shoot you! No, don’t go that way! Go that way!” They howled with laughter and froze in suspense as Billy the Kid sought to outmaneuver the sheriff who pursued him. The eerie scenes and mechanical wonders of German expressionist films terrified them: Siegfried’s battle with the huge dragon Fafnir the Great in Fritz Lang’s *Die Nibelungen*; the spooky sleepwalker Cesare’s kidnapping of the beautiful Jane in Robert Wiene’s *Cabinet of Dr. Caligari*; in Murnau’s *Nosferatu* the sight of the ship tossing at sea, driven only by the breath of the vampire after rats had infected the crew with the plague. When the diva tore off the mask of the *Phantom of the Opera* revealing a deformed monster, José and his friends flew out of their seats and ran screaming into the streets. *The Man Who Laughs*, Paul Leni’s 1928 adaptation of a Victor Hugo story set in seventeenth-century England, made them cry as they saw Gwynplain’s lip cut and frozen into a smile. The tears flowed down Gwynplain’s cheeks like the tears of the clowns the boys had seen in the circus. The endless ways Charlie Chaplin maneuvered his body enchanted them and so did his person, his humble origins and demeanor, his generosity and sense of justice. *The Kid* filled their hearts as Charlie the Tramp rescued an abandoned infant and raised him. Would that they had had such fathers!

The friends’ fascination shifted as their hormones surged. Rudolph Valentino and Ramón Novarro seduced them. The swarthy good looks of these romantic Latin heroes infused confidence and opened new possibilities for the poor, dark-skinned boys from remote Indian Oaxaca. The young tailors cut and sewed Valentino’s tight pants and gaucho shirts. They bought short black boots and curved their sideburns. They purchased the wildly popular Valentino sombreros put out by the Tardan Hat Company.

When in the *Four Horsemen of the Apocalypse*, Valentino danced the tango, the young men picked up the dance. José learned to whistle ragtime, jazz, and other tunes he heard at the movies. His musician friends transposed his whistling into notes and played the tunes at the fiestas the boys organized. Dressed like Valentino, perfumed and combed, they performed the tango, Charleston, and foxtrot with barrio girls no more materially endowed than they but wearing their hair short and wavy and their dresses loose and flowing so that their bodies moved freely to the music. It was at these dances that José renewed his acquaintance with his childhood friend and future wife, Guadalupe Delgado.

The major political movements of the Mexican Revolution did not influence José. These engaged, benefited, and organized campesinos, service, and industrial workers. He was an artisan. A devout Catholic, he had no interest in the revolution's campaign against the church. But neither was he a political Catholic. As noted, he paid no attention to the church's censorship of popular entertainment. Although he did not share the intense dislike his sister Antonia expressed for the anticlerical Benito Juárez, neither did he revere the hero's anticlericalism so central to the Revolution's ideology. He respected him as a fellow Oaxaqueño and defender of the patria. But most of all, he adored Porfirio Díaz, the dictator overthrown by the Revolution and demonized by its rhetoric. For José, Díaz was a staunch patriot, the architect of national progress, and an illustrious Oaxaqueño.

Distant from the Revolution's redemptive political mobilizations, José was nonetheless swept up in the energy of his times. If social, economic, and political turmoil led to movements of despair, anger, and militarization in other parts of the world, Mexico at the end of the 1930s entered an extended period of social and political pacification and demilitarization fueled by expanding economic opportunity. José Zúñiga imagined this opportunity. Like Al Jolson in *The Jazz Singer*, he wanted to break out of his provincial and familial confines, follow his dreams, and improve his life. For this, he had come to Mexico City along with thousands of others. José lived in an authoritarian regime where elections were controlled, laws often arbitrarily applied and the police corrupted, independent political action discouraged, and censorship and repression common. Yet he did not consider himself unfree or his aspirations trounced. In Mexico City he never belonged to a union, where so many of the period's political battles were fought. He remained a quasi-independent artisan, sewing men's and later women's clothing from his home workshop on contract from tailors and later small companies higher up on the chain of production and marketing in this complex, burgeoning industry.[3] His notion of freedom had deep artisanal roots in Mexican history that translated well into Hollywood paradigms. For José, Hollywood modernized an old idea of freedom, introducing the notion of individual struggle for "success," which meant "moving up." José identified with Clark Gable as Rhett Butler in *Gone with the Wind* because he saw him fighting for his personal liberty against the chaos and wreckage of civil war and the capricious whims of a selfish, aristocratic woman. But he also admired that woman, Scarlett O'Hara, for her indomitable will and tenacity in navigating the same conditions of adversity and rapid change. He liked Joan Crawford because she was tough, beautiful, and hardworking in her rags-to-riches roles. And could she dance!

He loved *Scarface*, that first and most violent of Hollywood gangster films, in which Paul Muni played the intrepid Tony Camonte, modeled after Al Capone. The gangster fought his way from the bottom to the top of the Chicago crime rackets through personal charisma, manipulation, and endless gunfire. These were all—Scarface, Rhett Butler, Scarlett O'Hara, Joan Crawford's many characters—successful conquerors, rebels against society, full of energy, often fighting outside and against law and convention. "It depressed him," Pepe remembered, "when Scarface turned coward and surrendered himself to the police." On the other hand, José loved Paul Muni when he played noble heroes who advanced "civilization": the steadfast Juárez defending the patria against foreign invaders in William Dieterle's *Juárez* (1938), Frédéric Chopin's mentor in *A Song to Remember* (1945), and Émile Zola in *La vida de Émile Zola* (1937). These were all propagandistic antifascist productions of the Second World War. Muni fascinated him because of his versatility as an actor. What a feat of talent and superb makeup was Muni's transformation from a struggling young writer to an aged bourgeois *hombre ilustre* in *The Life of Emile Zola*! And his character! His brave defense of a man (Alfred Dreyfus) wrongly convicted of a crime! Years later, Pepe told his father that Muni himself had been a committed democrat who stood up for freedom. "Maybe that's why I liked him so much," he replied.

José Zúñiga's personal quest for liberty and plenitude unfolded in the context of the war and the years of opportunity that followed in Mexico City despite the problems of scarcity, censorship, and mounting Cold War paranoia. Ironically, wartime productions of films like *Juárez* and *A Song to Remember* strengthened his resolve and deepened his secular faith as a Mexican: they were stories of steadfast small nations resisting foreign conquest. He followed the events of the war in newsreels shown in Mexico City theaters, he had lived through the city's blackouts, and he admired the Mexican Air Squadron 201 that flew in the Philippines. Probably, the Allied struggle for "democracy" moderated hostility he might have harbored against the United States as a perpetual invader of Mexico. In any case, he did not recognize the propagandistic intent of *Los Tres Caballeros*, the film Walt Disney made to strengthen Latin American support for the Allied cause.[4] He considered it a "tribute to Latin America," with its shots of Patagonia, the gaucho of the pampa, and the samba dancers in Bahia. He learned from it. "Mostly it pleased my father to see Mexico there—the beach at Acapulco, the canals of Xochimilco, the island of Janitzio in Lake Pátzcuaro, and the Tehuana beauty of his native Oaxaca singing the *Sandunga* he knew so well." Pepe remembered,

"He told me what a pleasure it was to hear Dora Luz sing Agustín Lara's "Solamente una vez," so popular on the radio."

Although the Zúñiga family's living quarters in the Colonia Guerrero were dark and cramped and money was scarce in the 1940s, José knew well how to tap into the entertainment that was everywhere in the central city: movie theaters, radio stations, parks, boxing and bull rings, wrestling arenas, gyms, live theaters, nightclubs. He embraced its pleasures and its messages, and many of these he shared eagerly with his family. It was José's cultural capital that made life for the family not just tolerable but exciting, enchanting, and promising. Every year he took the family to see *Holiday on Ice* at the auditorium in the upscale Colonia Roma. Here Disney stories and other Hollywood movies came alive in graceful skating, spectacular side effects of changing colors, smoke, fire, and snow, and the music of Cole Porter, Rodgers and Hammerstein, and Jerome Kern. In his son Pepe's opinion, "These were exquisite moving paintings." The family went regularly to the *lucha libre* matches. Although sectors of the middle and upper classes and even many in the popular barrios thought lucha libre violent, the Zúñiga family (like thousands of others) found it an immensely engaging art form.

Founded in Mexico City in 1933, the Empresa Mexicana de Lucha Libre commercialized an ancient sport, drawing thousands to the Coliseo and small arenas. In 1954, the Director of Physical Education of the Secretaría de Educación Pública, together with the president of the Confederación de Deportes Mexicanos, inaugurated the Nueva Arena, which could accommodate 20,000 fans.[5] Although more liberal than Greco-Roman wrestling or jujitsu, lucha libre had its rules, holds, and maneuvers perfected by the best *técnicos* or *limpios*. These rules were made to be broken by the outrageous *rudos*, like the famous Cavernario Galindo, who moved in the ring like a caged panther and delighted in biting the foreheads of his opponents. The public supported the técnicos or the rudos, replicating metaphorically a real struggle in their daily lives between their sympathy for the rule of law and convention and their impulse to subvert and mock them in order to survive, enjoy, or push ahead. Técnicos like Tarzán López, Wolf Ruvinskis, and El Santo—well appointed in their elegant capes, agile, spectacularly prepared, and stoic in the face of crude abuse—fought off rudos like Murcielago Velázquez, who opened his cape to let loose a storm of bats. Once he climbed into the ring with a viper, killed it with his teeth, and then hurled its corpse into the stands. The rudo Gardenia Davis appeared dressed in a luxurious robe and with his valet, who combed his hair, sprayed him with perfume, and delicately removed the robe. As the public screamed "*¡Puto! ¡Joto!*" Davis, with an arrogant smile and a gardenia in hand, exhibited his perfect musculature.[6] "Then he would enter the ring and fight like a tiger," Pepe laughed.

The Zúñiga family rooted for the técnicos, none more ardently than Lupe, who would jump to her feet waving her arms and hands, denouncing the umpire for bad rulings and shouting instructions to the wrestlers. "Hit him in the eye!" she screamed. Fans in the seats above shouted at her to sit down and shut up—and on one occasion dumped cups of urine on her head. Furious with his wife, José got up, grabbed the family, and snarled, "Let's get out of here." In these years, as new publics created themselves in interaction with the spectacle and with each other, the participants took measures to contain spectator involvement when it got out of hand. Traditionally, popular entertainment in Mexico City had been a rowdy space for attacking and mocking authority. Lucha libre, violent and raucous as it seemed to many, was by comparison a space of modern discipline that still left room for subversion; the audience regulated itself in its avid participation, while the wrestlers' rules of engagement were as clear to all as the rudos' attractive and hilariously outrageous negation of those rules.

The Zúñiga family returned many times to the matches. José Zúñiga bought the boys a scrapbook in which they pasted the wrestlers' pictures. Its introduction instructed the children: "Thus, Mexican youth can follow the moves of la Lucha illustrated here and staying clear of bad inclinations, dedicate the majority of its time outside of study to practicing sports; only then will we forge a strong patria of which you will be very proud."[7] The boys could identify every wrestler and every move.

With strong support from his father and his mother, Chucho took up swimming and boxing. He swam at nearby pools and trained at a local gym. As an adolescent, he participated in the city's golden gloves competition. He pursued sports in order to discipline himself, to please his parents, and to not turn out like his mother's brother, the violent assassin Manuel. Pepe learned to swim and with his friends frequented the pools in the east of the city that were all the fashion with the young. But he never pursued sports. He did not accompany his father to the Friday night boxing matches at the Arena Coliseo. "Once in a while I would go to the bullfights with him," Pepe noted. "I liked the candy, the popsicles, and the soft drinks. But, really, I found the spectacle brutal and boring."

José took the whole family to the nearby Follies Bergere to watch the sensual dancing of the scantily clad Tongolele, whose picture he displayed in the apartment. Born Yolanda Ivonne Montes Farrington in Spokane,

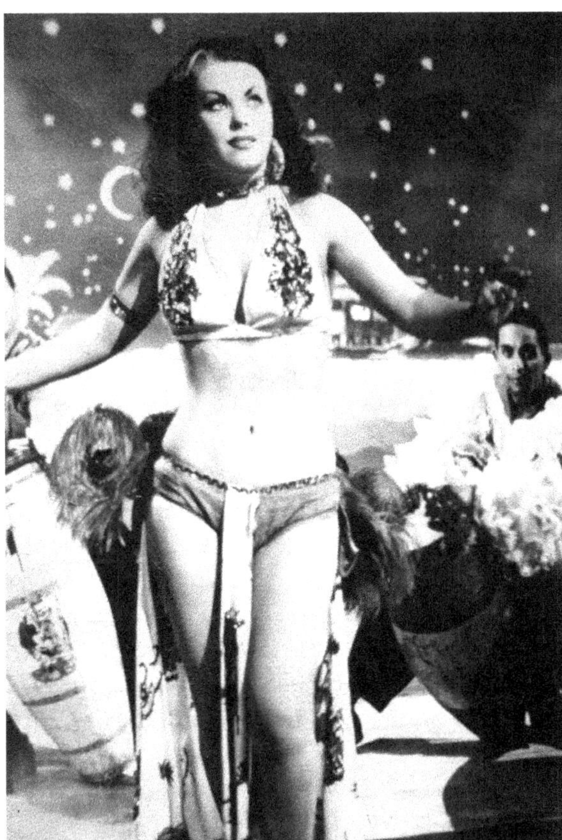

Figure 4.2. Tongolele. Black-and-white photograph, ca. 1950.

Washington, she was, as noted, the first of the city's "exotic dancers." Combining mythic notions of Africa and Tahiti, she took the name Tongolele and, to Caribbean drums and the Hawaiian ukulele, she danced in a bikini, sometimes embellished with sleek, long gloves, sometimes with a sweeping tale of frilly feathers (see figure 4.2). Tongolele did not pull Lupe to her feet like the lucha libre wrestlers. Rather, she simply hung her head in shame. The children stared openmouthed. José was enraptured.

What Pepe liked most to do with his father was go to the movies. José Zúñiga was not a formally educated man. He had left school after third grade. But for José, as likely for many others, a sense of empowerment and dignity came from learning through accessible, noncondescending media and from teaching others through them. José saw the radio as one such medium. The movies were another. He was a true connoisseur of film and an enthusiastic teacher. As Lupe and Chucho fell asleep in the movies, José Zúñiga took Pepe two or three times a week to one of the many theaters within walking distance of their vecindad: the Odeón, the Briseño, the Isabel, the Monumental, and the Capitolio. Often they would go afterward to one of the Chinese cafés on Santa María la Redonda Street or San Juan de Letrán Avenue, where they talked about the show over biscuits and café con leche.

José shared with Pepe his fascination with and understanding of cinematic techniques used to elicit fright, suspense, and wonder. At the Ciné Isabel, they watched the horrors of *Frankenstein*, *Phantom of the Opera*, *Dracula*, and the *Wolf Man*. Bela Lugosi's gruesomely made-up Dracula terrified Pepe as the count morphed into a bat. The scariest was Frankenstein. As Pepe watched the huge monster come alive with fireworks of electricity exploding from his neck, the boy could not look. He buried his face in his hands.

Of course, these terrifying monsters were similar to those, like the Serpent Lady, he had seen at the fair in Oaxaca, but cinema created them with innovative techniques and performances that provoked stronger, new sensations mixing fright with pleasure. José explained to his son how Frankenstein had been put together. He talked of Lon Chaney's laboriously applied makeup as the werewolf who prowled the dark Welsh countryside in *The Wolf Man*. Both father and son came to sympathize with some of these freaks—above all, the grotesque Quasimodo, who leapt from the tower of Notre Dame to save the beautiful Esmeralda from the gallows.

José saw cinema as a work of art—a study in plasticity, movement, and emotion—based on evolving technology. He talked to Pepe of the shift from silent film to sound. He admired Greta Garbo for her talent in making the transition. He quoted her famous line, "I just want to be alone," which they heard her speak in *Grand Hotel*. José loved Garbo's gorgeous and expressive face; he took Pepe to see *Anna Karenina*, *Camille*, and *Ninotschka*. He transferred to his son his awe at cinema's ability to display, expand, deepen, enhance—rather than violate—the physicality and emotion of the human face and body.

Father and son loved Hollywood musicals for their sheer exuberance. They saw *Show Boat* and *Rose Marie*—Jeanette MacDonald's singing reminded them of Lupe's. They took in the extraordinarily choreographed dances featuring big bands, huge choruses, and endless, curving art deco staircases to tap up and down on—the many Busby Berkeley films in which the overhead camera captured the shifting squadrons of dancers, as marching soldiers, as buds opening into full flower—creating kaleidoscopes of changing, glittering forms. Most of all, they loved Fred Astaire and Ginger Rogers, whom they first saw in the *Gay Divorcee* and *Top Hat*. Astaire was about "letting go"—bursting into tap anywhere and anytime—on a ferryboat, in a park kiosk, on the walls and ceilings of a hotel room, on a nightclub dance floor. When he danced with Rogers—to "The Continental," to "Cheek to Cheek"—they were sublime. In his tails and top hat, he beckoned to her—a shimmering jewel of organdy, satin, ostrich feathers, and pearls. As he swept her into his arms, they moved with an aristocratic elegance in a conventional manner, although their bodies were more closely and loosely intertwined and their smiles spoke an intimate joy. Then they would burst out on their own over terraces of sleek glass. Their athletic bodies seemed to fly across the floor, gliding low, leaping high, circling round each other, his tails flying, her skirt twirling—every graceful movement captured by the traveling camera. Astaire and Rogers showed, writes historian Morris Dickstein, that class was not a question of birth or money but of style—a coming together of motion, energy, pleasure, and skill.[8] In dance, they effected a transformation similar to that wrought by Agustín Lara in Mexican popular music. Like Lara's boleros. the music Astaire and Rogers danced to—the compositions of Jerome Kern, George Gershwin, Cole Porter, and Irving Berlin—and the very tap dance at which Astaire excelled—owed their vitality to a once despised popular culture—in the case of the United States, to the African Americans and vaudeville, and in the case of Lara, to the brothels nestled in the city's popular barrios like Guerrero and to the Afro-Cubans who had created the bolero and the *danzón* and brought it to Mexico in modern ships, old boats, and the new recording industry at the end of the nineteenth century.[9]

At the Ciné Mina, father and son watched Tarzan with Johnny Weissmuller and musicals like the *Glenn Miller Story*, *Rhapsody in Blue*, and the *Al Jolson Story* that inevitably repeated the tale of the immigrant or poor boy coming up from nothing and struggling to become somebody, usually a performing artist. These films were the equivalent for José Zúñiga and his son of the nineteenth-century bildungsroman, the bourgeois novel of male self-construction. They served as guides, models, and inspiration in their desire to mold themselves: to "become" and to "move up." The George Gershwin story, *Rhapsody in Blue*, particularly touched Pepe: "The neighborhood in New York City where he grew up had even more people—poor people—than the Colonia Guerrero. The vitality of New York City, the traffic coming and going, the horns honking, the spectacle after spectacle of music—'Swanee'! How my father loved Al Jolson!

All those Gershwin songs were in the film—''S Wonderful,' 'Fascinating Rhythm,' 'Embraceable You,' 'I Got Rhythm.' Then came the best—'Rhapsody in Blue' performed in the huge concert hall with the largest orchestra I'd ever seen. It began with that big, elegant swoop—then solos of the jazz instruments, the clarinets, the saxophones, trombones. There was even a banjo. Then Gershwin on the piano with that beautiful theme, I can only call it one of the most romantic pieces I have ever heard. The audience had been bored and skeptical, but by the end of the piece, they were clapping like mad and jumping to their feet. Then I wanted to hear more classical music. I wanted to be a pianist. Gershwin's parents had helped him a lot even though they were poor. My parents would not have been able to pay for my lessons, but even so, I was just eight years old, and I wanted to be a pianist!"

There would be no piano lessons. There would be more movies. Father and son loved Ingrid Bergman and Charles Boyer in *Gaslight*, Humphrey Bogart in *Casablanca* and the *Treasure of the Sierra Madre*, and Norma Shearer in *Marie Antoinette*. They watched the adventure stories of imperial conquest of the world's "lower orders," full of deceit, black terror, magic, animal revenge, and occasional loyalty to their new white masters: Gary Cooper in *Bengal Lancers*, Robert Mitchum in *White Witch Doctor*, Cary Grant and Douglas Fairbanks Jr. in *Gunga Din*. "To view cinema," said José to Pepe, "is to know more and more about life. More and more about the world."

But what world? More than primary school and more than Cri-Cri, the movies created an ideological, historical world for Pepe—a romantic Eurocentric world. Hollywood films of dance, verve, and struggle in the United States did not create a sense of awe about the society to the north. Any admiration for the United States was tempered by films like the Mexican *Las espaldas mojadas* (*The Wetbacks*), which portrayed the miserable treatment of the Mexicans who migrated north. Hollywood film represented U.S. society as the present and future of an expansive "body and soul." For viewers in many parts of the world, it created an encounter with a capacious, promising modernity.[10] According to Hollywood film itself, the United States had little history and less "culture"—defined in modernist terms as art, literature, and refinement. If José Zúñiga Sr. had cut his teeth on German film, Hollywood movies continued to portray Europe as the center of history and culture, interpreting its literature and celebrating its heroes and heroines—*The Hunchback of Notre Dame*, *Frankenstein*, *Camille*, *Anna Karenina*, *Marie Antoinette*, *Wuthering Heights*, and others. The rest of the world existed for Europe's conquest

(Africa and India); pleasure, intrigue, and subversion (Rio, Buenos Aires, and Acapulco); or as an example of exotic backwardness and tyranny (the Middle East and China).

Years later, Pepe would send his father endless postcards describing the old movies he was seeing in Paris and the places he visited that reminded him of the movies they had seen and conversation they had shared. "Knowing you like history," he wrote in 1972, "I am sending you this postcard of the tomb of Napoleon. It gave me goose bumps to approach it and to remember this great man." "Notre Dame reminded me of Charles Laughton and Maureen O'Hara in Victor Hugo's novel," he wrote in another.[11] From Vienna, he sent him a postcard of Johann Strauss and wrote of their seeing together *The Great Waltz*, the 1938 film of the composer's life. He also sent one with the portrait of the Empress Elizabeth, wife of Franz Joseph II, immortalized for Pepe in the movie *Sissi*, with Romy Schneider. He told his father he had trekked five hours through the Vienna woods to see the chapel where they married. He reminded his father that Franz Joseph was the brother of Maximilian, who had ruled Mexico. He noted the portraits he had seen of Elizabeth and Franz Joseph: "One cannot help but compare them with those of the archduke and his wife that hang in our Chapultepec Castle and form part of our history."[12]

However, Pepe's father exposed himself and his son to greater complexity rendered in film. A connoisseur of the medium as an art form, his taste was eclectic and ecumenical. Characterization fascinated him—the complex psychology of love, jealousy, vengeance, of surrender to love or to raw passion. He was as much interested in the adverse and the perverse as in the melodramas of glamour, success, and conquest. Not that these psychic aspects of human experience were new. Rather, cinema made them public and visible, open to the spectator's exploration and reflection. José introduced Pepe to film noir and to Italian neorealist cinema. The noirs—films like *Dillinger*, *The Maltese Falcon*, *Double Indemnity*, *Laura*, *Murder, My Sweet*, *Crossfire*, *The Postman Always Rings Twice*—were set in Los Angeles or San Francisco, sometimes Chicago or New York, on dark, slick streets lit by flashing neon signs, in smoky nightclubs, short-order restaurants, one-room walk-up apartments in cheap hotels with pull-down beds and hotplates, police headquarters, bleak train stations, or else in lonely beach houses, highway diners, and Lake Tahoe mansions stranded in dark woods. Noir characters were drifters and grifters, private eyes, femmes fatales, criminal gangs, crooked authorities—the police, the district attorney, the judge. Their props were guns, cigarettes, trench coats, whiskey, molls, and strapless dresses. Their complicated plot structures captivated audiences as they emerged through flashbacks and the multiple narratives told by characters who knew, forgot, imagined, and lied. Tortuous dances of violence and sexuality in a world of betrayal and deceit, they were hard-boiled, hypermasculine films—brimming with misogyny, homophobia, and homosexuality muted by the censors. Their heroes, played by Humphrey Bogart, Fred MacMurray, Ray Milland, Dick Powell, Robert Ryan, and Robert Mitchum, were antiheroes—mature, not handsome, often passive, anguished, alone, alcoholic. Noir films brought tough, evil women to the screen—not just jaded prostitutes and gun molls but icy middle-class women ready to kill their husbands or lovers in order to move up, women who turned the conventional housewife upside down—like Lana Turner in *The Postman Always Rings Twice* and Barbara Stanwyck in *Double Indemnity*. These films fascinated Pepe and his father.

Noir films were deliberately subversive, intended to challenge bourgeois ideology, particularly as this ideology was rendered in the Hollywood melodrama of "happy endings," the triumph of good over evil, of sentimental humanism, and didactic moralizing. They were, according to James Naremore, popularly accessible expressions of high modernism: of surrealism's attack on bourgeois convention, existentialism's preoccupation with alienation, ennui, and gratuitous violence, of German expressionist cinematography; of modernism's fascination with the primitive and its deprecation of the New Woman.[13] European émigrés made many of the films and influenced their development—Murnau, Fritz Lang, Billy Wilder, and Alfred Hitchcock. Pepe would study noir films much more carefully when he saw them in Paris, after sixties' youth had turned them into art films in their redemption and canonization of popular culture.[14]

There were no children in noir films, just scheming adults looking for a way out of their traps, a way to game the system, or the opportunity to act out their rage. By contrast the Italian neorealist films José and Pepe saw were about children—De Sica's *Bicycle Thief (Ladri de biciclette), Shoeshine (Sciuscià Ragazzi)*—caught with or without their parents in the grips of desolate poverty and an amoral struggle for survival in postwar Italy. These films were more explicitly focused on the poor, committed to the use of nonprofessional actors and to ethnographic documentation, in the spirit of Marxoid art after the Russian revolution. They captured the poor's cannibalistic preying on each other and the indifference and brutality of the law and social institutions. When a youth steals Antonio's bicycle, indispensable for the job he has finally managed to secure, he and his son Bruno set out through the streets of Rome to find it, only to be harassed and defeated by people like them and the police. In *Shoeshine*, an older brother and partner trick two innocent shoeshine boys, Giuseppe and Pasquale, into taking part in a robbery. Arrested and sent to a youth detention center, the boys' fast friendship is broken by police manipulation. Pasquale accidentally kills Giuseppe. Both films end in tears that reaffirm human love in the midst of moral and material squalor. In these films, as in those of the early Fellini and the work of Pier Paolo Pasolini—all of which Pepe would enthusiastically see many times over—stories of abject tragedy are tinged with Christian humanism totally absent from film noir. In noir, there was no redemption.

Scenes, settings, and characters from these films could have been transposed to the Colonia Guerrero, with its undercurrent of violence, abusive sexuality, hustling, and illegality. Guerrero's streets bred delinquency. The *vecindades* bred quarrels between and within families. Like Antonio's wife in *The Bicycle Thief*, Guadalupe Zúñiga pawned precious belongings so the family could survive, and like Giuseppe and Antonio in *Shoeshine*, Nicolás was sent to reform school. In a conversation about these foreign films, a friend asked Pepe why he preferred them to Mexican films of poverty. Pepe responded: "If it's what you see every day around you and you don't like it, why would you want to see it in the movies? Why would you pay for that?" Then he complicated his response. He did not much like the series of Ismael Rodríguez, *Nosotros los pobres* and *Ustedes los ricos*, two iconic films of Mexican cinema in its Golden Age. These melodramas romanticized poverty in a corny way. Rodríguez, said Pepe, wanted to inflate the virtues of poverty according to his own fantasies. "Pure fantasies! Why should a rich woman want to abandon all her comforts to go and live in a *vecindad* with the 'virtuous' poor as Mimi Derba's character did in *Ustedes los ricos*? Maybe some people identified with Rodríguez's films because they made them feel less screwed. But not me." He continued, "For me living in a poor neighborhood like the Guerrero where they filmed a lot of movies, I didn't want to see the poverty that surrounded us. I just didn't want to see it. There were movies like *Prisión de Sueños* and *El Quinto Patio* filmed just behind our *vecindad*. Some people want to think there is dignity in poverty, but not me. In this period, I was entering adolescence and I wanted to continue studying. I wanted a career, I wanted to progress." But despite his desire to "progress," perhaps even because of it, he liked Buñuel's classic film *Los olvidados*, a brutal, quasi-neorealist representation of violence, betrayal, and abuse in the Cinturón de la Miseria (the belt of misery) near the Nonoalco bridge, just a few blocks to the north of his home. He saw the film in 1952, when he was fifteen years old and was forming some critical judgment. His father disliked the film. "This cruelty cannot exist," his father commented. "Yes," responded Pepe. "This cruelty can and does exist."

Father and son also differed in their opinions about Mexican actors. José Zúñiga Sr. admired the elegant and aristocratic Jorge Negrete, with his well-trained baritone voice. He thought that Negrete, like Fred Astaire, had "style." But he had not much patience with Pedro Infante, a man of more humble origins and demeanor. Pepe liked Infante's less theatrical, less academic, and less pretentious voice, as well as his versatility as an actor—he played the role of carpenter, boxer, policeman, vagabond, cowboy, priest, and the great composer of waltzes, Juventino Rosas. If Pepe disagreed with the message of *Nosotros los pobres*, he liked the music sung by its star Pedro Infante. Every Friday with Margarita, the then wife of his Tío Manuel, he went to the newsstand of Doña Inez to buy the weekly publication that carried the words of the songs then playing over the radio and in the movies. They learned all the songs of Pedro Infante and sang them in the *vecindad* for whoever would listen. One day they even saw Pedro Infante at XEW studios. He was there dressed in the uniform of the transit police to promote his latest film, *ATM*!

Negrete and Infante were macho men, always conquering women, but there was a difference between the proud, patriotic, sonorous bellowing of Negrete:

I am Mexican, my land is brave,
Word of the macho, there's no other land
More beautiful and brave than my land.[15]

And the sweeter, more tender, and democratic song "Amorcito Corazón" that Pedro Infante sang as Pepe the carpenter in his overalls, T-shirt, and gymnast's muscles, to his girlfriend Celia (Blanca Estela Pavón) in *Nosotros los pobres*:

Sweetheart,
I want to kiss you,
Lost in the warmth
Of our great love,
I want to be, just be with you,
I want to see you in love
To dream in the sweet sensation of your kiss,

To tell you of my passion for you,
Compañeros through thick and thin,
Not even the years can weigh on us,
Sweetheart, you are my love.[16]

Infante represented a masculinity in transition: superior to and conquering women but at the same time tender in his relations with them, with children, and with babies; proud and hard at times but capable of torrents of tears of grief; agile with horses but enamored of men's modern technologies—the train, the motorcycle, the airplane.[17]

Pepe saw more cinema than his father, and he saw much of it differently. The sheer explosion of production, Technicolor, sound, special effects, and animation dazzled the boy and his cousin Nicolás. As they grew up, more and more cinema, above all from Hollywood, was made for children. Every Sunday after mass, the boys ran off to the matinees at the Odeón, Briseño, and Isabel theaters. At the Briseño, they saw the serial adventures of *Flash Gordon*, *Tarzan*, *King Kong*, *Daughter of the Jungle*, and *Captain Wonder*. Packed with children, the theater shook with their screams and the banging of their feet on the balconies' wooden floors. An incredible energy drew all into the experience. They followed the escapades out loud as their fathers had. They helped the hero along, "*Dale, dale . . .*"—"Give it to him!" Children who had seen the film would narrate what was going to happen next. Some liked this information, and others told them to shut up. They would see the films in episodes that always ended on a note of suspense and danger that would bring them back to the theater the following Sunday. Then when the episodes concluded, the cinema would show them again as a single movie. The Flash Gordon episodes went on for three hours. "If you hadn't eaten breakfast," Pepe commented, "You went home with a big headache."

Flash Gordon (Buster Crabbe) became Pepe's hero. White and handsome, he captivated Pepe as he struggled valiantly against the elements, slaying a dragon, withstanding a shower of flaming meteors, escaping a flood, and always defending his girlfriend Dale (Dahlia to Mexican children) from the forces of nature and the evil emperor Ming from the planet Mongo. When Flash and his allies, zapping their flash guns, hurling their fists, and drawing their swords, took on the enemy, the children stamped their feet wildly. As the enormous spaceship, spewing fire into space, rose toward the stars to music from Tchaikovsky's *Romeo and Juliet*, Pepe watched awestruck. The spaceship fascinated him. Its command center with its telephones for interplanetary communication and its screens that showed the battles going on in space anticipated television long before Pepe saw one. With all its electronic fixtures, he found the ship more fascinating than a car. Flash Gordon inspired his childhood art. He fashioned a spaceship from a piece of aluminum. He drew the landscapes of the planets, filling them with rocks, seas, and castle, much as these were depicted in Flash Gordon's adventures. "Flash motivated me to learn the position of all the planets at school. I learned them by drawing them. Saturn was my favorite," Pepe recalled.

He would not have noticed at the time how these films were wartime (both hot and cold wartime) depictions of the defense of the West against foreign invaders. The evil Ming was an Oriental despot with slanting eyes who sat on a high throne watching undulating belly dancers. He commanded an advanced scientific establishment that experimented with mind-altering drugs aimed at exterminating intelligent humans held in concentration camps. Flash Gordon, the American, aimed to liberate the good people of Mongo—a motley assortment of European-looking soldiers, nobility, and damsels out of scenes stretching in historical time from Robin Hood's Sherwood Forest to the near present.

From the time Pepe first heard the radio and saw a movie, the technology of sound and image enchanted him. He thought he was witnessing magic as he listened to the voices and music come out of the Philco box. He turned it around and saw the flashing bulbs. Maybe, like the genie coming out of Abu's bottle in *The Thief of Bagdad*, the sound came from the bubbling bulbs. Entranced by the magical effects of *The Thief of Bagdad* and Abu's genie, in Oaxaca Pepe had made himself a cape and pretended to fly while projecting candlelight against the wall that captured his shadow in flight. In Mexico City, he delighted in the mystifying figure of the *Phantom*, particularly his costume, his flowing black cape, and the beautiful green mask with slits for his eyes and eyebrows. From his father's cutting scraps, Pepe made several masks and climbed up to the roof in the night. Donning a mask, he transformed his world into one of total mystery, looking up at the moon and down on the immense cityscape glittering with lights and sounds. Like the spaceship he crafted from a piece of aluminum or dancing dolls he made from cardboard paper and cloth in imitation of those he had seen in *The Gay Divorcee*, the movies triggered flights of his imagination and built his artistic and mechanical skills.

Pepe began to view cinema with a sensibility distinct from his father's. His reading was not necessarily intended by the filmmakers. The children laughed hard at the films of María Félix as a wild woman challenging machismo. The story inevitably ended with the transgressive woman's domestication and subordination to patriarchal authority. This lesson was lost on the children, who instead identified with her rebellion. Like his other friends, Pepe had seen his father strike his mother, insult her for her cooking, and abandon her at night to philander. Pepe's father showed little affection toward Guadalupe, who was deeply in love with him. The children identified with their mothers' suffering—in part because it was their own suffering. Despite the deep love and admiration he had for his father, he thought him too strict and hard. The punishments he meted out often seemed excessive. When against his father's wishes he had gone to play on a set of swings in the park at Desierto de los Leones, he fell off the swing, and his father found him with blood and tears running down his face. Rather than respond to his pain, his father beat him so hard another man tried to stop him. "He's my son, you bastard, don't interfere," responded José.

The very presence of women and children in film and the focus on them seemed to promote a new appreciation for their rights to dignity, love, and selfhood. Children sobbed and sniffled in the theater when Cachita's mother died and the little seven-year-old girl, so sad and alone, had to sing in the school festival. Pepe and Nico felt Pedro Infante's overwhelming grief in *Ustedes los ricos* when he embraced the body of his baby, burned up in a fire. As he sobbed in desolation, Nico and Pepe cried with him. "What love from a father! What an unjust tragedy!" The children saw all of the Disney films many times over—*Snow White*, *Bambi*, *Pinocchio*, *Dumbo*. Snow White was the child who touched Pepe most deeply: this beautiful little girl, abandoned and cast into the forest by her wicked stepmother, taken in and cared for by a band of dwarfs, and finally rescued by the prince to the unforgettable tune of "Someday My Prince Will Come." He loved as well the child stars Shirley Temple, Judy Garland, and particularly Elizabeth Taylor, whom he watched in *National Velvet*, *Lassie*, and *Little Women*. He remembers Elizabeth Taylor in one of her less noted films, *Jane Eyre*. Seven or eight years old, she lived in an orphanage: the authorities punished her by making her stand for hours in the patio with heavy irons in her hands. She caught pneumonia and died. "What abuse!" remembers Pepe, "What cruelty to that little girl! The scene really affected me."

Of course, Pepe and Nico saw more than foreign films. They saw dozens of Mexican Golden Age movies: the romantic dramas of Pedro Armendariz, the classical ranchero films of Jorge Negrete, the comedies of Joaquín Pardavé—and Pedro Infante in all of these genres. They

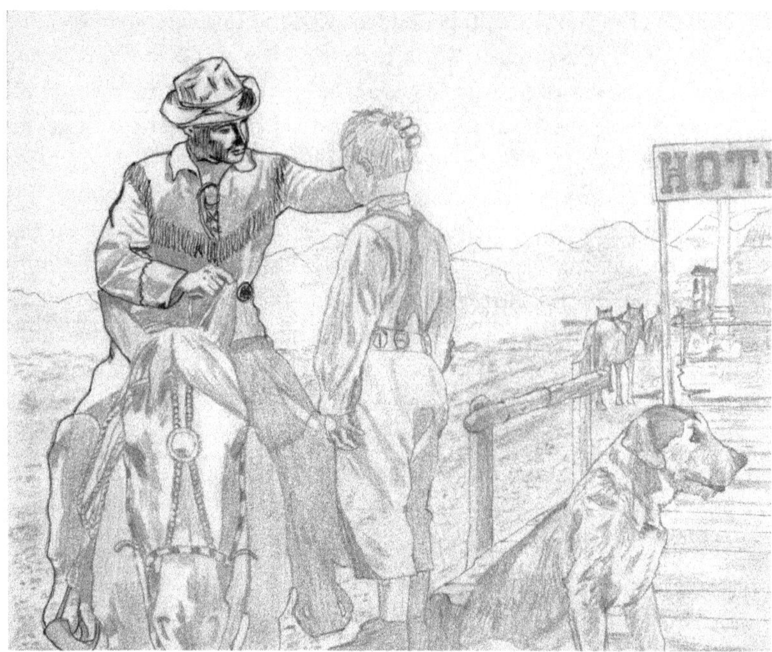

Figure 4.3. Pencil drawing by José "Pepe" Zúñiga, 1954.

watched the superfeminine and delicate Dolores del Río, the voracious, outrageous María Félix, and the beautiful, talented Marga Lopez. They took in many didactic melodramas in which a rebellion against authority threatened the integrity of the patriarchal family inevitably restored by the commanding, distant father or the loving, sacrificing mother or grandmother. A film like *Cuando los hijos se van*, with Fernando Soler and Sara García, reminded them that if modern children wanted to pursue new careers far from home, they should not forget their obligation to their parents. But if these films sought to nurture correct virtues in youth, there were other scandalous ones children could see in the 1940s before the ferocious campaigns of the Liga de Decencia, promoted by Ernesto Uruchurtu, the city's mayor from 1952. Pepe and Nico especially relished the sexy "rumba" films of Juan Orol, with the voluptuous dancers he had brought from Cuba: María Antonieta Pons and Rosa Carmina.

But the film that touched Pepe most deeply as he moved into adolescence was *Shane*. It came out in 1953, when he was sixteen years old. It was the only Western Pepe had ever liked, perhaps because it was an anti-Western. In the movie, a career gunslinger (Alan Ladd) comes to town to reform his life and finds lodging with a family of peace-loving, law-abiding farmers. The young son (Brandon de Wilde) worships him for his bravery, skills, honesty, and good looks; he contrasts him with his own father, whom he finds conventional, timid, and passive. Ultimately drawn into the local struggle between ranchers and farmers, Shane shoots all the bad guys and is forced to leave. The young boy runs after him, imploring him, "Shane, come back, come back, Shane!" Pepe heard Shane tell the boy, "No, I tried to become what I was not. You can't escape who you are. I will always be a fighter. But you, you grow up honorable. You take care of your parents." Pepe drew this moment of paternal tenderness (see figure 4.3). He copied it from a poster he had taken from the Ciné Briseño.

Shane reminded Pepe of the words of his cousin Alfonso, blond, tall, sensitive. He was, Pepe recalled, "fashionably dressed, very clean, handsome, and full of personality." Pepe was thirteen and Alfonso twenty-three when they bonded during Alfonso's visits from Oaxaca. They went to the movies often. They saw *Moulin Rouge*. The story of the deformed artist Toulouse-Lautrec moved Pepe deeply. He remembered Alfonso telling him after the movie, "In life you have to be what you are. You can be a taxi driver, or a tailor, or anything, but you have to be yourself. Don't let anyone tell you what you can and cannot be."

Pepe loved Alfonso very much. For Alfonso, he would make his pilgrimage to Juquila. Alfonso died of a heart murmur at the age of twenty-seven. The family received a telegram from Oaxaca. At seventeen, Pepe was devastated. He retreated to a corner and cried. His father asked him what was wrong. Pepe brushed him away. Then his father took him in his arms and said to him, "Son, don't think I do not understand why you are crying. You think I, who created you, don't know how you are, who you are?" His father bought him a bus ticket so he could go to Oaxaca to Alfonso's funeral. Over the years many differences would fray the bond between father and son, but they shared an understanding of the emotional complexity that lay outside and beyond the limits of convention—an understanding they had woven together in large part through their shared experience of cinema.

5. The Zúñiga Family as a Radionovela

Although José Zúñiga and Lupe Delgado united in the care of their children and their commitment to family well-being and improvement, sparks flew between them as they negotiated three moral codes. The first was religious: it united and kept them together. The second was clan loyalty. Having gathered their feuding extended families around them in Mexico City, divisions, quarrels, and mistrust ensued. The third we might call "modern"—those messages related to personal development and physical beauty, to affection and intimacy, to companionate marriage and the nuclear family. Often, the "modern" functioned as desire and sentiment that could create as much distance, insecurity, and disappointment as closeness.

On her saint's day, December 12, Lupe received postcards from female friends and relatives that represented the loving monogamous couple, content, beautiful, light-skinned, and fashionably dressed. We see here the mother seated embracing her cherubic child, both casting their adoring gaze upward toward the father, tall and straight, protective and warm (see figure 5.1). This was the Holy Family in its mid-twentieth century commercialized representation, full of joyous expectation, crafted from Hollywood movies, department store fashion, and hygiene mandates in the form of ads for Colgate Palmolive toothpaste, shampoo, and scented soap. It became the dream of so many women.

On his saint's day, José received postcards of bullfighters. As we have noted, he prominently displayed a photo of Tongolele on the wall of the

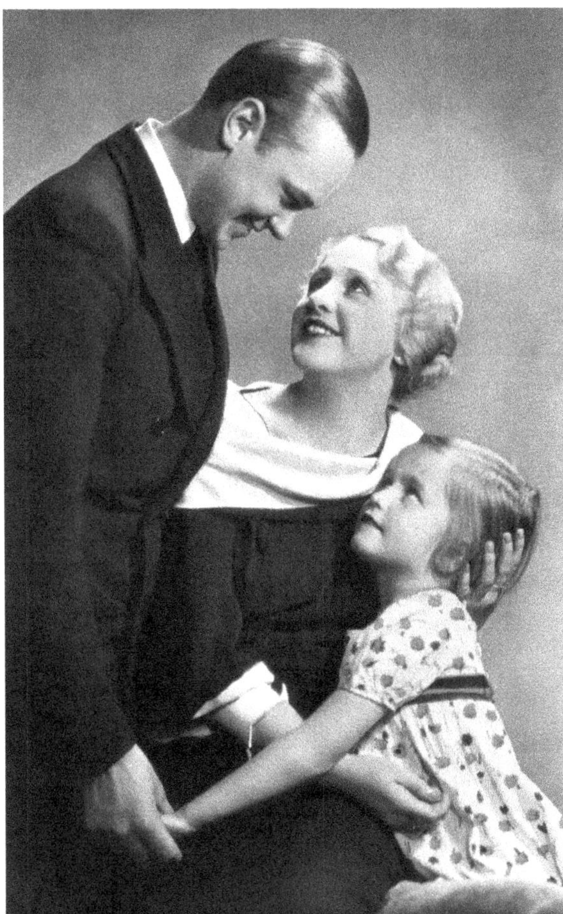

Figure 5.1. The "Holy Family." Hand-colored postcard, 1939.

apartment, and he kept another of a stripteaser he had seen at the Tivoli in a drawer. For all Lupe's cards that implied devoted monogamy, there were other messages—over the airwaves; in the movies; in the streets, clubs, and theaters of the Colonia Guerrero, and deeply rooted in life itself—that legitimized, even valued, a man's freedom to seek his pleasures outside of marriage. No one really knows about José Zúñiga's infidelities. His sons were convinced he had a great love, a woman named Lidia, who hovered in the shadows of their imaginations. Chucho remembered his father went out quite a bit to the clubs. Pepe thought he rarely stepped out but affirmed he was a "Don Juan." For certain, Lupe suspected him and was jealous of his possible adventures. Deeply in love with him, she suffered, according to Pepe, a sense of inferiority in relation to his beauty. "Her

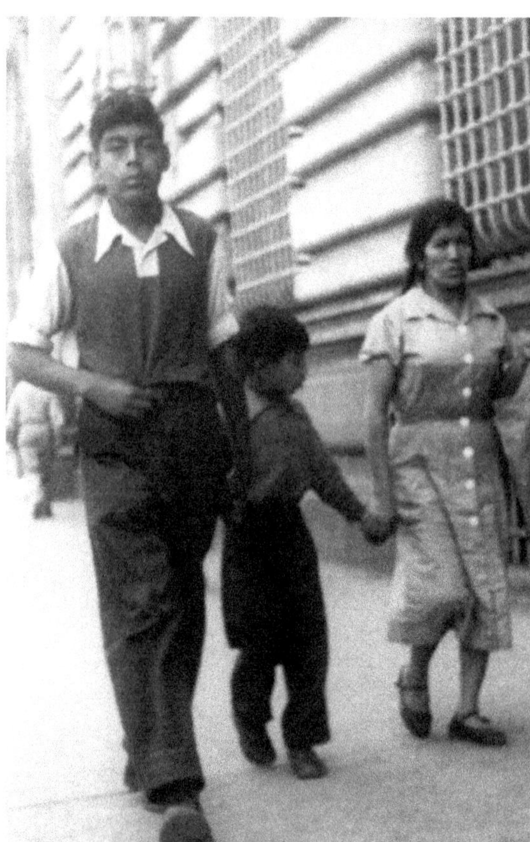

Figure 5.2. Pepe, Efrén, and Lupe. Black-and-white photograph, ca. 1951.

smallpox scars were less pronounced than she thought," he noted, "but they made her shy and insecure. Unlike my father, she never dressed fashionably. She sewed fashionable clothes for others but not for herself." Unlike her husband, she did not have models from cinema because she seldom went to the movies. We see her here in downtown Mexico City. She is walking with Pepe and Efrén, her last child, born in 1946. As always, she is on an errand critical to her family's welfare and survival (see figure 5.2). In this role in Mexico City, Lupe Delgado de Zúñiga excelled.

We have discussed the painful beginnings of this marriage born of an act of vengeance between families. The Zúñiga women—the mother Petrona, her daughters Antonia and Rosa, and her granddaughter Susana—brought their hostility toward Lupe to Mexico City. José considered himself a modern man in search of social mobility and success for himself and his nuclear family, but he was strongly traditional in his loyalty to his birth family. In his notions of morality, he seemed like Pedro Infante, the actor who disgusted him for his plebian conduct. As Carlos Monsiváis writes in his biography of the movie idol, Infante was above all "*un hijo de familia*."[1] Infante measured his personal success by his capacity to care for his parents and brothers and sisters. "If something makes me proud," he said, "it's having struggled always, having overcome misery, having given my parents a tranquil old age and having helped my brothers and sisters. . . . Even if it sounds off-key, I value myself for having been a good son and loving those of my blood, as I think it should be."[2] Of course, Infante also took care of his wives and lovers. Part of his notion of providing for them was to forbid them to work or develop any career. Pedro Infante sang as carpenter Pepe el Toro in *Ustedes los ricos*:

> How lovely is my woman,
> How well she knows how to cook,
> How great she is at sewing and ironing.[3]

For Infante, for José Zúñiga, and likely for many Mexican men of that period, wives and children formed part of a larger family the patriarch had to protect as a point of honor—the more so in José's case as he was his abandoned mother's only son. He was far more responsible to his nuclear and birth family than was his own father. Likely his own father's lack of responsibility prompted him to be so.

Yet he apparently harbored no bitterness toward his father, José Zuñiga Heredia, whom he brought to Mexico City just as he brought his mother, his sister Rosa, and her children (his sister Antonia was already there). He never knew his father until at the age of seventeen, he went to Orizaba, Veracruz, to find him. There in a restaurant, he met a pretty waitress who looked like him and bore the name Zúñiga. Eventually, she presented him to his father, who identified his son by a mark on his testicles, hereditary among Zúñiga men. Their encounter was cordial and brief. Years later, in his father's declining years, he brought him to live in Lerdo 17 because he felt that to be his filial duty. Here we see father and son in Mexico City (see figure 5.3).

Pepe remembers his *abuelo* as a kind man. He created no problems for Lupe, who cared for him. It was not the same with José's mother, Petrona. Although Lupe nursed Petrona in her last years, her mother-in-law never stopped accusing her nor did Susana cease with her stories of Lupe's infidelities. Tía Antonia and Lupe engaged in fierce physical battles. Lupe, small but strong, would punch out Tía Antonia, tall but inept.

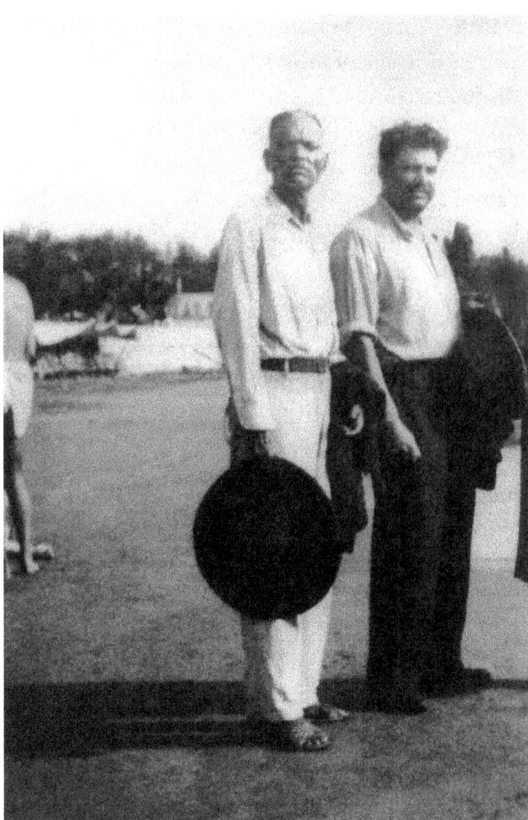

Figure 5.3. José (*right*) with his father, José Zúñiga Heredia. Black-and-white photograph, ca. 1954.

"My mother knew how to fight," Pepe remembers, "She hit with closed fists like a man. And my aunt was so stupid, kicking her and pulling her hair. Once, my mother broke Antonia's nose. Another time I saw Antonia, Susana, and Susana's sister Marta push my mother to the floor and beat her badly. Strong as she was, my mother was outnumbered."

"Much as the blows of my aunts hurt my mother, what hurt me was my father's attitude," remembers Pepe, "He didn't defend her." On the contrary, he made matters worse, his sons reflected later. He could abuse her. Chucho remembers his father telling him that he would never have married her had she not been pregnant. He wanted his meal at a precise hour, and if she served it late, he insulted her. "Get out of here, go home!" he ordered her once when she tried to follow him on one of his nights out, remembers Chucho.[4] "Her jealousies," Pepe noted, "put my father on the defensive and occasionally he hit her. My father was jealous as well. Listening to the accusations of the Zúñiga women, he did not trust my mother. Mama wanted to join the chorus at the Palacio de Bellas Arte to sing, but he would not hear of it. After she left Oaxaca, she never sang again in public. One day many years later, when I was studying at La Esmeralda, I heard her singing 'La Llorona,' that plaintive Oaxacan song full of mystery and grief. She was singing from the rooftop where she was washing. I had almost forgotten she could sing. Then I heard her voice, strong and beautiful, rising above the noise of the city on a sunny afternoon."

Lupe was an indefatigable mother and housewife, a brilliant hustler who invented every means possible to put dinner on the table, to dress her family and keep them healthy and clean, to make sure the bills were paid sooner or later. "She got so tired," remembers Pepe, "That she fell asleep at the dinner table. She missed mass on Sundays to catch up on sleep. She made frequent visits to the Monte de Piedad pawnshop to turn in her jewelry and pieces of cloth discarded by my father, anything that could bring her a little cash in those difficult first years in the city. She entered *tandas* where she and her neighbors pooled small quantities of money to secure loans. As payments were timed among the participants, the tandas helped her to calculate her costs and rationalize her spending." Through the friendships she forged with providers in the street, the market, and stores, among her neighbors, and with her Oaxacan networks, she secured access to goods and services. She had the gregarious talent and sharp perception necessary to build relations of confidence in a city permeated with public mistrust. She was the family's hustler, and in matters of daily sustenance, its public face. Without her deployment and accumulation of social capital, her husband's cultural capital would likely not have had as much magical and nourishing effect on their children.

She prepared excellent Oaxacan food. She bought from women who took the fifteen-hour train ride to sell *chapulines* (grasshoppers), *tlayudas* (giant baked tortillas), *hierba santa* (holy leaf) and *hierba de conejo* (rabbit leaf), *tasajo* (cured beef), *pan de yemo* (egg bread), and mezcal. "!Que sabrosos!" remembers Pepe. "Her *caldo de gato* (cat soup), her *sopa de garbanzo* (bean soup) covered with red chile sauce, her moles, her *guisado miltomatado* (green tomato stew). She prepared what she had available and sometimes there wasn't much—sometimes a chicken stew with little chicken, rice with tasajo with little tasajo. In the morning, we ate bread with coffee or chocolate with water, and at night a little milk. Not until I was nine years old did we drink much milk."

Out of duty to her family's needs and her own sense of justice, Lupe joined protests against high prices for basic goods in the years of scarcity and inflation. With neighbors, she built a barricade and blocked the street until the police came and dispersed the protestors with bullets. José raged: "Why are you going to these political meetings?" he badgered her. "You could get killed." She responded, "It matters a lot to me that my children can eat." "My mother was tough, decided, and risk-taking," Pepe recalls, "She was very active, not passive like my father, and she hated the PRI." Despite his identification with the audacious actors and characters in the movies, José Zúñiga was a man of a certain timidity and conformity. With her extensive relations in the neighborhood, Lupe responded to the needs of others—taking up a collection for someone's funeral or helping an old woman abandoned by her family. In the *vecindad* she always did her part in preparing for the posadas and in the fiesta of the Virgin de Guadalupe. She was, according to Pepe, like La Borola, the energetic mother in the comic book series *La familia Burron*, which Pepe, like so many others, read weekly without fail. La Borola, housewife in a vecindad, was always organizing her neighbors for some cause. José Zúñiga and his children were not so much in favor of these activities because many times she served their dinner late. "Ah, Lupe," declared her husband, "You are a candle outside the house but inside it's dark."

Lupe was capable of defending herself with her fists if she felt her honor or that of her family to have been offended. Pepe remembers when they had moved to the bigger apartment at 138 Soto Street, around the corner from Lerdo, Lupe hit a neighbor at the bottom of the staircase for some reason that he knew had to be defensible. Her son Efrén remembers that the women were taunting her—perhaps in the manner her brother Manuel had been taunted by acquaintances in the cantina many years before.[5] On another occasion, Pepe had to pull his mother out of a fight on the rooftoop with a prostitute who had robbed her laundry water. But with the passage of time, Pepe and his father waxed affectionate about Lupe. They compard her with Olan (Luise Rainer) in the movie *The Good Earth*: the Chinese wife and mother, totally sacrificing and suffering, who sustained her husband and her family in the midst of terrible natural disasters and her husband's infidelities and abuse. Pepe also thought of Lupe when he saw Fellini's *La Strada*: he saw Lupe in the figure of the faithful Gelsomina (Giulietta Masina), so exploited and intimidated by the tyrant circus performer (Anthony Quinn). Gelsomina always struggled to keep alive a tomato plant in the arid Italian countryside. Pepe also thought of Sara García, the eternal sacrificing mother and grandmother of Mexican film, always watering the flowers in her garden as a metaphor for holding the family together and enabling it to thrive. Ah, that was Lupe—making flowers grow out of rocky soil!

But as children, young men, and adults, neither Pepe nor Chucho considered their mother fully innocent. What bothered them was what irked them about their father—her loyalty to her birth family that sometimes outweighed her loyalty to her nuclear family. Lupe protected her brother Manuel, a murderer, an incurable drunk, and a marijuana addict. For smoking marijuana, the police arrested him once and sent him to La Castañeda mental hospital. But, as in the case of the murder he had committed in Oaxaca, he managed to escape.

"Manuel was just the opposite of my father," Pepe remembered. He had arrived from Oaxaca to live in the family's vecindad with Tía Clotilde. Manuel beat his wife Margarita so badly she finally escaped, leaving their son Manuel Jr. with Lupe. In another moment, he lived with María Luisa, a woman of vulgar dress and a face caked with makeup. She earned money as a waitress and as a prostitute. Manuel lived from her income. He also lived with men. Pepe remembers when he threw Ismael out of his apartment. He beat him mercilessly and cried, "Get out of here, you damned whore, I don't want to live with you anymore." Manuel did not consider himself homosexual, because he was the active partner in relation to the passive Ismael. The boys—Chucho, Pepe, and Nico—liked Ismael. "He was from Oaxaca," Pepe explained, "He was handsome and decent. We would often see him at the stands on Garibaldi Plaza where gay men sold food. When Manuel threw Ismael out of the apartment, Ismael said to him, 'Manuel, I hope you never have a "puto" son like me because he's going to cause you a lot of pain.' One of Manuel's several children, Javier, was born with sex organs of both genders. As a young man, he became a male prostitute. Manuel rejected him with his usual violence. Today, Javier is Nancy, a pretty, nice woman of sixty who lives happily with a younger man."

Lupe always protected her brother. To care for him had been her mother's last wish, her *manda*. But why, Lupe's children asked, hadn't she disciplined him the way she disciplined them? Why did she let him do as he pleased, just the way the Abuela Petrona let her orphaned grandson Nicolás run as he pleased? Lupe supported Manuel without question. Once, thieves robbed and beat her as she returned from the Monte de Piedad. With her dress torn and a black eye, she arrived home in tears of rage and impotence. When she said that part of the money she had lost was for Manuel, José flew into a rage. Another time, Lupe had put José's dinner on the table when Manuel came along, sat down, and ate it.

He did not bother to ask who it was for, remembers Chucho. When José arrived and demanded his dinner, she responded: "Wait a minute, I'm making it. Be patient." Manuel paid no attention to José and continued eating. José grabbed a plate and threw it at Lupe. "I am first!" he yelled. Manuel paid no attention and continued eating.[6] Pepe does not remember this incident. On the contrary, Pepe remembers that José was generous with Manuel. He taught him to tailor and gave him work from time to time. Once, he told Pepe to go down to the street to pick him up after he had collapsed in one of his drunks. "My father was a noble man," Pepe recalled. "He knew Manuel was a tortured soul. In his habitual binges, he would sob, pound his hands into the wall, and ask pardon for having killed his best friend in Oaxaca."

The distance between Lupe and José narrowed through the entertainment the family enjoyed together—above all, the programs they listened to on the radio that played all day in the home where they worked. These programs sentimentalized daily life, consecrated intimate love, and fostered communication. Doña Bremenilda and Don Casianito spoke of family happiness, achieved through *cariño*, respect, and responsibility. José wrote to them and and received a postcard, compliments of the sponsor, Casino Chocolates (see figure 5.4). It pictured the elderly couple in loving conversation. From her Clínica del Alma (Clinic of the Soul), "La Doctora Corazón" (Doctor of the Heart) provided advice to people who wrote her about their problems in love and tried to help them out of their tragedies and solitude. To sentimental music from the electric organ, she began her program: "Dear friends, write to me. Remember, I make your problems my own."[7] The family listened to *Solteras y Divorciadas* (single and divorced women), which aired different romantic dilemmas. These programs outed private feeling and provided scripts for dialogue, self-knowledge, and self explanation. In the Zuñiga home, they provoked animated discussions about who was to blame for the conflict—the man or the woman. Lupe and the children generally took the side of the woman. José was isolated but firm in his defense of the man. Moments of humor patched over the emotional distance between Lupe and José. When the voice of María Luisa Landín filled the room, José joked, "That's my sweetheart." "Silly," responded Lupe, "She can't be your sweetheart."

If the music of María Luisa Landín and Agustín Lara was forbidden or enjoyed in secret in many middle-class homes, for the Zúñigas, parents and children, it was an essential part of daily life, smoothing over the rough edges of material want, conflict, and mistrust. The impassioned and intimate music of the boleros created sympathy, shortening the af-

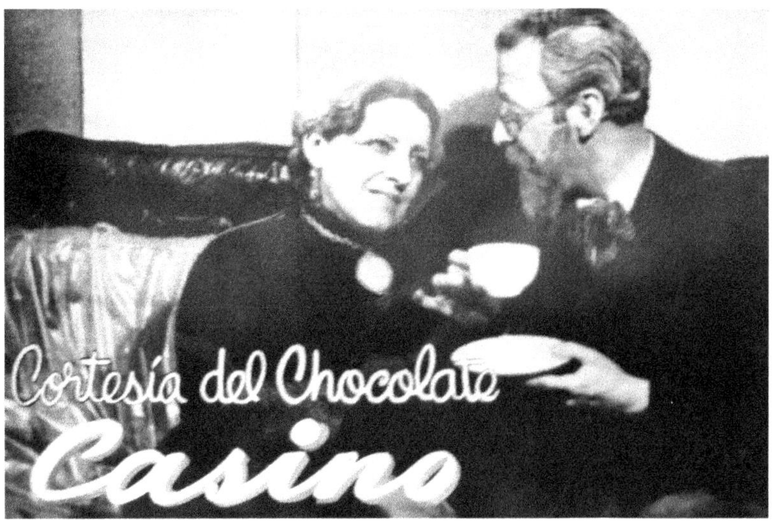

Figure 5.4. Doña Bremenilda and Don Casianito. Print advertisement, 1947.

fective distance between José and Lupe even if their thoughts wandered in different directions. When they listened to María Luisa Landín sing "Canción del alma," "Amor perdido," or "Injusticia," perhaps José was thinking of the mysterious Lidia. Lupe might give over to the deep sadness and frustration she felt over José's unreciprocated affection. "Cada noche un amor" reminded José of his years alone in the city. In it, Agustín Lara sang to a prostitute who had become his erotic obsession. María Luisa Landín's "Amor perdido" touched Lupe in her tender lament, full of self-deprecation. "Surely, you're happy without me . . . I was never yours. . . . You don't have to greet me when you see me. I am not hurt," the song goes. Then despite the tragedy, the song ends with "a round of applause for pleasure and love!"[8]

If radio programs and music created bonds of sympathy and solidarity among José, Lupe, and their children, the cast of colorful characters the family had assembled around them made for entertaining, instructive theater and considerable conflict. There was, for instance, the grandfather. Now at an advanced age, he spent most of his time in bed. José told the children that he had had a flamboyant past, heroic within the picaresque. Despite his dark skin, Pepe noted, he had been a dashing *galán*—almost two meters tall—fashionably dressed in broad-brimmed sombreros, well-ironed shirts, tight pants embroidered down both sides and sturdy shoes or boots depending on the occasion (see figure 5.5).

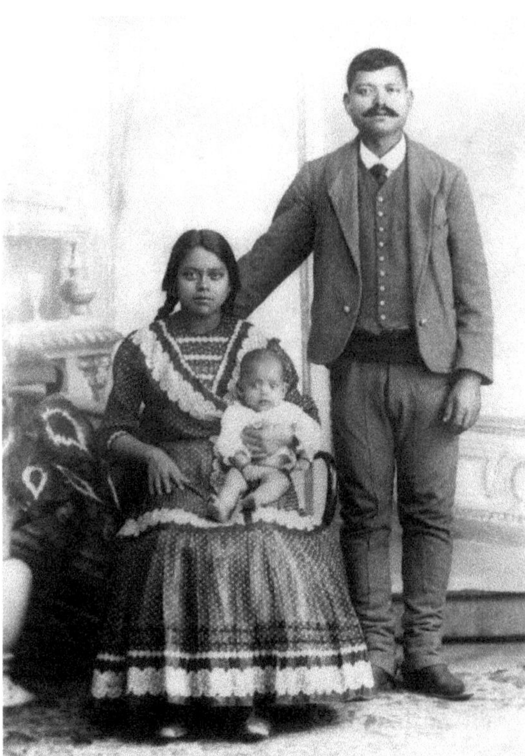

Figure 5.5. Filomena, with her father, José Zúñiga Heredia, and his baby son, José. Black-and-white photograph, ca. 1915.

Famous in his Oaxaca neighborhood for his daring and skill with a knife—an indispensable accoutrement in his day to the maintenance of plebian male honor—he had killed at least one man in a fight.[9] In the photo we see him at ease, proud, posed deceptively as the patriarch with his unfortunate daughter Filomena, the alleged victim of Lupe's father's lust. She is holding José Zúñiga Heredia's baby son, José.[10]

José admired his father's skills as a baker, a shoemaker, and an ice cream maker. He had been a draftsman and painter as well. He painted cards for Ancla, the Mexican bingo game, played during the days of religious festival. He decorated them with typical figures—death, the jug, the nopal cactus, the moon, the sun. He was a great womanizer, remembers his granddaughter Susana, who went to Orizaba to be near him. She worked in a department store and recalls how the salesgirls turned around to admire him when he entered—tall and arrogant—to buy underwear for his "sweethearts."[11]

The grandfather was proud of his collection of huge sombreros, attractive on a man of his height. Made of felt, they came in colors of coffee,

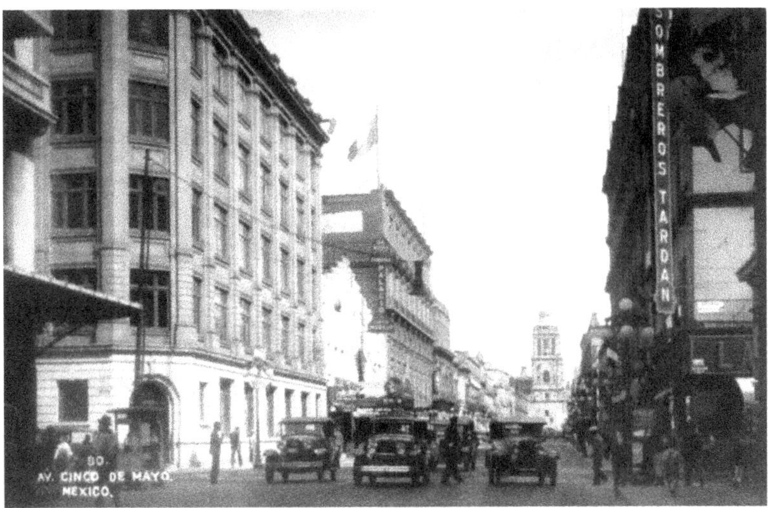

Figure 5.6. Cinco de Mayo Street in Mexico City. Black-and-white photograph, ca. 1930.

black, beige, gray, and cream, many with fancy embroidery. He brought them to Mexico City and told his grandsons that they would one day be theirs. The boys thought this was funny because they lived in a world where fashions changed quickly and they would never dream of wearing those sombreros. But they protested when, after the abuelo died, Lupe gave them to the *ropaviejero* (the peddler of used goods/Cri-Cri's Tlacuache) in exchange for pots and pans.

Everyone has his or her particular museum, collection of art, and memorabilia. Lupe kept the postcards she received on her saint's day in a small, sealed box. In another, she kept her rosaries, pamphlets of prayers, and her gold earrings, so prized by Oaxacan women. José put his on public display: the virgins of Juquila and La Soledad on their altars, the portrait of Porfirio Díaz on the wall, the photos of Tongolele and Rhett Butler (Clark Gable) kissing Scarlett O'Hara (Vivien Leigh). But in the children's opinion, their grandfather kept the most fascinating memorabilia in his trunk: an enormous collection of postcards. These depicted the wonders of modernity: the new municipal palace in Veracruz, the railroad station, the new penitentiary, the Rio Blanco textile factory, the Moctezuma Brewery looking like something between a cathedral and the elaborate municipal palaces built in the Porfiriato. Here we see one of the postcards showing automobiles crowding Cinco de Mayo Street as it entered the Zócalo in Mexico City (see figure 5.6). The Tardan Hat store is on the corner.

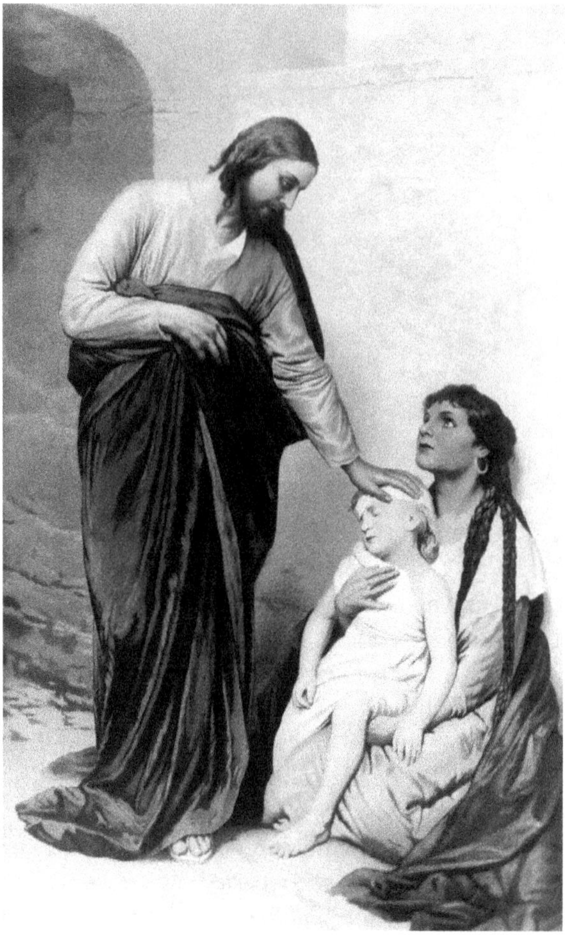

Figure 5.7. Black-and-white postcard, 1946.

The collection also testified to the abuelo's religious faith—one of the Santo Niño del Arbol, several of Christ suffering, carrying his Cross, and nailed to the Cross; the body of San Florencio wrapped in silver-covered brocade and encased in glass in the Church of San Juan de Díos in Orizaba. Baroque pathos stirred here beside and within the modern. Quite contemporary was the postcard of Christ blessing the forehead of an ailing child while the child's mother, very Mexican in her braids, gazes upward with hope at the holy man (see figure 5.7). According to Pepe, many Mexican homes displayed this picture. Movies too showed it as adornment in the vecindades.

But the pièce de résistance for the children—interspersed with bull-

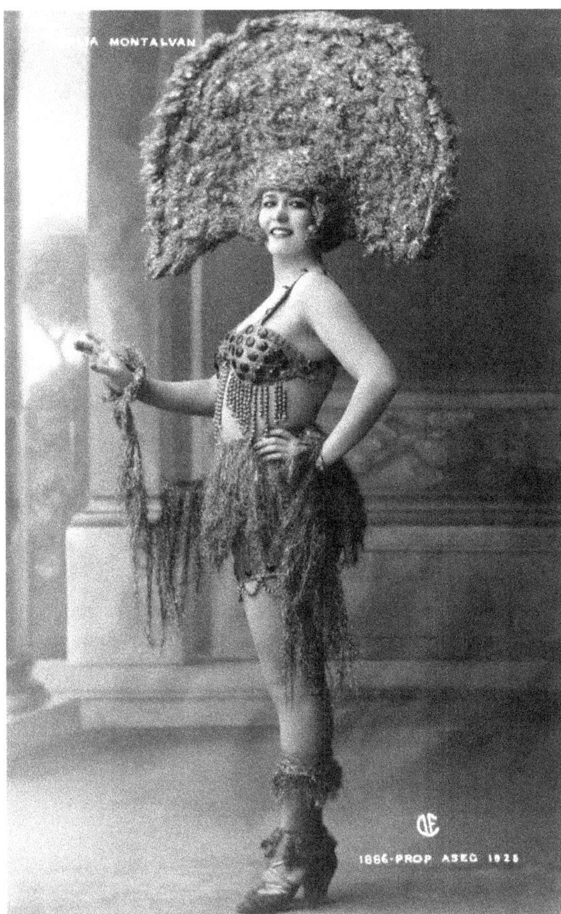

Figure 5.8. Celia Montalván. Sepia postcard, ca. 1925.

fighters exhibiting their elegant, indomitable virility—was the flush of nearly naked divas—the great *vedettes* (stars) of the first decades of the twentieth century—María Conesa, “La Gatita Blanca,” the unforgettable Celia Montalván (pictured in her short feather skirt and gigantic headdress; see figure 5.8), a Max Sennett girl posing in a bathing suit on a rock by the sea.[12] As evidence that desire survived into old age, the abuelo also had a photo of the contemporary Cuban star Rosita Fornes exposing her magnificent legs. There were more marvelous creatures, Pepe recalled. There was a whole collection of photographs of prostitutes in the brothels of Oaxaca that were sold under the table in stores in that city. There were photos of the abuelo with his girlfriends and many postcards with flowers and birds in watercolors his sweethearts sent to him. All these women had at one time or another enchanted the man. They complemented the photo of the Virgin of Guadalupe he placed on a tiny altar beside his bed. Unfortunately, Pepe said, when the abuelo died, Lupe burned the most sinful postcards on the advice of her priest.

Occasionally, the abuelo would give a peso or a few centavos to his grandsons. Nicolás loved to take him for walks. His favorite place to visit was the Calle Dos de Abril, where he relished a rush of libido at the sight of the prostitutes. He would flirt with them, smile, and doff his hat in a gesture of respect. When one beckoned him, he crossed the street to talk with her, but he returned to say that she charged the exorbitant price of fifteen pesos. The children also tormented him. They winced at the rancid odor of urine coming from his bed and bedpan. They threw breadcrumbs at him. One day, he rose up furious and growled, "Now, you're going to get it, boys!" Abuela Petrona screamed, "Don't you touch my children!" He hit her on the behind and drew his big knife. He would have stabbed her if someone had not intervened to stop him.[13]

From this moment, the Abuela Petrona never again spoke to her erstwhile husband. She hated him. They carried on like two estranged cats obliged to share the same space. Petrona did not follow the narrative of María Luisa Landín's songs; she would never pardon the man who had betrayed and abandoned her and her children. She lived in bitterness. To survive and raise her children alone, she became expert in manipulation, blackmail, and theater. She never learned to read, but she surely learned to count. Like her husband, she was intensely devout, but her conduct, like his, placed her a step removed from holiness. Without the privileges or the respect given to men, she learned as a woman to exercise her power indirectly. We see her here with her daughter Antonia in Mexico City (see figure 5.9).

As a grandmother, she could enchant her grandchildren with her ghost stories from Oaxaca. Efrén, the youngest child of Lupe and José, who had never lived in Oaxaca, loved these stories of terror and punishment for sin: stories of the Casa de Corredores, where the phantoms of the dead wandered at night; that of the Matlazihua, the woman who came in the night to unfaithful men and took them up the Fortín mountain to seduce and beat them; of the black dog who slept in the cemetery in the day and walked the streets at night, entering homes, barking, and attacking bad people.[14] Susana, who had lived with the abuela in Oaxaca and was a generation older than Efrén, remembers how she taught her grandchildren their prayers and took them to the church of La Virgin de la Soledad to spend the night before the virgin's feast day. She prayed and

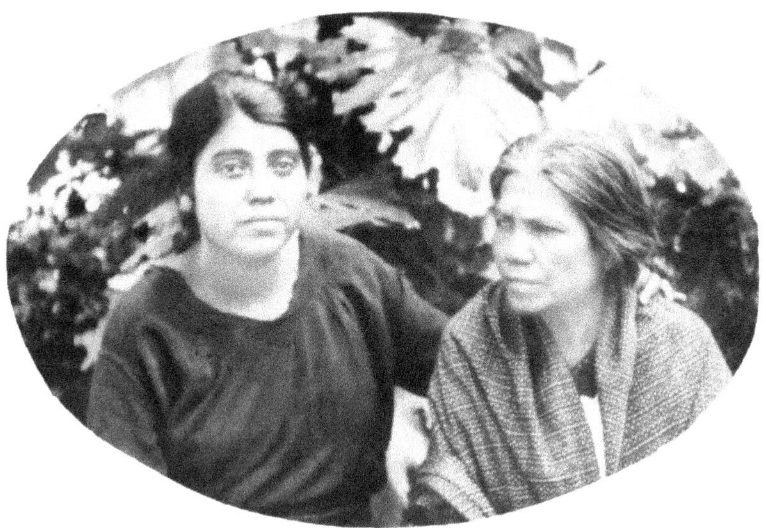

Figure 5.9. Antonia and her mother, Petrona. Black-and-white photograph, ca. 1947.

prayed while the children ate tamales and chocolate and slept. Susana remembers the moral of her stories. In one, a man who had robbed from the rich and now repented his sin of *ambición* drove the cart of death that rumbled over the cobblestone streets at night to awaken and panic people. In another, the abuela told of a wall where the rich buried their treasure. Those who looked for it and found it would die rapidly because "It is better not to be ambitious, it is better to be poor . . . to work, not be lazy, and not jealous of the rich."[15] Moral tales of the vice of envy Pepe Zúñiga had found in the songs of Cri-Cri and his school textbooks, but the texts and songs emphasized individual effort not as a negative expression of *ambición*, the way the abuela had meant it, but of productive creativity, patriotic duty, and self-fulfillment—indeed, as an obligation.

To survive as a single woman with five children (two of them abandoned by their children's fathers and another dead from an unfortunate sexual encounter), the abuela perfected her skills as an actress. She exhibited her talent not only in her telling of ghost tales but in the theater she created of daily life. For many years, she feigned imminent death, moaning, groaning, and complaining of pain. She cried out to Lupe to bring her hot bricks to soothe her aching stomach. One day, she gave Lupe a great surprise—"I think she's really dying," said Lupe. Once in the Briseño movie theater during Holy Week, when film showings of Christ's betrayal and crucifixion abounded, the family was watching *El mártir del Calvario* when the abuela suddenly stood up from her seat and began to scream and cry at the sight of the savior expiring on the cross. "*Jesús mío*, pardon us! Pardon us!" she cried. "Oh, *Díos mío*!" "Sit down, Abuelita," the children told her, but she carried on, absorbed in her grief. She was capable of mounting scandals that trembled like earthquakes and donning costumes that facilitated the task at hand. She went habitually to the Martínez del Alatorre market to beg. Positioning herself at one of the entrances, she covered her head and half her face with her rebozo and exposed her blind eye to elicit sympathy. "A favor for the love of God!" she would plead. The police arrested her, took her to the station, and robbed her of her money. According to her granddaughter Susana, everyone knew that the police robbed all the money from the beggars they arrested.[16] The police humiliated her further: they shaved her head. They brought her home. Not convinced of her misdemeanor, she returned regularly to the market. She even begged during a celebration in honor of Mother's Day held at Nicolás's reform school. This act caused much shame to the entire family but above all to Nico, who in this moment was trying hard to reform his conduct and adapt to the social and official rules of the day.[17]

Begging was a vocation for older women with few means of survival. In the older textbooks used in Pepe's primary school, these women functioned as emblems of poverty. They were intended to provoke generosity and charity in the hearts of the more fortunate. Begging was a skill Petrona learned from her mother. As her granddaughters Susana and Marta reflected years after, begging had a logic.[18] The abuela did not have a right to membership in the new system of social security that then provided a pension for those who worked in unionized industries. Further, begging was for Petrona an act of independence and autonomy, because in truth she had no need to beg, as José and Lupe gave her shelter and food. Listening to his cousins in the interview, Pepe understood what they were saying. He remembered a film in which Pedro Infante escaped from the prison at Islas Marías to look for his mother and found her, old, blind, and crippled, begging with twenty other women at the entrance to the Basilica of the Virgin of Guadalupe in Mexico City. But despite the pathos displayed to call forth a charitable response, Pepe reacted otherwise. He had little tolerance for this practice. In the newer school textbooks, these helpless women had disappeared in favor of figures celebrating work and productivity. He did not note their limited access to remunerative employment. Pepe remembered the swarms of begging women he saw on the Alameda in Oaxaca when he was studying at La Esmeralda. "They were like a plague. You couldn't eat in peace."

If Pepe's sentiments were not convergent with those that Petrona appealed to in the Martínez del Alatorre market, her other grandchildren were more receptive—at least to the spoils. Petrona accumulated a lot of fruit in the market and brought it to a public bathroom in Lerdo 17, where she opened her bags and distributed her booty to her grandchildren Nicolás and Teresa. She had taken charge of these children upon the death of their mother in Oaxaca. "My orphans! My orphans!" she would repeat. "My orphans need more support than the others." In the opinion of Chucho and Pepe, she spoiled them excessively—particularly Nicolás, who ran around dirty and unkempt. When José decided to send Nico to the Internado to inculcate some discipline in the boy, she begged, cajoled, and sobbed so that he would not go, and once he did, she begged, cajoled, and sobbed to get José to bring him home. Finally her son relented. Nico remembers his years in the Internado as the best of his life. "This damned woman," he reflected, "she did me so much damage. Because of her, I'm like this."[19] He referred to his rather informal life filled with many women, children, cigarettes, and a preference for tequila over eating. Fortunately, his uncle José had taught him to tailor. Unfortunately, it is a trade that mass production has severely harmed.

The money Petrona accumulated in the market she rolled up like the firecrackers she had made in Oaxaca. She stored these in her breast. According to her grandchildren, she acquired a considerable fortune and operated her own informal and clandestine bank. She lent her money to them with interest. There were many stories of the imagined fortune of Doña Petrona. First, her granddaughters Susana and Marta accused Lupe of having robbed her money on her deathbed. Lupe denied the charge. She said she had found some money but had given it to José. José defended his wife's word. Then the rumor spread of the abuela's hidden treasure. It was said that the abuela had given her money to Macaria, a Oaxacan neighbor who owned the restaurant on Pedro Moreno Street. Marta remembers when she asked her grandmother for a loan, she sent her to see Macaria. "I will fix it so another woman loans you the money," said her grandmother. Macaria lent her the money to buy a television set. She charged interest in pure silver. In this version of the story, Macaria and her daughter got the fortune of the abuela. According to Nico, Macaria used the money to buy a house on the corner of Lerdo and Magnolia. Nico and his sister Teresa thought that Marta got a considerable sum from her grandmother that she then very successfully invested in buying, selling, and renting houses.

When Petrona died in 1959, the family called Efrén Chávez Carreño, who had by then broken with his compañera, Petrona's daughter Antonia. Efrén loved Petrona. She had treated him well as the only grown man in the family apart from her son José. Efrén was the family intellectual. Among his many talents, he was a superb orator, a skill much admired in Oaxaca—the more theatrical, stentorian, and pathetic, the better. At her gravesite in the cemetery, he spoke of Petrona with deep nostalgia for the *patria chica* left behind—a sentiment expressed in much popular poetry, song, and film in those years. He began:

> With the expression of holiness in her Oaxacan face, Petronita Pérez has united us here for a moment of final goodbye. We always love you and Oaxaca, because you lived like Oaxaca, with the simplicity, the modesty, and the purity of our provinces bathed in grace, innocence, whiteness, and gentleness, like the precious azucenas flowers of our millenial hill, the Fortín. We want to celebrate you, dear Petronita, in whom we admire virtue that, to the shame of civilization, is disappearing. To see her at a distance with her immaculate white hair was to find consolation, peace, and quiet; to caress it and to kiss it was to stop on the road at a shelter of sincerity that was the bottomless spring of her heart. Those of us who knew her talk and her manner, without malice or spite, consider that with her absence we lose an irreparable treasure, not only for ourselves, but for Oaxaca, the *patria*, and Humanity. . . . Ay, Petroncita! We have come to deliver you into the arms of the earth, the mother of us all, at a moment when we find ourselves far from those beloved corners of the land of our birth. The *patria chica* saw us leave one day, saw us abandon its unforgettable places, the windings of Xochimilco, the barrio that cradled her childhood and youth. There is Carmen Alto, longing for her. . . . In the barrio of silk, of rebozos and indigo they will no longer see Petronita, the generous and cordial old lady, staunch defender of righteousness, devoted to Our Lady of the Helpless, faithful . . . to the goodness of Our Saint Petrona, Our Lady of Solitude, but the memory of you, Petronita, will linger there, the loving memory of you, of your politeness, your gift with people, your charity, your justice, . . . your purity, . . . humility, . . . simplicity, and . . . tenderness.[20]

Susana remembers everyone sobbed profusely. At that moment in 1959, Pepe was twenty-two and Chucho twenty-nine. The brothers could not figure out who Tío Efrén was talking about. Maybe he was thinking of his own mother, whom they knew to have been a good person. But Petrona—

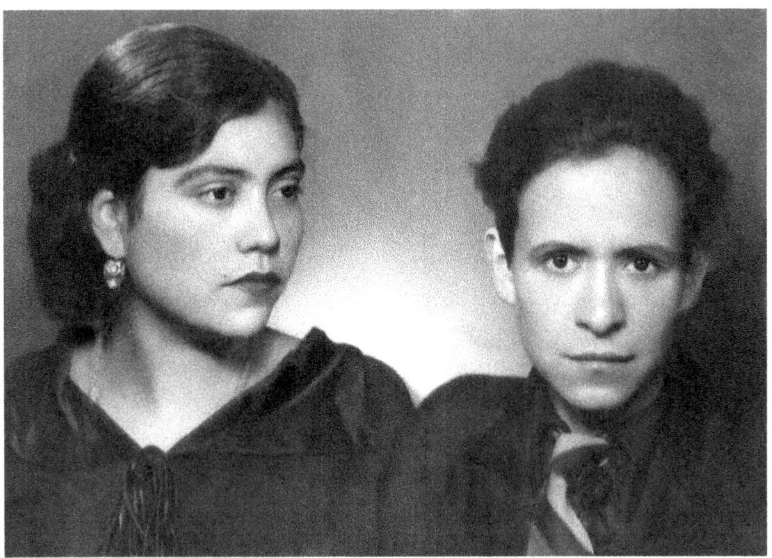

Figure 5.10. Antonia Zúñiga Pérez and Efrén Chávez Carreño. Hand-colored photograph, ca. 1938.

so vengeful, so bitter, so hypocritical? "How ugly it is for me to judge someone like that," reflected Pepe, "but that was what she was. But I have to admit, Tío Efrén had loved her a lot, and this was not the first poem he had written for her."

Efrén Chávez Carreño we see here in a photograph with his compañera, the beautiful Tía Antonia (see figure 5.10). He was a poet, writer, journalist, and painter. In Oaxaca in the 1930s, he worked for the newspaper *El Imparcial.* He performed in theater and radio. He applied his acting skills in his investigative reporting. He disguised himself at night in search of information for his articles, many of them critical of the state government. One night, the police entered his office, destroyed the printing press, and issued a warrant for his arrest for libel. Antonia was there but not Efrén. She went to warn him. He gathered some clothes, donned a wig and a costume, and left for Mexico City.[21] From there, he called Antonia to join him. They suffered a lot at first. They made tamales from what they could buy and sold them in the Alameda park. They crossed the street and slept, together with many destitute people, in the garden where funeral wreaths were sold and beside the ancient churches of Santa Veracruz and Juan de Dios and the Hospital Morelos that treated women—and later men—for venereal disease and would in 1948 become the very modern Hospital de la Mujer. Little by little, things improved for

Antonia and Efrén. They were able to rent an apartment at 17 Lerdo Street. They welcomed José there when he came to the city. Efrén got work in the government. Eventually, he broadcast the news on *La Hora Nacional*, the voice of the state transmitted every Sunday evening to all Mexicans who wanted to or could listen, among them the Zúñiga family. He worked at the Instituto de Bellas Artes, in the Secretaría de Gobernación, and the Departamento de Prevención. There, Carmen, sister of Susana and Marta, became his secretary and initiated her career as a public employee. Eventually, Efrén became editor of the magazine of Los Altos Hornos de México, the state steel company. He also wrote articles for the prestigious *Jueves de Excelsior* and the progressive magazine *Siempre!*

José Zúñiga Sr. saw him as a model of erudition, honesty, and high ideals. They talked for hours about Oaxaca—of its noble indigenous past consecrated at Mitla and Monte Albán and of its national hero, Benito Juárez. Efrén admired Juárez as a champion of the law and justice and as his country's liberator from imperialism. Although a man of faith, Efrén was an anticlerical like Juárez. José disliked Juárez's attacks on the church, but he shared Efrén's admiration for his patriotism. The Mexican Revolution of 1910 that seems to have registered little with José meant a lot to Efrén as a struggle against tyranny and injustice. With his love and talent for oratory, he recited romantic poetry and reminisced with José about the *patria chica*, its customs, its festivals, its legends. Efrén gave him two books, the only ones José owned: the Bible and *Don Quixote*. On Sundays he brought the children the comic strips from *El Universal*: *Mandrake*, *El Mago*, *Los Supersabios*, *El Reyesito*, *Maldades de Dos Pilluelos*, and *Tarzán*. Once, he took them to the Palacio de Bellas Artes, where for the first time they saw the murals of Rivera, Orozco, Siqueiros, and their Oaxacan compatriot, Rufino Tamayo.

The boys adored their Tío Efrén, but their Tía Antonia was another matter. She was "very beautiful, but slovenly and dirty," remembered Pepe. As noted earlier, she seldom bathed, reeked of sweat and perfume, spat on the floor, and urinated in the street. "She clashed with the culture of Efrén," Pepe noted. "She loved Efrén but she could never reach his height. She would give away his books to the ropavejero for whatever. She was so ignorant!" Her knowledge of politics and history was limited to her hatred for Juárez. Despite this, Efrén loved her although she abused him. One day, Pepe arrived at their door when Efrén was dressing. "I'll come back later," he told her. "No," responded Antonia, "Come in. Your uncle has a tiny dick, no?" Pepe didn't like that.[22] "How could she say such things about my uncle?" She gave him orders. "Hurry up, get going," she

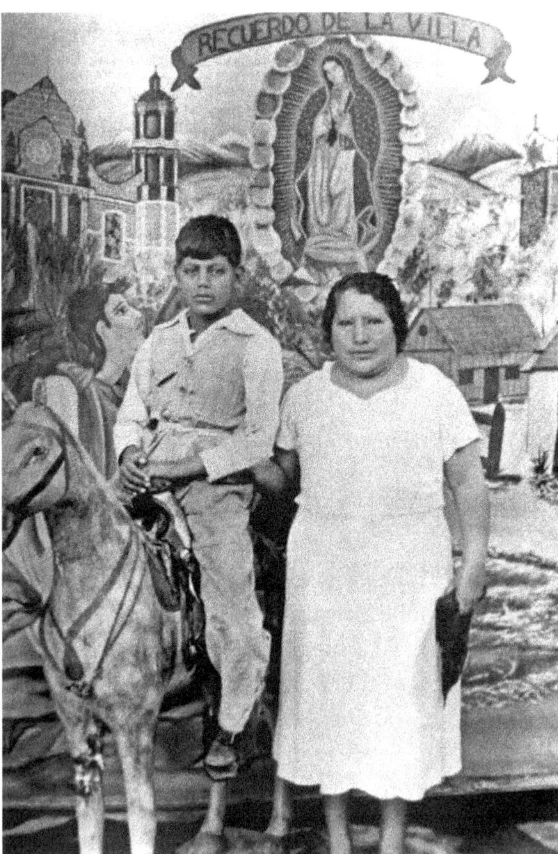

Figure 5.11. Tía Esperanza with Pepe at the Basilica of the Virgin of Guadalupe. Black-and-white photograph, ca. 1947.

would command him impatiently. She humiliated him in public. "You're worthless," she would say. "You serve for nothing." She called herself "*mula*," referring to her apparent incapacity to bear children. He wanted children. Finally, Efrén left Antonia and went elsewhere to create a family. "Like a man," Pepe judged, "He wanted a descendant for the Chávez Carreño family."

A frequent and favorite visitor was Tía Esperanza, pictured here with Pepe at the Basílica de Guadalupe (see figure 5.11). They called her "La Chapulina" (the grasshopper) because her brother, another journalist in Oaxaca, signed his articles "El Chapulín." She would come from Oaxaca carrying bundles of gifts. She would scour Lupe's shelves and throw out old and broken pots and pans and dishes and replace them with new cups, plates, and sheets. No used goods for her, everything had to be new. "For us, it was a fiesta when she arrived. With her baskets full of food, mezcal, and so many other things. We knew she would break the monotony of the house," Pepe remembered. "Get modern, Lupe! You can't live like this," she would say, and then she would gather the children and take them to the patriotic parades on Reforma Avenue or to the Basilica of the Virgin of Guadalupe or the National History Museum in Chapultepec Park. These were years before Jorge González Camarena, David Alfaro Siqueiros, and Juan O'Gorman painted their murals in the museum in a sweeping official narrative of Mexican history.[23] Pepe remembers the portraits of the Emperor Maximilian and his wife Carlota, their bedrooms and their furniture. He recognized them from listening to the radionovela *Maximiliano y Carlota* and because his father had told him about the movie *Juárez*.

Tía Esperanza, like Tío Efrén, admired the emperor's enemy, Juárez, the little Indian boy who grew up to become the liberator of his country and author of the famous phrase "Respect for the rights of others is peace." For Tía Esperanza, the figure of Juárez was a necessary response to the racism she detested. It was she who told Pepe not to bother about the color of his skin because he came from a noble race, the Zapotecs, who had built great cities and ceremonial centers. At that time, Alfonso Caso had discovered the rich contents of the tombs at Monte Albán. She had such faith in Pepe! Studying his drawings, particularly a portrait he had done of his father, she told him: "Pepe, your hands are worth gold. One day, you will be a famous painter."

Esperanza was an audaciously "modern" woman. As Pepe said, she was "much in the vanguard on questions of sex." She was a woman more in tune with the experimental, liberating spirit of the 1920s than the domestic conventions of the 1950s—more like painters Frida Kahlo or María Izquierdo in their direct, self-probing erotic, and sometimes scientific encounters with their bodies than the Mexican stars of the 1940s and 1950s, whose bodies mainly served to ignite the desires and imaginations of men or whose role was that of modest mother.[24] Esperanza made a cult of hygiene and cleanliness and insisted on bathing in the early morning in cold water on the patio. Lupe begged her to cover herself so no one would see her, but Esperanza had no shame. Like some of her compatriots in the 1920s, she had an iconoclastic faith in free love. Whether she was a free modern woman or a prostitute was a matter of opinion. "She didn't walk the street," remembered Pepe and Chucho. But she enjoyed the company of many prominent Oaxacan men—a well-known lawyer (father of her daughter María Luisa), a railroad worker in a responsible post who facilitated her many trips to Mexico and the many bundles she carried with her, a well-known surgeon, and a German engineer (the father of José's beloved friend Alfonso). She loved to talk about her lovers and the size and form of their sexual equipment. "We would ask her why she had so many lovers. She responded, 'Why not? One for a cough, the other for a cold.'" She talked this way in front of the family in part because there was no privacy in the apartment and in part because she was a rebel, independent, and in love with life and love. She commented, "You have to look at his crotch to see the baggage he's carrying." "Ay, sister," responded Tía Antonia, "you've always been a very frank *cabrona*." The aunts compared the history of their vaginas. "Tell me, sister," Antonia said to her when they were resting on the bed, "how many men have fucked you?" "Eh?" responded Esperanza. "I lost count. How many have you had?" "Very few," Antonia told her, "very few." "Ay," Pepe remembers, "although she was not pretty because she was fat, she had so much charisma. She must have been first class in bed! What a sensual woman!"

Esperanza laughed at her ignorance of the origin of babies until one day one dropped from her. "I was an idiot, a real idiot. Here was my daughter coming out of my vagina and I had no idea where they came from. How stupid and idiotic I was!" Seriously, she deplored the general ignorance of biology and sexual questions and would have supported sex education proposed by the government in 1932 but violently opposed by Catholic organizations. She herself tried to cure friends and relatives who suffered from venereal diseases with washes of permanganate, a treatment used by doctors prior to the arrival of penicillin.[25]

She loved to play practical jokes. She tied the penis of one of José's workers to a laundry line when he was sleeping on the cutting table. "With extreme care and delicacy, she slowly tied it," remembered Pepe, "Pinche Chapulina!" When the young man woke up and moved, he screamed with pain. Everyone enjoyed the joke, except the victim. On another occasion, she dressed up in José's clothes and put on one of his hats. She knocked at the apartment door late at night and inquired in a low, muffled voice, "Is Lupe there?" "Yes, she is," responded José, "but who wants to see her at this hour?" "Her lover," responded the deep voice. José flew into a rage and began to beat the stranger. "No! No! José! Lay off! Lay off! It's a joke!" Caught in his anger, he kept beating her. "José, don't hit me, don't hit me!" she cried. "Sensational!" Chucho and Pepe graded the joke. Another time, she went out on the patio in the dark of the night and began to moan and cry like the Llorona. "Oh my children! Oh my children!" she cried for the legendary lost babies. Pepe remembers, "My mother was so scared she froze and began to recite the Magnificat."

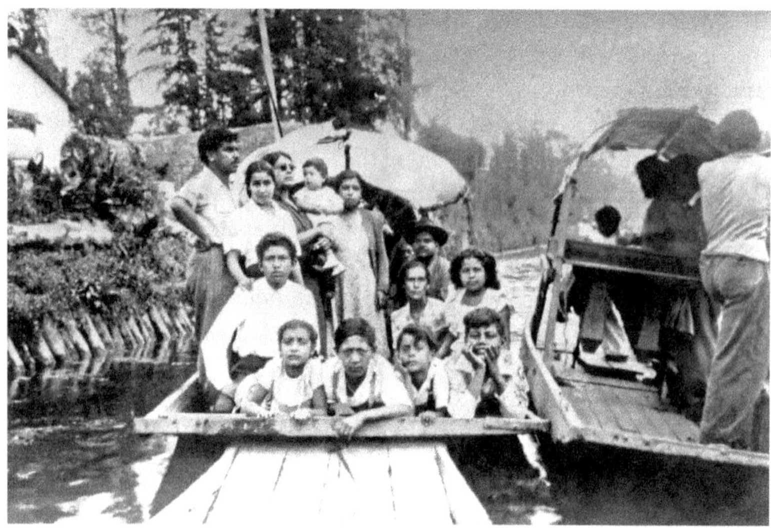

Figure 5.12. Outing at Xochimilco (Pepe, front right; José, third row, right, in hat). Black-and-white photograph, ca. 1948.

José Zúñiga liked to invite his guests and extended family on excursions to the floating gardens of Xochimilco, the park at the former convent of the Desierto de los Leones above the city, to the Molino de Flores in Texcoco, or to the nearby Teatro Margot on the Plaza Garibaldi to hear the trio Los Panchos. As we see in the picture, many could fit into the launch he rented to celebrate his saint's day in Xochimilco. It was his pleasure as a patriarch, a pleasure reminiscent of the nobleman's big table in the middle ages, a pleasure still enjoyed in modern Mexico (see figure 5.12). Of course, he paid for everything: the boat, the marimba that accompanied them and played songs from Oaxaca with the guests singing along, and the barbecue, the soda pop, and beer they enjoyed later at the benches in the market. These were occasions of much joy and harmony. They also cost a considerable amount of money that could have served Lupe to maintain the family. But, no. "You are my guests," he would say. Such was his principle.

Pepe did not completely approve of his father's extravagance. He thought his father was showing off to friends from Oaxaca all he had achieved in the city—above all for his friend Ezequiel (whose family we see in figure 5.12). They were longtime rivals. But José, Pepe knew, had little money. "My father was pretentious. He created something of a false image, a false reality." José had instructed Pepe to save. Pepe saved, but

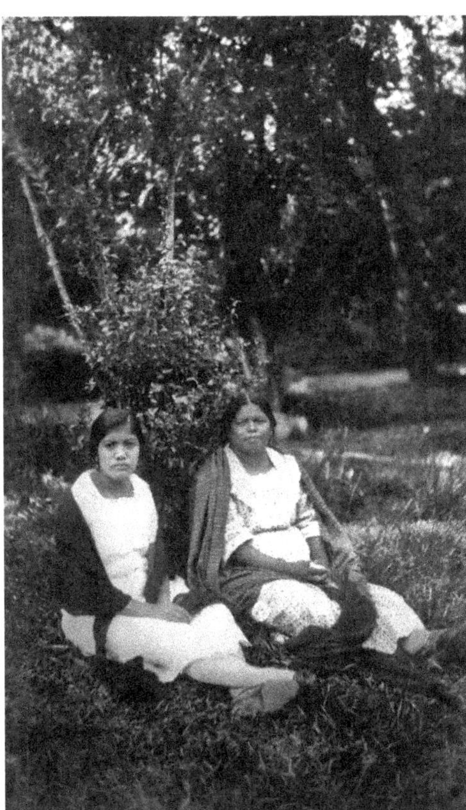

Figure 5.13. Lupe and Luz Carrizosa. Black-and-white photograph, ca. 1948.

his father did not. For José, to win the lottery was the only way to get rich. For Pepe, these customs were backward and undignified.

In addition to her work maintaining her family on a meager income, Lupe had to care for the guests and the workers who came to help José. Of course, she had the aid of Aunt Clotilde, although she was aging, and of her women guests, but most of the work fell on her. In the summer of 1948, Lupe broke. "Let's go," she said to her children, "I don't want to stay here anymore." They all cried. She took them, together with her sewing machine, three blocks away to Violeta Street, where her Oaxacan friend, Elvira, rented her a room with a bath and a kitchen. Elvira helped her find clients for her sewing. Luz Carrizosa, her godmother (*madrina*) from Oaxaca, came to her aid. We see the Madrina Luz on the right in the photograph (see figure 5.13). In her blue and white uniform, with her short hair and simple face, she looked like a nun to the boys—in the style of her friends Tía Clotilde and Tía Arcadia.

La Madrina Luz had succeeded as a migrant in the city. She was head housekeeper for the rich Lilienthal family in the elegant Colonia Roma. She was one of the children's favorite visitors to the apartment on Lerdo Street. Every Thursday afternoon on her day off, she would arrive with flowers, a blouse for Lupe, and sweet buns she had bought at the Flor de Mayo, a Spanish bakery in the Colonia Roma. Together with the aroma of fresh bread, Pepe remembers the fragrance of *naftalina* (moth crystals) from her uniform. In these moments of need when Lupe and the children were living alone on Violeta Street, Luz got Lupe work in the Lilienthal kitchen to supplement what she earned from her sewing.

For the children, the separation from their father was a disaster, a moment when the security of family life disintegrated. Efrén cried incessantly. "Aye, little brother, quiet down, quiet down!" Pepe tried to console him. Pepe hated the noise of the pedals of Lupe's sewing machine. He remembers there were no children in this vecindad and they had to pass the Christmas season in misery: there were no posadas. Perhaps Chucho suffered the most because he was oldest and was working with his father during the day.

Chucho recalls a bitter moment between the warring parties. Grandmother Petrona, her daughters, and her granddaughters told José that Lupe was running around with men and neglecting the children. One morning, Petrona, Tía Rosa, and her daughter Susana confronted Lupe on Violeta Street. She had the children with her. The women laughed and launched accusations. "Now see what you've done to my son," Petrona chided, "It's clear that Chucho and the baby are not his. What do you have to say about that?" Lupe did not respond. She stood silent. She turned to Chucho and said, "Hear that? Hear what your grandmother is saying? Go to your father and tell him I want to speak with him." The three women laughed more. Everyone marched to the vecindad at Lerdo 17. Chucho went up to the apartment. His father was still in bed. "My mother wants to talk to you," Chucho told him. José dressed quickly and went down to meet the women.

"What's happening here?" he asked impatiently. "You know what, José?" Lupe responded, "Your mother met us in the street and began to laugh at us. She said that Chucho and the baby are not your sons. We are here so that she can tell this to your face." "No! No! No!" retorted Petrona. "Son, what a huge lie! We didn't say anything!" Rosa agreed. "Tell the truth," insisted Lupe. "No! No! It's not the truth," wailed the grandmother. Raising her hands to God, she unleashed a torrent of tears. "No, Cuca!" insisted Lupe, "tell him the truth and don't lie." "Son!" sobbed

Petrona, "how can you believe her? There's a reason she's not living with you now." "Tell the truth!" demanded Lupe. "She's lying. Are you going to believe what she's saying, José?" "Aye, Tío," interjected Susana, "don't believe what my Tía Lupe says." José pushed Chucho aside and confronted Lupe, "Get out of here. I don't want to hear more gossip. You are making false accusations against my mother! Go!" Lupe left with the children.[26]

Pepe does not remember this incident. He remembers that his father had doubts and jealousies about Lupe's alleged conduct, but he recalls that Doña Elvira, a friend of both, convinced him that Lupe was being faithful and was taking good care of the children. "No, Don José, what they're saying about Lupe is not true. Nothing of parties, no one visits here. Trust your wife, José," Elvira told him. José began to visit Lupe in the apartment on Violeta Street. Pepe remembers having seen him "embrace her in a chair with a lot of affection. He became convinced that those were pure rumors against my mother. A little later, they reached an agreement. I was not there to witness it, but I know that my mother imposed conditions that he recognize her place as his wife and stop listening to his family's stories. In reality, my mother adored my father. It was not simply a question of affection but adoration—to the point of kissing his feet."

José met the conditions although he did not convince the Zúñiga women to abandon their battle against Lupe. Nonetheless, family life improved not only because José and Lupe had reached an understanding but because he began to earn more money. It was the moment at the beginning of the 1950s when scarcity yielded to a period of growth. José began to work for the Edwards Company, a society formed by Victoria Pimentel, a nightclub *fichera*, the tailor Efrén Torres, and Eduardo Alcocer, a wealthy man from Puebla.[27] Pimentel wanted to design daywear for the movie stars and singers. The successful company made dresses for individual clients and the big department stores, Palacio de Hierro, Puerto de Liverpool, and Sears Roebuck. It had a showroom in the Colonia Roma together with a workshop for many tailors, but José did his work at home. He contracted more workers, often as apprentices, normally Oaxaqueños known to the family. The Zúñigas moved to a bigger apartment on Magnolia Street, around the corner from Lerdo 17, and a few years later to an even bigger one on Soto Street, parallel to Lerdo.

The contract with Edwards lasted until the company decided to reduce its labor force to those employed in the big workshop in the Colonia Roma. Meanwhile, José earned well. He was an excellent master craftsman, instructing his workers in the trade, and a generous patriarch—giving them a little extra money, offering them food and lodging. There could be as many as fifteen or twenty workers, family members, and relatives and friends coming and going in the apartment at the same time. José was not totally traditional as a patriarch: he did not protect his workers when they got in trouble with the law, as Lupe had done with her brother Manuel and as the workers expected. His nephew Gilberto Colón, half-brother of Nico, never pardoned his uncle for not defending him against the authorities when they accused him of robbery. For Colón, José showed a lack of honor. For José, robbery was dishonorable and a crime that should be handled by the formal authorities, even if their own honesty was suspect. Nor did José protect his workers from accusations that they had violated women. Nico was expecting his uncle to defend him when the parents of a girl he had gotten pregnant came to the door demanding he marry her. José made him do his duty.

With more family income and greater access to goods and services, José and Lupe's youngest child, Efrén, had a different growing-up experience from that of his older brothers. He enjoyed new plastic toys and the metal skates his brothers had coveted and never received. He went on to secondary and preparatory school and the university. Most shocking for the family, he learned from his more middle-class friends to address his parents with the intimate "tu."[28] His older brothers would never do such a thing. The struggle for Pepe and Chucho as they entered adolescence was more difficult. Their father pressured them to become tailors. They sought more modern futures. Pepe wanted to be a radio technician and Chucho an auto mechanic. It was Lupe who secured their training and jobs.

6. "How Difficult Is Adolescence!"

At the age of fourteen in 1951, Pepe chafed at sewing shoulder pads for his father. One afternoon, he got drunk with his friends on Lerdo Street. "They all had nicknames: El Patón because he had big feet, El Macuca, after the daughter in the *Familia Burrón* comics, and El Tripa because he was razor thin. We would get together at the dances in Lerdo 20. I liked the dances because they were a chance to learn *danzón*. In one of these fiestas, we got some cheap red wine and took the bottles up to the *azotea*. I had never drunk but I did then. When we were really wasted, we went down and started drinking beer in the corner store. Evangelina Elizondo's 'Mambo 475' was playing on the jukebox. Out of my mind, I began to dance the mambo. I had never danced the mambo before and I never would again. 'Aye, Pepe,' my friends finally said, 'you're dead drunk. We're gonna have to take you home.' They carried me back to the *vecindad* on Magnolia. They had a hard time getting me up the stairs. They left me in the doorway, then ran like hell to avoid my mother. When she opened the door, I practically fell on top of her. She said nothing. She told me to go to bed. The next day, she told me to take a bath. By that time, we had a boiler heated with wood chips. She ran the hot water for me in the old tub with a shower faucet. When I had stripped down to my underwear, she opened the door and began to beat me with a thick electric wire. Pah! Pah! Pah! I covered my head but she struck me on all sides. Pah! Pah! Pah! 'I don't want you to turn into a drunk like your Tío

Manuel!' she cried, 'From now on, you're going to work. I don't know where, but you're going to get a job!'"

Lupe found him work in a nearby stove factory. "The work was awful," Pepe remembers. "I had to perforate metal pieces, one after the other. It was boring and they paid me a pittance. One day, some of the workers were lowering sheets of metal from a truck. They were three meters long and a meter wide. They asked me to help. They had gloves, and I didn't. I was on the ground and they were in the truck. 'Get a hold of this,' they yelled at me. I caught the sheets and they ordered, 'Go back! Go back!' They kept pushing the sheets at me, and they fell out of my hands. I looked at my hands. They were cut up and gushing with blood. 'Look, I'm cut,' I said. 'Wait! We'll cure you,' they said. They grabbed some dirt from the ground that was full of metal fragments and rubbed it into my wounds. The pain was excruciating! They laughed and laughed. Can you imagine? How cruel! Furious, I found a place where they couldn't see me. I broke down and cried from pain and rage. I felt humiliated, totally humiliated. At lunchtime, the workers usually went to the street to eat. I left at the lunch hour and never went back. I took refuge in the movie theaters with the little money I had on me. I went to the movies so my mother wouldn't know I had quit work. I remember seeing a lot of films then—that sad story of the Welsh miners, *How Green Was My Valley*, with Walter Pidgeon and Maureen O'Hara, and *Midnight Kiss*, with Mario Lanza and Kathryn Grayson. Anyway, when my money ran out, I couldn't hide anymore."

"Now I had to tell my mother. At first she bawled me out. Then she saw my wounded hands. 'Why didn't you tell me that right away?' she asked. Well, out of fear, just plain fear. I said, 'I don't know, Mama. I don't know.' My mother took me to complain to the owner of the factory in his offices near the house. 'Look at this, Señor,' she said. 'Your workers did this to my son. Pepe, tell him what they did to you.' I told him everything. The man asked me for the names of the workers. I hadn't the slightest idea. Anyway, I liked it that my mother made a fuss. My mother never tolerated injustice. She always protested and she was very tenacious in her protests."

"Life is capricious and one loses trust," he reflected later. "But finally, the factory experience changed my life for the better. If I had stayed with those guys (El Patón, Macuca, El Tripa), I would have ended up a drunken good-for-nothing. It was good that I had to promise my mother I would never get drunk again. How difficult is adolescence! Above all, for someone who is wandering around disoriented. I looked at my shabby clothes and my old shoes and I began to realize I had to work. I had always told my parents I wanted to be a radio technician. This is something I had always wanted to do since I first saw the radio and heard its sounds. My father didn't approve. But after the incident in the stove factory, my mother got me work with Señor José in his electronics shop on Belisario Domínguez Street a few blocks from our home."

The master took him as an apprentice without pay, as was the custom in artisan shops. The practice lent itself to abuse and exploitation that preoccupied the authorities, but in Pepe's case, the apprenticeship was invaluable. Don José had earned a diploma via correspondence with the Hemprill School of Electronics in the United States. He asked Pepe to read the big books Hemprill had sent to better understand the theory behind the practice. "Señor José called me 'secretary.' He would say, 'Secretary, so you know what you are doing you need to study these books.' They were the first theoretical studies I had seen about radio. I learned how the bulbs functioned for different purposes. I got to know everything that made up the circuits. When I was a child, I thought the sound was all magic made by the genie in the *Thief of Bagdad*. Señor José and the books opened up a new panorama: I began to understand the logic of how electricity flowed through these circuits to make sound."

Pepe read the books, learned the theory, and watched the maestro repair radios. He began to repair them, but principally he worked on motors of the jukeboxes that played 78 rpm records—Rocólas, Sinfónolas, and Wurlitzers. He went with another worker to fix them in the state of Mexico where he could enter the bars and cantinas as a minor. Here we see a photo of Pepe working in Don José's shop (see figure 6.1). All this was after Don José had tested his honesty. One day he gave him fifty pesos to buy parts in the Calle de la Dépublica de El Salvador. When he returned with the parts and the change, he had passed the test. Such trials were common because theft was common. One night, thieves dug a hole through a wall in the workshop and took out all the tools. Don José asked Pepe to stay guard several nights to see that the robbers did not return. He sent Pepe and another worker to the nearby market at La Lagunilla to buy new tools. There they found the tools that had been stolen from them and had to buy them back. Such trafficking was everyday stuff carried on with police complicity.[1]

He stayed a year and a half in this workshop. When his mother heard that the place would be torn down to build a hotel and parking lot, she looked for another position for him. Through the Madrina Luz, she got him work in the radio shop of Ernesto Pérez Medina, a Yucatecan, in the Colonia Roma, a good distance from home. Medina paid his bus fare and

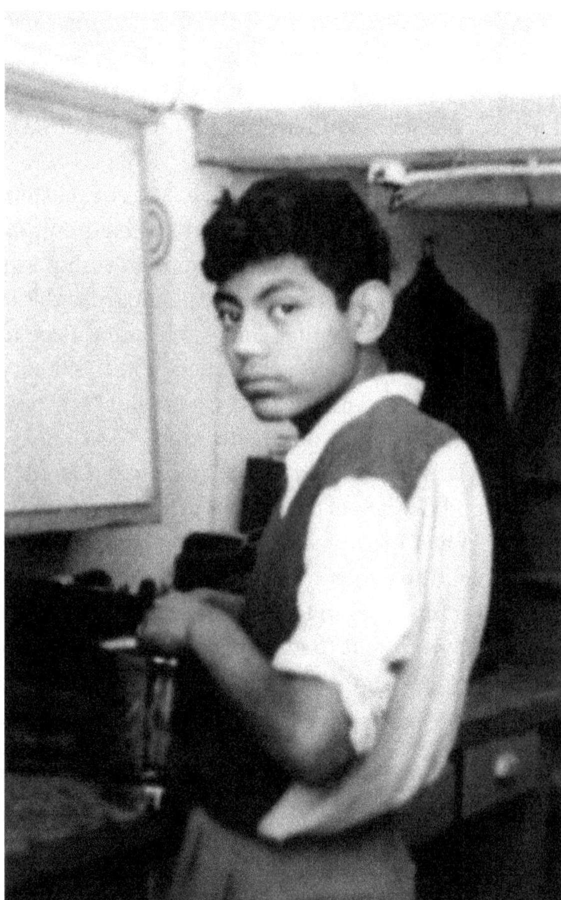

Figure 6.1. Pepe in Don José's shop. Black-and-white photograph, 1952.

a little extra that Pepe gave to his mother. In the two years he worked there, he repaired radios, record players, and electric blenders, a new appliance that was quickly becoming standard in Mexican homes.

As his mother had insisted, he no longer saw Macuca, El Patón, and El Tripa. Not all of them became the good-for-nothings he imagined they would. According to Chucho, El Patón ended up that way because his mother had spoiled him. El Tripa became an excellent boogie dancer and got work in a warehouse sorting merchandise. Macuca opened a store in the Colonia Dolores selling screwdrivers and pliers but died young of alcoholism. They did not, like Pepe and Chucho, acquire an *oficio*, a skilled trade. In any case, the last time Pepe saw them they were playing football in the street. That didn't interest Pepe. Some cousins had arrived

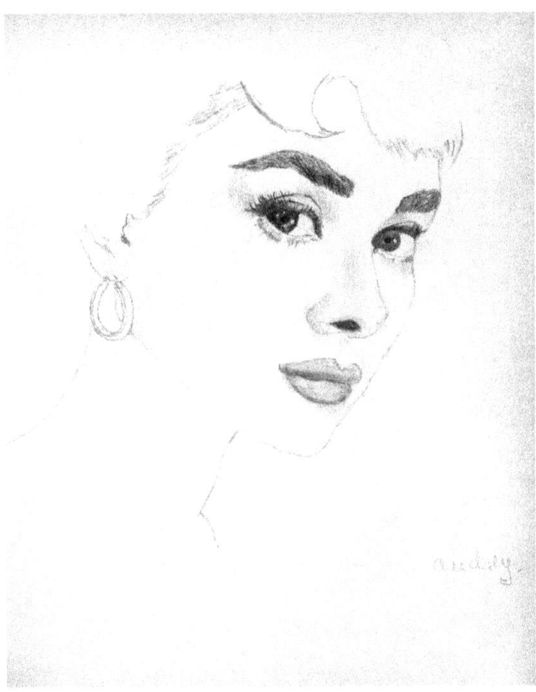

Figure 6.2. Audrey Hepburn. Pencil drawing by José "Pepe" Zúñiga, 1953.

from Oaxaca. With them and his cousin Susana, he practiced danzón at home. He also drew in the afternoons when he returned from work. He drew at the table where his father cut. They would listen to popular Spanish music over the radio and, at night, to the *Hit Parade*. They liked Perry Como when he sang "Don't let the stars get in your eyes, / Don't let the moon break your heart" and "Pretend" and "Wanted." "My father loved Doris Day. At the time she was singing 'Secret Love.' He liked the timbre of Eddie Fisher's voice, too. In 1954 he had a big hit with 'Oh, My Papa.' The sentiment of these songs was different from that of María Luisa Landín—clean and sweet, even "*cursi*"; almost devotional, upbeat, and very proper.[2]

Pepe drew portraits from photographs and drawings he saw in newspapers like *Figaro* and magazines like *Selecciones de Readers Digest*, *Sucesos*, a popular weekly, and *Ecran*, a movie magazine from Argentina. In *Figaro*, he read the film reviews of Efrain Huerta, a well-known poet. From the photos in *Ecran*, he drew the stars whose beauty touched his feelings and his sense of aesthetics. One such was Audrey Hepburn, who was all the fashion when *Roman Holiday* came out. In this drawing, he tried to capture her eyes (see figure 6.2). With time, he broadened

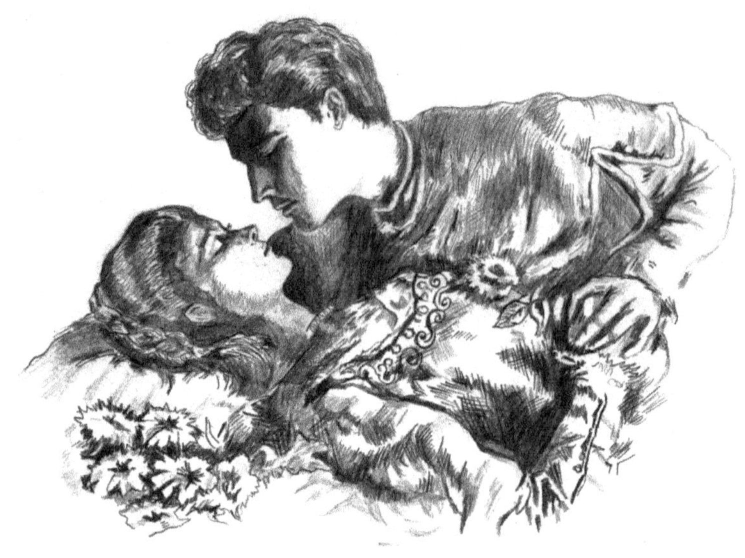

Figure 6.3. Romeo and Juliet. Pencil drawing by José "Pepe" Zúñiga, 1953.

his repertoire. From illustrations in *Sucesos*, he drew characters from Shakespeare: Hamlet, Macbeth, and, as we see here, Romeo and Juliet (see figure 6.3).

Since he first watched *Flash Gordon*, he was intrigued by outer space. In *Figaro*, he found articles on flying saucers sighted in Brazil, the United States, and many European countries. In one of them, George Adamsky of the United States claimed he had entered a flying saucer and traveled in space. He published a book Pepe bought, and he visited Mexico. Later, his story was proven false, but at the time it fascinated Pepe. It was a moment of science fiction movies. He remembered the film *The Day the Earth Stood Still*, directed by Robert Wise (1951). "This was a well-made movie," Pepe recalled. "The flying saucer lands in Washington, and a robot gets out with a man from space. They've come to tell the people that if they don't stop their wars with one another, they are going to destroy the Earth. The film had a very strong message of peace." The fear of nuclear catastrophe was likely more intense in the United States, where, as hysteria intensified in these years over a possible attack from the Soviet Union, people scrambled to build bomb shelters, and children hid under their school desks in air raid drills. In Mexico, the terror was less, but Pepe liked the film's pacifist message.

A little after his pilgrimage to Juquila in honor of Alfonso, Pepe left the shop of Pérez Medina and entered business with his friend Eduardo "El Loco" Mendoza, who lived in Lerdo 17. They opened a shop to fix jukeboxes and radios in Gulf of Bengal Street in Tacuba, to the west of the city. It was 1955. Pepe was eighteen years old, El Loco was twenty-one. El Loco was the son of a Spaniard who never participated in the fiestas in Lerdo 17. "He was a despot," remembered Pepe, "He made fun of the neighbors. He would take down the wet laundry from the clothesline to put up his own and when anyone challenged him, he would respond, 'Yeah, I tore off your damned pants full of shit.' I can assure you they were not full of shit. When someone came around asking for money to repair the vecindad or celebrate a religious event, he never gave a cent. He said he was an atheist. 'I don't believe in your *pinche* religious ideas,' he said. He was thoroughly disagreeable. He had no wife. There was no mother to take care of his children. He had a daughter and people said he had violated her. She left the *vecindad*, very young, just a teenager. And he didn't have anything to be so arrogant about. He dressed badly, like any worker. But he was a good electrician because he had taught El Loco and El Loco knew his trade. My father had asked the old man to string the electric lights around his Virgen de la Soledad. When we set up shop, many clients came because they knew his father."

Chucho lent them the money to start the business. Lupe had promoted Chucho's foray into the auto repair trade. But after he suffered an accident at work, he returned to master the tailor's craft with his father. At the time, in the mid-1950s, he was earning well. "We made a deal that we would repay Chucho in parts," Pepe remembers. "In the beginning, everything went fine, but when Eduardo repaired the jukeboxes, he would pocket the money for himself. I was repairing radios but he returned them to the clients and kept that money as well. There came a moment when he cynically told me he would not give me anything. I told Chucho. I had the keys to the store, and one day I went with my brother and removed all of his records. These records were his treasure. That's why we took them—all of them. We brought them home in a taxi. Right away and furious, he came to the house to get his records. I wasn't home but he left me a note: 'I have to speak with you. You stole my records.' When I saw him, I told him, 'No, they're on deposit until you pay me what you owe me.' He wouldn't hear of it. He insisted I robbed him. I told him, 'If you keep accusing me, I am going to break every one of those records.' 'Then, no, no,' he responded and gave me a sum of *lana* (dough), not much, and I returned the records, all the records, but I made him sign three letters of payment that obliged him to return all that he owed. We dissolved the business.

"When I gave him the letters, he said, 'I'm not going to pay you.' He claimed he had no money, but obviously he had money because he had just bought a motorcycle. Well, then, my mother intervened again and called my Madrina Luz, who got a written recommendation for a lawyer from Doña Lilienthal, her employer." Lupe and Pepe went to consult the lawyer in Las Lomas de Chapultepec, then the most luxurious neighborhood in the city. The lawyer turned out to be a bandit. He needed money to pay for a divorce. He took the letters of payment and embargoed El Loco's motorcycle. Then he sold it and kept the money for himself. "My mother, furious but always very smart, told the lawyer: 'What I want most, Licenciado, is for my boy to bring money home from his radio repair work.' The lawyer told her he had an uncle, Engineer Alfonso Bernal, who worked with RCA Victor in the Colonia Condesa. My mother went to see Engineer Bernal. She insisted we had no money and the lawyer had swindled them. The engineer said he was extremely sorry and responded: 'What I can do for you is give your son a job.' And that's how Engineer Bernal brought me to the central headquarters of RCA Victor."

One afternoon in the midst of the quarrel with El Loco, Pepe walked into a movie theater on the way to the shop in Tacuba. "I was very sad because I knew this was not going to end well. It was raining and I walked into the show and there I saw *Singing in the Rain*. It turned me on so much! Because like the title said, one shouldn't be sad and depressed, but happy even if it's raining. The film dealt with the transition from silent to talking film that my father had spoken to me about at length. I delighted in the technical processes of filmmaking shown in the movie, but what enchanted me most was Gene Kelly. My father didn't like Gene Kelly. He thought he was effeminate and not as elegant as Fred Astaire. But I admired his dancing. His feet! How he moved his feet! He was an acrobat, not just a great dancer. What a butt, so masculine! I adored Debbie Reynolds, too. How lovely when he sang to her from a ladder, 'You were meant for me. I was meant for you!' They had the same talent as Astaire and Rogers, but they danced and sang more intimately, more emotionally. These were moments I was not sure of my sexual preference, and I wanted a girlfriend. They were my dream of having a partner, faithful and loving.

"What tenacity the character played by Gene Kelly showed in his struggle against corruption and his drive to find his own way, his own destiny," Pepe remembered. "In the dance *Broadway Melody*, he arrives in New York, a city full of ambitious people and a lot of corrupt and cruel characters. Wasn't that what I was living? He wanted to become a great dancer on Broadway the way I wanted to be a radio technician. He encountered obstacle after obstacle, but he kept dancing and dancing, trying and trying. Then, in the film, came one of the most sensual dances I have ever seen in my life when Gene Kelly danced with Cyd Charisse. She danced with incredibly beautiful eroticism with her long legs, her hair cut *à la garçon* in the fashion of the 1920s. With her legs, her arms, her movements circling him, she seduced him. It was such a sensual struggle between them, as if they were making love, and then finally he conquered her. But she was corrupt. Her gangster boyfriend gave her a diamond bracelet and she took it. His bodyguards pushed Gene Kelly away. This was crushing for him, the way I was hurt by El Loco's betrayal, but he resisted corruption. He had to follow his path. He was looking for an ideal, as I was. I wanted to rise up [*subir de categoria*] like him. Gene Kelly left defrauded, but what saved him was his sense that he had the gift of dance. With what dignity and conviction he danced and sang *Singing in the Rain*. It's a dance permeated with feeling, without an ounce of sentimentality. There is too much movement, too much energy and conviction for that. He jumps over the puddles of water, he smiles into the falling rain. I think that what this dance tells us is that despite circumstances, one has to be happy—the rain and the puddles don't matter.

"The movie inspired me. I learned practically all the dialogues. I even tried dancing over puddles. Above all, I got the moral: dignity, always dignity. This hit me because my father spoke to me of dignity. Dignity is honor, he told me. 'Always have dignity in what you do.' That was a grand phrase! Never to be corrupt. My father had his problems with dignity in his relationship with Lupe. But my father did not want us to repeat his errors. Honor is very important. There was no dignity in the dishonest behavior of Eduardo and the lawyer."

So Pepe survived another bitter lesson in the public sphere of daily life. Thanks to the intervention of Engineer Bernal, "I really began my career in the workshop of RCA Victor." Engineer Bernal was something of a protector, in the traditional Mexican use and practice of the term—a social superior from whom Lupe sought a favor—but such protection was also modern, the result of networking and means of mobility that required technical performance from the beneficiary. It also brought new pleasures. Pepe received thirty-five pesos a week which he gave to his mother for the household. She gave him five pesos for his expenses and asked him to go every Saturday to the church of San Juan de Dios, on Hidalgo Avenue in front of the Alameda, to deposit three coins on the altar of the Holy Trinity. When after three months, he got a raise to fifty pesos a week, he did not tell his mother. He kept the fifteen pesos for himself. Not telling his mother did not seem to him an abuse of honor. It was not much money, but he could buy a few things he had always wanted. Like skates, but now he did not have much use for them. He bought toys for his little brother Efrén—toys that years ago he had wanted for himself. He invested his money in himself and his presentation. He bought a green turtleneck sweater that was in fashion at that moment. He bought Glostora and Brilliantine for his hair. Lupe had always put lard, then lemon, on his hair when he was a child. She said hair creams were for fairies (*maricones*). But her husband used Glostora, as did many men.

What a privilege to work at RCA Victor! It was the most important, advanced company in sound recording. Six technicians worked in the shop, along with several carpenters who built high-fidelity sets. Pepe learned to make and repair them—the record players and the amplifiers. What really delighted him was testing the equipment and the records in the new sound. The employees valued the gift of his extraordinary ear. In an enclosed booth, he checked the frequencies. He listened to Rachmaninoff, to Shostakovich, and to Rimsky-Korsakov's *Scheherazade*, the first record he ever bought for himself. He bought his father Eddie Fisher's records.

He gave up his lunch hour to listen to music. He listened to entire symphonies. "One gradually educates the ear, and for that reason, I can't bear the sound of people screaming or dogs barking." Then in 1958 came stereophonic sound! The first stereo recording he heard was *Taboo*, exotic music with drums, xylophone, and the euphonium, directed by Arthur Leyman. Then came the new records of Stravinsky, Khachaturian, Schubert, Schumann, Bach, and Beethoven. The radio stations that played classical music, XELA and Radio Universidad, decided to transmit the same music, one from the left and the other from the right. At home, he had a small FM radio and borrowed another to coordinate the sounds. He had heard the music of Silvestre Revueltas in the movies, but what a pleasure to hear his *Toccata for Percussion* with the different instruments coming from distinct places in the orchestra.

At the same time, he followed the transformation of visual production in the movies. When the Hollywood studios lost out to television, they experimented with new techniques to keep their public. In the Alameda, Real Cinema, and the Metropolitana, he saw the new 3-D films. "Films like the *House of Wax* and *Ticonderoga* gave the sensation that objects flew off the screen at the spectator like a ping-pong ball. 3-D didn't last long because it was too expensive. Then came Cinemascope. I read about it in the Spanish edition of *Life* magazine. Not only was the screen enlarged, but it captured stereophony in a bigger way with various channels for sound. They built new theaters to show these films. Today, many of these are arenas for religious revivals. The Ciné México in the Colonia de los Doctores was the first to project Cinemascope, and the first film was *The Robe*, from Twentieth-Century Fox, with Richard Burton, Victor Mature, and Debra Padgett. It was clever because Christian themes always drew the masses. It touched popular sentiments of faith and devotion that I also shared. I bought the record of the soundtrack, one of the first stereo recordings. In 1956, Paramount came out with Vistavision, with films like the *Ten Commandments*, a very long movie with badly done special effects. Cinema is believable when you see a film of science fiction or drama that seems very real, like a miracle well pulled off. It's a question of technique. Cecil B. DeMille's *Samson and Delilah* was good in this sense. Although the columns were made of cardboard, it seemed as if Samson (Victor Mature) was doing something extraordinary and miraculous when he destroyed them. Spectacular! Afterward our comic Tin-Tan did a terrific parody of this scene in *Lo que pasó a Sansón*. Pushing the columns with all his might, he said, 'I can't, I can't!' The crowd was cheering him on, 'More! More! More! Yes, Samson, you can! You can!' Obviously he couldn't. He started kicking the columns with his feet and pushing with his arms until he told the crowd, 'I can't because I'm not Victor Matur-é.'"

For Pepe the more profound revolution in film was not so much the flashy new techniques but an emotional, erotic one that probed individual psychology in new ways. When the Hollywood studios lost their family audience to television, they pressured the censors to lower the bar and began to explore the emotional turbulence and exploding sexuality of youth.[3] Young and talented actors, many of them trained in "Method acting" to express their inner feelings—the more conflictive the better—made these films that became transformative experiences in young people's construction of themselves. They were precisely the market the studios targeted. Much more explorative of interiority than films like *Rhapsody in Blue* or the *Al Jolson Story* that informed Pepe's childhood, they were the bildungsroman of a new generation. The most impacting brought to the screen the novels and scripts of splendid writers like Tennessee Williams and Gore Vidal, who wrote the screenplay for *Suddenly Last Summer*; Michael Wilson, who adapted Theodore Dreiser's novel *An American Tragedy* as *A Place in the Sun*; John Steinbeck and Paul Osborn, who wrote *East of Eden*; and notable directors like Elia Kazan

(*On the Waterfront*, *East of Eden*), Nicholas Ray (*Rebel without a Cause)*, George Stevens (*A Place in the Sun*), Joseph L. Mankiewicz (*Suddenly Last Summer* and *Julius Caesar*), and Vincente Minelli, who directed the film version of Robert Anderson's play *Tea and Sympathy*.

Seeing these films with his budding libido, Pepe drew their stars: Grace Kelly, Elizabeth Taylor, Marlon Brando, and above all, James Dean. "To draw was like writing for me. It came out of me with no effort. It thrilled me to reproduce a face with a pencil. It excited me to draw these beautiful, erotic faces. To capture the face of Grace Kelly was to capture pure beauty." Elizabeth Taylor had been his soulmate from childhood. He had followed her from the time he saw her as a little orphan cruelly abused in *Jane Eyre*, as an innocent, carefree child in *Lassie*, as a beautiful adolescent, bursting with energy and rebellion in *National Velvet*, as Amy in *Little Women*. Now in *A Place in the Sun*,[4] he watched her as Angela Vickers, a rich girl, daring, on fire, risk taking, speeding her stylish convertible, skiing at high speed on Loon Lake. Spoiled, innocent, and impulsive, she broke all social barriers and conventions in pursuing her love for George Eastman (Montgomery Clift), the ambitious employee of her father. "The close-ups of these lovers, the pure expressive faces of Taylor and Clift, were unforgettable," Pepe remembered. "They captured the tenderness and sincerity of Taylor in trying to understand and give herself to her lover who was so enigmatic and tortured by the conflict between his fascination for her and the fact he had gotten his other girlfriend, a plain working girl, pregnant. Their feelings expressed themselves not so much with words, but with the eyes, the movement of the lips, the gestures of the body. That's what those close-ups did."

He followed Clift and Taylor in *Suddenly Last Summer* (1960). In the film, Pepe explained, "Clift is the psychiatrist of the young Taylor, and this time she expresses her eroticism through her tortured soul. Her aunt (Katharine Hepburn) has her hospitalized in an asylum and wants to force her into a lobotomy, because she knows something about the death of the woman's son she doesn't want revealed. The girl is crazy and blocked because she cannot remember what happened on a Mediterranean beach with her cousin Sebastian. The homosexual cousin was tortured and eaten by a mob of poor delinquents. Gradually with the aid of the psychiatrist, she remembers that Sebastian was using her as bait to attract boys. In the movie, we see Sebastian's invisible hand pull her into the water. The boys come swarming behind a fence, peering hungrily through the wire. You see her body writhing in protest, her voluptuous breasts overflowing her bathing suit, the white suit against the smooth bronze of her sun-tanned skin. She goes down into the water then emerges like a mermaid, glistening water streaming over her body. She returns to the beach, takes off her bathing cap and shakes her thick, black hair in the breeze. How sexy! Finally we see this swarm of poor youth chasing Sebastian, always invisible. They kill him. It seems they devour him. She cries out like no one before had ever cried out in cinema. If you remember, it was before Janet Leigh screamed in *Psycho*.

"For me, the story revealed the victimization of a girl so innocent and so young, the hypocrisy and conventions of a repressive society and the institutions like the asylums that seem to have been torture chambers for youth that didn't want to conform. For me, the picture showed the levels to which corrupt adults were willing to go to maintain acceptable appearances and myths. It was very daring to treat the theme of homosexuality at that moment. I read a review in *Figaro* that made that comment, and right away I went to see the movie in the Ciné Variedades. I wanted to see it a second time with friends, but within three days, the censors—the Liga de la Decencia—had it removed from the theaters. I remember around the same time I saw *Tea and Sympathy* (1958), in which homosexuality was insinuated but not so openly. What's certain is that the young man (John Kerr) in that film is tormented by his father, by the schoolmaster, and by other male students for the way he walks and talks, his refined taste in music, his lack of interest in so-called masculine activities like sports. These men tormenting him were pretty much interpreted as insensitive thugs. It was so touching when the schoolmaster's wife (Deborah Kerr) decided to make love with the sensitive young man and said to him, 'I only ask that one day when you talk about this, and I know you will, you will be kind.' Those are words I will never forget."

Pepe drew Marlon Brando in many of his film roles. "I saw his first picture, *El Hombre*, a very honest treatment of soldiers wounded in the war. I read in *Ekran* that to prepare for his role, Brando put himself in a veteran's hospital to feel the experience and learn how to move in a wheelchair. In *On the Waterfront*, he played a lost youth on the docks of Hoboken, an accomplice of a crooked union mafia he felt he had to follow because his brother was its lawyer. Although the same mafia and his brother had destroyed his career as a boxer, he stayed loyal to his family. He took part in the murder of a worker who was going to reveal the corruption, but through his love for the victim's sister and the persuasion of a priest, he finally decided to denounce the mafia. He's tormented and indecisive, but he shows his tenderness in his care for the pigeons he keeps on the rooftop of the *vecindad*—very similar to our *vecindades*—and in his love for the

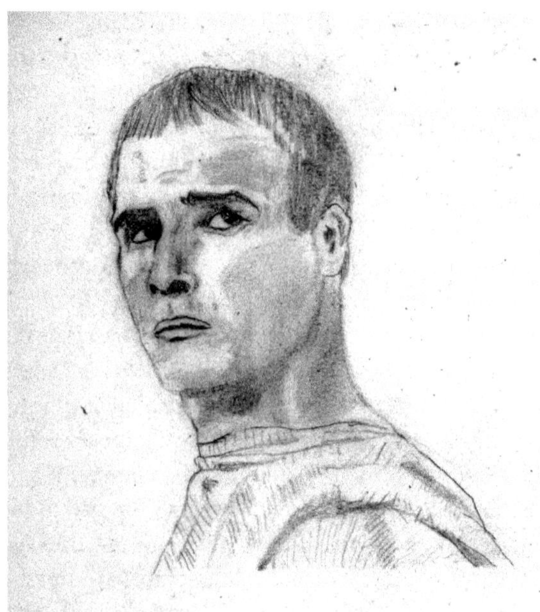

Figure 6.4. Marlon Brando in *Julius Caesar*. Pencil drawing by José "Pepe" Zúñiga, 1953.

girl. Through his love, his honesty, and his courage, he discovers himself as a person of dignity.

"How handsome was Brando! I always perceived beauty—the beauty of men and women both! I liked Brando's masculinity, his physique. I drew him several times—in *Julius Caesar* (see figure 6.4) and on the motorcycle he rode in *The Wild Ones*. I didn't like his violence in that movie, but I identified with his rebellion—and with him when he abandoned rebellion for his love for a girl. He decided in favor of tenderness."

Of course, the most rebellious and seductive was James Dean. "It was 1956. I was nineteen years old. I was doing my military service. I picked the black ball in the lottery so I only had to march on Sundays. We formed a guard in the parades down Juárez Avenue past the Alameda. One day as I was marching, I saw that the theater in front of the Alameda was showing *East of Eden*. I went. How Dean could show his agony, his indecision, his twisted feelings! I drew him many times (see figure 6.5). This anarchic, restless boy rebelled against his very passive, distant father and his mother, aggressive, independent, hard, and subversive—she ran a whorehouse. After, I saw *Rebel without a Cause*. Again, a young guy full of anarchic rage against his indecisive father, confused and passive, and his mother, strong but conventional. At the time, I had begun to rebel, particularly against my father. I love him very much and I looked for

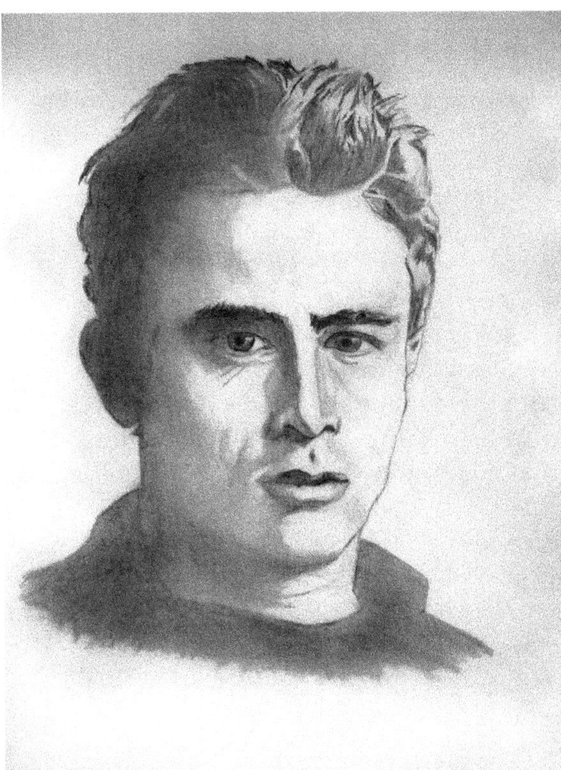

Figure 6.5. James Dean. Pencil drawing by José "Pepe" Zúñiga, 1955.

him to love me, but he was hard and aloof, very authoritarian, imposing, and limiting. He had punished me cruelly upon occasion—for instance, when I fell off the swing. Now he was pressuring me to bring more money home. He had taught me a lot, but at the time I was becoming more conscious of things, and all my father's defects suddenly became clear to me: his passivity, his conformity, his ingratitude toward my mother, his wasting of money with his friends simply to show off, the way he had forced me to work at cutting and sewing from the time I was a child. He dreamed of getting rich by winning the lottery. It was in those years that Chava Flores began to mock that kind of behavior in his songs about the vecindades. I liked Chava Flores's songs, but my father did not.[5]

"In Dean's movies, the struggle is individual, of a masculine hero, but the rage of youth is resolved and dissolved in love and friendship between them—in a solidarity of tenderness." Such solidarity Pepe also felt in Mexico. "Here, as in other places, Dean became the model of the moment," he recalled. "The department store windows displayed his clothing along with his picture. We already had jeans but Dean made them very fashionable. I bought a red vest and a red sweater. I could not afford the jacket. I did my self-portrait in the red sweater. It was an obsession with many young guys—not necessarily the poorest. I doubt for my old buddies, Macuca, El Patón, and La Tripa, Dean meant anything. But the students at La Esmeralda, where I entered in 1959, were into Dean. Many of them came from modest families like mine but they wanted to '*superar*' (move up), develop themselves, and create something—they wanted to discover themselves by doing something creative and new. I asked myself: why this rebellion? Was it because of poverty? For not being able to realize desires for development because of the limitations, the repression, both social and political, we felt around us? I felt deep down a sort of frustration that didn't have a name. I felt my limitations and the film *Rebel without a Cause* pushed me to want to move forward, to not be a conformist like my father."

Pepe found new friends in a class in radio and television technology he took in a program affiliated with the Instituto Politécnico Nacional, where youth generally from modest backgrounds prepared for technical professions. Engineer Bernal arranged his enrollment in this class that met at night on Abraham González Street between Bucareli and Cuauhtémoc. Here Pepe got to know two young men named Zúñiga—David and Xavier. "We called ourselves the 'Three Kings.' I was the black one, David the blond one, and Javier a rose color with black hair. By now it bothered me less to be called *negro* by my friends—it was sort of a label of solidarity. After class, we would hang out outside the Café de La Havana at Bucareli and Morelos, where the journalists met. We didn't have the money to go in. On the street, we would share our life stories and our ambitions. David liked to show off his muscles and talk about his conquests of girls. Javier and I criticized him for being macho and arrogant. Javier was a mountain climber. On the weekends, mostly Sundays, he and I would climb Ajusco and Las Ventanas near the city. We even went to the Fistol in Hidalgo state. We bought rope and hooks to climb. Sometimes we went with the explorers' club, the Mountain Cubs (los Cachorros de la Montaña). I liked to climb. I loved the danger of it. When we took night trips, we would pitch a tent and by lantern light talk into the dawn about our families and other things. I really loved these trips." In those years, mountain climbing like the Boy Scouts (Exploradores) was considered a clean and healthy sport for rising male youth.

"In addition to David and Javier, I also got to know a fellow named Enrique in the radio and television class. He convinced me to leave RCA

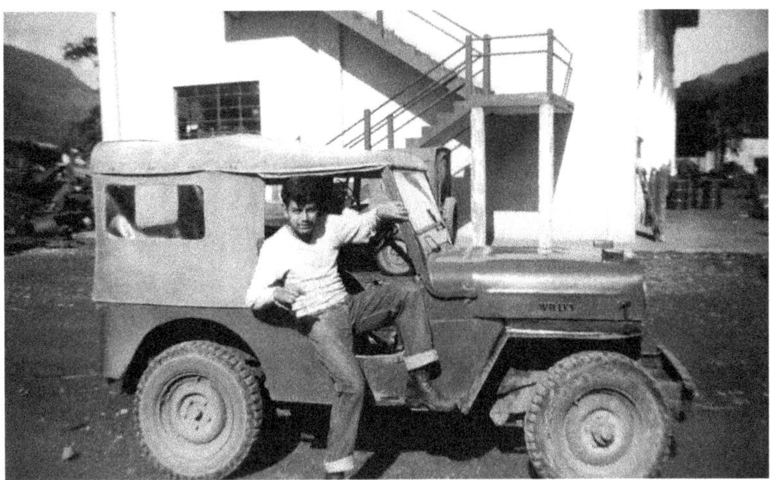

Figure 6.6. Pepe in Veracruz. Black-and-white photograph, 1958.

Victor to work for the Ingenieros Electro-Mecánicos Compañia de Alejo Peralta, a big, successful firm that was introducing radio communication between vehicles. Alejo Peralta became the director of the Instituto Politécnico Nacional in these years. The company installed telephones in the Federal District for domestic gas companies and the Tintoreria Francesa dry-cleaning chain. It also made possible the radio taxis, the first taxis to have a telephone in each car. The company immediately began installing mobile phones throughout the country. Now I began to earn some real money. Once I was trained, the company sent me to the sugar-producing zone of Veracruz to repair a system of telephones installed for a company owned by Cubans. I relished the opportunity to travel." We see him here getting out of a jeep at the Motzoronga sugar refinery in Veracruz (see figure 6.6).

Meanwhile, now that he was twenty-one and could enter the cabarets, Pepe explored night life in the Colonia Guerrero. Elvis Presley had arrived: "His music was everywhere and I saw his movies. He was no actor, but he could sing." In the Colonia Guerrero, Elvis had to compete with other music—the impassioned romantic laments of José Alfredo Jiménez, their pathos deepened by tequila, the "trios," and the mambo that held on to its performers and publics even after the government threw Pérez Prado out of the country allegedly for having set the National Anthem to mambo rhythm. But perhaps the biggest sensation of the 1950s was Celia Cruz, the Cuban singer, who had come to Mexico in 1948 as part of

Mulatas de Fuego. The Mulatas toured all of Latin America introducing the mambo in their scandalous bikinis. In the words of novelist Gabriel García Márquez, "they turned the world upside down."[6] In the 1950s, Celia Cruz came to Mexico with the Sonora Matancera. "They played in the ballrooms—the California Dancing Club and the Salón Los Angeles in the Colonia Guerrero where Chucho hung out," Pepe remembers. "They played a lot of Cuban rhythms like the *guaracha*, the *son montuno*, the *huahuanco*, and the *merengue*. I bought many of their records. I was working in RCA Victor when Celia Cruz's song 'El yeberito moderno' came out. She sang of a healer who cured with herbs. 'I bring mint for good people,' the song went. It was a tribute to her Yoruba religion and her Afro-Cuban culture. It was a huge hit and I loved it. Then she came out with 'Rock 'n' Roll,' a response to Elvis Presley, and it was an even bigger hit."

Pepe was exploring his sexuality. He went to the Tivoli to watch Calentan, Gemma, La Argentina Hermosa, and the "China" Sumukei strip as the male audience chanted: "Hair! Hair!" He was more excited by the public than the strippers. He decided to learn to dance seriously, but not the mambo or rock 'n' roll. As with his father's taste in film, Pepe chose the most refined dance, the danzón. Of Afro-Cuban origin, danzón had acquired in Mexico a high level of subtlety and elegance. The Mexicans subordinated its undeniable sensuality to strict rules. To perform it well was a work of art, an exhibition of exquisite, intimate aesthetics and insinuated sexuality. Carlos Monsiváis described it as "an erotic flight affixed to the floor."[7] For these reasons, Pepe chose to master it.

"I walked into the cabaret, La Hija de Moctezuma, near my house, with my military card. I drank some Cuba libres, or Bacardi rum with ginger ale, to work up my courage to ask a woman, a *fichera* with the gift of dance. The ficheras worked in the clubs entertaining male customers. You had to pay a peso a dance. It was prohibited for these women to leave the club and have sex, but it was possible to get away with it with a bribe. Chucho had done it from time to time, but me, no. I found a girl—I cannot remember her name—for the single purpose of dancing and we got to be good friends. She trusted me and I her, and she came to respect me. She was a superb dancer. She corrected all my errors. I went back again and again. If in a lot of dances, the man conquers the woman, in danzón the conquest is mutual and shared. She, the woman, takes the form of another individual, not an object. I. Danzón is about mutual tenderness and respect."

7. "Five Pesos, Two Pencils, and an Eraser!"

In the spring of 1958, Ingenieros Electromecánicos asked Pepe to cover intervehicle communication for Adolfo López Mateos's presidential campaign in Mexico's states. He jumped at the opportunity to travel. Then without explanation, the company canceled his trip. He thought Enrique, who had recommended him to the firm, had undercut him. Angry, as he made his way home that evening, he stopped at the door of the Esmeralda painting school in the Calle San Fernando in the Colonia Guerrero. Since his time at the Escuela Primaria Belisario Domínguez across the street, he had been curious about the school—particularly about the nude models he had seen through the windows. Now at the age of twenty-one, he knocked on the door and asked the attendant what he needed to enroll in a night class. "It was a kid's whim, nothing more," he remembered. "But when the guard told me, 'Very simple, you pay five pesos. You will need two pencils and an eraser.' 'Five pesos, two pencils, and an eraser!' I said to myself. 'Imagine that!' I immediately signed up for a class." At the time, he had no idea he would do anything more than learn about drawing.

Founded in 1942, the Escuela Nacional de Pintura, Escultura, y Grabado La Esmeralda traced its origins to the open-air painting and stone-sculpting schools the government created in the 1920s. These sought to nurture the spontaneity and intuition of students from the popular sector on the principle that art was an innate gift in the Mexican soul, particularly in those of the humble classes untainted by European sophistry. Diego Rivera, Frida Kahlo, Antonio M. Ruíz (El Corcito), and others founded the Esmeralda as an alternative to the formalism and rigidity of the Academia de San Carlos, the official plastic arts school founded in the late eighteenth century. They hoped to open popular access to art and art education although the school's program became more restrictive.[1] Classes in the full, degree-granting curriculum in painting, sculpture, drawing, engraving, and humanist studies met during the day. Night classes, for those who worked in the day, took students with no more than a primary-school certificate. When Pepe entered, night classes offered only drawing and did not count toward a degree. In the 1940s, the major muralists Rivera and Pablo O'Higgins and painters María Izquierdo and Manuel Rodriguez Lozano taught at the school. By 1958, this spectacular older generation had died or retired. The faculty still included distinguished artists: Raul Anguiano, Ignacio Aguirre, Feliciano Peña, Arturo Estrada, Enrique Assad, Benito Messeguer, Armando Carmona, Francisco Zúñiga, and Santos Balmori.

In 1958, the Mexican school of social realism, mostly based in mural painting and graphic arts, still held sway and particularly at La Esmeralda. It faced challenges from all sides as many prominent painters followed Rufino Tamayo and Juan Soriano in new directions. If José Luis Cuevas, the enfant terrible of the 1950s, led the rebel pack because he spoke the loudest of rupture (La Ruptura), many had declared their independence, including Mathias Goeritz, Alberto Gironella, Manuel Felguérez, and Fernando García Ponce. Even such recent graduates of La Esmeralda as Lilia Carrillo and Pedro Coronel followed informalism, the Parisian equivalent of New York abstract expressionism. Mexican school adherents despised the latter for its abandonment of social politics and democratic commitment, its celebration of art for art's sake, and dependence on the private art market. Abstract expressionism lent itself to the Cold War politics of the U.S. State Department, which exported it as an expression of individual freedom. In 1958 the Mexican government's Bienal honored David Alfaro Siqueiros, the only surviving muralist of the Big Three, but abstract expressionism was well represented in the exhibit.[2]

In its perennial role as referee between warring camps, the Mexican government at the 1960 Bienal honored the muralists' rival and critic Rufino Tamayo. The majority of works selected by governments from eighteen countries were in abstract or semiabstract style.[3] Behind this representation, Mexican school loyalists saw not just the Mexican state but a more concerted, aggressive strategy that linked the U.S. State Department and CIA to José Gómez Sicre, director of visual arts at the

Organization of American States, Jorge Romero Brest, director of the Argentine Museo Nacional de Bellas Artes, and his protégée, Marta Traba, founder and president of the Museo de Arte Moderno in Bogotá. For Mexican school supporters, these puppets of the United States opposed not just realist painting as a dated genre but all political painting.[4]

Pepe Zúñiga knew nothing of these struggles when he entered his night drawing class. He had scarcely heard of Orozco, Rivera, and Siqueiros. Years before Tío Efrén had taken him to see the murals of Diego Rivera, David Alfaro Siqueiros, and Rufino Tamayo in the Palacio de Bellas Artes. He did not like them and he did not understand them. He could not determine the gender of Siqueiros's main figure, which appeared to him to be a man with a woman's breast. "I did not yet have the eye of a painter," he commented. "Over time I came to respect them from an artistic perspective." When Pepe entered La Esmeralda, about the only famous painter he knew and liked was Jesús Helguera, whose compositions of mythical Aztec warriors and princesses were frequently reproduced on popular calendars hung in Mexican homes. As higher education did for thousands of young people in these years, La Esmeralda opened for Pepe a new galaxy of knowledge, aesthetics, and sensibility—a humanist cosmopolitanism that youth in many parts of the world had glimpsed as children through movies, radio, popular books, advertisements, and museum visits.

In general, Mexican youth's discovery was as uneven, fitful, and painful an experience as it was exhilarating and expansive. For Pepe, it began with the mastery of technique. Not surprisingly, Benito Messeguer, his first teacher at La Esmeralda, asked him if he had drawn before. Messeguer introduced him to formal technique (see figure 7.1). He taught his students the grades of pencils according to the quality of lead; what could be done with each in lines, shading, tones, and chiaroscuro; how to sharpen pencils with single-edged razor blades to achieve long, fine points that permitted shading with delicate crossed lines, instead of the powdered lead Pepe had rubbed with his fingers in his drawing of James Dean. Messeguer taught them how to work with charcoal pencils and to avoid stains, smudges, and tears in the paper through applying different erasers. He introduced them to grades of paper and the pencils and inks suited to them. He had them copy geometric shapes to capture volume, proportion, and shading on different sizes of paper to demonstrate the need for distinct pencil solutions. They drew objects—animal skulls, tree trunks, flowers, leaves, tablecloths, plates—to depict surface textures. The exercises prepared them to draw the human figure.

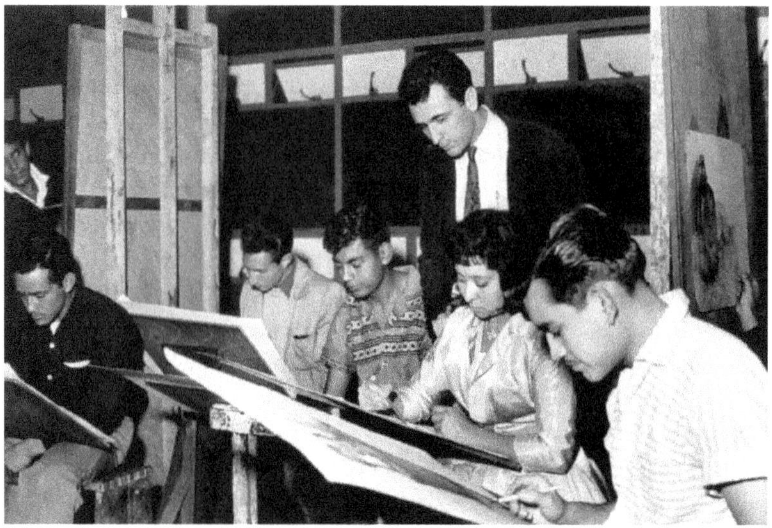

Figure 7.1. Benito Messeguer standing over Pepe. Black-and-white photograph, 1959.

Esmeralda models belonged to families—fathers, mothers, sons, daughters, cousins—some of them recognizable in the murals of Rivera and Orozco, like Doña Luz Jiménez, the model of female indigeneity and Mexican motherhood in murals and sculpture, or Don Melchor, who modeled for José Clemente Orozco's *Man of Fire* in the Hospicio Cabañas murals in Guadalajara. Pepe painted or drew both of them at the Esmeralda, but in Messeguer's second-year class, his principal subject was Don Timoteo. In the class, Don Timoteo and Melchor posed in different states of dress or nudity. After an initial moment of surprise, Pepe found the naked male body beautiful and sensual to draw. However, in his principal work that year, he drew Don Timoteo seated on a chair in work clothes with his sleeves rolled up (see figure 7.2). Pepe drew him quickly in pencil, capturing the wrinkles in his shirt and pants, the veins in his arms, and the contours of his fingers. The exercises he had been doing at home helped him to observe and capture the different textures of the skin and clothing. "Here, take the brush," Messeguer told him.

He had never used a brush. Working on craft paper in black, white, and red liquids prepared in a base of paste, his strokes gave line and volume to the figure. The eyes and mouth required more delicate brushwork. To the surprise of the class, he finished in two hours. His capacity to observe and his visual memory, sharpened by years at the movies, had given him speed and accuracy. But what caught Messeguer's attention was the

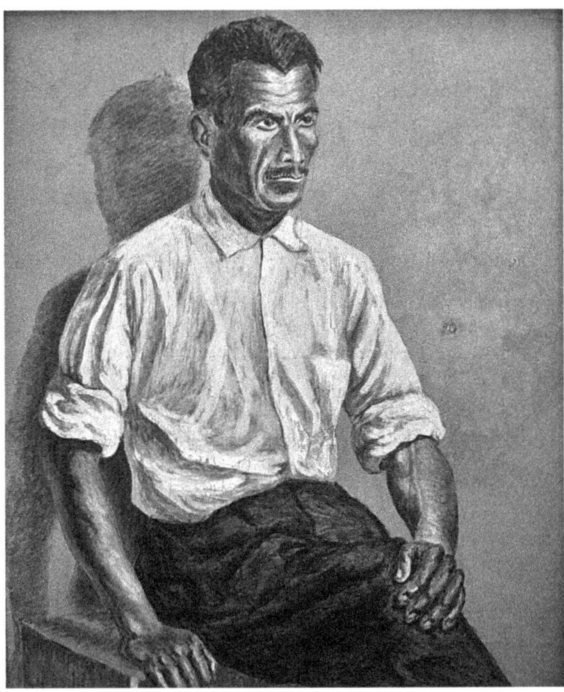

Figure 7.2. *Don Timoteo*, painting by José "Pepe" Zúñiga, 1959.

emotional vigor of the piece. "This is very Orozco," Messeguer told him, "You have expressive power, José. You feel your roots. You capture his character."

Pepe showed the portrait in July 1959 in an exhibit of Esmeralda student drawings at the Chapultepec Gallery, one of several belonging to the Instituto Nacional de Bellas Artes (INBA). The government of the state of Zacatecas cosponsored the show, along with the Jornadas Culturales de Artes Plásticas of the INBA and the Grupo Francisco Goitia. It featured lectures on Mexican art history and films on Mexican and world art, many produced by the U.S. Information Agency. Such sponsorship was typical of Cold War cultural diplomacy.[5] While this diplomacy served political purposes—inclusive of the desire on the part of the U.S. State Department to win over Latin American youth—it offered young people important opportunities.

One evening in the second-year drawing class, Messeguer asked the students if they had ever painted in oils. Pepe told him he was doing a painting at home. Benito asked him if someone had taught him the technique. He replied no. "I had bought the materials," he recalled later. "I had no training at all, but I wanted to do a still life. I put bananas, apples, and lemons on a napkin on a table together with a Chianti bottle. The Chianti bottle was my real challenge. I worked with colors of viridian and emerald green to capture the bottle's transparency, then I experimented with several colors, mostly whites, to get the shine of the glass. I struggled with this for days and nights—so long, the green bananas turned brown. Then, finally, I knew I had gotten it. I crossed myself and I started to cry. I said to myself, 'I think I can be a painter.'" Benito asked him to bring in the painting. He admired the work and said to Pepe, "If this painting had a figure in it, it would be completely Flemish in style." Pepe had no idea what Flemish style was, but he took it as a compliment. Messeguer told him, "There are a lot of electrical technicians, but there are very few painters. You have to be a painter." "Until then, I had no idea whether my teachers would find I had talent. I thought I would just stick to radios and stereos." Messeguer pushed him gently, "Right now you draw well, but you have much to learn about the figure, about landscape. You have to find your style."

To encourage self-expression but to impress upon them that the path toward artistic creation was difficult, demanding, and technical, Messeguer suggested they read the biographies of artists. He particularly recommended Van Gogh's letters to his brother Theo. Van Gogh was Messeguer's favorite painter, along with Rembrandt, Goya, and Orozco. "To paint is more than making a few lines and colors," he said, "It is deeper. The artist is someone who thinks and feels, who is contestatory, who never conforms. Consider this when you take up this career. You must always work with the truth." It was not about selling and becoming rich, he told them at a particularly sensitive moment, when the rise of private art galleries in the city had begun to outstrip those of the government.[6]

Pepe immediately bought the book of Theo's letters that had recently been published in Spanish.[7] The story of the Dutchman deeply moved him. Here was a young man growing up in a conventional, religious milieu much like Pepe's. Van Gogh wanted to follow in the footsteps of his preacher father and struggled to do so, evangelizing among the wretched miners and weavers of the Brabant. He gave them his clothing, his few worldly possessions. He noted the contradiction in the workers' worship of God and their unrewarded poverty. He painted them to express his feelings and his faith. Like Pepe, he painted for pleasure and self-expression, not to pursue a career. Pepe noted how Van Gogh had followed the French painter Jean-François Millet, with whom he identified for his capacity to transpose spirituality into painting. How moving for Pepe was Millet's *Angelus*, the peasant and his wife in their field in the late afternoon sunlight, their heads bowed in prayer as they gave thanks to God for the harvest they had brought in! From Van Gogh's story, Pepe learned that painters did not emerge full blown with a defined vocation, technical skills, and unique styles. They worked hard and long, and they could accomplish nothing without imitating the painters they most admired. Van Gogh's story inspired Pepe's struggle to become a painter.

Pepe took his technical training with the same seriousness he had applied to radio electronics. After two years of classes with Messeguer, he studied drawing with Raul Anguiano. Born in Guadalajara in 1915, Anguiano was a distinguished member of the Mexican school who had abandoned political painting in favor of portraits and picturesque, folkloric, and indigenous themes. When Pepe studied with him, Anguiano had recently published his drawings of Bonampak.[8] He had been part of the team exploring the Mayan region under the auspices of the Instituto Nacional de Bellas Artes (INBA) in 1949. Pepe learned a lot from this rigorously disciplined virtuoso.

The class centered on drawing of the female nude. The model was Marilu, a beautiful mestiza woman with "panther eyes." Sensual in any pose, Marilu excited everyone—teachers and students. Pepe drew her in many positions to delineate her body's anatomy with the purest line using a soft lead pencil or a pen with sepia-tinted ink (see figure 7.3). His best drawing filled the craft paper with her voluptuous form, but in reality, he said, "the only accomplished element was her face."

Pepe took his first painting classes in his third year with the Spanish maestro Enrique Assad. Once a student at the Escuela de San Fernando in Madrid, Assad loved to talk to the students about his friend Salvador Dalí. Assad had carved and painted wonderful puppets for the Teatro Guiñol, formed in 1932 in Mexico City by Graciela Amador, ex-compañera of Siqueiros, Angelina Beloff, ex-compañera of Rivera, German List Arzubide, and other artists on the left. Intended to create an agitprop art independent of the government, the Teatro Guiñol began with such consciousness-raising plays as *Comino Goes on Strike* but soon produced *Comino Brushes His Teeth* as the group joined state campaigns, performing in schools, parks, and playgrounds, promoting antialcoholism, hygiene, literacy, vaccination, and children's rights.[9] Now in 1961, Assad was an old man who lived on a pittance in the Colonia Guerrero. He always wore the same worn jacket and pants that smelled of age. In the winter, he wrapped a scarf around his neck and bound his rheumatic

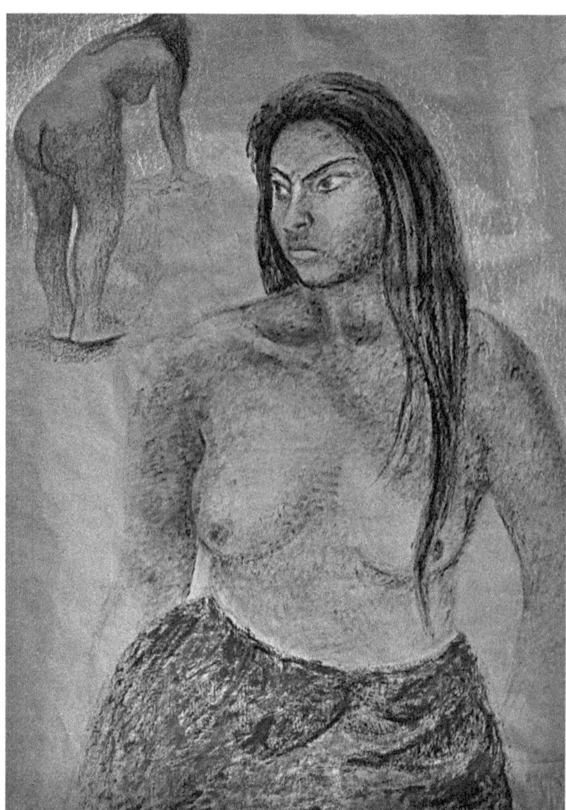

Figure 7.3. *Marilu*, pencil-and-ink drawing by José "Pepe" Zúñiga, 1960.

hands with bandages. He fed the pigeons in the school's patio. "He was very poor like a saint. He was a father to us all," Pepe remembered. "He handed out candy in the class along with paper and brushes. When he examined our work, he would tell us very gently so as not to offend us, 'You're doing well, child, but you ought to do another.' He brought in white cardboard paper and had us prepare it with a coat of green watercolor. He thought it would help us overcome our fear of painting on white, and if we didn't like what we painted, we could discard it." In watercolor, oil paints, and temperas, they began to copy simple objects he asked them to bring to class. Pepe brought a tin mask with green glass eyes he had found in the market, a conch shell, and a starfish. "Paint, son," Assad would say with his hands locked in prayer like a monk. As they began to work with diverse inert models, they used a type of cardboard paper with a base made from boiled animal dung, water, and titanium white. Blending the mixture with pigments, they used their brushes to achieve different color tones and transparencies. The maestro gave each student a large sheet of thin wood 180 by 90 centimeters and asked them to paint the living model, Doña Luz Jiménez.

Luz Jiménez had been the model for the feminine expression of *Mexicanidad*: Diego Rivera's iconic rural schoolteacher, flower vendor, tortilla maker, and washerwoman, Orozco's Malinche at the side of the conqueror Cortés, Jean Charlot's and Tina Modotti's essential mother, and Carlos Bracho's *Race*, sculpted as a family with wife and children kneeling before the patriarch. In sculpted stone—erect, stoic, full bodied, and braided—she guarded the monuments to the revolution and to President Alvaro Obregón. In her representation, she was always female nature and primordial essence versus masculine rationality and historical agency. Yet she was a pioneer in Nahuatl studies: language teacher, storyteller, and historian of indigenous experience, imagination, and traditions for international linguists, anthropologists, and students at Mexico City College and the Universidad Nacional Autónoma. In 1961, she was sixty-four years old. At La Esmeralda, she posed with practiced stoicism, her white hair pulled back in a single braid, her apron flowing over her now ample girth (see figure 7.4). She spoke little. She seemed timid and shy, never abandoning her enigmatic gaze. Yet Pepe found her eyes very expressive. Her eyelids had fallen with age over her haunting dark pupils. At first, he did sketches of her face and body in pencil and charcoal on green-coated paper. As he approached the large-scale painting, Assad told him to work his oils with a spatula to capture broad surfaces more rapidly. At first, Pepe did not like it, but the spatula served for the big surfaces of her skirt and apron. "With a few brushstrokes, I got through to the character of Doña Luz. Her very melancholy eyes were not at all easy to do, but I think I got them."

Pepe's notion of color was at that point intuitive. No professor taught about color in a theoretically sophisticated way, nothing beyond the distinction between cold and hot, primary and secondary colors. In his chemical class with Refugio "Cuca" Satarín, his only female instructor, he learned the difference between organic and mineral-based tints and how to prepare his paints, grinding colors with a mortar and mixing them with damar varnish of linseed oil and resin. She showed them how to prepare paper for different applications, mount their canvases, and seal their drawings and paintings. Cuca taught them the principles of painting alfresco that Pepe would practice in the classes of Armando Carmona, a strict disciple of the Mexican school. But Pepe was then more eager to experiment with colors, forms, and light in landscape painting.

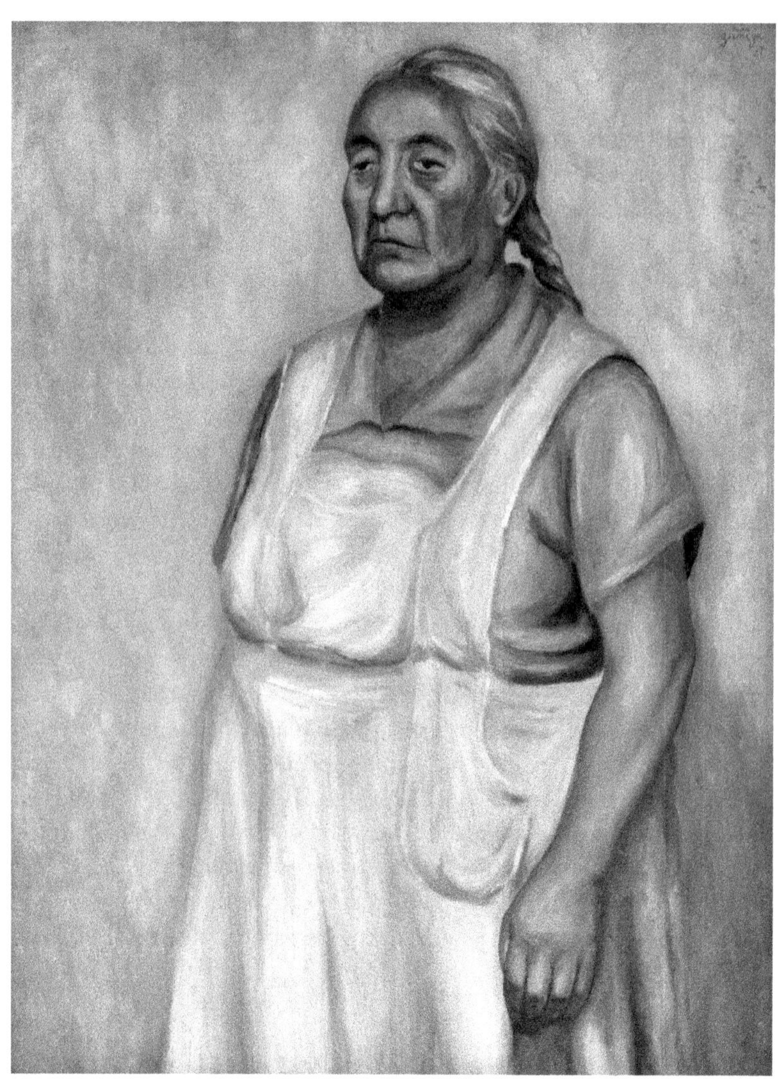

Figure 7.4. *Doña Luz Jiménez*, painting by José "Pepe" Zúñiga, 1960. See color plate 1.

Feliciano Peña, another unconditional member of the Mexican school who specialized in urban and rural landscapes, sent the students to the Peñon Viejo, the Cerro de la Estrella, and the Cerro de Chiquihuite and other nearby heights to paint the Valley of Mexico. Pepe used his frequent trips for Ingenieros Electromecánicos to paint in the open air—on a ruined hacienda in San Luis Potosí, the shores of Lake Chapala in Jalisco, and the sugar refinery in Veracruz. He imagined himself Van Gogh. He enjoyed applying generous quantities of paint to depict the multitoned smoke spewing from the sugar factory against the sun. In open-air painting, he learned to make quick decisions about color as it changed rapidly with the light of the day. He used his more frequent trips to Oaxaca to study how the colors of the built and natural environment changed at different altitudes in tandem with the journey of the sun.

In his first years at La Esmeralda, no professor was as important to Pepe as Benito Messeguer. Born in Tarragona in 1930, he was not much older than Pepe. His family had moved to Barcelona during the Spanish Civil War and took refuge in Mexico in 1944. He entered La Esmeralda in 1948 and studied with the muralists Diego Rivera and Pablo O'Higgins and the engraver Leopoldo Méndez, founder of the Taller de Gráfica Popular, all of them profoundly committed to social and political art. A fine engraver, easel painter, portraitist, and sculptor, Messeguer won first prize in 1956 and 1957 for his paintings in the Exposición de Nuevos Valores at the Salón de la Plástica Mexicana. Created by the INBA to compete with the upsurge of private galleries, the Salón exhibited and sold paintings at a relatively low commission.

Although mural painting lost ground to easel painting with the proliferation of the art market, Messeguer made it his signature genre. He took José Clemente Orozco's position: mural art was the highest, most logical, and purest form of painting and the most disinterested because it could not be converted into an object of personal wealth or hidden for the benefit of a privileged few: it was for "the people." To his murals, he introduced innovations: the use of acrylics, metals, and asbestos; careful integration of the composition with the architecture and function of the building; an exuberant expressionist use of color and form to theatricalize rhythm and movement, trending toward abstraction without abandoning social, public, and monumental art. With his students and friends, he painted murals on the new government buildings that went up one after the other in these years of prosperity: the housing complexes, the Instituto Mexicano de Audición y Lenguaje, the Hospital Infantil IMAN. In his mural painted in 1963 in the Narciso Bassols Auditorium of the economics school on the new campus of the Universidad Nacional Autónoma, he expressed his modernist conviction in the history of man the creator. Art historian Justino Fernández called him a "universal humanist." In praise of this mural, Rosa Castro wrote in the magazine *Siempre!*, "We do not want messages, we do not want political banners. We want works of art that take into account man and his needs."[10]

With his faith in individual creativity, he was bound to break with the dogmas of the Mexican school. In the early 1960s, he formed part of the innovative art movement Nueva Presencia. A response to the antihumanism of abstract art and the rapid commercialization of painting, Nueva Presencia was a nascent expression of the "New Left," protesting as much against the empty demagoguery of social realism as against authoritarian, capitalist states. It formed part of a neohumanist movement in painting that emerged at the end of the 1950s in diverse centers of the United States, Europe, and Latin America. Permeated by the existentialism of Sartre and Camus and the lament of alienation from corporate capitalism articulated by David Riesman, Nathan Glazer, and Reuel Denney's *The Lonely Crowd* and Beat poetry, its artists depicted a sense of the individual's solitude and anguish before the violence and banality of social existence. The peace promised at the end of World War II had evaporated. The specter of nuclear annihilation intensified in the mounting struggle between East and West, just as imperialist wars and military interventions against the anticolonial liberation movements heated up in Africa, Asia, and Latin America. Before the dehumanization and individual isolation wrought by war, the machine, and governments, Nueva Presencia affirmed the need for social solidarity and action.[11]

The movement began in 1962 when Messeguer and José Luis Cuevas started a publicity campaign against the jailing of David Alfaro Siqueiros. The government had thrown the famous painter in prison for criticizing President López Mateos. In that period of censorship, no newspaper would publish a paid-for, open denunciation. Nonetheless, the young painters managed to print 3,500 copies of their magazine, *Nueva Presencia*—likely with the aid of contacts within the government. They distributed it free to libraries, bookstores, galleries, museums, and universities. Newspapers and magazines then reproduced articles or entire issues of the publication. Nueva Presencia identified with the civil rights movement in the United States, world peace and nuclear disarmament, the Cuban Revolution, and anticolonial struggles. Bypassing the Old Left's call for a worker revolution, Nueva Presencia spoke to "all social classes, particularly professionals and youth."

"Art," Nueva Presencia argued, "should be an instrument of struggle in the nonviolent evolution and spiritual development of humanity." It celebrated personal liberty, human empathy, and emotional expression seeking to break free of societal, aesthetic, and political fetters. Its catalyzing philosophical statement came from Selden Rodman in his 1960 book, *The Insiders: Rejection and Rediscovery of Man in the Arts of Our Time*. Rodman critiqued abstract art as antihumanist, obsessively technical, a sterile and violent statement without feeling or commitment. Artists should recapture another Western tradition expressing the inner feelings of the self, a tradition he identified with Michelangelo, Rembrandt, Goya, van Gogh, and Rouault.[12] His favorite artist was José Clemente Orozco, who was also Nueva Presencia's emblematic painter—an iconoclast, an anarchist, a humanist, an expressionist. Nueva Presencia's emblematic poem was *Howl!*, Alan Ginsburg's attack on repression, conformity, and hypocrisy in the United States. The movement's emblematic music was jazz. In 1962, the photographer Nacho López and sculptor Pedro Cervantes (who was working with car fenders, traffic lights, and sidewalk cement) organized the exhibit *Fifty Images of Jazz* in the Novedades Gallery. The show celebrated "this music of liberty" that manifests "a total lack of inhibition and fear, a direct expression of the rhythm, intermittent, anguished, explosive and incessant of man."[13]

Mary Coffey has recently interpreted the movement as pessimistic and disenchanted, an expression of abject humanity degraded by the corruption and violence of the modern world.[14] Indeed, Nueva Presencia emerged at a moment of mounting questioning of social and political structures prior to the flowering of a social movement full of exuberant hope and visions of strawberry fields. Nueva Presencia was a precursor of and catalyst to that movement. It may have conveyed gloom, as in Cuevas's depiction of monsters, butchers, prostitutes, and wards of La Castañeda mental hospital. Yet Cuevas had not declared for gloom but for freedom and creativity in art, society, and politics. That spirit animated Icaza, Cervantes, and Benito Messeguer. As the ethos was also antielitist and democratic, it opened new worlds and possibilities to young artists. One suspects that for young male painters like Pepe it opened the possibility—indeed, the necessity—of unblocking feeling as had the Hollywood youth films of the late 1950s. Nueva Presencia had its equivalent in poetry in *Corno Emplumado*, a bilingual magazine edited in Mexico City by Margaret Randall, Sergio Mondragón, and Harvey Wollin that published young Latin American and U.S. writers (principally Beat poets) seeking a new language of personal liberty and social politics.[15]

It had its equivalent in theater in emerging works of expressionism and social criticism that grew out of the experimental push of Poesia en Voz Alta, formed in 1956 by Octavio Paz, writer Juan José Arreola, director Hector Mendoza, painters Juan Soriano and Leonora Carrington, and others.[16]

Pepe did not know of Nueva Presencia directly. He learned its principles and message through Benito Messeguer. In the early 1950s, Messeguer had helped in the creation of the Jardines del Arte, open-air alternatives to museums and galleries where artists could exhibit and sell their work to ordinary citizens who filled the parks on weekends. He taught at night at La Esmeralda to open possibilities to "the less privileged." "He loved the school's ambience," recalled his wife, Alicia (Licha) Uruastegui, "its sculptures of indigenous figures in wood and stone, a response to the staid Academy of San Carlos with its fake Greek statues."[17] He was instrumental in the early 1960s in getting night classes accredited for students who wanted to enter the degree-granting day program. His democratic politics and committed mentoring were not atypical of professors in higher education at this moment. Indeed, their dialogue with students was critical to the development of alternative movements in the arts, politics, and personal life in the 1960s.

"Look, boys," Messeguer told his students, "To be a painter is not just to put the brush to canvas. It's about cultivating yourselves, reading, traveling, feeling." He invited students to the apartment he shared with Licha in the Conjunto Habitacional Morelos, built by the government in the popular Colonia de los Doctores. A former *bailarina*, Licha was an economist and one of the first Mexican women to wear slacks—or at least, according to art critic Margarita Nelken, to look good in them.[18] They would put on records of folk music, vernacular and political. Pepe had never heard Catalan dances, Manolo Caracol interpreting flamenco, or the sensual, seductive singing of Mohammed El Bakkar from the streets of Cairo. New too for him were the songs of South Africa that Miriam Makeba sang to jazz rhythms in protest against apartheid.

Benito led discussions about art, history, politics, and music. Together with students from the night classes who came from humble origins, he invited well-known young artists like Arnaldo Coen, students from the day program who came from more privileged backgrounds, and rich ladies from Las Lomas de Chapultepec who loved art. "He would pose a question," Pepe remembers. 'For you, what is art?' he would ask. That's a very difficult question to answer because there are many roads to art. 'I think art is something in your veins. It's a gift,' replied one of the ladies from Las Lomas. They had more self-confidence to talk than we did. 'I wanted to be an opera singer,' she said, 'But I don't have the throat for it. I didn't have the artist in me.' That made me think. Yes, art is a gift and a passion. It is like love. You love your work [*oficio*] with the modesty and passion of an artisan."

"Benito was a provocateur. He forced me to speak and I learned to listen," remembers Pepe. Juan Castañeda, a skinny, tall young man from Aguascalientes who worked in construction in the day, was very shy and quiet. Benito made him talk. "Juan, what do you think of Picasso?" he asked him in public.[19] Daniel Manrique, who worked in a bed factory and lived in Tepito, a neighborhood even poorer than the Guerrero or Colonia de los Doctores, liked the get-togethers at Benito and Licha's because he met "guys as screwed by life as I was." The others, however, made him nervous and he clammed up. He thought Benito talked weirdly. He didn't use words like "fucked" and "screwed." Benito brought him into the conversation on the mentor's terms.[20]

In addition to Juan, whose father was a railroad worker, and Daniel, whose father picked up odd jobs between pulque binges, Elva Garma attended the gatherings. She was from downtown Mexico City near the Colonia Guerrero. Her father was a dental mechanic who made false teeth, and her mother was a housewife. Very shy, she was convinced of her limitations. She told her father she had no gift for study and wanted to go to a vocational school. She studied decorative domestic arts and worked in the department store Palacio de Hierro. At the insistence of her godfather, she entered night classes at La Esmeralda. She was one of the few women in the masculine ambience. Benito irritated her because he pushed her. He insisted she change her colors and try abstraction. She tried, she cried, and insisted she could do nothing abstract. She decided to stick with realism. Anticipating the feminist and kitsch art that would gain ground much later in the 1980s, she painted ironic, playful pictures of the dainty embroidery typical of the domestic arts school she had attended. She liked the get-togethers at Benito and Licha's. She fell in love with Juan, so withdrawn, gawky, and out of style in his checkered shirt and work pants. She was a tiny girl and he was a giant, but she felt "tenderness" for him.[21] We see her here (seated fourth from the left) at a Messeguer soiree with noted painter Arnold Coen (second from left). Benito is standing and Juan Castañeda is on the right (see figure 7.5).

Aurelio Pescina was another guest. Considered the most brilliant and promising student at La Esmeralda, he came from San Luis Potosí and supported himself in the city hauling hundred-pound sacks of sugar

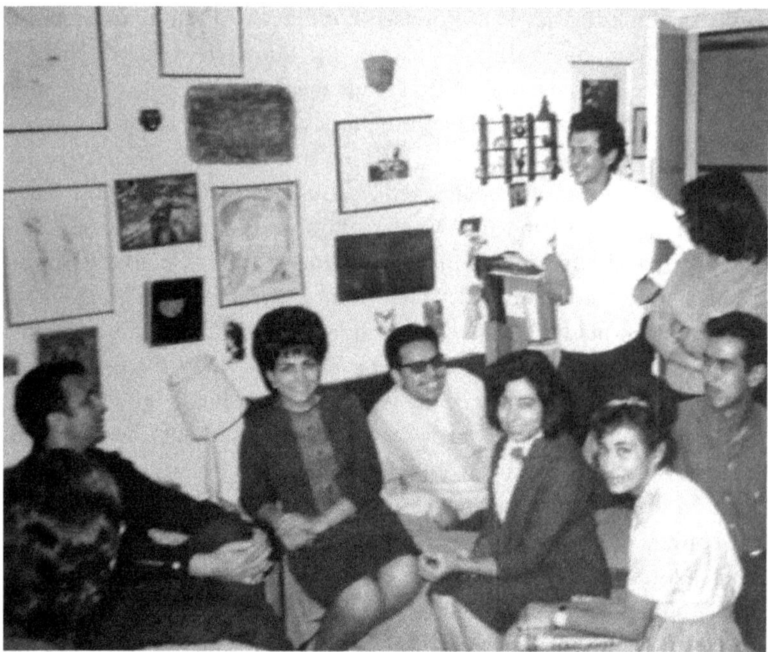

Figure 7.5. A get-together at Benito and Licha's home. Black-and-white photograph, 1962. From the private collection of Juan Castañeda and Elva Garma. Used by permission.

and grain in the La Merced market. He hardly had enough to eat. So Licha Messeguer snuck him into the cafeteria of the government investment company, Nacional Financiera, where she worked. Benito found him clients who wanted their portraits painted and hired him as an assistant on his mural projects.

Benito and Licha helped many of the students. Benito contracted Juan, who knew how to solder, to work on his sculptures. He took him to exhibits and forced him to participate in conservations with the artistic elite.[22] He organized exhibits of his students' work in government galleries. Later in the 1960s, he invited Pepe or Juan to stay in their home when he and Licha traveled; he offered them the use of his studio to paint.

When Daniel lost his job in the bed factory, Licha got him an apprenticeship and admission to the Instituto Politécnico Nacional to train as a mechanic.[23] He was thrilled to learn an oficio; it was something his father did not have. Years later, when he painted the walls of Tepito in honor of his neighborhood and its culture, he celebrated the mind-body skills of manual labor. He provided hammers to his female as well as his male figures.

Benito and Licha took Pepe to the movies to see Russian films, somewhat disappointing in their propagandistic nature, and the more innovative and strangely introspective works of Ingmar Bergman. Benito gave Pepe Robert Silverberg's new study, *Lost Cities and Vanished Civilizations*, which explored ancient Pompeii, Troy, Bangkok, and Chichén Itzá.[24] The book whet Pepe's thirst for travel! He recommended other books on technique in painting, the history of art, and more biographies of famous painters like Oscar Kokoschka, Goya, and Picasso. As book translation and publication flourished with growing international markets, Pepe could buy these books at discount prices in bookstores in the Colonia Guerrero. Daniel Manrique bought dozens from street sellers in Tepito who lined them up on the sidewalk. "Look, come! Culture's on the ground right here!" they hawked.[25] Daniel became so absorbed in reading that he left La Esmeralda to dedicate his free time to reading Sartre, Nietzsche, Kierkegaard, the surrealists, Argentinean novels, and histories of art. Licha and Benito were less successful in convincing Aurelio Pescina to read. He traded the books they gave him for pulque. Although he was talented, reflected Pepe, "He had no culture."

Benito and Licha deepened the students' understanding of the Mexican past and present. Benito spoke of the misery of the Otomi people he had witnessed when he taught at the Center of Fine Arts in Tula, Hidalgo. He explained the history and aesthetics of the Toltec warrior sculptures at Tula. He and Licha took them to the colonial convent at Tepozotlán. In the spring of 1959, they took the drawing class, along with the rich ladies from Las Lomas, to Oaxaca to visit the city, its churches, and the Zapotec religious centers of Monte Albán and Mitla. As a child, Pepe had visited these with his family. However, he noted, "Messeguer's explanation was more comprehensive from an aesthetic and historical point of view." It made him rethink the sense of shame he had about race. "I was Zapotec in my family origins and I marveled at Oaxaca's tradition of color." He returned many times with friends in these years as the proud guide to the culture and history of the region. In his painting, he opened to the color, light, and iconography of his birthplace. Pepe began to form a new dimension of his identity at a propitious moment when Oaxaca was on the verge of becoming a center for a contemporary art based in local traditions.

In 1962, Messeguer persuaded Pepe to move into the degree-granting day program at La Esmeralda. It was a difficult decision. His father insisted his art was a waste of time and pressured him to bring more money into the house. Messeguer got him a job teaching art in a private school and later in the Escuela de Verano (summer school) at the university. Pepe continued part-time at Ingenieros Electromecánicos and earned extra money installing stereo systems for his friends and professors and disc-jockeying at parties.

In the day program, Pepe encountered a new ambience. One expected a bohemian atmosphere in an art school, but the incipient social rebellion among the students was new. It was amorphous and contagious. James Dean was a hero. He spoke to what Pepe called "a kind of frustration without a name, without definition." The students felt surrounded by adult enemies. The government, the barrio, Mexican cinema, and parents began to denounce rebellious and anarchic youth. To be a student, remembers Pepe, "was negative because to be a student was to contest." Opposition fueled the rebellion, drawing the lines between the old and the new.

Take Pepe's friend Octavio Ocampo. He came from a well-off, religious family in the very devout town of Celaya, Guanajuato. He had spent years studying with the ultraconservative Legionarios de Cristo hoping to become a saint. Then he discovered James Dean, rock 'n' roll, Marilyn Monroe, and the pretty girls of Celaya. His brother had become "a rebel without a cause, with his long hair, red jacket and faded jeans." He told Octavio to turn up his collar, roll up his shirtsleeves, and sit in the movie theater with his legs over the seat in front of him. Octavio helped with his brother's rock 'n' roll band, first called the Sputniks, then the Golden Kings. "Apart from singing in English and dancing marvelously," Octavio writes in his autobiography, "they caused a big sensation among Celayan youth." They provoked resistance from everyone else. Once, a crowd at a fiesta tried to lynch them. On another occasion, a taxi driver refused to let them into his car with their instruments. Other taxi drivers and a bunch of baseball players defended the driver, and a battle broke out in the city's central park. Octavio's brother ended up in the hospital with a stab wound in his back.[26]

Perhaps because they came from more privileged, middle-class families (Octavio from Celaya, José Méndez from Torreón, and Armando Villagrán from Mexico City), Pepe's new friends had the self-confidence to rebel. Their work in scenography and costume design in the vibrant theater movement emboldened them too. They loved to act. Octavio and Villagrán did a hilarious imitation of Rita Moreno and her chorus singing and dancing "I like to be in America" from *West Side Story*. Pepe Méndez, "good homosexual that he was," imitated Andrea Palma, herself imitating Marlene Dietrich, as she embraced a wall, puffing on a cigarette, caressing her hips, and singing "I sell pleasure to men who come from the sea" in the classic Mexican film *La Mujer del Puerto*.[27]

His new friends smoked pot and they talked back. During a school trip to Yucatán, Professor Lorenzo Guerrero commented to Méndez in a restaurant, "Aye, Pepe, I think you like men because you keep looking at them." Méndez responded: "And you? What's it to you? Mind your own business. Don't stick your head in mine." Guerrero snapped back, "Méndez, don't be rude. I'll take away your trip allowance." "Take it," Méndez answered, "I'll get money from home." Méndez's directness shocked Pepe, but he was not himself exempt from a certain insolence that now penetrated the school. When Professor García Robledo told his class to get rid of their religious medals, several protested: "Hey! Wait a minute! I'm carrying Jesus Christ here on my chest and I'm not gonna dump him." On another occasion, García Robledo began his class with reference to painting techniques: "Now I've taught you the Fibonacci series, the harmonic door, the golden ratio, and the Cross of San Andrés." Pepe Zúñiga piped up, "Why don't you teach us the broom of San Martín?" The students burst out laughing to hear this reference to a black saint who was then appearing with his broom in a *telenovela*. "Out of the classroom, Zúñiga!" ordered the teacher. Armando Villagrán told this story to Gustavo Sainz, the novelist of 1960s youth culture. Sainz included it in his book *Compadre Lobo*, the history of a young, abused delinquent who discovers his artistic gift, his tenderness, and his homosexuality through his studies at La Esmeralda and his experience in the student protest movement of 1968.[28]

Although Esmeralda professors were demanding and brooked no impudence from students, they themselves contributed to and participated in the mounting insurgence. "Many of our teachers taught a sense of the social commitment of art and the conviction that the artist had to be contestatory," Pepe remembered. "We identified with those who encouraged the agitation, who made us see that the artist was not there to get rich but to pursue a noble objective." "If I wanted money," commented Pepe's friend Guillermo Zapfe, "I'd sell hamburgers."

Abetted by the availability of new books in translation, Pepe's professors opened his philosophical and historical horizons and gently nudged his religious certainties. In Adrían Villagomez's class on the history and sociology of art, he read Marx, the Bible, Darwin, the positivist Taine, the Marxist Plekhanov, and the *History of Western Art*, by Paul Westheim. He also tackled Wassily Kandinsky's *Concerning the Spiritual in Art*, the Russian painter's rebellion against bourgeois convention not to promote class struggle but to celebrate the expression of the individual subconscious in a mathematically informed abstract painting of vibrant colors. Plekhanov, Taine, and Kandinsky stressed the evolutionary nature of history and art as an articulation of context in time and space. Each text, together with the *Origin of the Species*, understood history as a progressive, secularizing process. Pepe noted that when Cennino Cennini, the Renaissance painter, gave instructions to the artist to recite the Our Father when he was grinding chicken bones in black pigment, it was in reverence for the craft and the truth according to his time and place. When he read Paul Westheim's *The Fundamental Ideas of Prehispanic Art*, he asked, if the Mesoamericans worshipped a pantheon of gods, could there be absolute truth in the Christian God? He got to know something of Buddha when he read Herman Hesse's *Siddhartha*, a cult book of the moment given to him by a Oaxacan friend who was practicing yoga.

Adrian Villagomez invited Pepe, Ocampo, Méndez, Villagrán, and Zapfe to his apartment in La Romita, a quiet, charming neighborhood on the edge of the upscale Colonia Roma on the city's southside. Over drinks, he provoked discussions about history, film, politics, and religion. He criticized the government for its abandonment of the poor. "He tried to transmit honesty," Pepe noted, "about what we ought to do—to take responsibility as painters and teachers." García Robledo also invited them to his home. As a Cuban, he was an ardent admirer of his country's recent revolution and an outspoken anti-imperialist. He was of course not alone: in the early 1960s, Octavio Ocampo and José Méndez joined others in making placards, banners, and posters for demonstrations in support of the Cuban Revolution. It was "our hope for a more just and free society," remembered Octavio.[29] Pepe recalls García Robledo loved to get drunk with them. "He talked to us about religion, politics, and sex. He criticized absolutely everything. We loved his aggressiveness. It turned us on. He was very contestatory, downright audacious. There was nothing conformist in him."

One night in 1964, García Robledo took Pepe to the studio of a student of the painter Juan Soriano near the Ciudadela. Soriano was there. In full rebellion against the Mexican school of painting and openly gay, Soriano was a big star in the Mexican art world. A graduate of the Academia de San Carlos, he had spent many years in Rome and Paris. Now he was teaching ceramics and sculpture at the government's Escuela de Diseño and Artesanias "La Ciudadela." At the party, Soriano invited the guests to dance the cancan. Locking arms and kicking up their legs to French music, the men sang, "We are the prostitutes! We are the prostitutes!" This bohemian camaraderie was even more outrageously amusing to Pepe than the parodies of his friends Méndez, Ocampo, and Villagrán. He did not find it unattractive. On the other hand, he felt García Robledo could go to excess with his aggressive bravado. "I was in parties with him," Pepe remembered, "where he got so drunk he tried to seduce all the women. He was an exhibitionist and very macho. He wanted to show us how easily he conquered women. We didn't like it much. It wasn't very dignified mauling a young girl. Once I heard him say, 'If I can't make love to this woman, I'm going to jump out of this window.' We caught him before he jumped. In 1969, he did jump out a window to his death. It was very tragic. But I have to say that we did not find his sexual aggression attractive. It was without tenderness and respect."

While these young men studied, parodied, and partied, they learned. As his friends worked in theater, they introduced Pepe to a wave of fresh, experimental works open to students at discount prices. They saw *Olímpica*, written in 1962 by Héctor Azar, head of Teatro Universitario based at the UNAM. Like Benito Messeguer he was born in 1930 and became one of the period's most dynamic young mentors, mobilizing a stunning cohort of students in acting, directing, costume design, and scenography. Juan Ibáñez, one year younger than Pepe, directed it "with energy and tenderness," wrote the critic Armando de María y Campos in the newspaper *Las Novedades*.[30] He staged it in the garden on the north side of the Alameda between the churches of Santa Veracruz and San Juan de Dios, the Hospital de la Mujer, and the market for funeral flowers. The staging impressed Pepe for its utter originality and because it was here that his Tía Antonia and Tío Efrén had first slept when they came to the city from Oaxaca. The play focuses on youth in a vecindad at the end of the 1950s and particularly on Eddy, an adolescent "like all adolescents" according to Azar, or certainly those of Mexico City, wrote the critic. Spoiled by his dominating single mother, Eddie is handsome, restless, disoriented, but full of dreams as he searches for opportunities that seem to elude him. Casandra (Casi) freezes in her Catholic soul fearful she will fall into sin as she becomes a woman; she cannot accept Eddie's invitation to go to the movies. Despite the daily intersection of lives in the vecindad, everyone seems alone. Eddy's older girlfriend commits suicide with the aid of her friends when she learns he does not love her. Another couple breaks up as the man leaves for the United States in search of work. The actors convey a breadth of feeling, wrote the critic, of innocence and its loss, illusion and disillusion, love and frustration, trust and mistrust. A classical chorus of women—beggars outside the portals of the church of Santa Veracruz—

chants in a language "at once poetic and realist."[31] Drunks outside a cantina add to the poignant realism. "The work spoke to our world, to our situation," remembers Pepe.

Pepe found still more moving Juan Ibáñez's production of *Divinas palabras* in the Teatro El Caballito near La Esmeralda. The presentation would win first prize at the International Festival of University Theater in Nancy in 1964. As in *Olímpica*, Ibáñez abandoned traditional sets of painted curtains and furniture. Abstract painter Vicente Rojo did the scenography. The action took place under a huge crown of thorns. Ibáñez moved the Valle Inclán story of sordid poverty from Galicia to Mexico. In this tale of brutalized human beings absorbed by greed, lust, and rancor, two women dispute control of a deformed, drooling orphan. One of them, Mari Gaila, takes off to exhibit him at fairs. Carried away by the sensual bliss she finds in a stranger, she leaves the orphan, whom the locals ply with liquor until he dies. She returns to her husband Pedro, the village sacristan, with no money and the corpse. Pedro exhibits the body to make money. When Mari Gaila runs off again with the stranger, she is caught making love by neighbors who stone her ruthlessly. Pedro stops them with the "divine words": "Let him who is free of sin cast the first stone." He takes Mari Gaila's hand, walks her to the church, and pardons her.

Like Valle Inclán, Ibáñez drew poetry and redemption out of the grotesque, sharpening the political anger that permeated the work.[32] It was similar to what José Luis Cuevas was doing in painting. The actors, all young, the majority without professional experience, intensified the power of the play. "The characters were all dirty and dressed in rags in a dark ambience of mystery and abandon," Pepe recalls, "As in *Olímpica*, you felt the poverty. You knew Ibáñez was expressing social discontent: why were so many people so miserably neglected? These were not pleasant works. They were denunciations."

Like the plastic arts movement of Nueva Presencia, these plays were expressionist productions representative of the new theater that came out of the movement Poesia en Voz Alta formed in 1956. Seeking to bury the tired, derivative realism of Mexican theater, Poesia en Voz Alta had introduced the work of T. S. Eliot, the absurd theater of Jean Genet and Ionesco, and above all, classical Spanish works in new frames and expressive forms. Rejected in the 1950s for being elitist, homosexual, frivolous, and decadent, Poesia en Voz Alta did not mesh well with the state's project for the "moral development of the masses."[33] But in the 1960s, the movement found its public and its creators in the same youth raised under this moral project but now chafing at its restrictions.

The theater movement reached the apex of experimentation in the mid-1960s, when Alejandro Jodorowsky introduced his "Panic Theater," probably the most iconoclastic artistic work in Mexico City in the early 1960s and similar to the denunciatory happenings being staged in Europe by groups associated with the Situationist International. In Jodorowsky's "panics," the relationship between actor and spectator, theater and reality, dissolved. The panic turned into a violent therapy session for all in what they did not want to see or admit for the sake of their own liberation from the distortions of a repressive society. Celebrating experience itself, "panic," wrote Jodorowsky, "always appears as the moment of spiritual birth."[34] Sponsored by the university's theater school, the panics enraged the Catholic Right and Oficina de Espectáculos, but as Angelica García writes, the censors became Jodorowsky's best allies.[35] Young people flocked to his productions. The new and progressive Mexican publishing house, Era, immediately published his explanation of his work. Eventually he got on television where he chopped up a piano.

In October 1963, Jodorowsky staged his first public panic at the Academia de San Carlos with the help of young rebel painters Manuel Felguérez and Alberto Gironella. In the show, "Monster Monster" appeared dressed in a dog's skin. He carried a white dove he bit and chewed into tiny pieces while a chorus danced a frenzied twist. Another recited a poem as he destroyed a mirror that was supposed to symbolize the narcissism of traditional poetry. A girl with a long blond mane dressed in net stockings entered on crutches. Screaming, "I'm innocent! "I'm innocent!" she wrenched pieces of raw meat from her breast and threw them at the public. Then she sat down on a stool and let a barber chop off her hair and shave her head. A boy nailed a girl to the wall and painted her dress, body, and face, while another caressed a woman in a bridal gown, threw her into a tub of blood, and washed her with a live octopus. The function ended with the entire cast hurling tortillas at the public.[36]

Today we might choke on the misogyny of this work of "liberation," but in 1963, the public did not know what to make of it. As one young man wrote in bewildered, tentative empathy: "The most extraordinary thing about it was its relationship to the public. They were part of the spectacle, and if there was not a reaction of fright, there was at least one of profound and startled questioning. I myself don't know what to say about my emotions: I felt disgust, horror, humor. Maybe I would say in general I liked it, but one wouldn't know what I meant. It was an attraction, how would I say?—outside of context, very unusual. It's more like an intellectual communion with something which undoubtedly is an adequate and representative symbol of our time, in which old responses just don't work anymore and we have not yet found something to grab onto."[37] That was the case with Pepe and his friends—all bound up in a creative, agitated search for a language of self and social expression they had not yet found. His friends told him about the panic at San Carlos. He went to see another in the Hostería Bohemio, near the San Hipólito Church on Hidalgo Avenue next to the Alameda. In the early years of the 1960s, these blocks of Hidalgo Avenue, with their old convents and churches and the Hospital de la Mujer, became a hub for new theater, bohemian revelry, and experimental painting on the part of young artists who had taken over a *vecindad* that had once been the convent of San Hipólito.[38] It was here beside the churches of Santa Veracruz and San Juan de Dios that Ibañez staged Olímpica. In this downtown center, the new, upscale Zona Rosa, and the neighboring Colonia Cuauhtémoc, along with the distant Ciudad Universitaria, the new language began to take form.

In his final years at La Esmeralda, Pepe took classes with two extraordinary artists. The first was Francisco Zúñiga. Born into a family of religious sculptors in 1912, he had studied art in his native Costa Rica. In 1936, he worked in Mexico with the painter Manuel Rodríguez Lozano and the sculptor Oliverio Martínez. He worked with Martínez on the colossal Monumento de la Revolución, where Pepe had played as a child. Principally a sculptor, Zúñiga was also an extraordinary draftsman, a great painter, and a lithographer. He sculpted many monuments for the state—in Veracruz, Monterrey, Zacatecas, and at the irrigation works in Valsequillo, Puebla. These were within the style and purpose of the Mexican school, but his indigenous women—Juchitecas, Yalaltecas, Yucatecas—moved beyond the archetype in their voluptuous sensuality.[39] At work or at rest, often with children, they breathed a new intimacy, energy, and sense of movement. Zúñiga explained: "My work isn't about morality or sociology. In me, it produces a more intense sensation of being alive. Not for sentiments of romantic humanism but perhaps to achieve the fullness of essential and meaningful forms."[40]

Zúñiga's women inspired Pepe's first sketches of Oaxacan women he drew in his now frequent trips to his home state. Such rendering of sensuality was where Pepe wanted to go. "The secret," he said, "is to understand the concept of drawing through volume. A sculptor's drawing is not the same as a painter's. Zúñiga didn't use lines until the end, but he achieved volume and form through shadings. One could hear music in those tones he created with a mixture of Conté crayons and charcoal." Through Francisco Zúñiga, Pepe learned more than technique. The sculptor did not copy nature in its human forms, nor did he seek to embellish or essentialize nature as Auguste Rodin had. He reduced the body to telluric form, to its volume, to a sensual elaboration of space.[41] Here we see the first efforts of the young Pepe Zúñiga in his drawings of the model Victoria in monumental form (see figure 7.6). It was a night class. Electric light from above illuminated her body. The figure emerges from darkness. The light shines not on her head but on her breasts, her abdomen, and her legs. Moving from clear to darker tones, casting her hair and other parts of her body in shadow, Pepe could capture the magic of light and call attention to the detail of her hands and feet. He produced a stylized drawing. Victoria was in fact small and short. He elongated her neck, extended her back and legs, and gave her a seductive pose—an arched spine, hands on her hips, with one leg pushed forward. When he saw her, the art critic Antonio Rodríguez exclaimed: "One wants to embrace her!"

In 1963, Pepe began to study with Santos Balmori. He entered his class as an auditor to learn about composition and the famous golden ratio, one of the basic principles of Western painting and architectural composition. Balmori was a master teacher. He was perhaps the most learned, independent, and erotic painter Pepe studied with; he would have a tremendous influence on Pepe's generation. Born in Mexico City in 1898 to a Mexican mother and Asturian father, he moved as a child to Argentina and Chile. In 1919 he enrolled in the Academia de San Fernando in Madrid, where surrealists Salvador Dalí and Remedios Varo were also students. From there, he went to the Grand Chaumière in Paris, where he made friends with Juan Gris, Vlaminck, Giacometti, and Maillol. He worked with Romain Rolland and Henri Barbusse on the newspaper that became *Le Monde*. He delved into Hindu philosophy and knew Rabindranath Tagore and Gandhi, whose portraits he painted. He illustrated for fashion magazines and the texts of Unamuno, Tagore, Gorki, and Upton Sinclair. He made posters for the League of Nations and the International Red Cross in its struggle against fascism and in favor of the Spanish Republic. He worked in factories. He socialized with young Latin Americans in Paris and attended the meetings of the left Peruvian political movement, APRA, led by Raul Haya de la Torre and Cesar Vallejo.[42] He moved to the port of Oran in Algeria, where an old Arab taught him to meditate.[43] During the Spanish Civil War he collaborated with republicans García Lorca, Unamuno, and Luis Felipe. When he feared he would lose his life in 1935, he sought refuge in Mexico. The government welcomed him with an exhibit of more than two hundred of his works in the Palacio de Bellas Artes. He joined the League of Revolutionary Writers

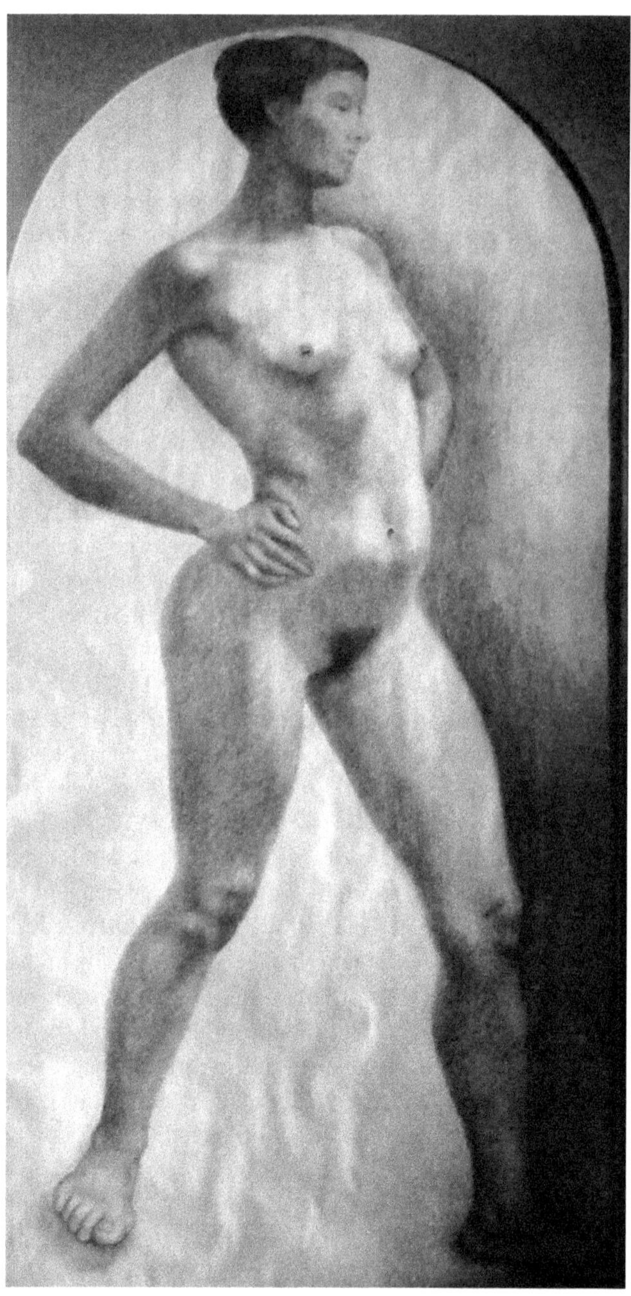

Figure 7.6. *Victoria*, drawing by José "Pepe" Zúñiga, 1965.

and Artists (LEAR) doing agitprop art for workers and campesinos. Loyal to the republican cause, he urged President Cárdenas to open Mexico's doors to children orphaned by Franco's troops. Cárdenas welcomed the 456 "niños de Morelia" in 1937. Balmori dedicated several years to their school in Michoacán.[44]

But although he became a professor at both the Academia de San Carlos and La Esmeralda, the Mexican school of painters never accepted him. They found him not just Spanish but very European in a period of intense Mexican nationalism. Although he was a master of line, color, form, shading, and above all, composition, his painting resisted categorization. A traveler in life and art, he constantly reinvented his work.[45] For that very reason, young painters seeking to break away sought him out: Juan Soriano, Pedro Coronel, Rodolfo Nieto, Byron Gálvez, Octavio Ocampo, Armando Villagrán, and Pepe Zúñiga.[46] In 1966, when students at San Carlos rebelled against the existing curriculum and teaching methods, they nominated Santos Balmori to direct the school. The Communist Party, influenced by David Alfaro Siqueiros, the spokesperson for the Mexican school, blocked his candidacy.[47] In general, Pepe noted, the art establishment treated Santos shabbily. For Pepe, Santos's situation in the 1960s spoke to the unbearable tension of the moment: could the individual artist emerge, survive, and prosper in a culture still pegged to the principles of corporatist thinking, cohesion, and loyalty? Toward the end of the 1960s, Pepe worked as his driver as Santos moved from one end of the city to another in his job as an inspector of night schools. "That job was a disgrace for such a man. They made his life impossible," remembered Pepe.

The painter Carlos Merida, one of Balmori's most consistent protectors in Mexico, wrote in his introduction to the 1936 exhibit that the secret to Santos's painting was his rhythm. Rhythm was for him the primordial principle of life and the universe and the basis of art—whether it was poetry, architecture, music, painting, sculpture, or dance.[48] Balmori captured rhythm through the bodies of women—not passive objects of male sexual desire typical of Western art but tall women of exaggerated musculature and vigorous movement. He painted them dancing, striding across the Oran desert, climbing staircases, reaching like Venus for the stars, jumping through flames, gathering conch shells and seaweed, arching their bodies toward the sky to embrace the spring, their breasts bared upward, their strong arms clasping blocks of stone; women embracing, playing with children, or screaming in terror as fascist bullets rained over them. He married three dancers: Thérèse Bernard in Paris,

Rachel Björnstrom in Stockholm, and Helena Jordán in Mexico City. In the early 1950s, he directed the Academia Mexicana de Danza for seven years during which time—together with Miguel Covarrubias, director of dance at the INBA—he created the most brilliant moments in Mexican modern dance.[49]

His composition classes at La Esmeralda centered on the Pythagorean concept of the golden ratio, about which he wrote one of his two books.[50] The geometric and mathematical concept of harmony in space had presumably guided Phidias in the design of the Parthenon, Renaissance painting and medieval church architecture, and much of modern art. Balmori's students learned it as a necessary concept. For him, it was more than a concept. Like most modern artists, he believed that painting radiated elements of its own nature, elements that worked through the artist's grasp of technique and his or her particular educated optic.[51] "In all my work," he wrote, "there is a fundamental desire: to reflect on rhythm. Elements of reality are parts of a totality. For me, this is an ideological principle. Rhythm is continual flow. To stop it is to die."[52] He studied Hindu philosophy, physics, mathematics, astronomy, and the work of dozens of artists one after the other. In his search for what he believed was a hidden depth and a universal integration, he moved from one plastic style to another, working finally in highly complex geometric abstractions. The golden ratio was for him the most consistent divine principle that could unlock the mystery of the universe. Art and dance critic Alberto Dallal called him a precocious postmodernist because he followed no narrative, told no story, believed in no vanguard, and reinvented himself incessantly.[53] He did not share with Pepe's other professors a faith in Enlightenment man or the perfectibility of history.

Pepe Zúñiga would interpret the mathematical and geometric techniques of composition as music on canvas: "The golden mean can be divided and subdivided infinitely, like primary and secondary notes in a musical composition that transmit silences and stridencies. The strident notes of Stravinsky are different from the baroque notes of Bach, but they are each integrated one with the other." Pepe intuited the radical posture of Santos not directly through any shared knowledge of Hindu philosophy but through his composition of erotic bodies in musical space. During a student trip to Yucatán, Pepe watched the sixty-six-year-old painter dive nude into a sacred *cenote*. It was an experience he would never forget.

8. Exuberant Interlude

Painting at the Museo de Antropología

In late 1964, in the waning days of the Adolfo López Mateos regime, the Mexican government opened seven new museums, the most spectacular of which was the Museo Nacional de Antropología. With this project, the government moved to solidify a cohesive nationalism at a fragile moment. In the first months of his administration in 1959, railroad workers launched strikes that provoked military intervention and the unprecedented jailing of 10,000 workers. In 1960 and 1961 sugar and textile workers and white-collar employees—telegraph operators and telephone workers, pilots and stewardesses—walked off their jobs. In 1960 the conservative press, political parties, and civic associations in major cities launched protests against the introduction of a free, obligatory, and singular series of primary-school textbooks. From the 1960s, university students launched left-oriented protests in Puebla, Hermosillo, Morelia, and Mexico City. The Cuban Revolution of 1959 deepened the fault lines in Mexican politics. This fresh, untested promise of social redemption and liberation challenged the Mexican regime's pretension to fulfilling the promises of the 1910 revolution. In 1964, Pablo González Casanova published his scathing critique of the revolution's social and political consequences. While the economy continued to grow, what was known as the Mexican Miracle began to dim as problems surged with population explosion, mounting unemployment, urban traffic and housing congestion, and increasingly impoverished campesinos, to whom the revolution had promised land and dignity through agrarian reform.

The United States responded to the Cuban Revolution with interventionist aggression and placed heavy demands on the Mexican government to denounce Cuba, a position untenable to the PRI's progressive wing, the small left opposition parties, intellectuals, and artists, and a growing sector of the public, swelled by legions of students. Many of these adhered to a new opposition movement, the Movimiento de Liberación Nacional, led by Lázaro Cárdenas, informal chief of the PRI's progressive sector. Offsetting the MLN were the organized forces of the party's right wing, identified as Alemanistas for their association with ex-president Miguel Alemán (1946–1952). President López Mateos used economic prosperity and his considerable negotiating skills to prevent open ruptures. Among his many moves, he allowed greater freedom of the press, endorsing *Política* as a more radical complement to *Siempre!*, the officially tolerated magazine of critical opinion.[1] At the same time, the state reinvigorated its already strong cultural apparatus, in part to embrace and channel the energies of youth.[2]

In a bold, sweeping gesture in 1964, the regime created seven new museums not only to pull the nation together but to enhance international prestige at a moment of heightened cultural diplomacy and increasing tourism. These included the museum built at the pyramids of Teotihuacán, amid a spectacular refurbishing of the ancient site; the colonial museum at the convent of Tepozotlán, outside the city on the expanded highway to Teotihuacán; the Museo de la Ciudad, housed in the old Casa de los Condes de Santiago y Calimaya in downtown Mexico City; the Anahuacalli, which housed Diego Rivera's collection of Mesoamerican art; a museum of natural history in Chapultepec Park, which replaced the old museum of hygiene; and the Museo de Arte Moderno, also in Chapultepec Park, which would display paintings of the Mexican school while broadening and diversifying the representation of Mexican artists.

Across the street from the Museo de Arte Moderno was the crown jewel of the state's cultural project, the Museo de Antropología, conceived as Mexico's singular and distinctive contribution to humanity and universal culture, a concept promoted by UNESCO in the aftermath of World War II.[3] At the museum's entrance, water cascades from a vast canopy. Its stem is a bronze column, sculpted from bottom to top by José and Tomás Chávez Morado, with symbols of the indigenous origins of their country and the historical struggle of a mestizo nation to reach the present moment of clarity, integration, and peace represented in the figure of a dove and a man wrapped in olive branches.[4] In their design, architects Pedro Ramírez Vázquez, Jorge Campuzano, and Rafael Mijares reached the pinnacle of high modernism. Functionalist in its embrace of the spectator, the museum's structure, its integration with its natural surroundings, the materials used in its construction, and the symbolism in its design all emanated from Mesoamerican roots. Like the new buildings of the Torcuato di Tella Institute in Buenos Aires, opened in 1963, the Museo de Antropología was a modernist masterpiece constructed at a moment of rising prosperity and optimism against a backdrop of social turmoil and mounting contention.[5]

The Museo de Antropología was more than state of the art: it was spectacular and path setting in its museography, designed to display and interpret in didactic simplicity and luminous spectacle the history, art, and material life of ancient and contemporary Mesoamerican cultures and to create archives, libraries, workshops, labs, conference rooms, and auditoriums for study, discussion, and diffusion, all within a monumental space of rare, quiet beauty. This massive undertaking brought together every level and talent in the Mexican labor force—experts in archaeology and anthropology, bricklayers, glassworkers, carpenters, solders, metal and electrical workers, and engineers of every type. Joining them were teams of artists led by prominent painters of diverse affiliation—Mexican school stalwarts such as Pablo O'Higgins, José Chávez Morado, Jorge González Camarena, Raul Anguiano, and Frida Kahlo's students Rina Lazo and Arturo García Bustos, as well as those independent of the school (e.g., surrealist Leonora Carrington), and those opposed (e.g., Rufino Tamayo, Manuel Felguérez, Mathias Goeritz, Gilberto Aceves Navarro, and Rafael Coronel).[6] Esmeralda painters and sculptors Luis García Robledo, Fermín Rojas, and Gloria Pimentel created replicas of the bas-reliefs, sculptures, and murals that could not be moved from their tombs at Monte Albán. Esmeralda sculptor Rafael Guerrero made the human figures, animals, and wares that filled the stunning reproduction of the grand market at Tlatelolco.

Mexico's indigenous peoples so readily marginalized by the country's modernizing craze served as advisors and creators. They worked with the teams of anthropologists who claimed to have visited every living original culture in Mexico and gathered information not only about the past but contemporary practices, beliefs, and material life. Not relegated to a position of simple informants in the creation of themselves as objects of display, Mayans, Zapotecs, and Nahua speakers came to the city to work in the museum, where they advised and built their own exhibits. Men, women, and children filled the central patio with work tools, hunting arms, clay, wood, cotton, and straw. From these they built replicas of their homes and work sites and made their ceramic utensils, clothing, and toys. Out of cane, workers from Morelos built a typical Nahua granary. Outside the Maya gallery, Yucatecans reconstructed the temple of Ochob using original techniques and stones they had brought from the peninsula.[7]

From February 1963 to the opening on September 17, 1964, people worked three turns around the clock. The process was not without creative contradictions. Head architect Pedro Ramírez Vázquez and a team of engineers and archaeologists proposed to rescue Tlaloc, the ancient god of rain, for the nation and the world. Tlaloc had been sleeping for centuries in a riverbed in the town of Coatlinchán, twenty-four miles outside Mexico City. To lift the god, who was 8 meters tall and weighed 168 tons, they worked over a year building an immense truck with several steel flatbeds, many Goodrich Euzkadi giant tires, and a cable apparatus for lifting the deity. To transport him to Mexico City, bridges and highways had to be reinforced. The people of Coatlinchán were not pleased. They sabotaged the truck and the road built for its exit. When they cut the cables suspending the god and sent him crashing to the ground, the government sent in the army. Pedro Vázquez Ramírez went to the town to try to convince the residents of the extraordinary significance of the sculpture to the national patrimony and to Mexican history. He told them how important it would be for the greatest number of Mexicans to be able to see Tlaloc in the museum. The villagers would not budge. Then the old schoolteacher got up and told them that the stone was like the grass, the lake, and the shore and that the god himself would always protect them. To the architect's surprise, the people turned to him and said: "You can take him."[8] In fact, as Sandra Rozental has recently shown through extensive interviews with the people of Coatlinchán, Vázquez Ramírez's tale of a community superstitiously attached to an ancient god obscured the real story. The rock was not an object of religious veneration or the source of rain but part of village space, a place of recreation, and passage to the mountain where residents pastured animals and gathered firewood. To part with it, village officials had negotiated with the government for a new school, a health clinic, irrigation works, and a paved road. The riot occurred because many, sensitive to the arrogance of federal authorities and engineers, felt they would be betrayed and would not receive these benefits. However, the notion of their primitive religiosity made for an urban legend in Mexico City. The dramatic entry of the now celebrated deity, gigantic and prostrate on his flatbed hauled by two enormous trucks, was televised. The national cathedral on the Zócalo lit up the night to welcome him. As he moved slowly down the boulevard of La Reforma, people were awestruck, for the skies opened and huge torrents of rain fell upon the city in the normally dry month of April. It was, of course, the work of Tlaloc. While the people of Coatlinchán got their instruments of modernity—school, road, clinic, and wells—the rumor ran among the citizens of the capital and the press that the subsequent drought had to be blamed on the authorities for having left the humiliated god prostrate for weeks on his giant flatbed. Not until the authorities turned him upright on his feet did it rain.[9] This would suggest the museum offered to the proud moderns of the capital an alternative subjectivity, if only imagined (sometimes in jest), and a possibility for reinterpreting the nation's history and cultural legacy.

Pepe Zúñiga and his Esmeralda friends, Pepe Méndez, Octavio Ocampo, Armando Villagrán, and Aurelio Pescina, were all invited to paint. Joining the Esmeralda contingent was their friend Guillermo Zapfe, who took evening courses there. A graduate of the prestigious Colegio Alemán and of the Instituto Politécnico Nacional, Zapfe was, in Pepe's opinion, the most intellectual of his friends: the only one who really understood Kandinsky's theory of color. Zapfe directed the workshop for drawings that would decorate the glass in the gallery introducing the history of the American peoples as uncovered by archaeologists and anthropologists. Ocampo joined him there. Villagrán worked with Luis Covarrubias painting transportable murals.[10] Pescina joined Raul Anguiano's team in the Sala Maya. Pepe first worked with Luis García Robledo's group in the Sala Oaxaca.

For Pepe and his friends, creating the museum's murals and its ethnographic maps became an experience of reverence, irreverent exuberance, and exhilarating learning about their country and its past, about art, and about themselves as aspiring youth. What an opportunity for these young men! Pepe remembers: "The government decided to spend everything possible to make it one of the greatest museums in the world. So many artists were there! *Medio mundo!* They paid us by the hour, very well and they gave us the finest materials. We worked with much passion. We were given the liberty to work in our own languages, our own styles. I was leaving the Esmeralda, and I had a good foundation to search for a style. In the museum, we were a very big family of artists enriched by our communication." Established artists recruited young talent from a diversity of backgrounds. Rogelio Naranjo came fresh from Morelia and the leftist student environment of the Colegio de San Nicolás and Michoacán's university. In the RCA Victor warehouses in the Calle Egipto, where many of them worked, Naranjo was timid and quiet, but he would shortly gain fame when Carlos Monsiváis invited him to illustrate for *La cultura en México*, the celebrated cultural supplement of *Siempre!*[11] He would become a major caricaturist for progressive magazines and, as the press opened up after 1970, for mainstream newspapers. Byron Gálvez came from Hidalgo, where his campesino father played in a jazz band. He had recently graduated from San Carlos and was enjoying his first solo exhibit. He painted in the Sala Oaxaca. Pedro Banda, who had come from humble rural roots in Tamaulipas to La Esmeralda in 1949 and never abandoned his thematic focus on campesinos, took a leave of absence from the Secretaría de Educación Pública, where he was working on textbook illustrations, to join the team of Regina Raull. "The pay was immensely better," he recalled.[12] Aurelio Pescina, the Esmeralda student from San Luis Potosí who hauled meat in the Merced market, was sought after by many team leaders for his extraordinary drawing capacity. Javier Arévalo came from Guadalajara to work with fellow Jaliscense González Camarena. Eugenio Brito came from Chile; he was at the time a visiting artist with the government's Organismo para la Promoción Internacional de la Cultura (OPIC).

Pepe Zúñiga forged a close friendship with Brito and with Guillermo Ceniceros. Ceniceros came from Monterrey. The son of a carpenter, he had worked as a boy in manual labor, then industrial design, at the giant machine manufacturer FAMA. The company paid for his schooling and would have provided him with a scholarship to the Instituto Tecnológico de Monterrey had he not gravitated to the fledgling Escuela de Artes Plásticas at the state university and a small circle of young painters eager to break into a more cosmopolitan world. There he met Esther González, a teacher who had turned to art. They came to Mexico City in 1963. Between teaching art at a private school and caring for two young children, she focused on engraving while Guillermo went to the museum. Soon after, he would join the workshop of David Alfaro Siqueiros. For Guillermo, to paint with Siqueiros was a dream come true, as he had long worked with industrial materials, the master muralist's forte. In 1964 at the museum, Guillermo was learning about his own country. He worked on the exhibits of the Mixteca, western Mexico, and Veracruz. With the aid of photographs taken by the North American anthropologist Barbara Dahlgren, he painted the Seris, Purépechas, Triquis, and Totonacos in their festive dress for Luis Covarrubías's ethnic maps.[13]

For Pepe too the museum was an unprecedented opportunity to learn about the history of his country while at the same time creating it. Shortly after entering the project, he transferred from the Sala Oaxaca to the team

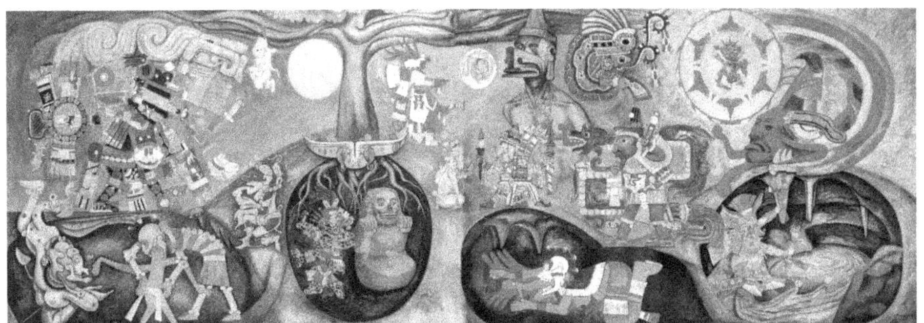

Figure 8.1. *Los dioses de Mesoamérica*, mural by Raúl Anguiano, 1964. Reproduction authorized by the National Institute of Anthropology and History.

of Raul Anguiano, who offered him more money and a better painting opportunity in the Sala Maya. Anguiano assigned Pepe a mural with the theme "gods of Mesoamerica." Advising him were the Campeche-born archaeologist Román Piña Chan, who had recently published *Culturas y ciudades de los mayas* (1959) and *Bonampak* (1961), and Alberto Ruz, who had excavated much of Palenque and uncovered the tomb of the Mayan ruler K'inich Janaab' Pakal in 1948. Anguiano had accompanied Ruz and illustrated the trip. Pepe began to read voraciously: Paul Westheim's *Las ideas fundamentales del arte prehispánico* (1957), Alfonso Caso's *Pueblo del sol* (1953), the Codices Borgia and Mendoza and other materials in the old museum's library. His trip to Palenque with Santos Balmori helped his understanding. He took time out to visit the Museo de Antropología in Jalapa, Veracruz, to see the recently uncovered frescoes, graves, and huge terra-cottas dedicated to women who died in childbirth. Putting theory into practice, he experimented with color and composition. On the eighteen-square-meter canvas, he started with the golden ratio, creating a harmonious hierarchy of spaces occupied by twenty-three gods and goddesses of death, water, air, and fire—Tlaloc, Ehecatl, Mitlantecutli, Chalchicuitle—framed by the magic of the Maya sacred tree, cenotes, jungle, and sky in brilliant tones of red and blue (see figure 8.1). "The content and the colors were completely Mexican," he recalled. "All these treasures of magical thought."

In the RCA Victor warehouse, the young painters and sculptors worked up to twenty hours, from early morning until late into the night, high on caffeine and the excitement of the collective experience. They painted to the light symphonic music of Tchaikovsky and Rimsky-Korsakov. Pedro Banda recalled that from time to time, Pepe played Bach over the radio he brought with him.[14] Rogelio Naranjo remembers that Raul Anguiano played Ravel's *Bolero* over and over.[15] They listened as well to the new folkloric music from Chile, Colombia, and the Argentine pampas. They heard the Mexican urban balladeers José Alfredo Jiménez and Chavela Vargas, soulmates in songs of desire and loss they sang in long nights at the Bar Tenampa in the Plaza Garibaldi. "Chavela Vargas!" recalled Pepe. "How daring! With her strong, impassioned voice, this women sang '*desde las tripas*,' her desire for another woman."[16]

It was an ambience of creative, energy-charged *relajo*.[17] Raul Anguiano, who loved attention, had his model Juan pose nude on the scaffolds. Painters and carpenters responded with whistles. Juan relished the applause. When Pepe's girlfriend Emma showed up in the afternoon to have lunch with Pepe, Villgrán would call out, "*¡Negrura! Aquí viene tu blancura!*"[18] The racial epithet bothered him less now: it was uttered affectionately among friends in a moment of solidarity and rupture. Emma's tight white dresses showed off her sexy body. She had a long wavy mane of chestnut-colored hair that reminded Pepe of the Chicana singer Vikki Carr. When Emma came around, Villagrán whistled and Pepe Méndez called her beautiful. Pepe enjoyed showing her off.

In the evenings after payday, the young painters would go to the Fondo del Recuerdo restaurant in Bahia de Las Palmas Street, where they drank *toritos* of *aguardiente* with guanaba or pineapple and listened to Veracruz music. For Guillermo Ceniceros, just getting to know the music and the food was a learning experience about Mexico. They talked about painting, anthropology, how the murals were going. They discussed the different artistic styles and histories of their team leaders and the errors they thought some were making on the job. They talked about new exhibits and experiments—among them, Jodorowsky's now famous and oft-repeated "*pánicos*." Pepe remembers that although they talked a little about politics, they noted how lavishly the government was willing to spend on the museum to impress the entire world. They commented on how the press never reported the number of workers killed and injured in the construction, particularly in the building of the spectacular waterfall at the museum's entrance.

The young men continued their conversations elsewhere. In Villagrán's house in the Calle Melchor Ocampo, they drank rum. Some smoked pot. Pepe did not because it reminded him of his Tío Manuel. They went to the movies to see the Beatles' *A Hard Day's Night*. "What a daring film and John Lennon!" remembers Pepe. "That's when I began to love the Beatles." On Bajío Street in Zapfe's studio, which he named Vaticueva after the *Batman* comics, they drank and listened to music. Pepe heard Joan Baez sing for the first time. "Wow, how well she sings in Spanish!" Pepe noted. "*Claro, pinche negro*," replied Zapfe, "didn't you know her father was Mexican?" Then Zapfe played the newly recorded Misa Criolla (creole mass) composed by Argentine folklorist Ariel Ramírez. The music was part of Pope John XXIII's reform movement within the Catholic Church, which would be marked in Latin America by the theology of liberation, its option for the poor, and the introduction of folk music and guitars at mass.

The friends also got together at the home of Esmeralda instructor García Robledo on Bolivar Street, near the Viaducto in the south of the city. He would play African music from his native Cuba, not the commercialized Sonora Mantancera they heard over the radio and at the clubs but a more primitive, rougher music—"authentic," as it was called in that day when "authentic" became a keyword. Also a connoisseur of baroque music, García Robledo put on his recordings of Bach, Vivaldi, and Frescobaldi. The music of the Ave Marias reduced the young men to tears.

Similar feelings Pepe experienced when he saw Pier Paolo Pasolini's *Gospel according to St. Matthew*, released in 1964. So different from the sentimentality of Hollywood religious spectacles or Mexican Catholic iconography, Pasolini's Christ was, in Pepe's words, "very human"—an ordinary young man speaking with contained but uncompromising anger against the materialism of society and the abuse of the powerful. He preached to poor and simple people, the real residents of Basilicata, Italy, in their own arid, poverty-stricken habitat, made more austere by the black-and-white photography of the land and close-ups of the human face. The fiercely radical interpretation of the Catholic Marxist and homosexual director was rendered more moving and profound by music from Bach's B Minor Mass and St. Matthew Passion and by the Missa Luba, the new African mass performed with Congolese instruments. Odetta sang the spiritual "Sometimes I Feel like a Motherless Child" as the three kings came to visit the Christ child along with the children and mothers of Jerusalem.[19] "The music was unforgettable!" remembers Pepe, "Pasolini's films are completely unique!"

A deepening intensity of human feeling went hand in hand with expanding sensual experience. The moment could be ribald and wild—like the time Pepe, García Robledo, Pepe Méndez, and Fermín Rojas went to Acapulco on a lark. They drove in the Datsun Pepe had bought from García Robledo with the good money he was earning. He had taught himself to drive on a Mexico City street, and as green as he was at the wheel, they made it to Acapulco. Thoroughly drunk around 11 PM one evening, they headed to the Playa Pie de la Cuesta to see who was more macho. Illuminated by the car headlights, they dove nude into the shark-infested open sea. Or the experience could be one of sexual excitement. He loved to go with Emma to a dark intimate bar where they danced *danzón*. They meshed beautifully together. Or the experience could be one of solitude touched by the powerful trumpet of Miles Davis interpreting the *Concierto de Aranjuez* of Joaquín Rodrigo as if alone and mourning in the silence of a great Moorish plain or the same masterwork interpreted in close, interior intimacy by the Modern Jazz Quartet with John Lewis at the piano and Milt Jackson on the vibraphone. Pepe heard them over Radio Universidad's *Jazz en la Cultura*. A Cuban friend had given him the recording of Davis's *Sketches of Spain* when it came out in 1960. He bought the MJQ record when it became available in 1964.

In the summer of 1964, trucks transported the murals and maps done in the RCA Victor warehouse to the Museo de Antropología. The artists headed there to hang and complete them. "It was just splendid," recalled Pepe, "to see all those people working. It was like a huge, teeming city inside the building, with hammers pounding, machines polishing, a dissonant chorus of voices without music." Pepe's mural went with him and Anguiano's team to the Sala Maya, where they watched a construction worker crash into the cross of Palenque with his wheelbarrow, breaking it into pieces. It was soon restored and they kept on working, each assigned to a particular detail in the murals—the sky, the trees. Six painters contributed to the mural Pepe had designed. Then Anguiano came, gave it three brushstrokes, and signed his name to it. It was disappointing not to be recognized, but the experience of the teamwork, of exploring indigenous culture, of painting, most of all of being in the museum made it all worth it.

"You would enter the museum," he said, "and just breathe the spirit of the indigenous, this love to recover something—art, legends, poetry. It was so inspiring!" He remembered the eerie sound of the conch shell that would echo the length of the museum, from the Sala Mexica over the long reflecting pool to the waterfall at the entrance. Once in the Sala Mexica he stood in front of the ferocious goddess Coatlicue as the electricians were putting in lights to illuminate her. In a moment, the lights went out and he stood face to face with the sacred goddess to whom thousands of sacrifices had been made—she with her skirt of writhing snakes, her necklace of human hands and hearts. Literally terrified and deeply humbled, he stepped back slowly.

Otherwise there was little time to contemplate. The painters worked day and night, sometimes sleeping on the floor "because the commitment was so strong to complete this museum." The day before the opening, Octavio Ocampo remembers commenting to Pepe Méndez, "This is going to be a catastrophe!" as they scanned the "total disorder of scaffolds, tools, wires, paint buckets, rubbish and garbage and people running every which way shouting, everyone trying desperately to finish their work." Security threw them out at dawn the day before the opening so another crew could clean up and install plants, flowers, and patriotic paraphernalia inside and outside the building.

The young artists were not invited to the opening on September 17, 1964. They watched it on television, with all the dignitaries (foreign diplomats, ministers of education and culture, representatives of the United Nations and other international organizations, museum directors, anthropologists and archaeologists, historians) and the music of Mexican composers Moncayo, Castro, and others.[20] "We cried," remembered Pepe, "We could not believe that all the disorder of a day disappeared as if the flowers had bloomed there in the entrance forever." "Everything was perfect!" recalled Octavio Ocampo, "The gardens with their flowers, trees, and newly trimmed lawns; the floors cleaned and polished, all the rooms in marvelous order. Once more the Mexican Miracle!"[21]

9. Private Struggle / Public Protest

1965–1972

Five long years of private struggle followed Pepe's exhilarating collective experience at the Museo de Antropología. It was a private struggle not in the sense of utter solitude, for he interacted with friends, family, lovers, and increasingly iconoclastic cinema, theater, and music. He began to break into the commercial art market while responding to opportunities federal and state governments opened to young artists. His experience was private in relation to the public explosion that engulfed the city between 1964 and 1968—a youth movement that began with the strike of medical interns, swelled in a mobilization against the university administration in 1966, and culminated in a tsunami of student protest against repression and authoritarianism in 1968. While he shared many sentiments, principles, and visions that energized the student movement, he lived a different moment as he struggled to create his own work—painting at once disciplined, expressive of himself, and recognized by others.

If he began to exhibit regularly in 1966, it was not the first time. Since 1958, he had been in show after show for Esmeralda students, most of them sponsored by Mexican federal art agencies (under the aegis of INBA) with cosponsorship by Mexico's states and by foreign governments. They sought to capture youth's diverse and experimental creativity, a particular form of contestatory creativity facilitated by the unprecedented expansion of higher education. Perhaps no government moved as energetically as the Mexican in mobilizing its prodigious cultural apparatus to channel these youthful energies and to showcase Mexican cultural achievement to the world. Mexico's hosting of the Olympic Games and Cultural Olympics in 1968 followed the flurry of museum openings of 1964.

Enabled by new wealth and in search of both regional cultural identity and cosmopolitanism, Mexican state governments joined the list of sponsors. The business sector—both private and state-owned industries and associations—got into the act. They were sensitive to proliferating art markets and the notion that aesthetics brought prestige to the mundane and increasingly maligned business of producing goods and making money. They saw that U.S. multinationals sponsored exhibits and contests, opened their own galleries, and built their collections.[1] The rise of the art market favored easel painting. In the increasing number of competitions and exhibits, young artists like Pepe found venues for recognition and communication. The student protests of 1968 took place within this milieu of expanding opportunities and benefited from them even though artists directly involved in the protests voiced hostility to both state and commercial sponsorship.[2] Taken together—those who responded to traditional modes of exhibit and those who did not—young artists broke apart old cultural monopolies to introduce a plethora of languages speaking to distinct, often new publics.

For Pepe Zúñiga, neither the development of a style nor public recognition came easily. For a while after the museum work ended, Pepe focused on Emma. He had known her since they had lived in the same vecindad in Magnolia, she with her husband and three daughters. She was four years his senior. The Zúñigas had moved around the corner to the vecindad on Soto Street when in 1963 Emma asked him to repair her record player. "You have changed a lot," she commented upon his arrival. "You're very handsome." "No, my father is handsome and my grandfather, not me," he demurred. "No," she responded, "you are handsome." She asked him how he was doing in school. When he said he was doing some pencil portraits at home, she asked if he could do one of her. "But won't your husband be upset?" he asked. "Don't you know I am divorced now?" she answered. In repeated visits, he did her portrait (see figure 9.1). It was pleasing to draw her—it was as if he were caressing her cheeks and her long, chestnut-colored wavy hair.

But it was also intimidating because he feared her children would see them, and she herself had begun to make advances. When he finished, she asked how much she owed him. When he said nothing, she insisted on having a party. It was her saint's day, and he brought her a record of the popular Cuban singer, Olga Guillot. She served her guests equally

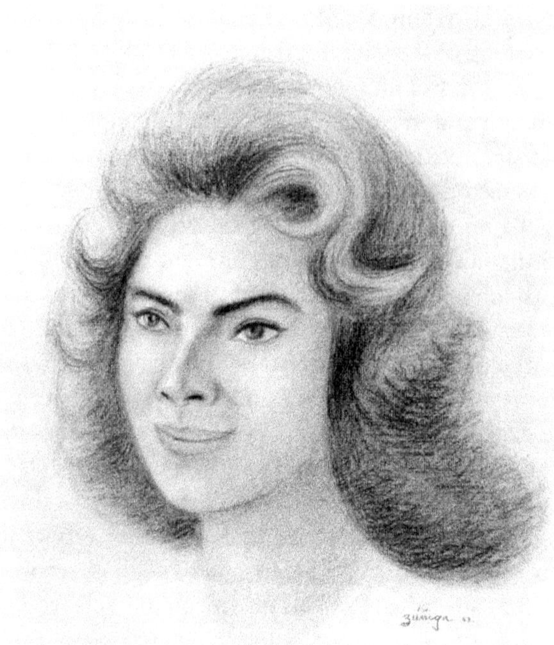

Figure 9.1. *Emma*, pencil drawing by José "Pepe" Zúñiga, 1964.

popular Cuba libres. She sent her children to bed, and Pepe and she began to dance. They danced beautifully together.

After that, they began to go to intimate bars in different parts of the city that served a well-off clientele. She insisted on paying. He did not like it, but she earned more money than he. She worked for a homeopathic doctor. She gave him a religious medal with "Love and Hope" engraved on the back. She brought him flan and *gelatines*. She told his mother she wanted to do his laundry. Lupe would have none of that. Pepe had tender affection and respect for Emma: his was not a conquest like those of his professor García Robledo. But one day, when he was visiting Emma at her apartment, Guillermo, her ex-husband, appeared and gave him ten minutes to vacate the place. He left in a hurry. That ended his romance with Emma. Years later in Paris, he would paint *Homenaje a Emma*, exhibited at the prestigious Salon de Mai and bought by the Musée d'Art Moderne.

He was in his final year at the Esmeralda. He had missed the 1964 school year as he had gone to the museum while the Esmeralda buildings were remodeled. When he returned, his friends had graduated. He was frustrated and angry. He thought he had learned everything there was to be learned there. He knew from memory the muscles, bones, and flesh of every model. He wanted to find his own style, his own mode of expression. He wanted to go abroad because he was not sure he could find his voice in Mexico. He had watched a film at La Esmeralda about the geometric painter Victor Vasarely, who received foreign students in his Paris studio. Pepe wanted to go, but there was no way. Instead, he had to sit through boring classes.

In class, Fernando Castro Pacheco had explained repeatedly the difference between Apollo (Phidias, Michelangelo, and Rodin imitating nature) and Dionysus (French Impressionism's willful transformation of color, form, and composition). The students had had enough of the classics. Joking with one another, they would say, "That's Apollo. No, it's Dionysus. No, it's Apollo." They called him "Castro Pachuco" after the Chicano street dandies imitated by Tin-Tan in the movies. It was not a compliment. Pepe took him on. He was a student leader now. He challenged the director when he denied a student the opportunity to take the annual trip to Yucatán. Castro Pacheco responded to Pepe, "Zúñiga, you think a lot of yourself but you're nobody. I'm going to ask you in five years what you've achieved as an artist." Years later, Pepe would have the pleasure of telling him he had been invited to show at the Salon de Mai in Paris.

But in 1965, Pepe Zúñiga had no way of knowing where he would be in five years. When he graduated from La Esmeralda, he felt even more at sea. It was as if someone had cut the umbilical cord that tied him to the creative life. He had no place to paint, no supplies, and only sporadic exchange with his former classmates and professors. From his parents he had learned the artisan's commitment to craft, but they could not understand his creating in a new form. His father particularly feared the life of misery that would follow from his dedication to painting. He kept demanding money from Pepe for the family. He had cut off the legs of Luz Jiménez in Pepe's painting to use the wood of the frame for his own purposes. His mother was more supportive, but both parents harped at him to find a wife. They were afraid of Emma because she was divorced, and her ex-husband could take revenge. His father wanted to present him to other women. Whenever he brought a girl to the house, his mother called her *nuera*—"my daughter-in-law." He kept busy installing new stereo systems, repairing radios, and acting as disc jockey at parties with his records and sound equipment. But he earned money irregularly as he was painting and taking courses in engraving at the OPIC, the government agency that prepared traveling exhibits and offered classes and exhibition opportunities in its galleries.

Often he did not have enough money to put gas in his car—that symbol of independence and success that now seemed to elude him. He was haunted. He had long feared turning thirty with nothing to show for himself. He saw the film *La Dolce Vita*—again and again. He focused on the relationship between the reporter, Marcello, indecisive, adrift, dispersed in his energies, and the sensitive intellectual Steiner who talked of art and literature and to whom Marcello looked to set him on the path to serious writing. Pepe identified with Marcello and saw Steiner in his new mentor, the art critic, historian, and journalist Antonio Rodríguez. But in the film, Steiner mysteriously committed suicide after murdering his two children. Marcello descended into a life of meaningless partying and cheap publicity making. The movie perplexed Pepe as he approached the age of thirty. He thought he had accomplished nothing. His life had no apparent reason. Films, the books he had read, the professors he had had—all of these had encouraged the idea of individual creativity and self-expression through high art, but could he get there? Could he break the constraints of his academic training to discover his own style? He was not concerned about "notoriety" or "sales." He was not looking for a deeper universal truth. He was looking for his own identity.

He did not have the camaraderie of the students at the Academy of San Carlos when they joined the 1966 rebellion of university students, overturned their curriculum, and declared it rot. They rejected most of their professors in favor of experimental workshops advised by innovative artists they themselves chose: abstract painters Manuel Felguérez and Vicente Rojo, iconoclast José Luis Cuevas, the maverick Santos Balmori, and Spanish painters Antonio Rodríguez Luna and Francisco Moreno Capdevila, both of whom had been involved in Nueva Presencia.[3] The San Carlos students launched a social movement. By contrast, Pepe was alone, cut off from the student milieu, and dragged down by its negative image with the public. "The student was seen as a *persona nula*, a threat, something dangerous, as if we had tramped on all aspirations. I saw it in other friends. We were all '*andando en esa onda*.'"[4] And behind it festered his personal anguish: "It was a clash of ideas I could not resolve. I just couldn't say what I wanted to say, 'Good, I am going to be a painter.'"

In fact he was not utterly alone. He had teachers with whom he kept in contact, partly because of his skills as a sound technician. They provided him with advice, support, and reading materials. Sculptor Fidencio Castillo had given him Rodin's *El arte*, published in Spanish in Buenos Aires in 1955. Like Bach's music or Orozco's *Man of Flames*, the French sculptor's pensive, anguished, and heroic sculpting of the human figure was much in vogue in the neohumanist ambience that predated the political cataclysm of the late 1960s. Pepe was drawn by the master craftsman's extraordinary command of technique and by his capacity to render emotionally charged beauty. He relished his advice, "One has to learn to be a man before being an artist." Yet Rodin was an interpreter of nature in an orthodox and academic manner. He was Apollo while Pepe looked for Dionysus. In that sense, *Letter to a Young Painter*, by the English art critic Herbert Read, spoke more directly to his concerns. Esmeralda sculptor José L. Ruiz gave him the recently translated book. This treatise on the history of modern art moved Pepe, particularly the advice Read provided the young painter. Read wrote eloquently of the task of translating sensation and internal sentiment into a material visual language. Such "virile," expressive communication required mental clarity, discipline, and power.[5] With the modernist conceit inherent in the neohumanist language of the day, Read argued that the artist's exaltation of life set him apart from "the majority of people of our modern civilization . . . alienated beings, slaves of the machine, robots in a demolished land," bereft of the "joy of creation."[6] Struggling alone, the artist would find new symbols to express feeling. In creating his own world, he would uncover "a new land" and "widen the area of coherent consciousness."[7]

Read's advice, like Rodin's, was similar to Steiner's counsel to Marcello. Their faith in the individual creator of "fine art" and "high culture," above the corruption of the market and banality of popular culture, predated the integration of contemporary popular culture into the canon. Similar convictions animated Antonio Rodríguez. He was a distinguished publicist of the Mexican mural movement, whose history he wrapped in an aura of revolutionary romanticism full of utopian faith in the militancy that would bring about the redemption of "*el pueblo*."[8] Rodríguez had been the general secretary of the Portuguese Communist Party before seeking asylum from fascism in Mexico in 1939. Acquiring Mexican citizenship, he quickly became a prominent journalist, writing in many newspapers about aesthetics, social suffering, and politics. Although he renounced political affiliation, he was, like the Comintern, a believer in the PRI's "bourgeois democracy" and its stated commitment to development and social justice. He was an intellectual of the state. He lived in the Colonia del Periodista, constructed by the government to keep journalists loyal.[9] To be an influential, principled journalist in this period, one had to write critically within state parameters while discreetly pushing those parameters toward greater freedom of expression. And so he did. In 1952, he had written a novel about the misery of the Otomi living in the Valle de Mezquital. In 1967, he published his exposé of the failures of land reform in the henequen industry of Yucatán. When President López Mateos asked him, "*No he tenido ninguna cortesía con Usted*. How can I help you?"[10] Rodríguez responded to this subtle form of corruption. "Señor Presidente, personally I need nothing. I am fine, my work is good. If you want to help me, do something for journalism. I would be very pleased if journalists could have a meeting place." He suggested to him a building downtown on Filomena Mata Street. The government restored the building and gave it to the Club de Periodistas. Shortly after, the club created an art gallery where Rodríguez organized exhibits. One of them consisted of cartoons about the Mexican Revolution. A member of the club locked the building because he thought the work too critical of the president. Don Antonio disagreed. He found a plumber to break the lock and reopen the exhibit for the public.[11]

In the 1950s, Rodríguez edited *Espacios*, a magazine read throughout Latin America that explored issues of urbanism and modern architecture. He was the first in Mexico to insist, through prominent exhibits, that photojournalism should join the ranks of "high art."[12] The magazine *Siempre!* was founded in his home in 1953. With government permission, it served as an important journal of critical, plural opinion. He wrote for it weekly. Artists, writers, and students conversed in his living room. His intimate friends were the painters Messeguer, Capdevila, and Santos Balmori, the writers Salvador Novo and Andres Henestrosa, the composer Carlos Chávez. The enemies Siqueiros and Tamayo felt equally at home there, as had Rivera and Orozco.

Don Antonio met Pepe at an exhibit in 1964. Messeguer introduced them. Shortly after, Rodríguez asked him to install a stereo system in his home. From there began a long friendship. As in *La Dolce Vita*, Rodríguez played Steiner to Pepe's Marcello. If these were wobbly moments for Pepe, they were for Don Antonio as well. In turbulent, iconoclastic times, Pepe and Don Antonio became mutually important to one another in redefining a sense of art, self, and politics in Mexico.

Rodríguez found himself in the center of a fiery artistic polemic. We cannot reduce the battle to one between the Mexican school and the new tendencies encouraged by Tamayo, Cuevas, Goeritz, and the abstract artists who had risen to prominence. Don Antonio had promoted abstract painters like Vicente Rojo and Manuel Felguérez. For him, the struggle was more complicated. It came to a head on the night of February 2, 1965, in the recently opened Museum of Modern Art. In the competition and exhibit *Artistas Jovenes de México*, sponsored by the U.S. multinational Esso, the jury chose a painting to be sent to a Latin American exhibit planned by the Organization of American States in Washington.[13] The jury had split over the prize: art historian Justino Fernández opted for Benito Messeguer's neohumanist painting *Mimetismo*. Rufino Tamayo swore he would never give a prize to "a painting of that tendency." He and writer Juan García Ponce wanted the prize to go to the abstract work of Juan's brother Fernando. Characteristic of the negotiating will of the authoritarian regime, José Luis Martínez, INBA director, worked out a compromise: the Museo de Arte Moderno would buy Messeguer's painting and García Ponce would win the prize. Messeguer told Martínez that the decision discriminated against a prominent artistic tendency and reeked of nepotism. At the inauguration, he interrupted Martínez's speech in protest, and the fur began to fly. Messeguer's allies jumped to his cause, denouncing the CIA and OAS art director, José Gómez Sicre, for their imperialist campaign against realist art. They targeted José Luis Cuevas for his close association with Gómez Sicre. Cuevas, Messeguer's one-time ally, loudly defending the prize. "Go to Washington, traitor! Sellout to the OAS!" they jeered. Olga Tamayo stood up in her bison fur coat and shouted, "It's the *ardidos comunistas*! *Los ardidos comunistas*! They ought to know the hammers and sickles have fallen!" Alicia Messeguer threw her drink at Cuevas. Cuevas and Francisco Icaza got into a fist fight. Messeguer and Antonio Rodríguez separated them while protesting the jury's decision.

In the weeks and months that followed, the controversy raged in the press, government corridors, and public fora. One side declared the Mexican school dead and called for liberty of expression, and the other railed against U.S. imperialism—an argument with sharpening resonance as the U.S. military had just invaded Santo Domingo and was ramping up its war in Vietnam. But the United States was not the central issue in what was at once a more local and international debate. The old ex-muralist, Roberto Montenegro, who had never been on the political left, wrote in *Lunes de Excelsior*: "It's marvelous! These are magnificent things! It doesn't matter if the traditional Mexican school has been abandoned. The young should paint what the moment dictates!"[14]

Don Antonio was in the thick of the polemic. He understood that a sea change was under way. He had always considered himself a vanguardist—supporting Le Corbusier in architecture, championing concrete and other experimental music.[15] His objections to the Esso exhibit jury's decisions related more to nepotism than to artistic style. For similar procedural reasons, he resigned from the planning committee the government created for its proposed exhibit *Confrontaciones*, which would show the many artistic styles emerging in Mexico. He did not challenge the exhibit's purpose but the decision to choose representative artists before seeing their work.[16]

Don Antonio was not opposed to change. He simply wanted to guide it. He feared anarchy and the loss of plastic traditions and painting technique. As director of Difusión Cultural at the Instituto Politécnico Nacional, he was in a good position to do so. Those in charge of Difusión Cultural at the UNAM were at the time sponsoring new work in every area of the arts: painting, theater, film, literature.[17] The IPN, poor brother to the university, offered technical and scientific training to a less elite student body and had little cultural programming.[18] Although the government gave him few resources, Rodríguez wasted no time in sponsoring art exhibits, musical concerts, a cinema club, and lectures—many of the latter featuring prominent Mexican journalists he invited to speak to student writers.[19] With his humanist faith, Don Antonio hoped to end "the divorce between science and poetry so that these unite in the mission to provide plenitude and freedom to man."[20]

Don Antonio had a particular interest in promoting the work of students from the less elite art school, La Esmeralda. In March 1966 he invited five of them, including Pepe, to exhibit at the IPN. In the exhibit's catalogue, Rodríguez expressed his ambivalence about the transition. The spirit of rebellion had gone out of the once powerful mural movement, he wrote; it had become sterile, dogmatic, and asphyxiating. Against this routine, young people had rebelled, but if they intended to deny all value to the masters or to create a new dogma in place of the old, they were on the wrong track. "Today's young artists," he wrote, "face the possibility, indeed the obligation to create an art free of all prejudices, complexes, and dogma." He was pleased to present these young men from La Esmeralda who rose to that challenge.

> They confront their responsibilities without old or new dogmas, without the obligation of obedience to their predecessors, but also without the urge to negate their historical value. Theirs is not the posture of the nihilists who want to destroy the universe to recreate it from zero; but neither is it to continue down well-traveled roads.[21]

In the exhibit, Pepe showed one of his first attempts at neofigurative drawing. In *La epoca actual*, he experimented with the concept of accident using a splotch of ink dropped on paper to create a human figure with visible head, shoulders, and thighs but arms and legs diluted in space. Thematically within the spirit of existential angst expressed by Nueva Presencia, Pepe had been thinking about the disaster at Hiroshima and the threat of nuclear war when he drew it. A critic described it as "the figure of a man not yet fully formed. Neither monster nor a perfect being, it is more a nebulous mass not yet integrated."[22] At the same time, this man adrift and not fully formed reflected Pepe's feelings about himself.

Don Antonio saw in Pepe the potential to create new painting without abandoning the Mexican legacy. He followed him with respect, affection, and support. He invited him to participate in a tribute to David Alfaro Siqueiros that he organized in Cuernavaca and in the ex-chapel of La Concepción in Mexico City in honor of the seventieth birthday of the painter, who had recently been released from jail. Pepe went to hear Rodríguez speak at the university and the IPN. He gave Pepe books—the ones he had written about Yucatán, about the Otomi, and about Diego Rivera, José Clemente Orozco, and the populist engraver José Guadalupe Posada. He invited Pepe to his home. "Don Antonio helped me to discover new musical languages," he remembered. It was the first time he had heard the *fados* of Portugal—a gritty, uncommercialized folk music similar to the flamenco and Catalan music Messeguer had played. Don Antonio introduced him to John Cage's concrete music and showed him the chaise longue designed by Le Corbusier he had in his living room. "He moved me a lot. He gave me a lot of support," reflected Pepe. "He saw in me a painter's vocation, a gift he wished he had had."

Pepe's friends provided support as well. The Zúñiga family apartment was full of tailors and relatives. There was no good place to paint. Like Van Gogh, Pepe wanted to leave this conventional ambience to find inspiration in the camaraderie of other young painters. He rented a studio around the corner with the sculptor Cuauhtémoc Zamudio, his colleague from La Esmeralda. It became a meeting place for them—Guillermo Ceniceros, Gerardo Cantú, Guillermo Zapfe, and Armando Villagrán. From Ceniceros, experienced in the use of industrial materials, Pepe learned more about technique, especially the use of acrylics and creation of new textures. Zapfe introduced him to contemporary folk music and to the Chinese calligraphy he used in his abstract paintings. Zapfe's knowledge of art history and theory enriched their discussions.

As Cantú, Ceniceros, and Zamudio were from Monterrey, they had direct contact with Francisco Guzmán de Bosque, director of the INBA in Nuevo León. He issued an open invitation to the young artists of Mexico City to exhibit in Monterrey. He intended to develop more artistic activity in this wealthy industrial city, which lacked a plastic arts tradition but had a growing market for painting.[23] Pepe began to exhibit in Monterrey.

It was the creative process that was more solitary and more difficult. Pepe continued to paint in the studio and in a room his father enlarged for him in the apartment. He listened to Messeguer, "Remember, José, painting is like a lover. Don't neglect it or she will abandon you. You need to paint at least one or two hours a day with discipline and love." Messeguer continued with his advice: "Paint to learn. Paint for yourself, and if someone buys your painting, very well. But don't be an egotist: don't paint and then hide your work so no one can see it. That would be selfish. You will get to know people who appreciate art and you will win prizes and friends. You will have everything."

"I came to figurativism in my last years at school," Pepe remembers, "In 1965, I did a series of Juchitecas, all of them stylized in juxtapositions of purples. Many artists had painted these women of Oaxacan Isthmus of Tehuantepec—Miguel Covarrubias, Waldemar Sjolander, Valetta Swann, Diego Rivera, Frida Kahlo, and Francisco Zúñiga. Why not me? I was from Oaxaca and had made sketches of the Juchitecas during my visits to the isthmus. In some, I painted fat women in the form of triangles and thin women in other triangles. I wanted to abstract their forms. I was interested in volume. I was influenced by the voluptuous women of Francisco Zúñiga. But inside, I was suffering. I was conflicted about form. I began to play with materials. I drew with both hands. That's a skill. A skill is one thing and finding a style is quite another. I didn't want to go completely abstract: I wanted to leave the academy, not reality. I abandoned oils for acrylics because they gave me more control over color and form. I experimented with new textures, with pigments, finishes, and sand that I worked with new techniques. I wanted to go more quickly, produce more. Now I know that there are many roads to follow to accomplish what I was looking for. I began to create a very dark palette. I believe this is because I greatly admired my fellow Oaxaqueño Rufino Tamayo, born in the barrio of Carmen Alto like me. I tried to follow him in color and textures. At the time, he worked in a dark palette—reds with neutral, almost humid colors. But I didn't know how to work with grays, and as Maestro Tamayo said: 'For colors to sing and vibrate you have to use grays.' His solutions were a mystery to me. I painted a series of horses and fish, all abstract in form. I tried to filter them in an ambience. I imagined the fish in the depths of the sea and the horses in the night. All very dark. I wanted to achieve a certain elegance that created textures, textures of wetness or of stone.

"I lost a lot, I broke a lot, I threw a lot into the garbage. Some things I gave as gifts because they had no value for me. All of this was part of my road toward the purification of form, a synthesis of everything, an effort to be more direct and frank. But this only comes from passion when one feels desire. Sometimes I cried, sometimes I laughed, sometimes I took a drink. I locked myself in. I didn't want anyone to interrupt me. I remembered what Bentio had told us: 'When you are working, you have to apply all the senses you have. If you have twenty senses, use them all.'"

Pepe's now very aged Tía Clotilde passed her days in a chair. She leaned over a table resting her head on her arms. "I did sketches of her and then I painted her in a simplified manner with brushstrokes that were not academic but very free. I painted two figures of Clotilde, one next to the other." The painting is almost abstract with her body represented in concentric circles. "I was trying to apply the golden ratio. I did not completely achieve it. But the painting in black, white, and ochre uncannily captured the fatigue of her years. I showed it in Monterrey in 1967. The collector Terry Haas bought her."

Terry Serrano Haas was one of the wealthy women of Monterrey who directed the commercial art gallery Arte AC, the only one in the city apart from the government gallery run by Guzmán del Bosque. Pepe thought she bought it out of sympathy to compensate for the failure of the exhibit. The gallery planned the exhibit to show Pepe's work. He invited his parents. It opened in June, the hottest month in Monterrey. The women who ran the gallery prepared a cocktail party for two hundred people. Very few came. "I didn't care so much that people didn't come," Pepe reflected. "What bothered me was my father's attitude. After he had drunk a lot of wine, he told me that painting was not economically viable for me and I should dedicate myself to radio electronics."

Terry Haas also bought a painting of Juchitecas now done in brighter colors. Fernando Guzmán del Bosque liked these. He wrote in the newspaper *El Porvenir* that he found in Pepe's work an "authentic, innovative *Mexicanidad*," nothing of "this repetitive, unoriginal and self-referential internationalism":

> This young painter expresses and interprets Mexico, its landscapes, and above all in his compositional themes, the majority based on popular life in a very picturesque corner of our beloved Patria, of

> this Oaxacan folklore. He delights us with his fresh and radiant colors, because his rich palette blends composition with technique, movement with sentiment, the legitimate pride of our plastic inheritance.[24]

Around this time, Pepe met José Luis Gaitán. He was from Michoacán and worked in a pencil factory in Coyoacán. "He was handsome," Pepe remembered. "He reminded me of Franco Nero and Richard Burton." He knew nothing about painting, but he inspired and supported Pepe. José Luis loved to watch him paint. He modeled for him and helped him to prepare his brushes and his materials (see figure 9.2). Pepe's parents liked him and enjoyed having him around. When he was painting in the room his father had enlarged for him, José Luis would tell him, "Your mother says you can't leave until you've painted a lot." José Luis accompanied him to exhibits. "My friendship with him was very intimate. It inspired me for all the five years I was with him. So much so that I began to win important prizes." José Luis, he says, set him free.

José Luis accompanied him in his moments of disappointment and exasperation. One day Pepe received a telegram informing him that he had won first prize in a student competition sponsored by the cigarette company Tabacalera La Moderna of Aguascalientes. The prize was for 10,000 pesos. Never had he entered a contest and never had anyone paid him so much for a painting! At the time, he did not even have enough money to put gas in his car, so he and José Luis took the bus to Aguascalientes. When he arrived, the director informed him that he had been disqualified because he was no longer a student. He protested saying that he was a student in the OPIC. The director dismissed him. "I told José Luis 'Take that painting and I'll take the other and we're getting out of here.' I was crying because I considered the whole thing completely unfair. Then the director said to me, 'We can make an arrangement if you agree to share the prize with two painters from San Luis Potosí.' Later I learned that he had a deal with the people of San Luis Potosí who always took first prize in this contest. At the time, I told him, 'I'm not sharing anything. I'm taking my paintings.' We went back to Mexico City with the two paintings, without the 10,000 pesos, and completely broke. I went to the authorities at Bellas Artes to complain but they wouldn't give me the time of day. What corruption! In the end, those paintings ended up in good hands. Years later, Elena Olachea, director of the José María Velasco Gallery of the INBA, bought one and a politician from Monterrey bought the other for the Moctezuma Brewery collection."

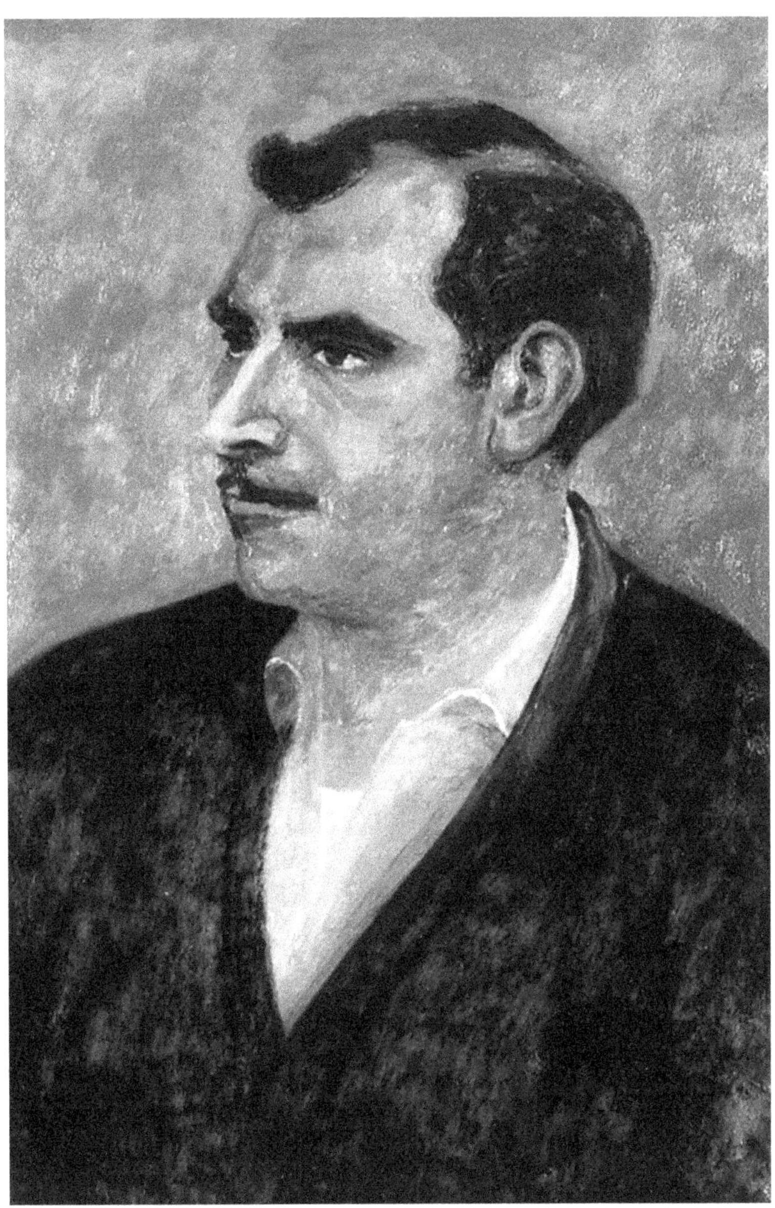

Figure 9.2. Pepe's painting of José Luis, 1967.

In the city, they went to the movies. They saw *cursi*, conventional films, like *Camelot*, that pleased the eye and melted the heart. More often alone, Pepe saw works that smashed every sentimental, aesthetic, and social convention. Pasolini's *Teorema* came out in the spring of 1968. In the movie, a young man (Terence Stamp) with the face and body of Michelangelo's David visits a bourgeois home in postwar, newly prosperous Milan. It is a sterile fortress of stone, an ornate, spiritually empty box situated on a manicured lawn behind high walls. The stranger gently seduces every member of the family, including the maid. He is God, Jesus, or the Holy Spirit. He teaches not through words or good deeds but tender sexuality. As in *The Gospel according to St. Matthew*, Pasolini renders the encounters through powerful full-screen portraits of faces—but this time, with repeated shots of the stranger's crotch. To the music of Mozart's Requiem, the only words in the film are uttered upon his departure in the confessions of each he has touched. The son has discovered his homosexuality and will express his soul through painting. The daughter has discovered her sexuality is not a sickness. The mother confesses that she was interested in nothing in her world of false ideas and endless accumulation. The stranger's love has filled her life and destroyed only her bourgeois reputation. The father tells the stranger that his caresses have destroyed him, he has lost himself, his identity, his idea of order and possession. Only the maid says nothing, kisses the stranger's hand, and returns to her village. When the stranger departs, each, save for the servant, disintegrates. Their superficial values block them from more substantive transformation. Only the maid can translate the stranger's love into good works, for her traditional popular culture has not yet been contaminated; surviving on nettles, she heals the sick and wounded.[25]

Pepe had lived his life in popular culture; he knew there were good and bad people there and not saints. He knew less about the bourgeoisie but did not care much about them. They did not cause him jealousy or anger—after all, some of them were buying his paintings. And as he was not much into consumerism, Pasolini's critique washed off him. But the plastic genius of this Italian director captured the tender carnality of love that moved Pepe deeply, as did his assault on Catholic repression in the name of goodness and liberation. Pepe found *Teorema* to be a more positive film than another iconoclastic movie of that year—Jodorowsky's *Fando y Lis*. Based on a script by Fernando Arrabal, Jodorowsky rendered this voyage of two lovers to the promised land of Tar in surrealist scenes of brutal misogyny and grotesque characters. The film could be read as the director's assertion of liberty of expression in re-creating childhood dreams that captured the complexity of sexuality. But *Fando y Lis* overdosed. Forced to drink her own blood, the actress, Diana Mariscal, suffered a nervous breakdown, Pepe recalled. At the opening in Acapulco, the genius of Mexican Golden Age cinema, Emilio "El Indio" Fernández, is said to have brandished a pistol at Jodorowsky who fled the theater.[26]

That year of 1968 opened well for Pepe. The Mexican government planned to complement the Olympic Games with elaborate Cultural Olympics featuring dance, painting, theater, and music. In the government's opinion, Mexican prestige in the world depended greatly on its cultural achievements and projection, which now went hand in hand with cosmopolitan industrial modernity.[27] As the first government outside Europe, the United States, and Japan to host the Olympic Games, the regime intended to spotlight Mexico's achievements. The festivities began with national artists and were to conclude in the fall at the time of the games with international guest performances. The government intended the Olympics to celebrate youth.[28] Opportunities multiplied for young artists. Guadalupe Solorzano, director of INBA's Chapultepec Gallery, invited Pepe to show his work at collective exhibits in December 1967 and spring 1968. He was painting variations on familiar themes—horses and Juchitecas. Guadalupe called them "*estas mujeres que son de tu tierra*." He painted now in brighter colors and more refined composition. In one show, he won honorable mention from a jury that included José Luis Cuevas.

Then the year turned tumultuous. In May, students at the Sorbonne in Paris took over the streets, battling police. If they protested specifically against an antiquated, authoritarian, and hierarchical university structure, they saw it as a microcosm of a bureaucratized, repressive state and society, anathema to the needs and sensibilities of an exploding student population. They registered their sympathy for the Vietnamese in their struggle against imperialism. Young workers quickly joined them, taking over factories and initiating a general strike of ten million people. Although similar student protests in major cities, capitals, and campuses of the world had preceded these events, the significance of Paris as the modern historical center of culture and revolution, together with the social breadth of the movement, grabbed more attention in Mexico. Antonio Rodríguez wrote at length about the Paris uprising in *Siempre!*[29] In July in Mexico City, vocational school students began to fight, first against each other and then against the police who invaded their schools. On the eve of the Olympic Games, the government wanted no disorder. So the repression escalated with the protests that expanded to the preparatory schools, the IPN, and the UNAM. The demands were few and specific. They focused on state violence. The energy and sensitivity propelling them was amorphously yet stridently libertarian.

In the beginning days of the movement, Pepe went to see *Cementerio de los automóviles*, performed by students of the university's Escuela de Teatro. Throngs of young people lined up in the street for a chance to get into the Teatro Jiménez Rueda, a new INBA theater near the Colonia Guerrero. They packed the aisles to see this play set to the music of the Beatles' "Yesterday" and "Let It Be." Director Julio Castillo had transposed the script of Fernando Arrabal to a Mexican setting. Castillo had grown up in a modest neighborhood bordering the Colonia Guerrero and had trained with Jodorowsky. Like Juan Ibañez, who had directed *Olímpica* and *Divinas palabras*, Julio Castillo was very young, just twenty-four years old. Felida Medina, Pepe's classmate at the Esmeralda, did the stunning scenography. She and her team (this was the self-consciously collective work of students bonded by a commitment to art, egalitarian politics, and community) had salvaged wrecked cars from all over the city, discarding all but the twisted, rusted, burned-out frames in which the characters of the play lived.[30] The cars were an obvious critique of consumerist modernity, the wreckage they caused, and the exclusion they engendered. Felida's changing lighting illuminated the different stories of these marginal people, "vagabonds of the street living in the poverty zones," Pepe recalled. One was about making love: "The lights went out," Pepe remembered, "but you knew what was happening." In one automobile carcass, a woman gave birth to a baby of unknown paternity. In a third automobile lived an army officer with a lesbian and in another, a conventional couple. The story developed as an allegory of the crucifixion. The principals were three hippie youths. Emanu as Jesus and his two friends, representing the apostles Peter and Judas, arrived to play music to rescue the poor from their misery. With them was Dila (Mary Magdalene), whose gigolo lover had forced her into prostitution. His violence she transformed into tenderness in her friendship with the boys. She protected Emanu, a mute, effeminate lad who knit sweaters to protect beggars from the cold but whose trumpet symbolized for one critic the rifle of revolution. Sensing his challenge to the social order, the authorities announced a reward for his capture. His closest friend betrayed him, turning him in to a couple of street performers—secret police agents among their peers—the same couple who had earlier made love in their automobile carcass. The crucifixion took place virtually: the police beat the ground rather than Emanu, and Dila marked in red pencil the lashes on his back. The police tied him up in the tire of a car, then crucified him on a bicycle. As the audience heard a little doll repeat what she had said throughout the play, "I love you very much, tell me a story; I love you very much, tell me a story," the figure of Emanu was projected in film on a sheet as he escaped over a viaduct into beds of flowers. Suddenly the Technicolor of the flowers turned to damaged, blurred black-and-white film as Emanu ran frantically to a place where he found the wounded body of Comandante Che Guevara. The play ended as the boy, smiling and making a victory gesture with his hand, waved goodbye to the dying *guerrillero*.[31]

The critic François Baguer dismissed the production as irreverent and blasphemous. María Luisa Mendoza, an avid supporter of new theater, judged the crucifixion magnificent "as the Señor likes it and commands it."[32] Most were overwhelmed by its freshness and the sentiments of pain and love and gentleness so powerfully transmitted by the actors. Writing in *Impacto*, Ilya Engel was ecstatic. "What is your name? Love. What is your name? Jesus Christ. What is your name? They call me Che Guevara. What is your name? Love and progress," he wrote.[33] Pepe Zúñiga was carried away. "It was much more powerful than Bunuel's *Los olvidados*," he recalled. "It was very sad, very moving—to see the way the young actors projected their emotions. I cried, but I also felt a love for life. I was excited. It made me think. It made me question myself. Not only the actors, but the effects—the lights, the films projected on the sheet, the Beatles' music. The shells of the wrecked cars were unique sculptures, works of art. It was a repudiation of the authorities, a rebellion. It was about our poor, those with little education but the will to overcome (*superacción*). We are neither bad nor good, it's the circumstances that turn us bad and thwart us. One lives saturated and surrounded by this ambience; part of it is about loving and being loved, and another part is revolting and disgusting. The poor cannot get out because they are censored and kept down. There was more and more rancor and rebellion in youth in those days, and I identified with them."

The play was a call to change, and he could see metamorphosis in his friend Felida Medina. Pepe remembered her as a proper bourgeois girl in Messeguer's night class. One of the very few women there, she always came with neatly coifed hair, light makeup, and very "feminine" dress. Years later, she complained to Pepe of the attitude of the men at La Esmeralda—always wanting to seduce her instead of accepting her as a thinking, sensitive, creative person. By 1968, she had transformed herself. Now she was in pants, her hair long, no stockings, no bra, no makeup. And she was transforming Mexican scenography as Julio revolutionized theater direction. The critic María Luisa Mendoza was thrilled: "We are witnessing the slow but inevitable advance of women of talent." Felida herself remembered: "We traveled around the city in our jeans covered with paint, moving between our theater work and taking baskets of food to the student protestors. We invaded opera performances at the Palacio de Bellas Artes. We entered the boxes and totally shocked the bourgeois audience decked out in their bouffant hairdos and their ties. We were interested in art for its own sake, not as a status symbol."[34] They were themselves a roaming theater of liberty and defiance, the very spirit of the student movement that gathered force, taking over the streets, unleashing its message on the walls, telephone booths, buses, tree trunks, and statues, in the markets, from the rooftops of cars, balconies, and windows, at family dinner tables; singing, dancing, shouting, carrying placards, waving flags, and marching in absolute silence. Theirs was the same spirit that drove Tommy Smith and John Carlos to shatter the script of the Olympic Games with their black power salute. Whether they sought to "get back to the garden," as Joni Mitchell sang the next summer at Woodstock, or to make a socialist revolution, they changed the world with their bodies, gestures, and images more than their words.[35] They captured the joy and hope that had eluded Nueva Presencia.

Through the summer, the marches mounted, drawing greater crowds as well as police attacks and mass arrests. It was a moment of exhilarating defiance for those who threw their energy into the movement. Juan Castañeda and Elva Garma, Pepe's friends from Benito Messeguer's parties and still students at La Esmeralda, made posters and placards for the demonstrations and together with other students stood guard at night to protect the school from police invasions.[36] Fear and danger heightened the exuberance. "Even when we were not students," Pepe recalled, "the police could arrest you at any moment for the simple crime of being young and looking like a student. I was concerned about my brother Efrén. He was studying architecture at the university and had thrown himself into the student movement." Pepe participated in some marches. Although not directly involved, he was deeply sympathetic with the cause.

At the time, he had grown close to Eugenio Brito, the Chilean guest artist at OPIC. "He had a beautiful vocabulary," Pepe remembers. "He was a great intellectual. I loved the way he spoke Spanish, and he also spoke French. He told me a lot about Europe. I really wanted to go. That's why I was painting now in a frenzy." Brito gave him a vicuña poncho; he said he would need it to keep warm in Paris. Brito talked to him about politics. He told him the Mexicans were apathetic and submissive; they did not know how to defend their rights. In Chile, Brito told him, politics were mother's milk—children grew up talking about them. So many political parties made for militant citizens who knew how to defend their rights. Pepe protested, "Well, look at us Mexicans now! What do you think we are doing?" Brito introduced Pepe to the political protest music of Victor Jara, Violeta Parra, and Quilapayún. When Jara came to sing at the university, Brito introduced them at a reception in the home of the Chilean cultural attaché. Eugenio gave Pepe a book of Pablo Neruda's poems about birds of his native Andes. The poetry touched Pepe deeply. He began to translate Neruda's images into painting. He rendered them in increasingly sophisticated composition and form achieved through color, line, texture, and volume.

On August 1, university rector Barros Sierra led a march of 50,000 against government repression and violation of university autonomy.[37] They marched down Insurgentes Avenue toward the central city. On August 13, 300,000 protestors reached the Zócalo for the first time. Tanks, soldiers with bayonets, and police expulsed them. Bloody encounters continued into September. On September 18, army tanks and trucks rolled onto the university campus. On September 23, Barros Sierra announced his resignation. That evening, police occupied the Politécnico's Santo Tomás campus amid fierce student resistance on and around the campus and at the giant housing project, Tlatelolco-Nonoalco, where police battled with students as they occupied Vocational School Seven. The unprecedented scope of these invasions of legally autonomous space shocked the city, provoking ever greater waves of indignation from hitherto quiescent citizens and prominent intellectuals. Protestors stained red paint onto the government's white doves of peace hung over the city in honor of the Olympic Games. Everywhere people raised their fingers in the V sign of peace. But with such intimidating repression, the crowds at the marches had begun to dwindle. When the National Strike Council called a mass meeting at Tlatelolco, the Plaza de Tres Culturas, for October 2, about 10,000 came. Not only fear kept them away. Like many others, Pepe got partly there only to find the streets barricaded by army and police.

Just as the explosive youth movement was symbolic of the dramatic changes rocking Mexico City, so was the site of Tlatelolco. The largest urban renewal housing project in Latin America inaugurated in 1964, Tlatelolco-Nonoalco represented a feat of modernist architecture and engineering: 12,000 apartments, multiple schools, daycare centers, hospitals, clinics, sports fields, theaters, and stores. It housed as well the new building of the Secretaría de Relaciones Exteriores where, in 1967, thirty-three nations signed an important treaty of nuclear disarmament. Pedro Ramírez Vázquez designed its exquisite tribute to "Tres Culturas": the recently restored pyramids and ruins of the ancient commercial town of Tlaltelolco, site of the largest market in Meso-America; the colonial church of Santiago Tlatelolco and college where noble Nahua youth recorded and painted their history under the direction of Franciscan friars Pedro de Gante and Bernardo Sahagún; and modern mestizo Mexico, represented in the gigantic work of urban planning and slum clearance dubbed by Carlos Monsiváis as "modern Mexican utopia without vecindades."[38] Like the government's relationship with youth, Tlatelolco-Nonoalco captured the potent contradictions of state beneficence and creativity, repression and destruction. The new high-rise apartment buildings rose from the demolition of the Buenavista railroad yards, warehouses, roundhouse, workshops, and residences, including the north end of the Colonia Guerrero. The railroad workers belonged to one of the country's most militant unions; the government had jailed thousands in their strikes of 1958–59. They also worked for a dying industry eclipsed by trucks, buses, and cars. The project had promised them and other residents new homes, but in fact it displaced 7,000. It had demolished a big swath of the Colonia Guerrero's southeast. To reach the project and to alleviate growing traffic congestion, the government built the huge Prolongación de la Reforma, razing buildings and breaking up the narrow streets that for Pepe, his family, and thousands of others had constituted a seamless neighborhood. Because of its proximity to the Santo Tomás campus of the IPN and in defense of Vocational School Seven, dissident students had chosen to meet here on October 2, ten days before the Olympic Games were to begin. The students believed the Mexican army surrounded the plaza to protect the Secretaría de Relaciones Exteriores. The students did not know that members of the army's Batallón Olímpica dressed in plain clothes had infiltrated many buildings including the Santiago-Tlatelolco church.

That afternoon at the Zuñiga apartment on Soto Street a few blocks away, the family watched the helicopters gather overhead. They had never seen them before. It was very strange. In the afternoon around six, they watched them launch Bengal flares. Then they heard explosions. "Must be firecrackers," said Pepe's father. "No, the explosions are not like firecrackers," the family said. These were guns spewing bullets into the crowd. "We had never heard such a thing. We had never imagined," recalled Pepe, "that there would be such a massacre at this meeting. Children, women, and innocent people died there. They closed the doors so no one could

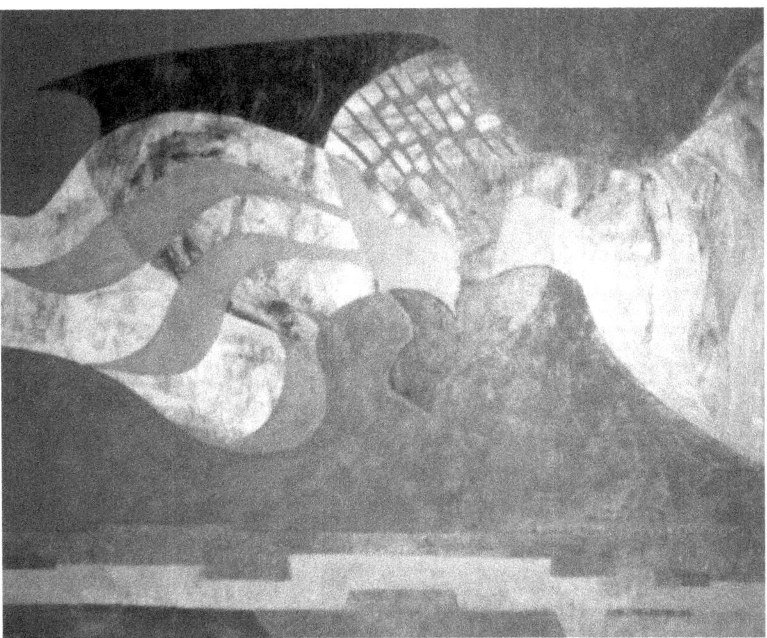

Figure 9.3. *El pájaro de Tlatelolco*, painting by José "Pepe" Zúñiga, 1968. See color plate 2.

escape. What confusion! What a crisis!" As the police and army jailed scores of young people and dead and wounded bodies disappeared, a huge, heavy pall bore down over the city. People were stunned, scared, and grieved. Nothing like this had ever happened.

For some time, Benito Messeguer and Antonio Rodríguez had been telling Pepe to paint something of the poverty in Mexico. He had tried, but he could not do it—at least not well or to his taste. It was not within his sensibility to condescend, to monolithize, or to depict a condition whose complexities he knew well and from which he wanted to escape. Instead, after Tlatelolco, Pepe painted an elegant bird, the symbol of peace wounded and falling from the sky over a terrain of pre-Hispanic ruins (see figure 9.3). In a reversal of the symbolic positioning of the Mexican nation in the bronze column at the entry to the Anthropology Museum, Pepe's bird did not soar upward toward freedom, clarity, and peace but plunged downward toward its death. It was the only painting Pepe ever did in fiery colors of orange. He entitled it *El pájaro de Tlatelolco*—"The Bird of Tlatelolco."

As deafening and terrifying as the repression was, it hastened official efforts to win over youth. In the early winter of 1969, Guadalupe Solorzano invited Pepe to a solo exhibit at her INBA gallery. He painted in a frenzy to prepare and, with José Luis's support, managed to get together twenty-six paintings of birds, mares, fish, a grasshopper—the *chapulin* of Oaxaca—and an impressive eclipse of the sun. He worked in brighter colors and mixed techniques to achieve different textures. His parents came, of course. So busy was he setting up the sound system to play the Beatles that he hardly noticed the gallery had filled with people, lots of them young. In the course of the afternoon, he sold ten paintings. When he handed his father 35,000 pesos, the older Zúñiga wept. "Wow, son, I guess you won't die of hunger," he said. "I guess not, Papa." His father never questioned him again. Pepe was to be a painter.

His picture appeared in several major newspapers—a serious young man looking something like Che Guevara with his beard and mustache (see figure 9.4). In *Novedades*, the influential critic Jorge Juan Crespo de la Serna called him "a talented Oaxacan. . . . He's no upstart or autodidact. . . . There's originality in his deliberate plastic language. He will go far."[39] Noting that Zúñiga was one of the young artists to whom Solorzano had opened opportunities not otherwise available, Ignacio Martínez Espinosa in *La Prensa* wrote that Zúñiga had justifiably won "the praise of the public." These were works of good quality, he noted, expressing "personal passion" and the "desire of a restless spirit to reach greater heights."[40] Enrique Gual found Zúñiga "drowning in the raging vitality of youth." The feverish painting was "not fully ventilated," but rather "blindly struggling, blemished by innocence." He noted "chromatic violence and daring, rapid formal syntheses, and graceful displays of true talent. Everything here is struggle, pushing, and frenzied disorientation." Entitling his article "Zúñiga, el futuro," he concluded he was a real artist who had now to begin to "restrain and refine the real possibilities of talent he possesses."[41]

Antonio Rodríguez was gentler. He wrote in his presentation of the exhibit: "In his liberty is the effort the artist has made to get out from under what the academy imposed as obligation and constraint. This newfound freedom does not reflect an anxiety to obey the demands of the moment, to conform to the impositions of the market, the galleries, or the critics." He placed Zúñiga within a telluric Mexicanidad: "The painting flows from Zúñiga's creative imagination in pure and spontaneous form, with the simple aim of realizing a dream, a desire, perhaps anxiety or pain. The work is as 'natural' as a volcanic landscape erupting and settling over the centuries, like a crust of the earth made up of many layers of clay, like the juice of fruit ripened by many tropical suns, or a fire that will never

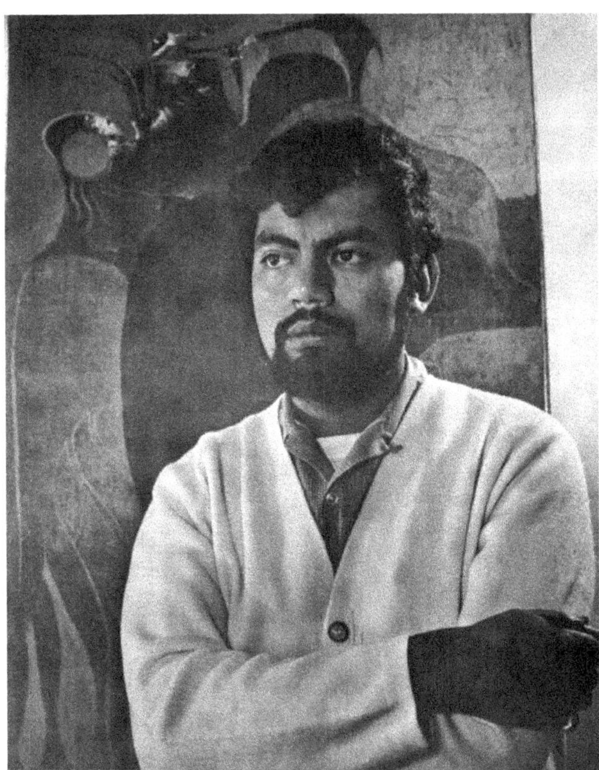

Figure 9.4. José "Pepe" Zúñiga. Black-and-white photograph, 1969.

go out. . . . A great draftsman, he restrains his lines because he resists the easy route . . . his color for me comes from the living core of Mexico. I find a rich expression, fertile invention, and impassioned song."[42]

Pepe visited Don Antonio frequently now—sometimes to be part of intense discussions of politics and art with Messeguer and Francisco Moreno Capdevila—sometimes to talk with him alone. He encouraged him to go to Paris. "José, you need to leave this place. You have to have another vision of the world." He taught him to eat Gouda cheese without consuming the wax. "When you get to France," he told him, "you are going to eat many types of cheeses." He helped him apply for and finally win the scholarship of the French government. "Don Antonio was my spiritual father," Pepe said. "I was like a son to him." The more so as his son Cristóbal had died in the protests. Don Antonio visited the Zúñiga family in the Colonia Guerrero. Pepe showed him all his early work. It was on this occasion that Don Antonio noted the majestic stylization of the model Victoria Pepe had drawn in Francisco Zúñiga's class at La

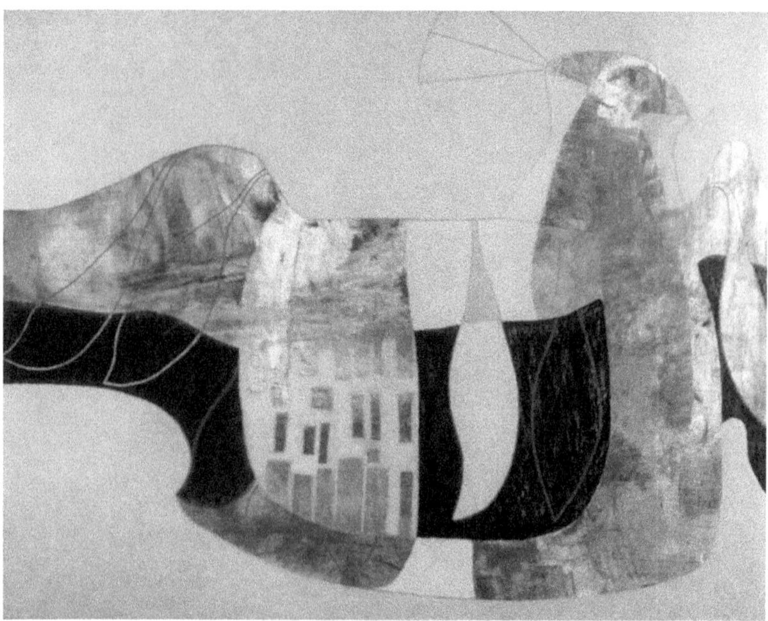

Figure 9.5. *Variaciones de ave número cinco*, painting by José "Pepe" Zúñiga, 1970. See color plate 3.

Esmeralda. Rodríguez said to his father, "You have an exceptional son. He has real talent."

In 1970, Pepe's *Variaciones de Ave Número Cinco* shared first prize at the Salón de la Plástica Mexicana with a painting by his friend Guillermo Ceniceros. In this work, Pepe reached a new level of refinement (see figure 9.5). He painted a giant bird with an oversized beak in a complex of rectangular and curved forms using pigments, different brushes, and spatulas to create a series of textures in grays and black on a yellow base. He divided the composition, a successful execution of the golden ratio, in zones of textures, shapes, line, and color. To lighten the heaviness of the middle section, he created Klimt-like rectangles of gray-green suspended in space. He did not then know the work of Gustav Klimt, but when he saw his paintings later in Vienna, he recognized the similarity. He refined the whole painting with details: thin lines descending from the bird's beak and red ones outlining the feathers. For him, it was musical, its strident yellow a loud forte, its blended grays and yellows a soft pianissimo. The Museo de Arte Moderno acquired it, and in the fall of 2013 it formed part of the retrospective exhibit on La Esmeralda.

Despite the pall hanging over the city and in many ways because of it, more opportunities opened now for Pepe and his friends, none of them close to the elite of abstract painters—Fernando García Ponce, Manuel Felguérez, Vicente Rojo, Lilia Carrillo—consecrated by the new intellectuals of the 1960s—Carlos Monsiváis, Juan García Ponce, José Emilio Pacheco, Carlos Fuentes, and José de la Colina.[43] In the course of the decade, art broke out in new directions, buoyed by the demographic explosion, the expansion in higher education, political mobilization, and a growing economy that drove an art market always eager for innovation. While new private galleries opened, Pepe and his friends, for the most part, still depended upon public sponsorship and the competitions convoked by Mexican industrialists in the private and state sectors. The CONCANACO (Confederación Nacional de Comercio) contest in 1969, convoked "to project new values in Mexican art," explicitly sought to channel youth's exuberance into the big tent of the "Mexican family" and the national narrative of Mexican history as artistic essence. Young painters created within "a historical tradition dating from the origins of our integration that expresses the sensibility of our aboriginal races."[44] Of the 7,000 works submitted from all over the country, 310 were chosen for exhibit in Mexico City in the fall of 1969. Practically all of these were rendered in diverse neofigurative or abstract styles, some coldly geometrical, others, like Armando Villagrán's winning *Adan y Eva*, rendered in magical realism overflowing with color and dance of pre-Hispanic allusion. Pepe had three paintings in this show. The press noted that "no one already anointed participated."[45]

Pepe exhibited and competed for prizes with his friends Armando Villagrán, Guillermo Ceniceros, and Gerardo Cantú. They pulled other friends into the whirl of contests and exhibits. Guillermo Zapfe got wind of the competition sponsored by the Sahagún government firm that made railroad cars. At the time he was short on money. "*Pinche negro*," he said to Pepe, "You have been winning these contests. Tell me how I can participate. If you tell me I have to paint trains or railroad tracks, . . . or whatever the hell I have to paint, help me!" "No, Zapfe," Pepe told him, "don't prostitute yourself. Look, you've already got your own style. The only thing you have to do is make sure you do it within the maximum parameters of the contest." Zapfe took first prize. They celebrated by getting drunk in his studio, the Vaticueva on the rooftop of a vecindad on Bajio Street.

Another afternoon, Pepe met his old friend Daniel Manrique in the Jardín de Arte in San Angel, where Daniel was selling his paintings. Although Messeguer and others had created the open-air art shows to

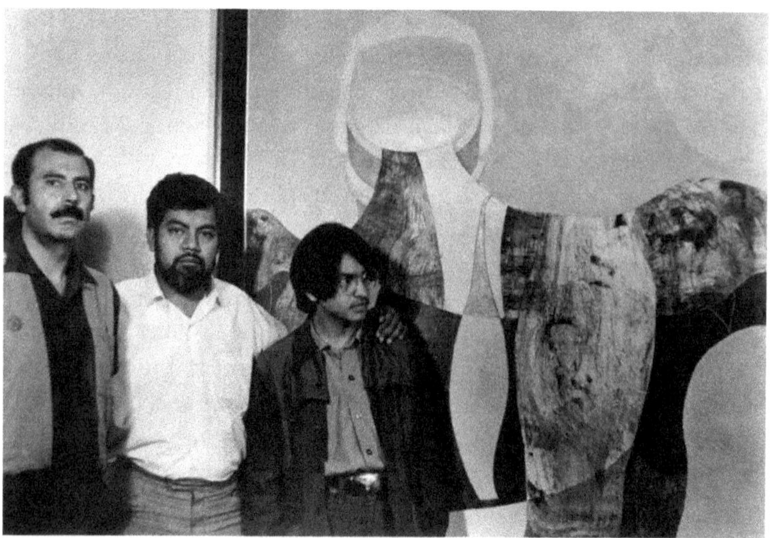

Figure 9.6. *Left to right*: José Luis, Pepe, and Pepe's cousin Arturo Colón. Black-and-white photograph, 1971.

strengthen the public presence of painting, for Pepe, to sell there was to admit mediocrity. He told Daniel he could get him into the exhibit circuit. Soon Daniel had a show with two other friends at the Instituto Francés para América Latina. They called it *Protesta Ambiental* (Environmental Protest). Daniel exhibited three paintings: one of a toilet with a tie, another of a Coca Cola bottle in the form of a crucifix, and another depicting an old Volkswagen raping a girl and a rich boy raping his motorcycle.[46] Daniel anticipated the iconoclastic, denunciatory work of young artists in the 1980s.

In January 1970 Pepe had a solo exhibit at the Instituto Francés. His was made up of less rebellious work in form, content, and style. In 1971 he won first prize in the contest sponsored by the state steel company, Altos Hornos de México. His painting, done in the manner of the *Ave Número Cinco*, depicted a figure that represented the foundry's steelmaking process in the form of a muscular male body, stylized but reminiscent of images of heroic worker masculinity within the Mexican school. When the telegram arrived, he feared someone had died. He had had the same fear when he received the telegram from Aguascalientes years earlier. This time, he had really won, and no one disqualified him. The family, with José Luis, happily went to the fancy Hacienda de los Morales in upscale Polanco to watch him receive the award (see figure 9.6).

Pedro Vargas, Agustín Lara's famous interpreter, sang. Altos Hornos gave the painting to President Luis Echeverría for his personal collection. When Pepe showed Antonio Rodríguez the pamphlet of Altos Hornos with a photo of the firm's president presenting Pepe with a check for thirty thousand pesos and a note indicating the painting had been given to Echeverría, Rodríguez took out his pen and crossed out Echeverría. As Minister of the Interior in the Díaz Ordaz government, he had been responsible for the massacre at Tlatelolco. Rodríguez had always been faithful to the regime. For him to blot out the president's name was an act indicative of a disintegrating revolutionary family.

Rodríguez played a role in Pepe's receiving a scholarship from the French government to study at the École des Arts Decoratifs in Paris in 1972. It had taken three years to get the scholarship. In 1970, scholarships had been canceled owing to the student protests, and in 1971, another student had won. Before leaving for Paris, Pepe learned from his friend Eugenio Brito that an earthquake had damaged the art school at Viña del Mar in Chile. With the help of Octavio Bajonero, Pepe's engraving teacher and director of the OPIC gallery of Santo Domingo in Tacubaya, Pepe organized an exhibit to raise money for the school and to support the democratically elected socialist government of Salvador Allende. Sixty-seven painters donated their work including José Luis Cuevas, David Alfaro Siqueiros, Rufino Tamayo, Fernando García Ponce, Vicente Rojo, Benito Messeguer, Raul Anguiano, Francisco Moreno Capdevila, Antonio Rodríguez Luna, Santos Balmori, and Juan Soriano. Around the union of art and democracy, the warring Mexican painters could come together. Brito would know now, thought Pepe, that the Mexican people were neither passive nor submissive.

10. Subjectivity and the Public Sphere

The Mature Art of José "Pepe" Zúñiga

In September 1972, Pepe Zúñiga boarded an Air France jet bound for Paris. Renewing and stretching his ten-month fellowship to attend the École des Arts Decoratifs, he stayed until December 1975. He returned to Paris in 1981 to complete his master's thesis. He came back to Mexico in 1983. His European experience marked him profoundly. He says it set him free. Often while there, he wished he could stay. Back home, he often wished he had. He felt he was more recognized there than he was in Mexico—he had exhibited in many places—not just the prestigious Salon de Mai in Paris, but elsewhere in France, and in Padua, Sardinia, and Montenegro. Nonetheless, he returned home. He became a professor and later director (1991–93) of La Esmeralda. He taught, painted, and exhibited primarily in Mexico City and lived in the family home on Soto Street in the Colonia Guerrero.

Although the focus of this book has been Pepe Zúñiga's education as a child and youth, the effects of the freedom-seeking, affective subjectivity forged through this education can only be demonstrated through subsequent events and processes. In this final chapter, we look at Pepe Zúñiga's mature art and that of his friends and age cohort as part of an uneven, partial, but nonetheless rapid process of democratization in Mexico, particularly in Mexico City. It began in the 1970s with the opening of the public sphere and the electoral system that eventually broke the PRI's control of the press and monopoly of political power. To a large degree, the young rebels of the 1960s created the pressure, the subjectivity, and, as they matured, the citizens for this democratization. Not fully liberated from the behaviors and conventions they decried, they nonetheless contributed to a transformation of politics, social mores, and artistic expression.

In 1987, Carlos Monsiváis left the directorship of *La Cultura en México*, the supplement to *Siempre!* he had edited since 1972. In his opinion, while the magazine had created a model for linking political criticism to culture, it no longer played the singular, vanguard role it had in the 1960s. Now it was one of several such magazines circulating in the public sphere along with an increasingly open daily press and a huge academic and international publishing apparatus. In addition, television had contributed to a massification and industrialization of culture.[1] José Agustín, a member of the editorial team that succeeded Monsiváis, lambasted the *Siempre!* supplement: he criticized its disdain for Mexican culture (from muralism to popular culture) and its authoritarian practices of consecrating some and destroying or marginalizing others.[2] He declared there was now neither political nor cultural hegemony in Mexico but rather a multiplicity of outlets for diverse opinion and aesthetic positions. Colloquial street language and lumpen literature had been mainstreamed. Cultural actors of diverse sorts had access to television, and aspiring artists and writers had access to workshops.[3] Both Monsiváis and Agustín wrote in the midst of a severe economic crisis begun in 1982 and the subsequent onslaught of neoliberal cuts in government spending. Yet both noted the government's critical continued support. In the arts, the state remained the major patron. It sponsored exhibits and museums and had introduced new cultural centers in the popular neighborhoods of Mexico City. In a program of decentralization, it financed Casas de Cultura, regional museums, art and literary competitions in Mexico's states—often complemented by support from banks and corporations, now ever more serious collectors, donors, and publishers. In the visual arts, art criticism flourished in Mexico City's major dailies, all of which had acquired cultural supplements. Art journalists formed a professional association in defense of freedom of expression. Although negatively affected by the economic downturn and the earthquake that devastated central Mexico City in 1985, private galleries rebounded in the 1990s as venues for painters, sculptors, and installation and performance artists in an increasingly globalized cultural marketplace.

As mature artists, Pepe and his friends from La Esmeralda and the Museum of Anthropology whom we have met through his story contributed to the diversity and vitality of this public sphere and its cultural landscape. They paint in different styles. Aside from participating in the making of dozens of Mexican and Hollywood films and designing sets for Mexico City theater, Octavio Ocampo made an exceptionally successful career painting portraits of celebrities in surrealist complexity—among them the Mexican presidents Miguel Alemán and José López Portillo, Jane Fonda, Jimmy Carter, Cesar Chávez, Marilyn Monroe, John Lennon, and the Virgin of Guadalupe. His unique style draws from the world of entertainment in which he has been immersed. A powerful easel painter of his native northern mountainscapes and of sensitive, thoughtful women, Guillermo Ceniceros has executed monumental murals commissioned by Mexican state and federal governments and wealthy entrepreneurs. Thousands who pass through the Copilco or Tacubaya metro stations can follow his colorful, powerfully narrated stories of the Aztecs' journey from Aztlán to Tenochtitlán, of the Spanish conquest, and of world (not just European and Mexican) art. His recently completed mural, *History of the Mexican People through Their Constitution*, rises five stories high in the Cámara de Diputados. Before his death in 2010, Daniel Manrique dedicated himself to painting the walls of Tepito. Whereas Oscar Lewis had rendered Tepito grim, violent, and pathological in his 1961 classic *The Children of Sánchez*, Manrique, who knew it much better, drew out its extraordinary vitality, turning its culture into a source of local pride and artistic activism. In the 1970s and 1980s, Manrique's Tepito Arte Acá made the barrio's culture not only legible but obligatory reading for the elite and middle classes whom it had terrified and disgusted.

Rogelio Naranjo became one of Mexico's most illustrious caricaturists, his piercing political criticisms ever more present in the gradually more open Mexican press. Byron Gálvez enjoyed a successful career, kicked off in 1964 when the actor Vincent Price bought up all the works from his first solo exhibit. In his mature painting, Gálvez combined elements of abstract and figurative art with expressionist verve to create a powerful personal language of sensual form and color. Guillermo Zapfe won recognition for his abstract painting based on his rendering of Chinese script and graphic techniques. In 1984, he took first prize in the second Bienal de Pintura Rufino Tamayo, established by Tamayo with support from the Instituto Nacional de Bellas Artes and government of Oaxaca. Zapfe taught with Pepe at the Esmeralda until his death in 1992 at the age of 59. Aurelio Pescina moved to San Luis Potosí but returned on weekends to sell his folkloric and telluric paintings in the Mexico City Jardines del Arte. Never successful in the manner of his youthful colleagues, this most-sought-after painter at the Museo de Antropología in 1964 died at the age of 48. Armando Villagrán died young as well from alcoholism after a successful career in commercial design.

Juan Castañeda, building on his early experience in construction work and as assistant to Benito Messeguer, focused on metal sculpture and trended in painting toward pop art: he depicted women's fashions, stylizing the paper pattern, the mannequin, and the living model. He became director of the new Centro de Artes Visuales of the Aguascalientes Instituto Cultural, the catalyst for local creativity, exhibits, and the integration of a broader Mexican and international artistic production. Like Juan, other friends and Pepe himself have participated in this process of artistic decentralization. Javier Arévalo, Cuauhtémoc Zamudio, and Gerardo Cantú—all of whom painted with Pepe at the Museo de Antropología—became major artists working out of Guadalajara and Monterrey, respectively. Guillermo Ceniceros exhibited, created murals, and opened museums in Durango, where he was born, and Nuevo León, where he grew up. Byron Gálvez's sculptures and murals adorn the city of Pachuca in his native state of Hidalgo. Pepe Zúñiga taught and exhibited in Oaxaca, which became the most important of Mexico's regional art centers under the leadership of Francisco Toledo.

Felida Medina early on launched a spectacular career as a scenographer. She belonged to the world of theater that produced some of the city's earliest and most articulate feminists. Pepe's female painter friends moved more slowly into the public light—out of modesty, self-effacement, subordination to family, and, most likely, the dominion of men in their field. But move they did. Elva Garma teaches at the university in Aguascalientes. Since she painted works of traditional women's embroidery as a student at La Esmeralda, Elva had practiced a playful, ironic feminism. As her husband, Juan, dressed women in high fashion, Elva began to undress them. She paints canvases of postcards protruding from envelopes to reveal a shapely leg in a fishnet stocking or a bare breast. In their sheer plastic elegance and humor they parody pornography. She renders icons of Mexican nationalism with surrealist, Dalí-esque humor and in terms of a feminist critique, a gentle version of the neomexicanist style that arose in the late 1980s. She paints lucha libre wrestlers and landscapes so luxuriant that she cannot resist a leafy branch, a flower, a bit of a tree trunk, jumping out in three dimensions onto the frame. She is commercially successful with a devoted national and international following. Esther González, wife of Guillermo Ceniceros, worked with new materials in engraving for many years. In the 1970s and 1980s, she won prizes in engraving, painting, and drawing in the Salón de la Plástica Mexicana.

Recently she completed her "thesis," a large exquisite opus of Byzantine religious painting. This work involved many years of intense study and journeys through the Balkans and Turkey as Esther sought and found in Byzantine religious symbols the pure essence of the element of the symbol itself—pure form, she says, with no previous lineage or possibility of manipulation.[4] Many of her Byzantine paintings she has done on Mexican *amate* (bark) paper, and many she has exhibited in the Balkans. In 2011, she contributed a portrait of Sor Juana Inés de la Cruz to the new women's museum in Mexico City and has been recognized as a singular Mexican woman painter by Elisa García Barragán, director of the Instituto de Estudios Estéticos of UNAM.

Guillermo Ceniceros refers to his generation as "forgotten." As many of them including Guillermo are widely recognized as distinguished individual painters, it is perhaps more accurate to see them—as he also does—as an age cohort (mostly born between 1935 and 1945) wedged between more celebrated cohorts—artists identified with the Ruptura (José Luis Cuevas, Manuel Felguérez, Vicente Rojo, Lilia Carrillo, Fernando García Ponce) and the politically radical collectives that came out of 1968 and spawned a deeply iconoclastic art in the 1980s. While close in age to some of the Ruptura artists, Guillermo and Pepe's cohort was still studying when the abstract artists won dominance in the mid-1960s. Although they supported the political protests of 1968 in different ways, they were for the most part out of school and launching careers when radicalism swept institutions of higher education and drew younger artists and activists into collectives that challenged "bourgeois" art—its individualist character, its commercialization and state dependence, its exhibit sites, publics, award system, and lack of political power and intent. In the 1970s, both the elite of abstract artists and the "*grupos*" eager to bring art to the masses through alternative media (posters, fliers, Super 8 film, wall art, happenings, etc.) suppressed the spirit of individual liberty central to the youth movement of the 1960s and to the Ruptura movement itself. In the words of art critic Teresa del Conde, they "deindividuated."[5] Although del Conde wrote that no one paid any attention to them, the grupos' public art contributed to the opening of the public sphere: they regarded it as a necessary representation of alternative, democratic opinion in a still controlled and censored environment, and they set the stage for a vigorous expression of artists from the popular sectors.[6] But at the same time, they subordinated themselves to rigid structural paradigms in politics and culture in the interest of overturning the "system." By the end of the 1970s, these movements had all imploded, under the weight of their own self-imposed repression, the difficulties of collective work, and their rejection of the market and state support. One of those that persisted was Tepito Arte Acá. Firmly rooted in the community, never dogmatic, never associated with the university or the radical political movements it spawned, Tepito Arte Acá served as inspiration, catalyst, and model for subsequent community-based artists and art movements.

Art historians and curators jump immediately in their post-1970s narrative to a cohort of identity artists born in the late 1940s and 1950s. They emerged in the 1980s from the disbanding of the grupos, to which many had belonged.[7] They worked in the midst of a series of disasters. The Mexican Miracle vanished in 1982 with the collapse of the peso. Neoliberal shrinking of public expenditures followed. In 1985, the earthquake leveled large swathes of the city and buried thousands of citizens. It shook faith in technology and the built environment. By the late 1980s, the AIDS epidemic claimed hundreds of lives in a shockingly short period of time. Each destructive catastrophe fostered creativity. The economic downturn required new, individual strategies for survival and brought thousands of women into the labor force to enlarge the base for feminist perspectives. Out of the earthquake emerged active, militant citizens from the popular barrios. The AIDS epidemic catalyzed the formation of an equally active, militant gay community and its supporters. Within this ambience, young artists, most of whom were born between 1950 and 1960, particularly feminists, gays, and urban punk artists, adopted Mexican symbols—patriotic, religious, historical, artistic, and quotidian—to challenge the repressive sociopolitical order and the modernist aesthetic regime.[8] Unlike previous generations, they explicitly linked sociopolitical repression to patriarchy and heteronormative sexuality. Much in keeping with postmodernist philosophy (Judith Butler, Michel Foucault, Julia Kristeva, Jacques Lacan), they depicted the body—most often their own in a fiercely autobiographical, unabashedly individual public style—as a social-political field scarred by society's withering inscriptions.[9] Commenting on the work of Enrique Guzmán (1952–1986), Carlos Monsiváis wrote: "He gives to bad taste a clear intentionality . . . his most appropriate still life—in a panorama of romances presided over by toilets—consists of a bottle of mineral water and a toilet plunger."[10] In *O Santa Bandera*, dedicated to Guzmán, Nahum Zenil (b. 1946) painted himself, his anus penetrated by a pole bearing the Mexican flag.

Usually strongly figurative in the interest of reaching a broader audience with a clear political-social message, these artists often catered to specific, emerging publics and were comfortable with practices of self-promotion necessary in an increasingly global, competitive market.[11] One of the most sensitive paintings representative of this generation is *Me quiero morir*, by Julio Galán (1959–2006). In the center of this work, Galán painted a fragile, almost androgenous adolescent boy. Christopher Robin, the pampered, protected middle-class child, has come into sexual-affective awareness. He is in pain. His eyes are closed, his mouth turned downward. He is on the verge of tears. His arms and delicate thin fingers rise upward in the muted anguish of a religious martyr. His wrists are cuffed on one side by a chain of heavy metal rings and on the other by a slender, braided, seemingly embroidered chain. Separating the discretely masculine from the discretely feminine, these chains meet to create behind him a map of Mexico. Out of his jacket pocket rises an oversized Mexican flag. The portrait is framed in middle-class kitsch—chains of pink flowers and curlicues painted on wood. Above the boy's head is a string of *papel china* that decorates every Mexican fiesta. The sheets of paper spell out MEQUIEROMORIR. Said the painter from Múzquiz, Coahuila, "Painting allowed me to breathe. I was dying." Galán spent most of his career in New York, where he fashioned himself as a walking artistic performance—he could show up straight, transvestite, or queer.[12]

If we look at a cohort of painters of Pepe's "sandwiched" generation exhibiting in Mexico City in the 1970s and 1980s, we see a different sensibility from that of painters Galán, Guzmán, and Zenil or the political works of the graphic and performance artists.[13] We uncover certain shared tendencies in technique, subject matter, and intent in a group that is predominantly male with strong female participation. Although some may paint murals or work in engraving, sculpture, or architecture, their easel painting is a highly conscious individualized art, an expression of personal feelings and visions, sentiment and ideas, biographies and memories, and their imagined unconscious within an orthodox format of composition, technique, and standard Western notions of beauty. As work of personal expression, it is subjective in ways that social realism and geometric abstraction pretended not to be. Many incorporated new materials, but few ventured into video, mixed media, or installation or performance art as these gained ground in Mexico City's public sphere. They were for the most part formally trained in Mexico and abroad (Paris, London, New York). Most had attended La Esmeralda or the Academia de San Carlos, where some participated in the 1965 rebellion and/or all drew inspiration from Santos Balmori and Antonio Rodríguez Luna. They judged each others' work—and critics judged them—on the basis of formal techniques of composition, color, line, and volume. Good art for them and their critics combined mastery of technique with emotional and intellectual power and imagination. Many were fascinated within a modernist frame with the autonomy of painterly qualities and problems of perception and communication.[14] Their work revealed different degrees of philosophical and conceptual depth. They were inspired by surrealist painters and magical realism, expressionism, and existentialism, cubism, Oriental philosophy and calligraphy, Greek sculpture, even art nouveau. Some remained resolutely figurative in the midst of fashionable abstraction in the 1970s. Others experimented with, then abandoned, abstraction. Women artists—Susana Sierra, Irma Grizá, Irma Palacios, and Beatriz Zamora—stayed more or less abstract.[15]

Critics inevitably hailed them as expressing liberty in new poetic languages even as they depicted different existential positions. Although they strongly separated themselves from traditional plastic nationalism and stylistic dogma, most drew to some degree on a Mexican repertoire—pre-Hispanic sculpture and symbols (José Francisco, Xavier Esqueda, Carlos Olachea, Irma Grizá, Leticia Ocharán, Leonel Maciel), regional landscapes (Guillermo Ceniceros, José Francisco, Leticia Ocharán, Leonel Maciel, Pepe Zúñiga) and degraded cityscapes (Falfán), local flora, fauna and their indigenous representations (Emilio Ortiz), objects of popular culture ranging from traditional toys, embroidery, and boleros to a replica middle-class living room in 1960s Mexico City (Emilio Ortiz, Xavier Esqueda, José Francisco, Leonel Maciel).[16] They used such a repertoire as background or symbol to reveal the individual psyche or as metaphor or pretext for expressing the painterly self.

They necessarily claim distance and individuation in their easel painting from the historical narrative of the Mexican school and its iconic bodies—the muscular industrial worker, the poker-faced, pajama-clad campesino ready to strike with machete or gun, mother earth, the Virgin, or the prostitute. They are nonetheless, unlike younger radicals, mostly disembodied in their painting despite their commitment to expressing themselves. Male artists might paint the body as metaphor or symbol of existential angst or the female body as incarnating beauty, inspiration, emotion, sexuality, or sin and degradation as represented in centuries of Western art. By contrast, female artists Susana Sierra, Beatriz Zamora, and Irma Grizá do not paint this classical female body. While it is clear to the viewer that the women's paintings represent a tremendous force of body/mind/emotion and are distant from the depersonalized, highly masculinist geometric structuralism that dominated Mexican abstract art in the 1970s, the body itself is absent from their rationally thought-out explosions of color, form, and rhythm. Although Beatriz Zamora paints only in black forms, lines, and textures, black represents for her a primordial freedom.[17] By contrast, the work of Leticia Ocharán (b. 1942) is embodied but not in a classical fashion. In murals, paintings, and engravings, she lyrically, sensually, and graphically depicts female genitalia in and out of love acts in her desire to break the Western code of sexual/gender representation.[18] She anticipates younger feminist artists who use the female body to unmask patriarchy, but her expression is more positive than iconoclastic. She affirmed women's right to sexual pleasure.

The male artists' expression of themselves—their feelings, subconscious thoughts, dreams, nightmares—are mostly cerebral rather than corporeal. In this opening up of their souls, many drew inspiration from the female surrealists who had worked and lived in Mexico—Remedios Barro, Leonora Carrington, and Alice Rahon—just as younger artists like Julio Galán and Nahum Zenil looked to Frida Kahlo as a model for their thoroughly embodied autobiographical painting.[19] Although several (Emilio Ortiz, Alfredo Falfán, Byron Gálvez et al.) expressed in their representation of the male body the existentialist sentiment of Nueva Presencia—that is, a distinctly masculinist, existentialist solitude and anguish before a brutal world—theirs is less an exploration of the body than an intellectual position symbolized in the human figure. Nonetheless it is an expression of individual masculine emotion and subjectivity. These male painters seemed unafraid to reveal their lack of psychic control and emotional vulnerability. This expression of vulnerability is most acute in the work of Arturo Rivera (b. 1945), the only artist who paints (exquisitely) medicalized, tormented, and fragile naked male (and some female) bodies. His is not the social-political statement made by Julio Galán, Enrique Guzmán, and others born after 1950 nor that of early 1960s existential solitude in a hostile world. He paints his own palpable inner terror. In an interview he gave in 2006 to Miguel Angel Ceballos for *El Universal*, he discussed his childhood fascination with fetuses in formaldehyde, dessicated animals, rats he dissected, operations he watched in hospitals, and bones he recovered from the common grave at the Panteón Nacional.[20] He told the journalist that he painted to avoid slipping over the edge into insanity. He had inherited depression from his father and suffered paralyzing panic attacks momentarily soothed by alcohol, marijuana, and, most effectively, painting. Within the overall trajectory of this period in Mexican painting, Rivera's public outing of his inner terror speaks to an ongoing opening up of masculine sensibility and emotion, a rational, sober admission of vulnerability as opposed to Paz's depiction of masculine emotional outbursts in states of inebriation.

In a partial, fragmented way, these men bring into public view the feminization of male sensibility we have detected in Pepe's life and in the youth movement of the 1960s. Feminization we have been careful to define with reference to a socially constructed essentialism identified with the Enlightenment: women as feeling, love, and openness versus masculine closedness, rationality, science, and history. When we search for such expression in the painting of this group, we need to consider that within this paradigm, modernist painting had remained a highly masculinist art form. It was not as acceptable an outlet for the expression of male sentiments of self and love as the genres of literature, poetry, drama, and music. Young Mexican rebels of the 1960s were much more at ease with emotion in the latter genres than in painting, despite young painters' desire for such self-expression. In the Mexican school, they could find models in sculpture as Pepe had in Francisco Zúñiga's sensuous rendering of Mexican indigenous women. However, mural painting had been militantly, often violently masculinist in its emphasis on class struggle. It was exceptionally repressive of the symbolic feminine.[21] For Mexican school painters, woman was no muse, no expression of positive sexuality, fantasy, and pleasure, but rather a fertile body that produced food and children or a mother who cared for children and soothed male suffering. She stood by sacrificing while men made history and was there to pick up and nurse with tearful tragic stoicism those who had fallen in that epic. Or she herself had fallen into despicable prostitution. Diego Rivera was an exception in his iconization of the women of the Tehuantepec Isthmus. He painted them as symbols of sensuality and sexuality uniting the eternal female of Western art to fashionable primitivism. Frida Kahlo transformed the Tehuana as a painterly symbol when she took Tehuana garb to declare her agency and to explore and express her body and inner feelings as a modern woman.

When we look at the painting of several men in Pepe's age cohort in Mexico City, we encounter an appropriation of the broader Western paradigm of the feminine to express an expanding range of their own emotional experience. Critics noted how in the early 1980s, Alfredo Falfán abandoned the darkness of his existential work associated with Nueva Presencia and his later engagement with geometric abstraction to celebrate a newfound freedom he expressed in a riot of color and erotic female bodies.[22] Guillermo Ceniceros's most sensitive and emotionally moving easel painting is of women. His female figures are more than traditional muses. In their intelligence, sustained reflection, and palpable sympathy, they are *compañeras*.[23] Byron Gálvez's gloomy, stranded male figures are reminiscent of early 1960s existentialism, but his female figures, seemingly deliberately juxtaposed, are an ever-expanding explosion of color, liberty, sensuality, and movement. If they have an African core and form drawn from Picasso and resemble the muscular bodies of Santos Balmori's women striding across the desert and beaches of North Africa, they are in their voluptuous, pulsating sexuality distinctly American. Critic Roberto Vallarino saw them as at once Afro Cuban and dancing to jazz. "Byron's women speak of love and desire," he wrote, "They are *bloques de ternura*—blocks of tenderness."[24]

In Leonel Maciel, the feminization of male sensibility is depicted not through the mature female body but rather in the fantastic, radiantly colored dreams of children. In his 1981 exhibit *Las cosas de niños*, he painted to engage children in a romping nocturnal train ride full of games, candy, toy carts and airplanes, singing crickets, ice cream cones, cats, grandmothers, and jumping elves—as if the songs of Cri-Cri had come alive in Maciel's wild, outsized figures frolicking in the tropical exuberance of his native Guerrero.[25] Children were not his only medium. In 1988 at the Instituto Francés de América Latina, he exhibited paintings inspired by the bolero, the popular ballad of love won and lost, of passion and pain interpreted by both female (e.g., María Luisa Landín) and male vocalists (e.g., Agustín Lara) that had shaped the romantic sensibility and vulnerability of his generation as well as that of his parents.

At the subjective level of the citizen creator or viewer, the feminization of masculinity in this easel painting expresses a sensibility of tenderness and empathy. It is a subtle, indispensable way of communicating an anti-authoritarian sentiment and longing for freedom and expression that animated members of this generation in their youth and matured with them and the city's social-political expression. It has been every bit as important to a democratizing public sphere as rights-claiming poster art or antipatriarchal performance art. Indeed, in this particular city, these appear to have been complementary, even creatively interdependent, despite their likely disagreements about the definition of art.

In Pepe Zúñiga's painting in the 1970s and 1980s, the feminization of masculinity takes a further turn. In 1984, he presented *Primavera* in an exhibit at the Estela Shapiro gallery, one of several he had had there and in other places in the city after 1977. Gone from this carefully created composition of seductive color were the gangly geometric shapes, the violent oranges and yellows, and the thick paste he had applied to canvas in the late 1960s. For some time, critics had noted a new delicacy in his work achieved through meticulous control. The formidable analyst Raquel Tibol noted that he trusted "more in the constructive than in the tensions of the spirit, more in controlled elegance than in improvisation."[26] Hugo Covantes found his paintings full of "*pulcritud y limpieza*" (beauty and purity). "Zúñiga," he wrote, "seeks an order distinct from nature's, transforming its terms, bringing the plastic idea to a sensation of form, converting an element of nature into a more general concept within a language of these forms."[27] Antonio Rodríguez explained his maturation in essentialist terms. He wrote that Zúñiga's innate *Mexicanidad*—located in a delirium of color, light, passion, spontaneity, and tropical magic—had been tempered by the refinement, rationality, and opaline light of Paris and the ancient cultures of the Mediterranean filtered through the crystalline luminosity of Delphi, Corinth, the Parthenon, Crete, and Sardinia.[28]

In *La primavera*, we see he now worked with grays, for which he had earlier envied Rufino Tamayo (see figure 10.1). Blues, greens, aquas, violets, and white predominate. The colors could be blurred and their contrasts softened. We also see the artist's own essentialization as waves of bright greens (Mexico) are filtered through a (European) window into pastels of lemon and beige. He now painted thinly to draw out the weave of the canvas. Reducing matter to visual textures, he sought to convey a serene, spiritual quality.[29]

In this painting, Pepe does not probe his subconscious. Rather, he conveys the experience of loving sexual communication. The mountains undulate as human bodies in affectionate embrace. They are a metaphor for the body that pushes against modernism's constraints, for while they may represent the eternal feminine, they are interchangeable male/female bodies lacking gender specificity. He had painted something similar but less subtle in 1977 in *Cazadores de amantes*—two lovers of unclear gender identity engaged in oral sex. In *Tema para un poeta*, exhibited in 1990 at the Instituto Francés de América Latina, he is more explicit (see figure 10.2). He paints the erect penis of a man emerging from the sea. Inspired by a poem of the Colombian writer German Pardo García, he painted a male figure, a stylized phallic silhouette, wrapped in a placenta through which flow female genitalia. The placenta mirrors the masculine body—it not only embraces and protects it, it replicates, shadows, and appears to be part of it.

None of the sexual, spiritual darkness that tortured the poet Pardo

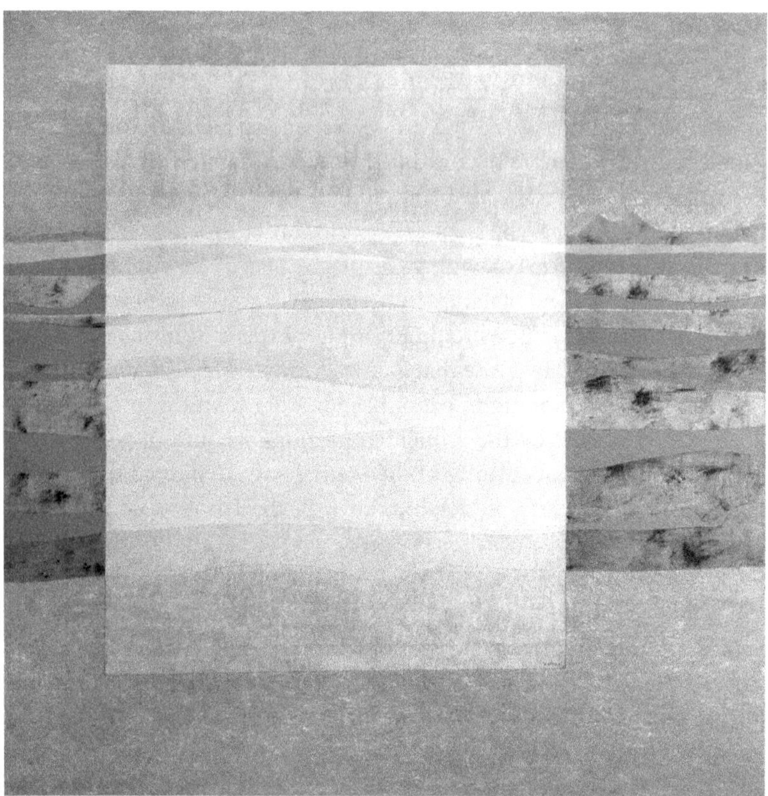

Figure 10.1. *La primavera*, painting by José "Pepe" Zúñiga, 1984. See color plate 4.

García came through in this painting. There was no conflict, no hostility, no complexity—none of the violence, struggle, and "frenzied disorientation" Enrique Gual had detected in his work in 1968. Now Pepe Zúñiga knew what he wanted to say. Although critic Francisco Fernández wrote that his lack of drama was a potential weakness, giving his work a decorative potentiality, he recognized that in simplicity was also strength.[30] The artist's rendering of sexuality shorn of objectification and abjection, of violence, brutality, or lust—those expressions of unequal power that scar the body and the soul—had a communicative force. Leticia Ocharán noted that "He paints for his time." "Love populates his work!" she wrote enthusiastically in the cultural supplement to *Novedades*. In *Segun el cristal como se mira* and other works exhibited at Estela Shapiro's gallery in 1984, Ocharán saw "men loving women, men loving men, women loving women." "These genitalia are loving," she exclaimed. "They inspire

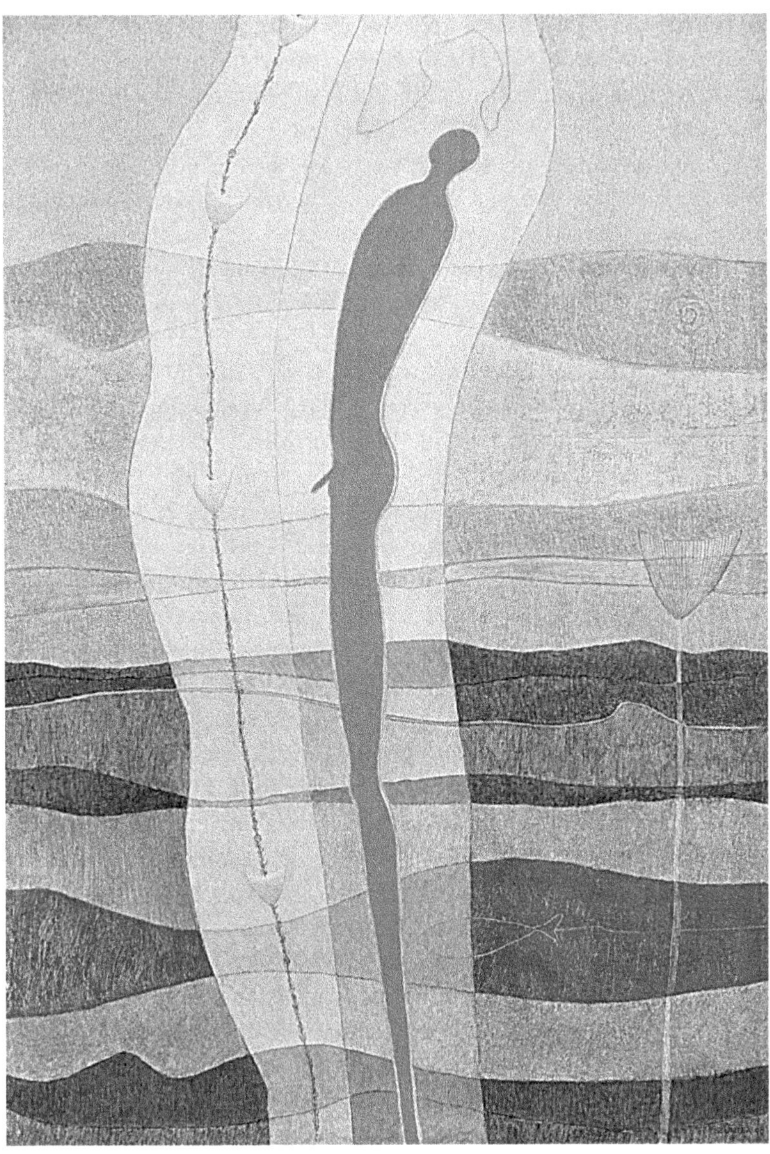

Figure 10.2. *Tema para un poeta*, painting by José "Pepe" Zúñiga, 1990. See color plate 5.

tenderness and need to live in communion with the heart."[31] As noted, Ocharán was one of the first women artists in the post-1960 period to explore female sexuality as an expression of pleasure and a right, an important statement in a country and an art world dubbed *mojigato* (prudish, repressed, and hypocritical) by art historian and critic Jorge Alberto Manrique.[32] She was also a major art critic writing for various cultural supplements of the daily newspapers, new cultural/political magazines, like Octavio Paz's *Plural* (1972–1976), and ephemeral ones, like *Zurda*, that attempted to break new artistic and political terrain in the 1970s and 1980s.[33]

Through Zúñiga's chromatic window, wrote critic Julio Amador, "He lets us slip into the loving encounter."[34] His human figures possessed a palpable skin. "Their intention is to touch and to be touched by the intimacy of the spectator."[35] "When people went to my exhibits," Pepe told me, "they said my painting was more tempered and measured—more thought out. A little more intellectual. A little less visceral. Rationality won out over emotion but as a means to communicate feeling. I was looking for a language that everyone could understand. This level of eroticism in figurative composition was not typical of my generation. It was something I was developing through experiences in my personal life. It is not the obvious eroticism of my Oaxacan compatriot Francisco Toledo, who renders sex in naked candor, or José Luis Cuevas, who rendered it through the grotesque and marginal. Nor is it like Nahum Zenil's self-portraits of penises and phallic objects. Nahum is ten years younger than I am, another generation. These are great painters, but I was trying to do something else. I was trying to create an aesthetic eroticism. It's difficult for me to explain from where it comes. But Mexico is such a hypocritical country in sexual matters—so repressed! When I got to Europe and traveled, I saw the museums and I saw how the people lived. It was not the perversion people thought but rather a freedom if we are speaking of eroticism. Many of us don't know our own bodies. If through a visual language I could motivate people into communion with what I was feeling, then I could give something as an artist.

"On a personal level, I began to have my intimate, sexual experiences and as a sensitive person, I began to project them. I read that the artist intuits what is latent in society, what wants to get out and be free. I think that is true. I must mention again the repression I felt in Mexico and that other young people suffered, particularly from their parents. The mere fact of wanting to be a painter! My father objected! Listen, remember that he even mutilated my painting of Luz Jiménez—he cut off her legs!

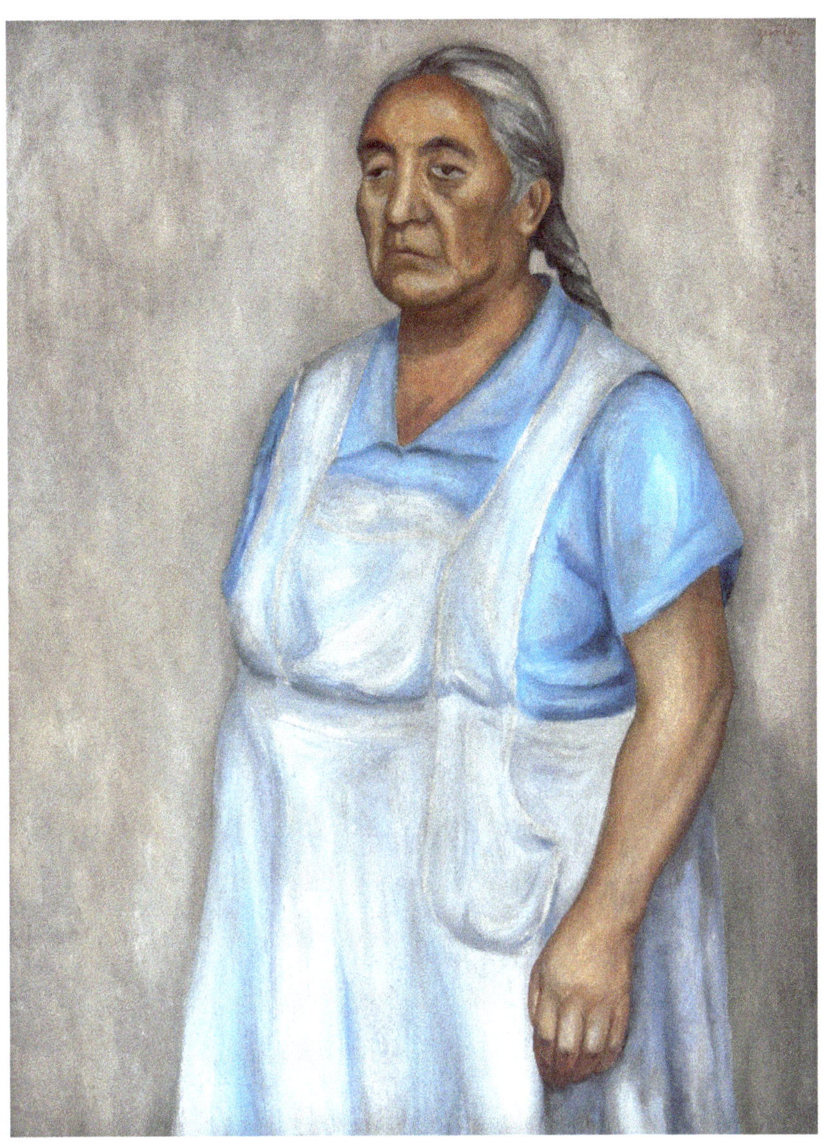

Plate 1. *Doña Luz Jiménez*, painting by José “Pepe” Zúñiga, 1960.

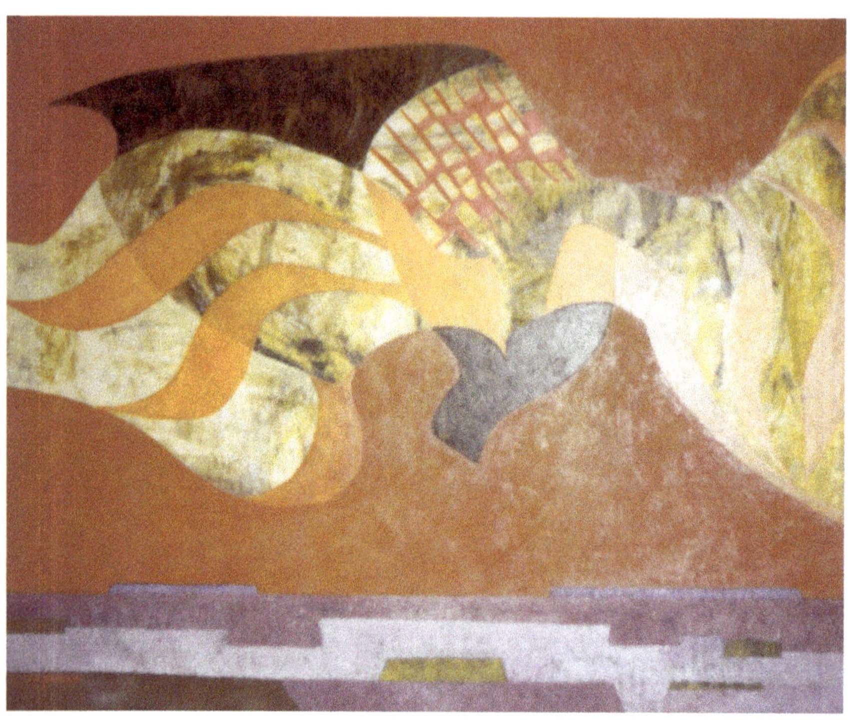

Plate 2. *El pájaro de Tlatelolco*, painting by José "Pepe" Zúñiga, 1968.

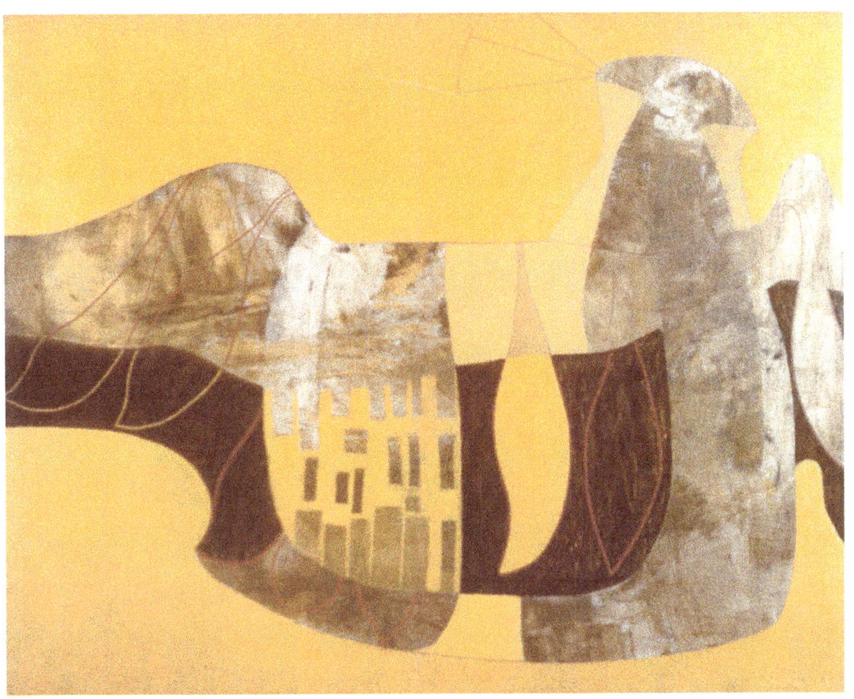

Plate 3. *Variaciones de ave número cinco*, painting by José "Pepe" Zúñiga, 1970.

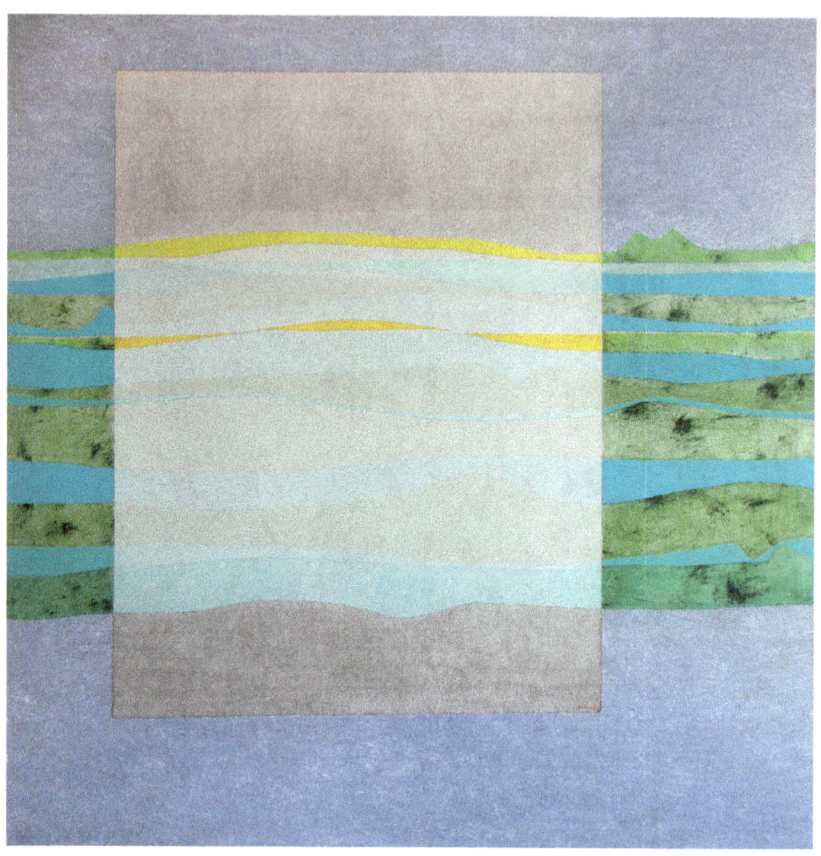

Plate 4. *La primavera*, painting by José "Pepe" Zúñiga, 1984.

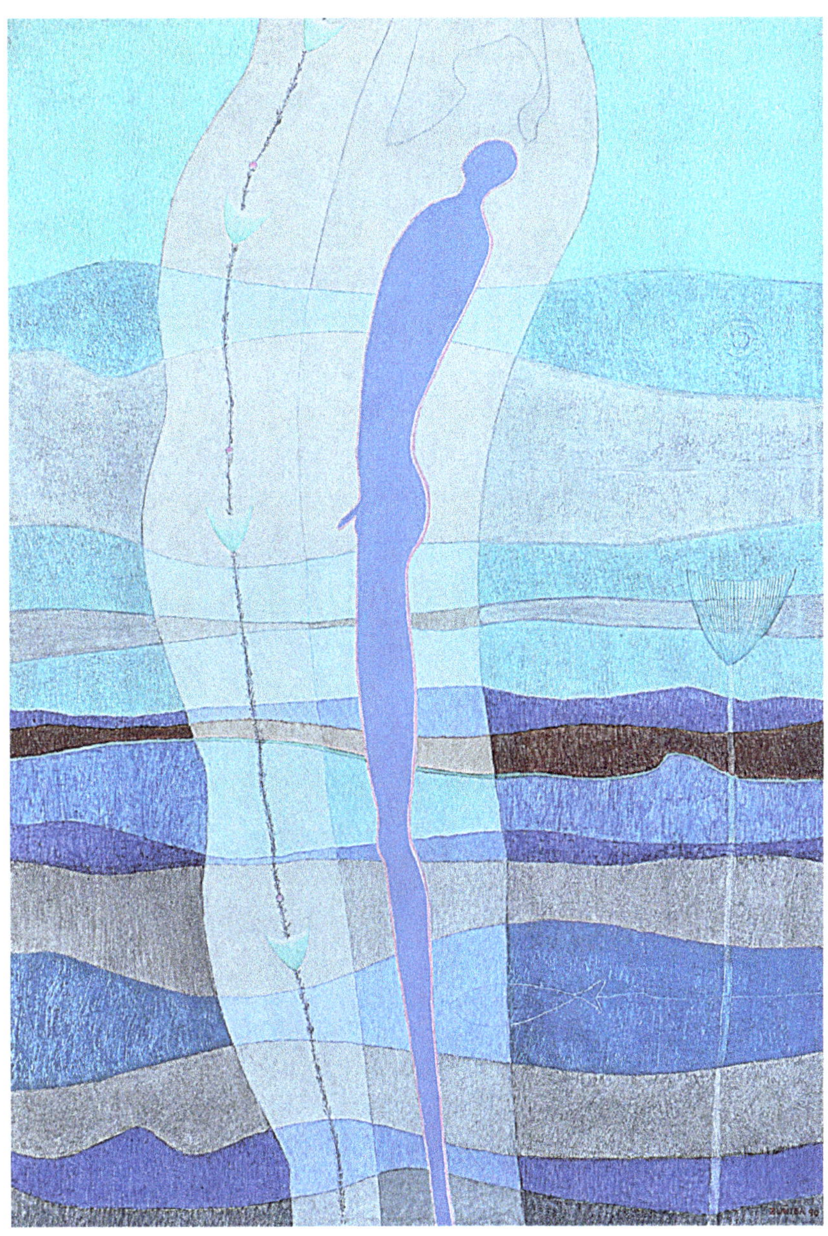

Plate 5. *Tema para un poeta*, painting by José "Pepe" Zúñiga, 1990.

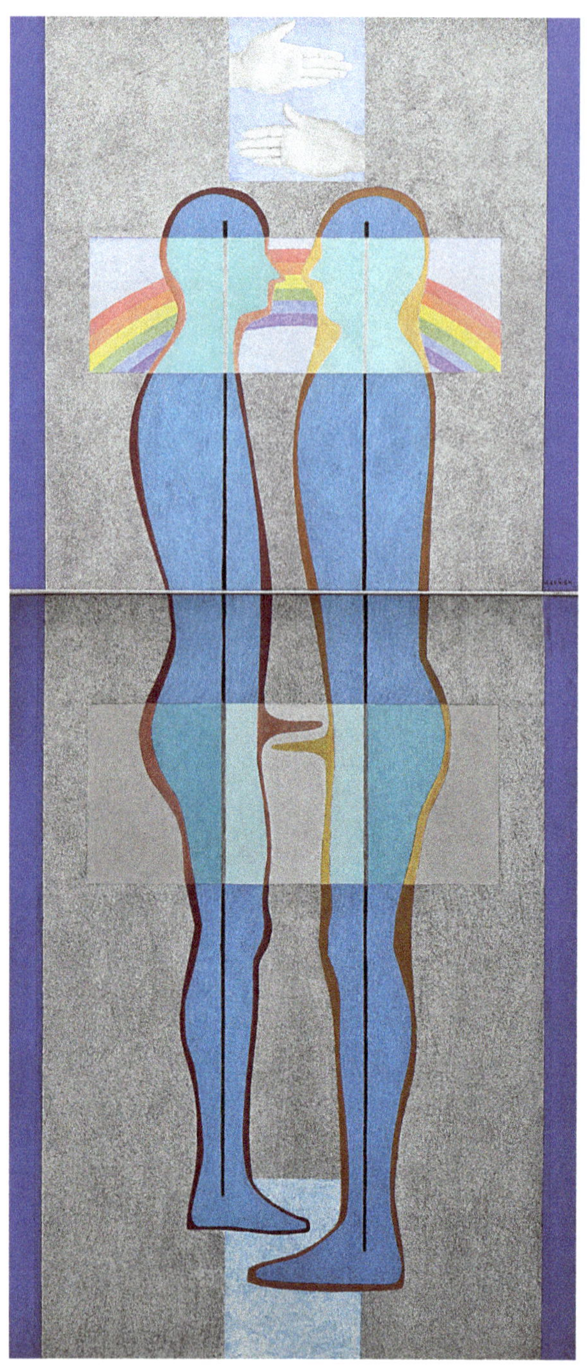

Plate 6. *Homenaje a un amigo conocido*, painting by José “Pepe” Zúñiga, 1992.

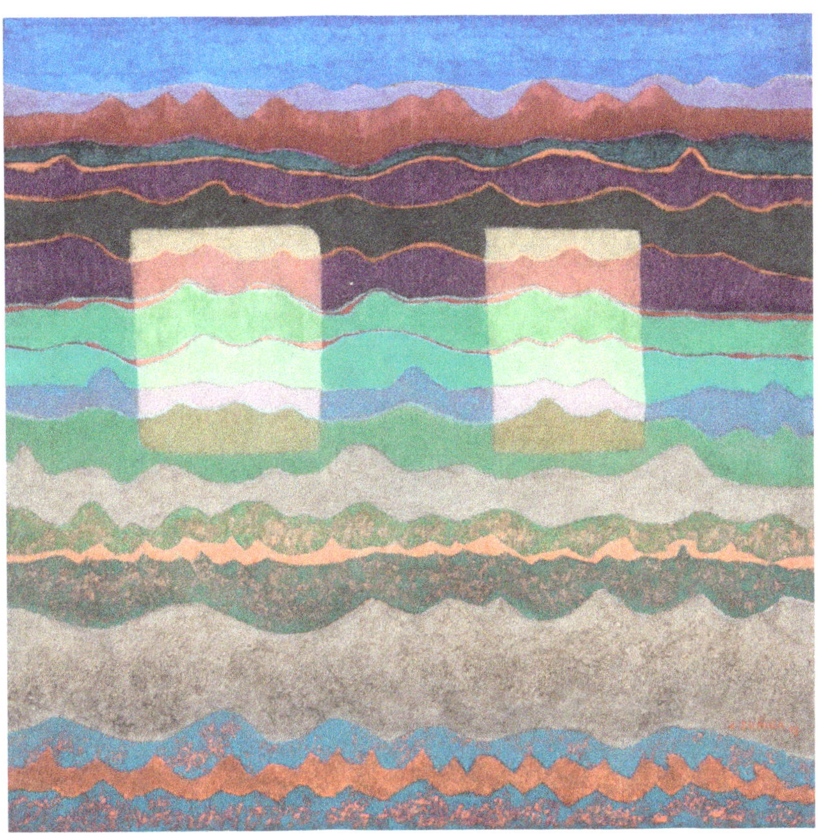

Plate 7. *Paisaje Zapoteco*, painting by José "Pepe" Zúñiga, 1998.

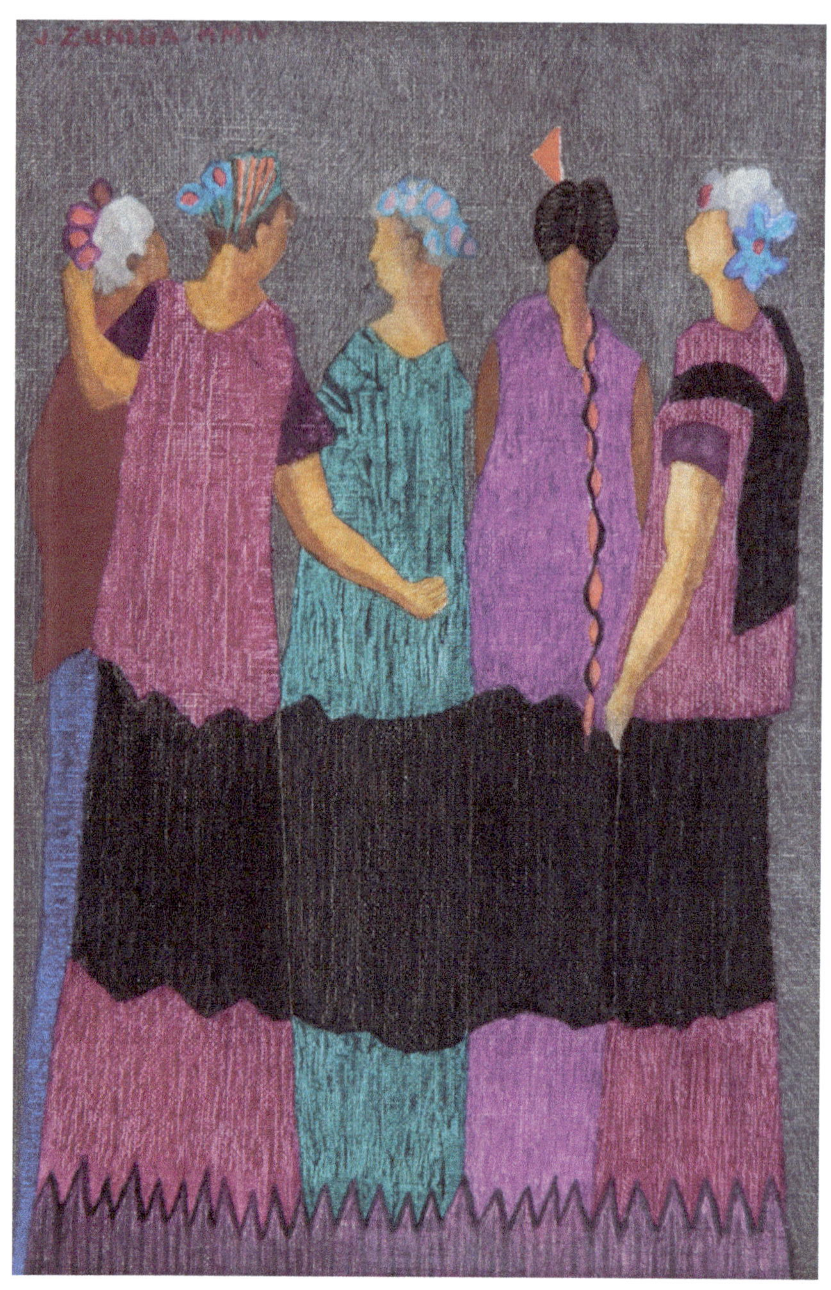

Plate 8. *Las Juchitecas*, painting by José "Pepe" Zúñiga, 2004.

Later on he was more accepting but he always said I was a teacher, never a painter, because a painter was thought to be full of vices, homosexual, full of stupidities. By contrast, the Europeans valued the artist, and Europe set me free!"

What inspired you in European art, I asked. "So much that it is difficult to say precisely what, but beginning with the small sculptures of female figures I saw in the Louvre. Then I melted upon seeing Rodin's sculptures of nude men and women, especially *The Walking Man*, cast in bronze without head or arms, yet poised for vigorous stride. I am speaking of the visual experiences I might have had because I really didn't learn much in my classes at the École des Arts Decoratifs. I had already studied many years and was way ahead of the other students. My professor recognized this and let me travel in return for giving him sketches of what I saw. And I traveled everywhere—to England, Spain, Italy, Yugoslavia, Germany, Holland, Belgium, Greece, Vienna, Turkey. Shortly after I arrived, I went to England and visited Felipe Ehrenberg and his wife, Martha Hellion, who were living in a commune in Exeter where everyone was into astrology, sex, and marijuana. I hated marijuana. It reminded me of my Tío Manuel. Felipe was experimenting with making stencil art on mimeograph machines; soon he would turn to mail art and photographing garbage in the London streets. I wasn't into that kind of experimentation. I was interested in the classics that I had learned at La Esmeralda and had seen in the movies. I visited so many countries, museums, and cathedrals. The churches inspired a whole series of paintings I later did. I sent my parents dozens of postcards describing my experiences at the shrine of Lourdes, viewing Christ's shroud in the cathedral of Saint John the Baptist in Turin, visiting the Byzantine church of Saint Nicolas and the monasteries in the hills high above Kotor in Montenegro, watching the marvelous clock on the Strasbourg cathedral when it struck at noon.[36]

"In Paris, cinema played a role in my development: I saw hundreds of movies at the cinématheque in Paris, many of them black-and-white silent films my father had told me about. I saw them now with the eye of a painter. Silent film is above all an art of the visual, an art that talking films push out. My father had understood that and helped me to see it. In Paris, seeing those films of German expressionism, like Fritz Lang's trilogy of the Nibelungen, helped me in working with contrasts of black and white and shading. I also took up photography and eventually abandoned my usual sketches for a camera shot. The photograph could capture rapidly and faithfully what I had seen, and in taking it, I framed compositions sensitive to space, volume, form, and shading.

"In relation to the human form, my experience in Sardinia was key. In 1975, Giuseppe Sciola, who had worked in Mexico on the Marcha de la Humanidad with Siqueiros and with Daniel Manrique in Tepito Arte Acá, invited me to paint in his village of San Sperate. A staunch leftist, Sciola had turned the village into an open museum of murals, sculptures, and paintings depicting local life and politics done by artists from different countries and by the residents. Some were very political and others more spontaneous like my own. He assigned me the entire wall of a house of a campesino family, and I painted a mural inspired by the book of Neruda poems Eugenio Brito had given me. I saw so many swallows and other birds in the brilliant, sun-drenched sky. I painted the birds flying toward a sun of liberty and a male figure flowering from the earth. In this figure, Sciola's sculptures of men carved out of tree trunks inspired me. His figures were not erotic. They were cadavers—a form of political protest. I didn't want to paint dead bodies. I wanted to paint the human figure with phallus erect, because it was more sensual for me. In the San Sperate mural, I painted the male figure blooming from a plant reaching toward the sky and sun for his freedom and fulfillment.

"It's difficult for a painter to explain the origins of his work because with time, one's language changes and what was once empirical and improvised becomes more reasoned, intellectual, and daring. After Sardinia, I went to Greece. That trip was decisive for me. I found Athens an ugly city. It was dirty and the people ordinary and poorly dressed—far from beautiful. I thought I was at the Plaza Garibaldi or the Lagunilla market in Mexico City, but I smelled gyros instead of tacos. When I climbed up to the Acropolis, I began to sense the grandeur of the culture. I stayed there all day watching the changing light illuminate the monuments. The anthropology museum was full of real works of art I had only seen in copies in books in Mexico City. There was Zeus, god of the sky, or maybe Poseidon, his brother, god of the sea and earthquakes. It was a magnificent sculpture of the male body in full muscular strength, his right arm poised to hurl—as someone said, caught at a moment of pause in the full potentiality of his coming movement. What exquisite beauty! And the korai, these female figures sculpted in marble—tall, slim, erect in their simplicity. Many had no heads as if they had been decapitated. I did fifteen paintings of the korai without heads and without legs and feet but with much color. Some saw these as misogynist, but for me they were sensual. I don't know if they were misogynist. I also painted male figures without heads or feet.

"But the height of my experience of Greece took place in a sauna. I was not accustomed to go to saunas. I was told I would find beautiful bodies there. I went and found ordinary fat men, but then a youth entered. He was like an Apollo. He was spectacular. He was muscular, but not with the physique of a body builder. Those bodies didn't attract me. He was a man—imagine a Greek sculpture!—of regular size, not very tall, not short, with a sensational body, a totally Greek body. He was a prostitute. I did many paintings and drawings of this man. I showed them in an exhibit in Mexico—*Memories of Greece* it was called. I admire the human body. I consider myself an aesthete. I love beauty. I love to contemplate it, caress it, feel it. When one encounters it, in personal life, too, it's marvelous. One reaches communion. To make people feel communion as I felt in doing my paintings—that's what I sought."

But how could he say his aestheticization of affectionate sexuality came exclusively from his European experience, with Mexico cast into the darkness of repression? Were not his best paintings a visual expression of the Mexican *danzón* he had learned and loved—a controlled performance of sexuality, the more beautiful for its graceful insinuation? Were not his renditions of germinating nature akin to Cri-Cri's butterfly, so beautiful as she emerges from her cocoon that all the animals and insects of the forest can but strike up in symphony? Didn't Cri-Cri's songs sing of the child's right to tenderness, love, and pleasure? Wasn't Agustín Lara a poet of love and desire? Didn't María Luisa Landín, with her warm, melodic voice, exalt the tenderness of passion over the wounds of betrayal, abandonment, and loss? Didn't Tía Esperanza delight him with her brazen flaunting of prudery and female subjugation, her bold love for her own plump body and the ample phallus bulging beneath the cloth of her lover's crotch, her bantering with Tía Antonia about the history of their vaginas? Hadn't his father helped him to see the aesthetics of affective sexuality rendered in film? Wasn't Pepe's marginalization of conflict, struggle, and material want to reify and to aestheticize pleasure a legacy from his father? Wasn't his father's celebration of pleasure enabled by the effulgent sensuality of the world of entertainment that pulsated through central Mexico City in the 1940s and 1950s? Wasn't Pepe's own imbibing and expression of these popular experiences in his art a contribution to the sexual opening among Mexican youth that came of age in the 1960s?

So what did Pepe mean by repression in Mexico? He responded, "It was about the weight of religion in the family. The idea that if you were thirty and not married, there was something wrong with you. The idea you were not a man until you had slept with a woman. That showed your machismo. You began with prostitutes, and I have to tell you, we had unpleasant experiences, Nicolás and I. For a man to love a man was sacrilege, something evil." His protest was not against a repressive Mexican sexuality per se but a particular heterosexual normativity based on the male-female dyad, the dichotomy of the Virgin (bride and mother) and the whore (female object of carnal pleasure and expiation) and the denial of same-sex love, its relegation to the margins of perversion, exotic spectacle, and abuse. And Pepe knew that abjection and lack of protection. How brutally his Tío Manuel had beaten up and pushed around kind Isaac! How miserably cruel his rejection of his own hermaphrodite baby! And the boy became a prostitute in his youth! José Méndez, Pepe's outspoken friend from La Esmeralda, had his throat slit by his lover, who was said to be suffering from AIDS-related dementia. The lover then slit his own wrists and was found dead in a bathtub of bloody water. In the provincial city of Torreón, where they lived, the press turned the tragedy into a sensational scandal. These experiences of dehumanized marginality were too many. He had had painful experiences as well, but he did not want to talk about them.

On September 17, 1985, José Zúñiga Sr. died. Pepe was teaching at the Taller Rufino Tamayo in Oaxaca when his brother Efrén called to tell him his father had suffered a stroke. Pepe made it back to the city in time to say good-bye to this most important person in his life. On September 18, the family buried him in the Panteón Nacional. On the morning of September 19, Pepe and his mother woke to a deafening roar coming from the north, ripping through Soto Street uprooting the trees and pavement. That was the path the earthquake took on that autumn morning, tumbling most of Edificio Nuevo León in the Tlatelolco housing complex, tearing through the streets and vecindades of the Colonia Guerrero, crushing mariachi musicians as they left Plaza Garibaldi at dawn, destroying the medical center to the south, burying thousands under cement, asphalt, glass, and debris. So damaged were Lerdo 17, where Pepe had grown up, and Lerdo 20, where he had enjoyed the fiestas, that they had to be razed. The earthquake would create new militant communities in the hard-hit popular barrios. Daniel Manrique took a leadership role in Campamentos Unidos, an organization of those committed to rebuilding the homes people had lost in the Colonia Guerrero and Tepito. Art became integral to their very public struggles for survival and justice throughout the city.

During that devastating time, Pepe had become caught up in the tragedy of the AIDS epidemic. Friends were dying left and right. The disease took Eugenio Brito, Pepe's Chilean friend who had introduced him to

Pablo Neruda in the 1960s, and indirectly it took Pepe Méndez. To have the disease recognized and treated, Mexico City's homosexuals and their many supporters forged another new community to fight government inertia, to combat those who saw the disease as the just retribution of God for sinful acts, and to insist on their basic rights as citizens. Among Pepe's close friends were doctors engaged in AIDS treatment.

Out of the AIDS campaign came the Semana Cultural Lésbica Gay, first organized in 1987. Pepe regularly contributed to this festival of painting and sculpture, dance, music, video, photography, and film, as did dozens of others from Mexico's art world. Repeated year after year and recently renamed the Festival Internacional por la Diversidad Sexual, the Semana opened space for the acceptance, defense, and insistence upon the right to expression and to civil and political equality for sexually diverse (and all other) citizens. In the public sphere it played a critical role in moving the marginal to the center and private struggles into a space of solidarity and legitimization. In a society in which homophobic sentiment penetrated daily life and the rule of law has often been arbitrary, the Semana insisted upon legal equality and protection to be implemented by a state of laws.[37] "Although it has brought together a small portion of the entire population," wrote Carlos Monsiváis, "the Semana has constituted for civil society critical proof of the way in which alternatives spaces have contributed to diversity and the democratization of Mexican life." In Habermasian fashion he noted, "The influence of rational judgment displaces prejudice."[38]

In the words of photographer and writer Alejandro Castellanos, the Semana created a "political construction of sexuality," affirming its heterogeneity, its legitimacy, its pleasures, and its abuses.[39] It has given visibility to a full range of human emotions in men, opening up the hermetically sealed masculinity described by Paz in *Laberinto de la Soledad* to display as much tenderness and joy as masochism and sadism, as much heterosexual as homosexual encounter.[40] It has exposed the effects of the subordination of women—brutality, deprivation, marginalization, and denial of rights. In its critique of patriarchy, it strikes at the heart of the Mexican political system and has paralleled and contributed to its gradual, uneven, and partial opening up—an opening up that has been most successful and deepest in Mexico City. Federal District governments under the leadership of the Partido Revolucionario Democratico have approved the right to abortion, promoted struggles against domestic violence, and legalized gay marriage.

The festival has taken place in the Museo del Chopo, located in the Colonia Santa María la Ribera, a "redoubt of aristocratic pretensions" from the Porfiriato, transformed in the course of the twentieth century by social revolution and rapid modernization into a popular barrio.[41] Like the adjacent Colonia Guerrero, Santa María la Ribera suffered major damage in the earthquake. The Semana's site signifies both a return of the city's cultural locus from the university, to which (for many) it had migrated in the 1960s, back to the center where it engages thousands of socially diverse citizens—from the most popular barrios to the exclusive new apartment high-rises of the wealthy. In this city of growing inequalities, forms of artistic expression, tastes, and demands differ. They are certainly more articulated today when everybody speaks than in 1960. Transcending differences is the impulse toward sexual and gender freedom and equality as a necessary element in democracy. If the Semana Cultural has drawn a primarily middle-class public, it complements and reinforces the sentiments and demands of thousands of young people from the popular barrios and distant Iztapalapa, Ciudad Nezahuaocoytl, and Chalco who march militantly in the city's grand Gay Pride Parade. This articulation links to transnational circuits and spaces now even more intensely, diversely, and complexly wired than they had been in earlier decades.

Pepe Zúñiga's painting *Homenaje a un amigo conocido*, shown in the 1996 exhibit, appears in the Semana's volume *Diez va un siglo*. In the painting, metaphor yields to more literal but still stylized depiction (see figure 10.3). Two naked men face one another. At three points, they are linked through Zúñiga's familiar rectangular filters: their erect penises, their faces with the rainbow flag of gay liberation behind them, and their hands above them. In contrast to much gender-centered painting that depicts the body as damaged by unequal power relations and social inscription, Pepe's painting affirms the body not as subjected but as agency—emotional, rational, creative, and in solidarity with like bodies. In a world that had disdained same-sex partnerships, *Homenaje a un amigo conocido* affirms them. There is something overly conceptual about this painting. One notes a solemnity in relation to other paintings, drawings, and photographs in this published collection of bodies less stylized, more realistic, more candid, more sensual, and in some cases more comic—a testimony to new territory opened by younger people. Yet Pepe's affirmation of egalitarian partnership is important and essential to the democratic ideal the Semana has celebrated.

We are all products of the constraints and possibilities of our time. In a postmodern world of multiple styles, genres, and markets, Pepe Zúñiga remains a modernist, an easel painter convinced that the artist speaks for

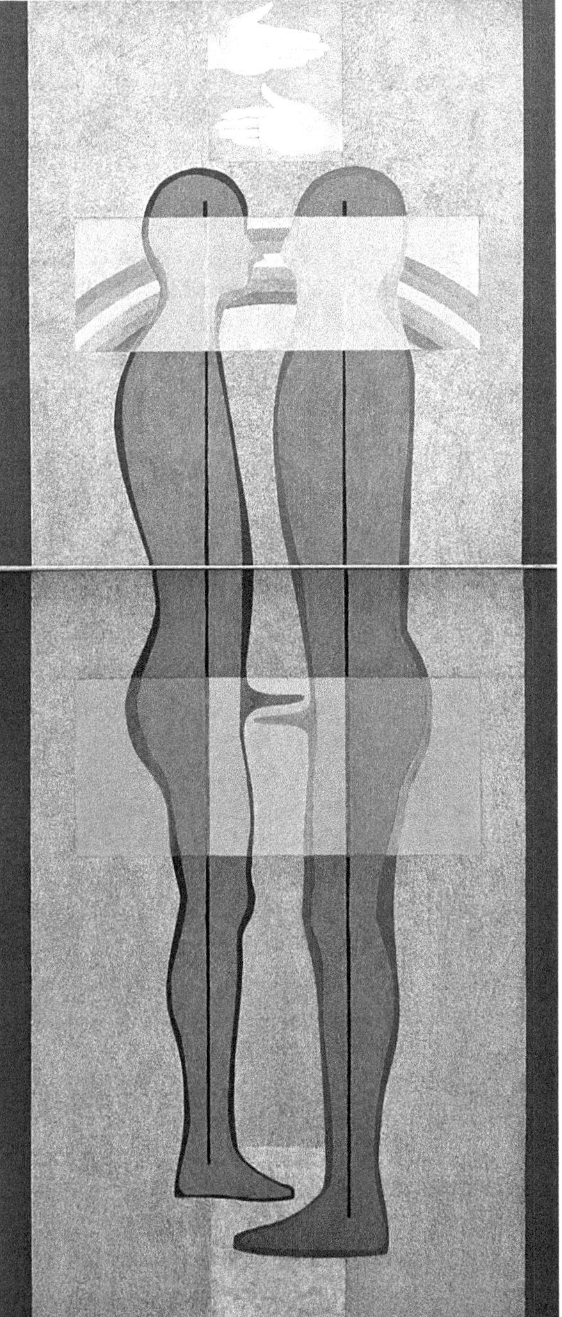

Figure 10.3. *Homenaje a un amigo conocido*, painting by José "Pepe" Zúñiga, 1992. See color plate 6.

society but from a perch above it and aloof from the market, as Herbert Read wrote long ago and Benito Messeguer taught him at La Esmeralda. Pepe never pursued a vigorous commercial strategy. Perhaps his position had deeper roots—perhaps it relates to his father's deliberate marginalization from market competition to dedicate himself to creative pleasure—in his work as a tailor, in his enjoyment of cinema, theater, dance, music, and sports. The essentialist dichotomy in much of Pepe's painting and thinking between a civilized, developed Europe and an underdeveloped, exotic Mexico came originally from the Hollywood movies he began to see with his father as a young boy—a dichotomy certainly reinforced by his professors at La Esmeralda and a strong but underexpressed assumption of the 1960s cultural and political offensive in Mexico City. This binary Pepe picked up on and benefited from in Europe. In Paris, they adored his dark-skinned "exotic" good looks and expected him to paint murals. He painted the mural in Sardinia and another at the École des Arts Decoratifs that contrasted Parisian and Mexican notions of light and color. He wrote his master's thesis at the École des Art Decoratifs on Mexican muralism.

Essentialism can be more than antiquated and banal. It can channel creativity and sensitive perception that both transcends and affirms it. Some of Pepe's best paintings are Oaxacan. In fact, the mountains in *La primavera* evoke those surrounding the city of Oaxaca. In the 1970s, when the iconic Mexican sun no longer broke through the polluted skies of the Valley of Mexico, it migrated to Oaxaca to illuminate the most defined and successful regional painting. In 1983, Andres Henestrosa, spokesperson for Oaxaca culture in Mexico City, identified Pepe with other major artists—Rufino Tamayo, Francisco Toledo, Rudolfo Nieto, and Rudolfo Morales.[42] He called them all "Indians," an identity that spoke as much to an ongoing reevaluation and self-articulation of Mexico's original peoples as it did to familiar essentialisms. Pepe went often to Oaxaca to teach at the prestigious Taller Rufino Tamayo and to exhibit. To a local reporter, he explained what he perceived to be a Oaxacan essence in painting: "a natural sensibility to drawing, colors and textures affected by the sun, a sensuality that makes the spectator want to reach out and touch the work, an aversion to the abstract."[43] When Pepe began to visit Oaxaca regularly in the 1960s, it was the sun and its effects that most impressed him—not the Zapotec symbols, culture, and folk art that fascinated Tamayo, Toledo, Morales, and Nieto. Yet Pepe Zúñiga's Oaxacan paintings express more than the region's light and color. They evoke memories of the mestizo urban culture of the city of Oaxaca and its migration to Mexico City.

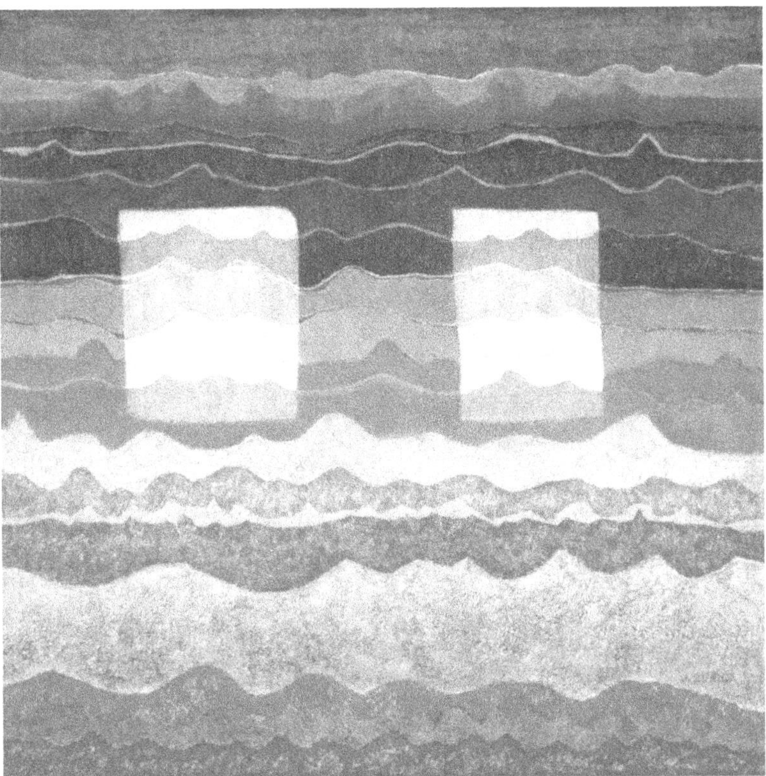

Figure 10.4. *Paisaje Zapoteco*, painting by José "Pepe" Zúñiga, 1998. See color plate 7.

In *Paisaje Zapoteco*, painted in 1998, the structuralism prominent in much of his painting softens in a lyrical dance of color, light, and textures capturing vibrating planes of mountains, forests, jungle, and beaches as these cascade from mauve-tinted peaks rising out of the altiplano downward to the sea (see figure 10.4). Pepe says these are the colors, shapes, and planes he saw on his many bus rides to Oaxaca. They are also the mountains and rivers, the gorges and precipices, he traversed as a youth when he made his pilgrimage with Chucho to Juquila to fulfill the *manda* his beloved Alfonso had made to the Virgin.

Las Juchitecas (2004) is one of several paintings he has done of the now legendary and certainly essentialized women of the Tehuantepec Isthmus (see figure 10.5). These figures are distinct from the semiabstract, geometrically stylized, and frankly cold Juchitecas he painted in the 1960s. These women, with their somewhat Grecian faces, form a communion of rhythm and beauty in the flow of the skirts and *huipiles* of purple,

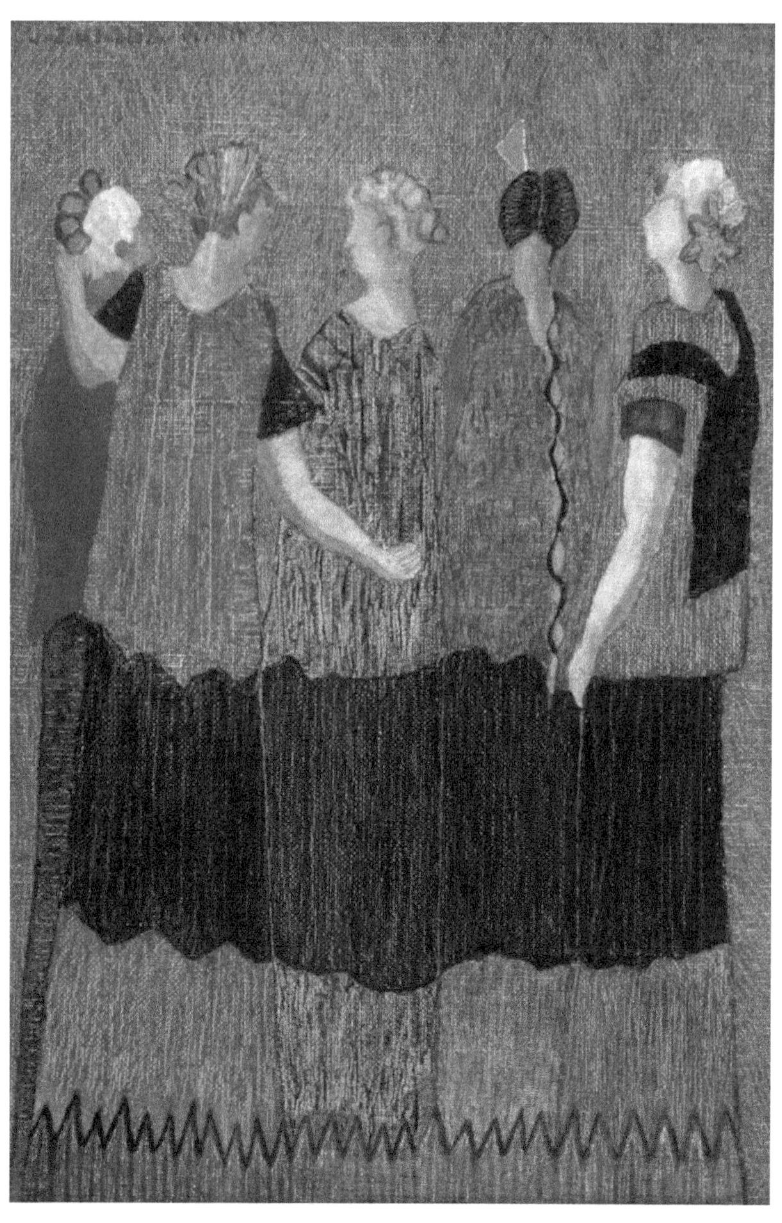

Figure 10.5. *Las Juchitecas*, painting by José "Pepe" Zúñiga, 2004. See color plate 8.

green, and black, the colorful detail of the clothbound flowers in their hair, the long braid laced with ribbons falling down one's back, and the union of their arms. "As Pepe Guizar wrote in his song, 'Tehuantepec,'" notes Pepe, "'the marimbas sing with the voices of women.' These women dance with women in the sexually more open society of the isthmus. I sketched them many times in the *velas* (fiestas) I attended in Juchitán, Tehuantepec, and Oaxaca."[44] The flow of the dresses recalls the skirts of his grandmother and aunts swishing along the floor; the banter that of Antonia and Esperanza recounting their sexual exploits; the grace that of the beautiful ladies dressed in regional costume, flowers in their hair, ladling cool, fruited water on the Day of the Good Samaritan in the heat of March.

Although he visits Oaxaca often and has worked there, he never formed part of the Oaxacan circle or any particular artistic circle for that matter. He is a Mexico City painter with a Oaxacan sensibility. He is retired now from La Esmeralda, from which he draws a pension. His mentors are long since gone: Benito Messeguer died in 1982 from leukemia, Antonio Rodríguez in 1993 at the age of eighty-five, and Santos Balmori in 1992 at ninety-three. The Estela Shapiro gallery, where he so often exhibited, closed many years ago upon Estela's death. Victims of neoliberalism and the privatization of the art market, most of the state-run galleries where he exhibited as a youth are gone as well.

Pepe does not much relate to the artistic expressions that have gained ground in the city's public sphere—installation and performance art, video and digital productions. He does not consider the graffiti that abounds in the Colonia Guerrero to be art. He never appreciated as art the personal costuming that has become almost de rigueur among artists. He found exhibitionist the posturing of Adolfotográfo, Adolfo Patiño, alias Peyote, the young boy from the housing projects who turned the mundane objects of everyday life (like Pepe's family's postcards) into installation and photographic art. Patiño always dressed in black—usually leather—with a long flowing raincoat.[45] No such performance for Pepe. He never abandoned his jeans except to don a traditional suit for exhibit openings. At a leisurely pace, he continues to draw, paint, and prepare exhibits from his home on Soto Street. He works in his studio, three floors above the rough, boisterous bustle, the strains of music, the smell of boiling grease, human soil, and automobile exhaust, the shrill sounds of the tamale seller's whistle, and, sometimes, the beating of the drums and clacking of the conch shells of neo-Aztec dancers. He paints to a Shostakovich symphony or a Mozart clarinet concerto, depending upon his mood. He watches many movies he buys from pirate vendors in Tepito.

He lives alone now. His mother, Guadalupe, died of a stroke in 1992. He remains close to his brothers. Chucho comes often to visit. At seventy-nine, Chucho is still an avid fan of Afro-Caribbean music and performs danzón with a group of senior citizen aficionados. Chucho's wife, Josefina, born in the Colonia Guerrero, has retired from a long and successful career as a secretary in the government, a typical path for women born in the barrio in the 1930s and 1940s. His brother Efrén, now in charge of architectural matters at the Palacio de Bellas Artes, lives a block away on Soto Street. He and his wife Susana raised three girls, all university graduates, one completing her master's degree in museum curating. Pepe is close to all of them. He sees less of Nicolás—an itinerant tailor, who would rather smoke cigarettes and drink tequila than eat. Nicolás has fathered many children, some of whom are in touch with Pepe. Cousins Susana, Carmen, and Marta live some blocks away in the Colonia Santa María la Ribera. Carmen has retired from a long clerical career in the government. Marta owns many buildings. Susana goes to church every day. "She is repenting," Pepe says, "for all the trouble she caused my mother and family." Some years ago, Pepe's Tío Manuel died in a ditch in San Bartolo Coyotepec near Oaxaca City—the victim of dereliction and alcoholism. But Pepe sees Nancy, Tío Manuel's hermaphrodite child, baptized Javier. While he keeps in touch with his biological family, he entertains with the patriarchal pride of his own father a small group of friends who have become another, intimate family.

He is an active citizen. He works with the residents of the vecindad, now divided into condominiums, on building safety and improvements. He votes independently and nonideologically on the basis of a candidate or party's record of contribution to the public good. He does not know if the police and justice system is less corrupt than before, but he knows that the Procuraduría down the street hauls in a new type of criminal, the crooked politician, the corrupt labor leader, and the drug trafficker. He likes that.

The colonia has lost people. Its population has declined with urban renewal, the earthquake, and a gravitation of activities away from the center that began in the 1950s and quickened in the 1960s. The colonia is dirtier because modernity has contaminated the air. Spewing exhaust is the incessant traffic on the three huge arteries that have broken up the streets Pepe walked as a child. People throw plastic bags of garbage, old sofas, chairs, sinks, and tires onto the street—they have much more to throw away now than they did in 1950. Some old vecindades still stand, but many live in new government-subsidized housing built after the earthquake. The dense economy of artisan production on the streets and in the vecindades has thinned out with the inexorable march of mass production. Manuel Buendía's carpentry shop is still there in the hands of his son Juan. Some continue to earn their living making goods and food from their homes; others work for the government; others drive taxis or repair cars.

Like the Esmeralda painting school, the movie and radio industries left long ago. There is still prostitution, but it is of a different sort: it is linked to drugs. Pepe seldom goes to the Plaza Garibaldi, teeming with mariachi players and the occasional tourist but not much else. The Teatro Blanquita, once the Teatro Margot where Pérez Prado dazzled with the mambo, still functions, but its shows have declined in quality, according to Pepe. The Chinese cafés where he so enjoyed talking with his father after the movies have shut down, and in the city where their biscuits were so prized, they are practically extinct. Gone too are the Tivoli, the Follies Bergere, and many cabarets, cantinas, and pulquerías.

Like many older residents, Pepe regrets the passing of the vecindades' vibrant social life that he had so much enjoyed as a child, but old forms of sociability have taken new paths and new ones have emerged. Religion continues to bond. The church of Santa María la Redonda, its altars, and its grounds are much better tended today by parishioners than they were in 1945. It is the only church in Mexico that features a mass with mariachis. Young crowds gather every twenty-eighth day of the month at the church of San Hipólito to have the priest bless their images of San Judas Tadeo, the saint of lost and difficult causes. Many seek strength there to overcome addictions, as do those who join the Colonia Guerrero's many chapters of Drogadictos Anónimos and Alcohólicos Anónimos. These options were not available a half century ago to Tío Manuel. Neighborhood associations have organized to press for housing and services and promote cultural life. The Union de Vecinos grew out of Jesuit initiative inspired by the theology of liberation articulated in the 1960s. Campamentos Unidos that mobilized in response to the earthquake continues to be a dynamic part of community life.[46] On Saturdays, youth from every neighborhood and social class in the city gather at the Tianguis del Chopo to exchange digital paraphernalia, old and new books, comics, movies, and rock music. They mount exhibits of painting, photography and sculpture and perform in multiple genres including that of self-presentation—their dress, their tattooed, pierced bodies, and hairstyles—dreads, mohawks, spikes, and bobs of many colors. Here one can pick up a copy of Alan Ginsburg's *Howl!*, an old Beatles recording, or a T-shirt with an image of Che Guevara: the long 1960s still signify for youth a period of vibrant rebellion, self-affirmation, and hope.[47]

Pepe appreciates the vitality of the Tianguis, but he is more likely to walk to the Alameda on the colonia's southern edge to take in a concert or opera at the Palacio de Bellas Artes. Across the street from the Palacio, the Museo Franz Meyer and the Museo de la Estampa occupy the ground on Avenida Hidalgo where the Hospital de la Mujer and the cemetery of Santa Veracruz once stood. There Tío Efren and Tía Antonia had slept along with dozens of other hopeful migrants when they came to Mexico seventy-five years ago. There in 1964 Pepe had seen Juan Ibáñez's presentation of *Olímpica* and deposited his coins in the church of San Juan de Dios. The ex-convent of San Hipólito, where in the 1960s young artists created in bohemian rebellion, has been magnificently restored by the Institution Nacional de Antropología and serves for art, cultural, and social events. The Hostería where Pepe first saw one of Jodorowsky's "*pánicos*" is now a hotel. These all form part of a postearthquake refurbishing of the city's center. On the other side of the Alameda, on weekdays the street buzzes with vendors and upscale employees of the high-tech and high-finance industries—most pegged to their cell phones. And on weekends citizens from everywhere flood the area, standing in lines to enter the many museums and creating their own art and entertainment on the streets.

The refurbishment is creeping into the Colonia Guerrero. Finally, the mansion built on Héroes Street by Antonio Rivas Mercado, the architect who led the city's beautification in the Porfiriato, is being remodeled as a historic site. From there, a committee works to organize events in honor of the Colonia Guerrero's 140th anniversary. Pepe is mounting an exhibit of painters who lived there. Brisa Avila López, widow of Daniel Manrique, is arranging a tour and photo exhibit of Daniel's many murals and sculptures that decorate street walls and the headquarters of Campamentos Unidos. A film festival will show, among other movies, *Los olvidados*, *The Children of Sánchez*, and *Prision de sueños*, which Pepe and Nico watched being made 1949. At the events to take place at the Salón de Los Angeles, where Chucho once carried the musicians' instruments, people will perform danzón. Of course, Pepe will be there!

Notes

Introduction: Portrait of a Young Painter

1. Elias, "Terrorism in the German Federal Republic," 229–98. Emerging scholarship on the global 1960s stays close to Elias's narrative particularly for the United States and Western Europe. See, for example, Marwick, *The Sixties*, and Suri, "The Rise and Fall," 45–68.
2. For literature, see, among others, Agustín, *La tumba*; Pacheco, *Las batallas en el desierto*; Sainz, *El compadre lobo*. For testimonials and biography, Poniatowska, *La noche de Tlatelolco*; Taibo, *'68*; on music, Zolov, *Refried Elvis*; Agustín, *La contracultura en México*; Rubli, *Estremécete y rueda*; Blanco Labra, *Rockstalgia*; Monsiváis, "De marzo de 1970," 91–114; on the arts, Debroise, ed., *La era de la discrepancia*; Goldman, *Pintura mexicana contemporanea en tiempos de cambio*; Hijar Serrano, ed., *Frentes, coaliciones y talleres*; McCaughan, *Art and Social Movements*; Tibol, *Confrontaciones*; on gender, Carey, *Plaza of Sacrifices*, and Frazier and Cohen, "Mexico '68," 617–60; for a powerful historical reflection, Hiriart, "'La revuelta antiautoritaria,'" 17–21; on festive street democracy, Guevara Niebla, *La democracia en la calle*; Jardón, *El fuego de la esperanza*; Soldatenko, "Mexico '68," 111–32. See also Zolov, "Expanding Our Conceptual Horizons," 47–73; Monsiváis, *El 68*. More directly relevant to the formal politics of the movement are González de Alba, *Los años y los días*; Revueltas, *México 1968*; Ramírez, *El movimiento estudiantil de México*; Pensado, *Rebel Mexico*.
3. Nasaw, "Introduction," 577.
4. Merleau-Ponty, *The Structure of Behavior*, 75.
5. Spiegel, "Comment on a Crooked Line," 412.
6. For a recent in-depth philosophical exploration of the term, see Ferguson, *Modernity and Subjectivity*; for a more accessible explanation, see Roper, "Slipping out of View," 57–72.

7. See de Certeau, *Practice.*
8. Kessler Harris, "Why Biography?," 626–28.
9. On memory and oral history, most helpful are Grele, "Oral History as Evidence," 43–99; Portelli, *Death of Luigi Trastulli.*
10. James, *Doña María's Story.*
11. Margadant, *The New Biography*, 25.
12. González y González, *Pueblo en vilo.*
13. It has been and still is such a prevailing view that to single out particular works may be superfluous, but it may be worth citing classical analyses such as Aguilar Camín and Meyer, *In the Shadow of Revolution*, and Hellman, *Mexico in Crisis.*
14. The Mexican Instituto de Seguro Social was founded in 1943 as a tripartite organization of government, employers, and workers to provide health care, pensions, and other social services to principally unionized workers.
15. Christopher Robin is a contemporary of Cri-Cri. He first appeared in the poem "Vespers," published in 1923 by *Vanity Fair* magazine before his big debut in the book *When We Were Very Young*, written by his father A. A. Milne and published in 1924 by Methuen. See Sedgwick and Frank, *Touching Feeling*, 42–43.
16. The classical study of childhood in Mexico City in this period that captures the multiple experiences of the well-cared-for and precociously stimulated middle-class child is a novel, Pacheco's *Las batallas en el desierto*, that in 1986 was made into a movie, *Mariana, Mariana*, adapted by Vicente Leñero and directed by Alberto Isaac. I am not alone in pursuing the idea of a mobilization for children in Mexico in this period. See, in particular, the excellent studies of Jackson Albarran, "Children of the Revolution," and Ford, "Children of the Mexican Miracle." Research on Mexican children is proliferating with five important books, Alcubierre Moya, *Ciudadanos del future*; Blum, *Domestic Economies*; Del Castillo Troncoso, *Conceptos, imágenes y representaciones*; Sosenski Correa, *Niños en acción*; Sanders, *Gender and Welfare in México*; collections such as Alcubierre Moya and Carreño, *Los niños villistas*; Sánchez Calleja and Salazar Anaya, eds., *Los niños*; Agostoni, ed., *Curar, sanar, y educar*; and articles by these authors and Galván, "Un encuentro con los niños," 221–32; Gudiño Cejudo, "Estado benefactor," 167–90; Sosenski Correa, "El niño consumidor," 191–222; Stern, "Responsible Mothers and Normal Children," 369–97; Vaughan, "Mexican Revolution," 194–214.
17. On the transnational campaign for children's rights in Latin America, see Guy, "Politics of Pan American Cooperation," 449–69, Jackson Albarran, "Children of the Revolution."
18. Jackson Albarran, "Children of the Revolution."
19. Sanders, *Gender and Welfare in Mexico.*
20. Lewis, *The Children of Sánchez.*
21. Claudio Lomnitz discusses the twentieth-century Mexican public sphere in terms of press censorship in "Ritual, rumor, y corrupción," 241–74. Pablo Piccato has done a rich, innovative analysis of the public sphere as press expression in the second half of the nineteenth century (*The Tyranny of Opinion*). For new work on the twentieth century, see introduction and essays in Sacristán and

Piccato, eds., *Actores, espacios, y debates*, particularly Piccato, "Honor y opinión pública," 145–78, Leidenberg, "Habermas en el Zócalo," 179–98, and Davis, "El rumbo de la esfera pública," 233–72. In his current work on crime journalism ("Murders of *Nota roja*"), Pablo Piccato argues that while censors monitored the political news, crime reporting encouraged reader engagement and commentary and permitted a critique of the corrupt police and judicial systems.

22. Habermas, *Structural Transformation*, 28–29, 36–51; for critical essays, see Calhoun, ed., *Habermas and the Public Sphere*.
23. Habermas, *Structural Transformation*, 155–94.
24. E.g., Mills, *The Power Elite*; Marcuse, *One Dimensional Man*; the classic work of Habermas's colleagues of the Frankfurt School, Adorno and Horkheimer, *Dialectic of Enlightenment*. Scholarly and artistic disdain for the mass media was general in this period and part of a modernist distinction between high- and lowbrow culture. Consider Adorno and Horkheimer, "The Culture Industry," 120–267; Read, *Cartas a un joven pintor*; Riesman, Glazer, and Denney, *The Lonely Crowd*; Goodman, *Growing Up Absurd*; MacDonald, "Masscult and Midcult," 1–75; or Fellini's *La dolce vita*. It is not surprising that Oscar Lewis entirely ignored the impact of movies and the radio on the Sánchez children, although he notes they were avid fans. Nor does Norbert Elías give the media their full due in the formation of 1960s rebels.
25. In his reflective essay on *The Structural Transformation*, Habermas acknowledges the seminal work of Stuart Hall, *Encoding and Decoding*, in influencing his reassessment of the media. See Habermas, "Further Reflections," 439–57.
26. On the sensorial revolution, see particularly Hansen as she draws on Walter Benjamin in "Fallen Women, Rising Stars" and "Benjamin and Cinema," 306–43. On community creation and sensorial revolution, see Lovigilio, *Radio's Intimate Public*.
27. Hansen, "Fallen Women, Rising Stars," 10–12.
28. On the formative role of cinema, radio, music, and comic books in Mexico, see, among others, Granados Chaparro, *XEW*; Loaeza and Granados Chaparro, *Mi novia, la tristeza*; Monsiváis, "Instituciones," 23–46, "Agustín Lara," 61–86, "South of the Border," 51–78, and *Pedro Infante*, 67–79; Rubenstein, *Bad Language* and "Theaters of Masculinity," 132–56. On radio listening experiences, see essays in *Tierra Adentro*, "Días de radio," and Robles, "Shaping Mexico Lindo." On cinema, see also Sosenski, "Diversiones malsanas," 35–64; on gender roles, behavior, and anxieties in cinema, see Tuñón, *Mujeres de luz*; Hershfield, *Mexican Cinema/Mexican Women*, and *Imagining the Chica Moderna*; de la Mora, *Cinemachismo*. On live theater and the negotiation of old and new gender behavior in the 1920s, see Eineigel, "Distinction, Culture, and Politics," 200–206.
29. On the imagined city, see Tuñon, *La ciudad actriz*, and Lara Chávez, *Una ciudad inventada por el cine*.
30. Interviews with Elva Garma, Elizabeth del Castillo Velasco González.
31. ATM abbreviates *¡A toda maquina!* In the 1951 film, Pedro Infante and Luis Aguilar play members of the Squadron of Transit Police in the Federal District.
32. See, among others, Poniatowska, *La noche de Tlatelolco*; Agustín, *La tumba*; Sainz, *El compadre lobo*, Taibo, *'68*.

33. Piccato, *City of Suspects*, 89–90.
34. Classic primary sources are Guerrero, *El Génesis del crimen*; Roumagnac, *Los criminales en México*; Ramos, *El Perfil del hombre*. Key secondary sources are Bliss, "The Science of Redemption," 1–40, and "Health of the Nation," 197–218; Buffington, *Criminal and Citizen*; French, *A Peaceful and Working People*; Piccato, *City of Suspects*; Gustafson, "'He Loves the Little Ones'"; Rath, *Myths of Demilitarization*; Stern, "Responsible Mothers and Normal Children," 369–397; Vaughan, *Cultural Politics in Revolution*, 40–44, 93–95, 177–84, and "The Modernization of Patriarchy," 194–214.
35. The Porfirian approach is well examined in Buffington, *Criminal and Citizen*, and Piccato, *City of Suspects*, and the revolutionary shift well explained by Bliss, "The Science of Redemption," esp. 2, 4–6, 8–9, 17.
36. On the increasing ability of Mexican working-class men to support their families through gainful employment between 1940 and 1970, see Thompson, "Households," 218.
37. Malanich, "Non-Normative Families." She bases her argument on Arraros, "Concubinage in Latin America," 330–39, and Therborn, *Between Sex and Power*. She also notes that the trend reversed after 1970. In Mexico marriage rates rose from 4 per 1,000 inhabitants in 1910 to 8.5 in 1942 to 11.4 in 1972 (Quilodran, *Un siglo de matrimonio en México*, 100).
38. On male domestic violence as socially perceived and legally handled in the Porfiriato into the 1920s, see Piccato, *City of Suspects*, 103–30. See also Buffington, "Toward a Modern Sacrificial Economy," 157–95. On protest against it in the press, see Gustafson, "'He Loves the Little Ones,'" 104–7; and in public education, Vaughan, *Cultural Politics*, 169.
39. Blum, *Domestic Economies*, and "Breaking and Making Families," 127–46.
40. On Porfirian conditions, see Piccato, *City of Suspects*, 40–70. The Porfirian poor often attended to their personal needs over series of spaces ranging from fetid tenements, *pulquerías*, public baths, the streets, and brothels. On the long-enduring role of the pulquería as a site of multiple transactions (drinking, eating, finding jobs, borrowing money, sharing the news, flirting, sex, fighting, and sleeping) from the colonial period well into the twentieth century, see Scardaville, "Alcohol Abuse and Tavern Reform," 643–71; Voekel, "Peeing on the Palace," 183–202; and Gustafson's analysis of newspaper and government reports in "'He Loves the Little Ones,'" ch. 5, 163–68; Pulido Esteva, "El 'cantinismo.'"
41. Sluis, "City of Spectacles," 203. On consumption and masculinity, see Macías-Gónzalez, "Hombres de mundo," 267–97, and "Lagartijo at the High Life," 236. Examining consumption and middle-class masculinity in Mexico City in the 1920s and 1930s, Susanne Eineigel notes that men consuming new fashions and entertainment were often labeled "fifi," or effeminate and frivolous. By the 1940s, that behavior had been mainstreamed. For her argument about the 1920s and 1930s, see Eineigel, "Distinction, Culture, and Politics," 119–20, 126.
42. On Pedro Infante, see Monsiváis, *Pedro Infante*, and Rubenstein, "Bodies, Cities, Cinema," 199–233. On Jorge Negrete, see Moreno Rivas, *Historia de la música popular mexicana*, 81.
43. Fromm's *The Art of Loving* was published in New York by Harper Brothers

in 1956 and translated and published in Spanish in 1966 by Paidós in Buenos Aires. For similar discussions about masculinity in the USA in the 1950s, see Gilbert, *Men in the Middle*.

44. Sainz, *Compadre lobo*, 161–63.
45. The bibliography has become immensely long. See, among others, Blum, *Domestic Economies*; Sanders, *Gender and Welfare*; Stern, "Responsible Mothers and Normal Children"; Vaughan, "Modernization of Patriarchy"; see also French, "Prostitutes and Guardian Angels," 529–53; all essays in Olcott, Vaughan, and Cano, *Sex in Revolution*.
46. In 1965, 26.3% of UNAM students and 15.6% of those in its associated preparatory schools were supported by blue-collar and peasant families. See Pensado, *Rebel Mexico*, 22, with data from Milena Covo, "La composición social," 28–135. The 1968 rebellion began among vocational high school students, the fastest-growing student sector of the Instituto Politécnico Nacional. Vocational students in IPN high schools increased from 4,666 in 1942 to 23,889 in 1966 (Pensado, *Rebel Mexico*, 29). Many leaders of the 1968 movement came out of the IPN, which had traditionally served the children of campesinos, trade unionists, and public sector workers. In *Refried Elvis*, Eric Zolov has shown enthusiasts of rock music came first from privileged groups but increasingly from the popular sectors.
47. In 1929, 32% of UNAM students were women; in 1961 only 20%. Of course, enrollments had mushroomed. Between 1961 and 1966, the number of female students rose from 11,444 to 16,766 (Pensado, *Rebel Mexico*, 30, with data drawn from González Cosío, *Historia estadística*, table XXIII, facing 72). Edward McCaughan, *Art and Social Movements*, 57, writes that only about ten of the hundreds of graphics from the 1968 movement preserved by Arnulfo Aquino and Jorge Perezvega contain images of women.
48. On the artistic rebellion or La Ruptura, see, among others, Cuevas, "The Cactus Curtain," 11–20; Goldman, *Pintura mexicana contemporanea*; Driben, *La generación de la ruptura*; del Conde, "Notas sobre la ruptura," 27–30; Hijar Serrano, *Frentes, coaliciones y talleres*, 149–62; Tibol, *Confrontaciones*, 1–100. On art movements coming out of 1968, most useful are Debroise et al., *La era de la discrepancia*, and McCaughan, *Art and Social Movements*.
49. García, "Alejandro Jodorowsky," 110–16; Jodorowsky, *Teatro pánico*; Medina, "Pánico recuperado," 97–111.
50. Monsiváis, *La cultura mexicana*, 355–68. See also Volpi, *La imaginación y el poder*.
51. The book generated enormous controversy retold in Villareal, "Gladiolas," 177–228. The Sociedad Mexicana de Geografía y Estadística launched a vigorous campaign and legal suit against the book as obscene, inflammatory, antirevolutionary, and subversive. Most intellectuals and journalists, including Fernando Benítez, Carlos Fuentes, Carlos Monsiváis, Rosario Castellanos, and Jacobo Zabludovsky defended the book on grounds of press freedom and as an exposé of the failures of the Mexican Economic Miracle. Kram correctly portrays the controversy as a significant opening up of critical public opinion. She notes that although Arnaldo Orfila Reynal lost his job as director of the FCE when he tried to publish a third edition of the book, he immediately went

to head up the new progressive publishing house of Siglo Veintiuno. While the FCE dropped Lewis's contract, the new avant-garde publishing company Joaquín Mortiz immediately published the third edition. It became a best seller.

52. Monsiváis, *La cultura mexicana*, 362.
53. With the publication in *Siempre!*, the cultural supplement became *La Cultura en México.*
54. See Paz, *Posdata*, 322–24; also García Canclini, *Hybrid Cultures*, 120–32; Coffey, *How a Revolutionary Art*, 130.
55. See, e.g., Pensado, *Rebel Mexico*, 74–80, and Zolov, *Refried Elvis*, 39–126.
56. Pensado, *Rebel Mexico*, 29.
57. Read, *Cartas a un joven pintor*, 21, 27.
58. On the recording industry, see Zolov, *Refried Elvis*, 21–26, 62–71, 91–103, 112, 162–74; on the book and journal industry, see Jean Franco, *Decline and Fall of the Lettered City*, 5, 10–11, 35–37, 43–50, 155–70, 185–88; Monsiváis, *La cultura*, 355–81. Neither Franco nor Monsiváis note the importance of the multitude of books translated into Spanish in the late 1950s and 1960s. Perhaps that is because of the inordinate importance of the new Latin American novel. The dependence of rebel youth on proliferating consumption has been noted in emerging comparative scholarship. See, for example, Marwick, *The Sixties*; Suri, "The Rise and Fall," and Timothy S. Brown, "1968." The most strident critique of the 1960s as an enlargement of capitalism in which youth movements played little more than a role in the transition from one stage of capitalism to another came from Fredric Jameson, "Periodizing," 178–209.

Chapter 1: Lupe's Voice

1. On Oaxaca in the late nineteenth century to the revolution, see Chassen López, *From Liberal to Revolutionary Oaxaca*. On elite attitudes toward race and ethnicity, see Poole, "An Image of 'Our Indian,'" 37–82. On the religious movement, see Overmeyer-Velázquez, *Visions of the Emerald City*, 70–97; Wright Rios, *Revolutions in Catholicism*, 31–112; Esparza, *Eulogio Gillow y el poder.*
2. On Oaxaca's artisan spaces, see Garcia Manzano, *Oaxaca*, 365–70, 378.
3. Loosely translated, "Attention, child! You're before the Señor!"
4. Interviews, Jesús "Chucho" Zúñiga, May 13, 2009, December 16, 2011. In the text, I note when Chucho is the source of information.
5. Federico Baena Solis, "Que te vaya bien."
6. The *arrabal* is loosely translated as slum.
7. Jesús "Chucho" Zúñiga, Oaxaca, May 13, 2009.
8. Jesús "Chucho" Zúñiga, Oaxaca, May 13, 2009.
9. A *galán* is a ladies' man.
10. A *manda* is a request and an obligation.
11. Jesús "Chucho" Zúñiga, May 11, 2009.
12. Jesús "Chucho" Zúñiga, July 1, 2006.
13. María Grever (María Joaquina de la Portilla Torres), "*Jurame.*"
14. Jesús "Chucho" Zúñiga, May 13, 2009.

15. *China poblana* is the national folkloric women's dress. On this day, see also García Manzano, *Oaxaca*, 161–62.
16. *Carrizo* is a form of bamboo that grows everywhere in the valley of Oaxaca.

Chapter 2: Enchanting City/Magical Radio

1. The population rose from 43,386 residents in 1910 to 100,200 in 1950. See Reynoso López, "La Guerrero," 15, 20. I thank Manuel Esparza for making Reynoso López's valuable manuscript on the history of the Colonia Guerrero available to me.
2. Interviews, Juan Buendía, February 9, 2011; Epifanio López, February 9, 2011.
3. Interviews with Jesús "Chucho" Zúñiga, Elvia Martínez Figueroa, February 9, March 14, 15, 2011. Also, Juan Buendía, February 9, 2011.
4. Interview with Elvia "La Boogie" Martínez Figueroa, March 21, 2011.
5. Interview, Nicolás Ramírez Zúñiga and Pepe Zúñiga, February 13, 2006.
6. Agustín Lara, "Señora Tentación." On Lara, see Carlos Monsiváis, "Agustín Lara," 61–86; Loaeza and Granados, *Mi novia, la tristeza*.
7. Interview, Nicolás Ramírez Zúñiga and Pepe Zúñiga, February 13, 2006.
8. Vaughan, "Primary Schools," 39–46.
9. It is a play on words: *La policía siempre vigila* and *La policía siempre en vigilia* (fasting, i.e., doing nothing).
10. Soler, *Cri-Cri*, contains, in addition to his songs, interesting reflections by Mexican artists and writers of the music of Cri-Cri and their own childhood listening experiences. In her dissertation, "Children of the Mexican Miracle," 175–193, Eileen Ford presents an insightful interpretation of Cri-Cri's songs in context.
11. Soler, *Cri-Cri*, 86–87.
12. Soler, *Cri-Cri*, 160–61.
13. Soler, *Cri-Cri*, 134–35, 138–39, 166, 172, 190–91.
14. Soler, *Cri-Cri*, 111.
15. Soler, *Cri-Cri*, 99–100, 105, 116–19, 170, 182, 183, 238, 241.
16. Soler, *Cri-Cri*, 95–96.
17. Soler, *Cri-Cri*, 268–69, 146–47, 258.
18. Soler, *Cri-Cri*, 255, 112–13, 154–57.
19. Interview, Elvia "La Boogie" Martínez Figueroa, March 14, 2011.
20. Soler, *Cri-Cri*, 102.
21. Interview with Jesús "Chucho" Zúñiga, May 13, 2009.
22. See Sedgwick and Frank, *Shame and Its Sisters*, 135–36.
23. Soler, *Cri-Cri*, 121–22.
24. Interview, Ivan Restrepo, August 15, 2010.
25. Interview, Jesús "Chucho" Zúñiga, Dec. 16, 2011.

Chapter 3: Pepe at School and with God, the Virgin, and the Saints

1. Delgadillo, *Poco a poco*, 48, 53–54, 62, 69–70, 74, 78, etc.; *Saber leer*, 18–19, 22, 31, 32, 37, 44–46, 60–63, 81–84, etc.; *Adelante*, 21, 24–25, 42–43, 51–54, 59–61, 64–65, 70–73, 83–85, etc.; Norma, *Rosita y Juanito*, 121, 126, 137; Basurto, *Mi patria*, 45, 56, 61–62, 69, 76, 82–84, 165–87; Cedujo, *Chiquillo*, 30, 32, 46, 112, 128; Camarillo de Pereyra, *Nuevas rosas de la infancia*, 31–35, 55–57, 64–67, 102–3,

163–67. These textbooks were all approved in 1941 (*El Nacional*, Feb. 22, 1941) and in 1948 (SEP Folder s/201.6, "Lista oficial de libros de texto para uso de las escuelas primarias y secundarias," 13 de febrero de 1948) with the exception of Delgadillo's *Adelante*, missing from the 1941 list but approved for 1948. I was unable to access editions of Norma and Camarilla de Pereyra published in the 1940s. Basurto's text has no date of publication (the earliest recorded date is 1941). There are many studies of Mexican school textbooks; the foundational text is Vázquez, *Nacionalismo y educación en México*.

2. Basurto, *Mi patria*, 79–84, 101–2, 135–36, 169, 201–2, 211–12, 131–32; Delgadillo, *Saber leer*, 30–31.
3. Basurto, *Mi patria*, 211–12.
4. Basurto, *Mi patria*, 83–84, 101–2, 169.
5. Delgadillo, *Saber leer*, 20–21.
6. See, e.g., Camarillo de Pereyra, *Rosas*, 95–101, 155–56, 162–63.
7. Delgadillo, *Saber leer*, 97.
8. Basurto, *Mi patria*, 140, 145, 148–49, 150–61.
9. Delgadillo, *Adelante*, 29, 37.
10. Basurto, *Mi patria*, 90–100.
11. See, e.g., Delgadillo, *Poco a poco*, 115, 137–38; *Saber leer*, 83–84, 186–87; Norma, *Rosita y Juanito*, 138; Basurto, *Mi patria*, 121, 142, 161; Cedujo, *Chiquillo*, 79.
12. Basurto, *Mi patria*, 103–8, 113–22; Cedujo, *Chiquillo*, 51–59, 68–69, 74, 79, 136.
13. For this transition, see Greaves, *Del radicalism a la unidad nacional*, 55–65, 141.
14. Basurto, *Mi patria*, 205–11.
15. Basurto, *Mi patria*, 105.
16. Delgadillo, *Saber leer*, 83–84; Basurto, *Mi patria*, 200–201.
17. Delgadillo, *Adelante*, 55, 71–73, 81, 128–29, 180–81; *Poco a poco*, 74, 166; *Saber leer*, 45, 62–31. See also Camarillo de Pereyra, *Rosas*, 55–57, 81–94, 121–25.
18. Greaves, *Del radicalismo*, 140–41; Delgadillo, *Adelante*, 24–25, 91–95, 105, 147, 154, 175; *Poco a poco*, 16–17, 27–28, 47, 57, 85, 105, 109, 143, 162–63, 166; Basurto, *Mi patria*, 26–27, 33–38, 163; Norma, *Rosita y Juanito*, 10, 12, 16, 20–24, 42, 59, 62, 67, 65, 75–77, 94–95; Cedujo, *Chiquillo*, 27, 40, 81, 104.
19. Basurto, *Mi patria*, 41, 42; see Cedujo, *Chiquillo*, 106–7.
20. Delgadillo, *Adelante*, 16–17, 44–45.
21. Basurto, *Mi patria*, 40.
22. Delgadillo, *Poco a poco*, 139; *Adelante*, 88, 93; Cedujo, *Chiquillo*, 81; Basurto, *Mi patria*, 21, 25.
23. Delgadillo, *Poco a poco*, 40, 48, 124, 133; *Adelante*, 79, 154; Norma, *Rosita y Juanito*, 17, 25; Cedujo, *Chiquillo*, 35, 110; Basurto, *Mi patria*, 43–44, 47.
24. Delgadillo, *Poco a poco*, 54–55, 70; Norma, *Rosita y Juanito*, 112; Cedujo, *Chiquillo*, 112–13; Basurto, *Mi patria*, 163.
25. Delgadillo, *Adelante*, 176; Norma, *Rosita y Juanito*, 17, 15.
26. Delgadillo, *Saber leer*, 383; Cedujo, *Chiquillo*, 7–12, 14–15, 19–20, 108–9; Basurto, *Mi patria*, 178–79.
27. Cedujo, *Chiquillo*, 44–50.
28. Cedujo, *Chiquillo*, 51, 129, 138, 139; *Rosita y Juanito*, 75–89.
29. Basurto, *Mi patria*, 196.

30. Basurto, *Mi patria*, 106.
31. Interview with Juan Buendía.
32. "Pelos! Pelos!"
33. Cedujo, *Chiquillo*, 44–48, 153–58.
34. Interview with Elvia "La Boogie" Martínez Figueroa, March 14, 2011.
35. Interview with Elvia "La Boogie" Martínez Figueroa, March 14, 2011.

Chapter 4: My Father, My Teacher

1. On the "fifi" in the 1920s, see Eineigel, "Distinction, Culture, and Politics," 119–20, 126.
2. Cited in Flores y Escalante, *Salón México*, 106.
3. For a sense of its complexity, see Flores Rivera, *Relatos de mi barrio*, 5–20.
4. Much has been written about these films as products of U.S. policy toward Latin America, some scholars interpreting them as blatant cultural imperialism and others examining them more from a Latin American perspective of appropriation. For hard-line criticism, see Burton, "Don (Juanito) Duck," 21–41, and "'Surprise Package,'" 131–47. For more nuanced analysis, see Fein, "Myths of Cultural Imperialism," 139–98; Pernet, "'For the Genuine Culture,'" 132–68.
5. On lucha libre in Mexico, see, among many others, Valero Meré, *100 años*, and Levi, "Masked Media," 330–72.
6. There is no exact translation for "*puto*" or "*joto*." *Puto* is a male whore, and *joto* a fairy.
7. "Así, pues juventud mexicana sigan los pasos de la Lucha que aquí aparecen y caminando alejados de malas inclinaciones, dediquen el mayor tiempo fuera de los estudios para practicar el deporte; solamente así forjarán una patria fuerte, de la que Ustedes mismos se sentirán orgullosos." Album, *Lucha Libre*, n.p, n.d., personal archive of José Zúñiga Delgado.
8. Dickstein, *Dancing in the Dark*, 360.
9. Dickstein, *Dancing in the Dark*, 361. Monsiváis, "Agustín Lara," 61–86. On bolero, also see Alejo Peralta Fundación, *Bolero*.
10. For her understanding of early Hollywood films as "vernacular modernism," see Hansen, "Fallen Women, Rising Stars," 10–22.
11. Pepe Zúñiga to José Zúñiga, Paris, Dec. 18, 1972, in personal archive of José Zúñiga Delgado.
12. Pepe Zúñiga to José Zúñiga, Vienna, July 26, July 30, 1982, in personal archive of José Zúñiga Delgado.
13. On high modernism and film noir, see Naremore, *More Than Night*, 17–25, 41–47.
14. For a discussion of reception in the 1960s, see Naremore, *More Than Night*, 25–37.
15. Esperón and Cortázar, "Yo soy mexicano."
16. Esperón and Urdimalas, "Amorcito Corazón."
17. On Pedro Infante, see Monsiváis, *Pedro Infante*, and Rubenstein, "Bodies, Cities, Cinema," 199–233.

Chapter 5: The Zúñiga Family as a Radionovela

1. "A son of the family."
2. Monsiváis, *Pedro Infante*, 50–51.
3. Monsiváis, *Pedro Infante*, 38–39. The song "Ni hablar mujer" is composed by Manuel Esperón.
4. Interview with Jesús "Chucho" Zúñiga, May 12, 2009.
5. Interview with Efrén Zúñiga, August 15, 2009.
6. Interview with Jesús "Chucho" Zúñiga, May 14, 2009.
7. *Crónica Urbana*, February 22, 2011 (757), Alejandro Rosales/Doctora Corazón. http://conexiontotal.mx/2011/02/22/crónica-urbana-128.
8. On the role of boleros in popular life in Mexico City, see, e.g., Monsiváis, "Agustin Lara," 80. The lyrics to the song composed by Pedro Flores are printed at the beginning of Monsiváis, *Amor perdido*. On boleros, see also Granados and Loaeza, *Mi novia, la tristeza*, and Alejo Peralta Fundación, *Bolero*.
9. On the knife, see Piccato, *City of Suspects*, 89–90.
10. If photography created archetypes and didactic models, it also fostered pretension and hypocrisy. See Chava Flores's famous song of the 1950s, "El retrato de Manuela." www.allthelyrics.com/es/lyrics/chava_flores/el_retrato_de_manuela-letras-1189766.html.
11. Interview with Susana Pacheco Zúñiga.
12. On the *vedettes*, particularly Celia Montalván, see Monsiváis, "Instituciones," 23–46.
13. Interviews with Nicolás Ramírez Zúñiga and Pepe Zúñiga, February 12–15, 2006.
14. Interview with Efrén Zúñiga, June 12, 2006.
15. Interview with Susana Pacheco Zúñiga.
16. Interview with Susana Pacheco Zúñiga.
17. Interview with Nicolás Ramírez Zúñiga, February 13, 2006.
18. Interview with Susana Pacheco Zúñiga and Marta Pacheco Zúñiga, Mexico City, June 15, 2006.
19. Interview with Nicolás Ramírez Zúñiga, February 13, 2006.
20. Efrén Chávez Carreño, "Para despedir a Petronita Pérez," April 7, 1959, personal archive of José "Pepe" Zúñiga Delgado.
21. Interview, Susana Zúñiga Pacheco.
22. She used the word *gallo*.
23. On these murals, see Coffey, *Revolutionary Art*, 78–126.
24. While the bibliography on Kahlo is extensive, it is less so on María Izquierdo. In relation to the body and sexuality, see Zavala, "María Izquierdo," 67–78, and *Becoming Modern*.
25. On syphilis and its treatment in Mexico, see Bliss, *Compromised Positions*, 99–126. Pepe is not sure of the treatment given to his father for the disease.
26. Interview with Jesús "Chucho" Zúñiga, May 11, 2009.
27. Ficheras worked in nightclubs entertaining men, inviting them to drink and dance. Although doing so was illegal, many engaged in sexual relations with the customers.
28. Interview with Efrén Zúñiga, August 15, 2009.

Chapter 6: "How Difficult Is Adolescence!"

1. Lewis, *Children of Sanchez*, 215–37, 356–59.
2. *Cursi* is close to the English word *tacky* or *sugary.*
3. Christensen and Haas, *Projecting Politics*, 110–12.
4. It was produced in 1951 but Pepe saw it later.
5. On Chava Flores's songs, see Guizar, "Crónica musical en México," 55–69.
6. On the Mulatas de Fuego, see Lam, "La leyenda."
7. Carlos Monsiváis, "Dancing: El Salón México," 51.

Chapter 7: "Five Pesos, Two Pencils, and an Eraser!"

1. On early years and intent, see González Matute, "La Escuela Nacional," 13–25.
2. On the rupture with the Mexican school, see del Conde, "Notas sobre la ruptura," 27–30; Goldman, *Pintura mexicana contemporánea*, 36–67; Driben, *La generación de la ruptura*; Hijar Serrano, ed., *Frentes, coaliciones y talleres*, 149–62; Cuevas, "The Cactus Curtain," 11–20; Frerot, *Mercado del Arte en Mexico*, 24–60; Goldman, *Pintura mexicana contemporánea*, 1–67; Monsiváis, *La cultura en Mexico*, 391–400. See also Tibol, "Introducción," i–xxiii, and *Confrontaciones*, which discusses the international and national politics of artistic rupture in Mexico in the 1960s, as does Goldman.
3. Goldman, *Pintura mexicana contemporánea*, 66–67.
4. Goldman, *Pintura mexicana contemporánea*, 38–67; Tibol, *Confrontaciones*, 1–33. On Jorge Romero Brest and the promotion of abstract art in Argentina and the Americas, see Giunta, *Avant-Garde*, 1–64, 300, 354.
5. Catalog, *Exposición de Escuela de Pintura Esmeralda*, July 1959, Galeria Chapultepec, Mexico City; personal archive of José "Pepe" Zúñiga Delgado.
6. In 1960 there were 25 private art galleries in the city; by 1970 there were 80, and by 1974, 124; Frerot, *Mercado del Arte*, 67–68, 103–4. These outstripped the state's organization of galleries, schools, museums, exhibits, and plastic arts organizations.
7. Published by Editorial El Ateneo, Buenos Aires, 1943.
8. *Expedición a Bonampak.*
9. Barreiro and Guijosa, *Titeres mexicanos;* Jackson Albarran, "Children of the Revolution," 166–95; Solís, ed. *Teatro para títeres.*
10. Information on Messeguer gathered from José (Pepe) Zúñiga, "Entrevista con Benito Messeguer," August 5, 1981 (recorded and transcribed), in personal archive of José "Pepe" Zúñiga; Rodriguez, "Abró nuevas rutas en el arte mural," and "La pintura mural"; Castro, "Nuevos Luces al muralismo mexicano"; "Falleció ayer Benito Messeguer," *Excelsior*, October 21, 1982; "Benito Messeguer: Fue pionero en exhibir las obras de arte en los jardines y calles de la ciudad," *Excelsior*, March 18, 1983; Fernández, Catálogo de la Exposición. All from Carpeta Benito Messeguer, Centro de Investigación, Documentación, y Información de Artes Plásticas (CENDIAP) Instituto Nacional de Bellas Artes.
11. Shifra Goldman has written the most comprehensive history of Nueva Presencia: *Pintura mexicana contemporánea* (esp. 1–110). See also Tibol's excellent introduction to that book, xx–xxiii. Material here is taken from both of these sources.
12. Rodman, *The Insiders*, 11–13, 26–30. Rodman's book came out of an exhibit,

New Images of Man, held at the Museum of Modern Art in New York in 1959. On Rodman in Mexico, Goldman, *Pintura mexicana contemporánea*, 68–84. She argues that Rodman served as a catalyst rather than a guide to Nueva Presencia, as Mexican participants thought his ideas not sufficiently linked to politics.

13. The quote is from Tibol, "Introducción," xxii–xxiii.
14. Coffey, *Revolutionary Art*, 150–51.
15. Anaya, "*El Corno Emplumado*"; Randall, "Asi nació el Corno"; Mondragón, "*El Corno Emplumado*"; Agustín, *La contracultura*, 228–29.
16. See Unger, *Poesia en Voz Alta*, 154–78. I discuss the movement further in this chapter.
17. Interview with Alicia Uruastegui.
18. Interview with Alicia Uruastegui.
19. Interview with Juan Castañeda.
20. Manrique, *Tepito Arte Aca*, 93–94. His words are "*algunas cuatesones tan jodidos como yo*" and "*chingada o jodido.*"
21. Interview, Elva Garma.
22. Interview with Juan Castañeda.
23. Manrique, *Tepito Arte Aca*, 102–3.
24. Published in English in 1962 (Philadelphia: Chilton), it was translated as *Ciudades perdidas y civilizaciones desaparecidas* and published by Editorial Diana in Mexico City in 1964.
25. "*Mire, ven! La cultura esta en el suelo!*" Manrique, *Tepito*, 172. Interview with Daniel Manrique and Emma Briseida Avila López.
26. Ocampo, *Yo metamórfico*, 25–29. On the youth rebellion associated with rock 'n' roll and James Dean, see Zolov, *Refried Elvis*, 39–61; Agustín, *La contracultura*, 112–18; Blanco Labra, *Rockstalgia*, 29–169; Rubli, *Estremécete y rueda*, 63–218.
27. "Vendo placer a los hombres que vienen del mar," lyrics by Ricardo López Méndez, music by Manuel Esperón, from *La mujer del Puerto*, directed by Arcadia Boytler, 1934. Lina Boytler does the singing.
28. Sainz, *Compadre lobo*, 313.
29. Ocampo, *Yo metamórfico*, 42, 43.
30. de Maria y Campos, "*Olímpica.*"
31. de María y Campos, "*Olímpica.*"
32. Velázquez Jiménez, "Divinas palabras."
33. See Unger, *Poesia en Voz Alta*, 154–78; Monsiváis, *La cultura en México*, 472–78.
34. García, "Alejandro Jodorowsky," 110–16; Jodorowsky, *Teatro pánico*, and "Metodo pánico," 80; Medina, "Recovering Panic," 97–111; Sánchez Puig, "La osadia Jodorowsky."
35. García, "Alejandro Jodorowsky," 100.
36. Jodorowsky, *Teatro pánico*, 73–80.
37. Jodorowsky, *Teatro pánico*, 80.
38. Interview with Elizabeth Del Castillo Velasco González.
39. See Moreno Villareal, *Francisco Zúñiga*, 1–31; González Ramirez, "La suave patria"; also, Oles and Molina, *Arte moderna de México*.
40. Zúñiga, "Notas autobiográficos," 18.

41. See Moreno Villarreal, *Francisco Zúñiga*, 15.
42. Bonifaz Nuño, *Santos Balmori*, 47.
43. Bonifaz Nuño, *Santos Balmori*, 48.
44. Bonifaz Nuño, *Santos Balmori*, 50.
45. Bonifaz Nuño, *Santos Balmori*, 9; Dallal, *Reflejo del ritmo*, 8.
46. Bonifaz Nuño, *Santos Balmori*, 9.
47. Librado Luna Cárdenas and Martínez Figueroa, *La Academia de San Carlos*, 83, 108–13.
48. Dallal, *Reflejo*, 11.
49. Bonifaz Nuño, *Santos Balmori*, 50.
50. Balmori, *Aurea mesura* and *El dibujo en la expresión plástica*, both published by UNAM.
51. Bonifaz Nuño, *Santos Balmori*, 1–8.
52. Dallal, *Reflejo del ritmo*, 10.
53. Dallal, *Reflejo del ritmo*, 8.

Chapter 8: Exuberant Interlude

1. *Política* stopped publication in 1967 for lack of funds and the refusal of the harder-line government of Díaz Ordaz to sell it paper.
2. For politics of the López Mateos and Díaz Ordaz presidencies, see Loaeza, "Gustavo Díaz Ordaz," 117–55.
3. On the museum as a key Mexican contribution to universal culture, see Torres Bodet, "Discurso," xiii, also published in *El Nacional* and *Excelsior*. Mexican educator and poet Jaime Torres Bodet had been Secretary General of the United Nations Educational, Scientific, and Cultural Organization (UNESCO) from 1948 to 1952. The Mexican government preferred this Paris-based organization dedicated to the "intellectual and moral solidarity of mankind" to U.S. and U.S.-dominated OAS cultural initiatives.
4. There is much written on the artistic and architectural politics of the museum. For a recent and penetrating analysis, see Coffey, *Revolutionary Art*, 127–77.
5. On the Buenos Aires museum as symbol of high modernism, see Franco, *Decline and Fall*, 5.
6. Other leading teams included Regina Raull, Iker Larraui, Fanny Rabel, Nicolás Moreno. For politics of their painting, particularly the innovative works in the museum by Goeritz, Carrington, Tamayo, and Coronel, see Coffey, *Revolutionary Art*, 148, 151–63.
7. Ramírez Vázquez, *El Museo Nacional*, 40–43.
8. "Ayer Cumplió 20 Años de Existencia el Museo Nacional de Antropología, construido por el Arq. Ramírez Vázquez," *Excelsior*, September 18, 1984, 1B, 3B.
9. Sandra Rozental retells the story in "Mobilizing the Monolith: Patrimonio and the Production of Mexico through Its Fragments." She has also made a film with Jesse Lerner about the uprooting of the stone, its transformation into a god, and its meaning for residents of Coatlinchán: *La piedra ausente*, coproduced by the Instituto Nacional de Antropología e Historia (INAH) and the Instituto Mexicano de Cinematografía (IMCINE), 2012. The film can be viewed at https://vimeo.com/80928830, password, festivales. For film footage of Tlaloc's journey on the flatbed truck, see www.youtube.com/watch?v=rJH2cwQE-hc.

10. Ocampo, *Yo metamofórico*, 43.
11. Interview with Rogelio Naranjo.
12. Interview with Pedro Banda; MacMasters, "Pedro Banda," 5, Sección Cultural.
13. Interviews with Guillermo Ceniceros and Esther González.
14. Interview with Pedro Banda.
15. Interview with Rogelio Naranjo.
16. *Desde las tripas* would literally translate "from her gut."
17. The Mexican practice refers to joking around, to a suspension of seriousness in relation to convention described, analyzed, and essentialized in detail by Portilla, *Fenomenología del relajo*.
18. Loosely translated, "Blackness! Here comes your whiteness!"
19. The film issued from a seminar of the Franciscan order in Assisi to which Pope John XXIII invited Pasolini in 1962. On the film, Roger Ebert, "Gospel according to St. Matthew."
20. Among many other newspaper reports, see "Homenaje al pasado," *El Nacional*, September 19, 1964; "Notables personajes de 23 naciones aquí asistirán en las fiestas patrias y la apertura de nuevos museos," *Excelsior*, September 12, 1964; "Inauguración del Museo Nacional de Antropología, *El Nacional*, September 18, 1964, 1, 8; Ramírez Vázquez, *Museo Nacional de Antropología*, 1–12.
21. Ocampo, *Yo metamofórico*, 44.

Chapter 9: Private Struggle / Public Protest

1. Frerot, *El mercado del arte*, 42, 77–78, 101–3.
2. These several movements are covered, described, and analyzed in Debroise, *La era de la discrepancia*.
3. Librado Luna Cárdenas and Martínez Figueroa, *La Academia de San Carlos*, 91, 108–13.
4. "Drifting on this wave."
5. Read, *Cartas a un joven pintor*, 34.
6. Read, *Cartas a un joven pintor*, 27.
7. Read, *Cartas a un joven pintor*, 32.
8. See, e.g., Rodríguez, *Mexican Muralism*.
9. Residents of the two Colonias del Periodista were diverse in their politics and métiers. Jesús Alvárez Amaya ("Una gira por Oaxaca en avión," 43) writes that they included reactionaries and militant communists, poets and police reporters, directors of newspapers, cartoonists, and poster designers for bullfights. Further information on Rodríguez taken from Carpeta Antonio Rodríguez, CENIDIAP, interviews with Pepe Zúñiga, Ivan Restrepo, August 24, 2011, and Cuahtemoc Rodríguez and María Antonieta Fernández Moreno de Rodríguez, and essays in Galindo Quiñones, *Antonio Rodríguez*.
10. Roughly translated, "I have not had the opportunity of doing you a favor."
11. Related by Ivan Restrepo, interview, Mexico City, August 24, 2011; see also Restrepo, "Antonio Rodríguez," 205.
12. On urbanism, see Magdaleno, "Antonio Rodríguez," 129–56. On photography and photojournalism, see Monroy, "México," 176–82, and "Haz la luz," 143–67.

13. The incident is described by Tibol, *Confrontaciones*, 19–22.
14. As cited from *Lunes de Excelsior*, May 9, 1966, by Tibol, *Confrontaciones*, 93–94.
15. On Rodríguez and avant-garde music, see Estrada, "Antonio Rodríguez," 63–75.
16. Antonio Rodríguez to Jorge Hernández Campos, November 30, 1965, published in Tibol, *Confrontaciones*, 40.
17. See Monsiváis, *La cultura mexicana*, 358–65.
18. Interview with Ivan Restrepo.
19. On his activities as director of Difusión Cultural at the IPN, see Restrepo, "Antonio Rodríguez," 206–7; Aguirre Garcín, "Antonio Rodríguez en el IPN," 23–27.
20. Cited by Aguirre Garcín, "Antonio Rodríguez, Difusión Cultural, Labor, Metas, Razón de Ser," 23.
21. Catalog, *Exposición de Pintores Jovenes de la Escuela Nacional de Pintura la Esmeralda*, IPN, March 1966, personal archive of José "Pepe" Zúñiga.
22. Unidentified newspaper clipping, personal archive of José Zúñiga.
23. Interviews with Guillermo Ceniceros and Esther González, Mexico City, Aug. 16, 2009, and March 11, 2011.
24. Newspaper clipping from *El Porvenir*, June 1967, n.d., personal archive of José Zúñiga.
25. On *Teorema*, see Pasolini, *Teorema*; Canby, "*Teorema*."
26. For contemporary reviews of the film, see Ayala Blanco, "Lo mejor"; Bracho, "La opinión," 4. Jodorowsky defended himself and the film in an interview with Zabludovsky, "De Fando y Lis," 43, 70.
27. See Zolov, "Showcasing the 'Land of Tomorrow,'" 159–88; "Discovering a Land," 234–72; Rodríguez Kuri, "Hacia Mexico 68," 48–50, 52–53.
28. Rodríguez Kuri, "Hacia Mexico 68," 50, 68.
29. As articles in *Siempre!*, June 1968, pointed out, student rebellions were ongoing or had preceded those in Paris—in Berlin, Bonn, Brussels, Rome, Turin, Cairo, Tokyo, Rio, Buenos Aires, Caracas, US campuses, Madrid, Prague, Warsaw, London, Essex, not to mention Sonora, Puebla, Michoacán, and Tabasco. However, the focus was on Paris. See Rodríguez, "Francia hoy," 19, 70.
30. Interview with Felida Medina.
31. Resume of Pepe Zúñiga, see also Cachorro, "Cementerio de automóviles"; Baguer, *El teatro*; Mendoza, "El teatro"; Engel, "Teatro"; Reyes, "El cementerio de automóviles"; Rabell, "La pasión." These are photocopies in the personal archive of Felida Medina and their page numbers are not indicated.
32. Baguer, *El teatro*; Mendoza, "El teatro." In Spanish, she wrote "como al Señor le gusta y como Díos manda."
33. Engel, "Teatro."
34. Felida Medina, Interview.
35. This is the argument of Michel de Certeau (*The Capture of Speech and Other Political Writings*) about Paris 1968. The language of the movement was more in gestures, bodily performance, and spontaneous utterances oral, written, and painted.
36. Interviews with Elva Garma and Juan Castañeda.

37. The many accounts of 1968 share this very basic narrative of events. Here, I am drawing on González de Alba, *Los dias y los años*, 65–162.
38. Monsivais, "Los días del terremoto," 54.
39. Crespo de la Serna, "Miscelanea de Exposiciones," personal archive of José Zúñiga.
40. Martínez Espinosa, "José Zúñiga exhibe sus pinturas," personal archive of José Zúñiga.
41. Gual, "Zúñiga, el futuro," personal archive of José Zúñiga.
42. Rodríguez, "Presentación" (1969), personal archive of José Zúñiga.
43. Frerot, *El mercado del arte*, 26.
44. CONCANACO, *Primer concurso nacional de pintura*, personal archive of José Zúñiga.
45. "Ceniceros, Urban, Villagrán posibles ganadores del concurso de CONCANACO," personal archive of José Zúñiga.
46. Manrique, *Tepito Arte Acá*, 217.

Chapter 10: Subjectivity and the Public Sphere

1. As cited by Cabrera López, *Una inquietud*, 334–36, citing Monsiváis, *La cultura en México*, March 5, 1987, and *Proceso*, March 2, 1987, 45. On expansion of the public sphere in politics and the arts in this period, see also Pérez Rosales, "Trayectoría," 59–65.
2. As cited by Cabrera López, *Una inquietud*, 339, Agustín, *La cultura en México*, August 13, 1987, 37.
3. Cited by Cabrera López, *Una inquietud*, 343, Agustín, *La cultura en México*, 38.
4. Tsaseva, "Ester González"; García Martínez, "Forma y simbolo."
5. del Conde, "Richard Rocha," 6a. On the "grupos," she wrote: "In relation to the masses they wanted to reach, no one paid any attention to them. It's likely that contemporary graffiti artists have had much more success."
6. On the grupos, see, among others, Vázquez Mantecón, "Los grupos," 194–99; Hijar Serrano, "¡Muera el arte burgues!," 216–17, 218–41; *Frentes, coaliciones, y talleres*, 219–420; McCaughan, "Gender, Sexuality," 105–8; Goldman, *Dimensions of the Americas*, 133–34; Aquino Casas, "El 68." On the hegemony of the abstract, see Pérez Rosales, "Trayectoría," 59–60, and on grupos, 62–63.
7. Most analytical and representative of this narrative are essays in Debroise, *La era*, esp. "Me quiero morir," 276–82; Navarrete Cortés, "Symbolic Production," 289–97.
8. The style known as neomexicanism is treated in Debroise, "Me quiero morir," 276–81, "A Kitsch Dandy," 204–7, and *La era*, 301–23; Mendoza, "El neomexicanismo"; Revista Electrónica, "Efemérides"; Jiménez, "Me quiero morir."
9. See esp. Sánchez, "El cuepro de la nación," 138–39.
10. As quoted in Revista Electrónica, "Efemérides."
11. See Debroise, "Me quiero morir," 276–77. See the painting and quote at Figueroa, "Julio Galán."
12. Debroise, "Me quiero morir," 276–81.
13. I made this selection drawing from the exhibit catalog collection in the library of the Instituto de Artes Gráficas de Oaxaca. It includes Guillermo Ceniceros

(b. 1939), Xavier Esqueda (b. 1943), Byron Gálvez (b. 1941), Irma Grizá, Alfredo Falfán (b. 1936), José Francisco (b. 1940), Leonel Maciel (b. 1939), Leticia Ocharán (b. 1942), Carlos Olachea (b. 1940), Emilio Ortiz (b. 1936), Irma Palacios (b. 1943), Arturo Rivera (b. 1945), Susana Sierra (b. 1942), Beatriz Zamora (b. 1935), Guillermo Zapfe (a bit older, b. 1933) and, of course, José Zúñiga (b. 1937). It is not an exhaustive coverage. Among others, it does not include two extraordinary Oaxacan painters, Rudolfo Nieto (b. 1936) and Francisco Toledo (b. 1940). Although Nieto studied briefly at La Esmeralda, he early sought an extra-academic artistic independence that appears to have been more intense than the artists above. Francisco Toledano is in a class by himself, recognized as a major artist in the 1960s. He early began to depict sexuality, his own and that of Isthmenian Zapotec culture through local flora and fauna. He is more regionally identified than the above artists and considered by many to be Mexico's most outstanding artist.

14. On painterly qualities' autonomy, see, e.g., García Martínez, "Guillermo Ceniceros"; Taracena, "José Francisco"; Elizondo, "Arturo Rivera"; Sánchez, "Irma Grizá"; Vallarino, "Byron Gálvez," 8–13.
15. Irma Grizá can introduce figuration and tell stories.
16. Mountainscapes of Durango and Nuevo León in Ceniceros's painting *Guillermo Ceniceros*, 80–92; Tabascan landscapes and pre-Hispanic symbolism in Francisco, *José Francisco*; Guerrero landscape and pre-Hispanic symbolism in Maciel, *Cosas de niños*; popular toys, images of flora and fauna, pre-Hispanic sculpture in Ortiz, *Emilio Ortiz*; on Carlos Olachea and the landscape of Baja California, *Carlos Olachea*; pre-Hispanic iconography and middle-class family living room in Esqueda, *Xavier Esqueda*; Aztec mythology in Grizá, *Realidades suspendidas*; degraded urbanscape in Falfán, *Alfredo Falfán*.
17. On female abstract artists Beatriz Zamora, Susana Sierra, and Irma Palacios, see Fernández, "Cinco Pintoras Abstractas Mexicanas."
18. Hijar Serrano, *Leticia Ocharán*; González Pagés, *20 Obras*.
19. Teresa del Conde notes Magritte and Ernst influenced Emilio Ortiz's surrealist painting. She does not mention the women surrealists; del Conde, "Emilio Ortiz."
20. Ceballos, "Arturo Rivera." See also del Conde, "Las pistas de Arturo Rivera"; Elizondo, *Arturo Rivera*; Debroise, *Arturo Rivera*; Elizondo, "Arturo Rivera," 216–19.
21. On gender and the Mexican school, see Zavala, *Becoming Modern*.
22. *Alfredo Falfán: Lo Imaginal*, texts by Rufino Tamayo and Fernando Gamboa.
23. See paintings, Ceniceros, *Guillermo Ceniceros*, 103–23.
24. Vallarino, "Byron Gálvez," 12–13. Agustín Arteaga makes the reference to Apollo and Dionysus and to Gálvez's male and female figures in the same catalog, 6–7.
25. Samperio, "Las cosas de Maciel."
26. Tibol, "Las estilizaciones de José Zúñiga," unidentified publication, ca. 1977, personal archive of José "Pepe" Zúñiga.
27. Covantes, *La onda, Novedades*, November 13, 1977, personal archive of José Zúñiga.
28. Rodríguez, "El sol negro"; "José Zúñiga: Pintor," 5; "José Zúñiga y el juego";

"Zúñiga"; and "El refinamiento"; Amador, "El secreto deseo," 15–16; Berryhill, "Mexican Art International"; personal archive of José Zúñiga.

29. Ocharán, "Del hueco"; Berryhill, "Mexican Art International"; personal archive of José Zúñiga.
30. Fernández, "La responsabilidad"; Rodríguez, "Zúñiga"; Amador, "El secreto deseo," 16; Dallal, "José Zúñiga"; personal archive of José Zúñiga.
31. Ocharán, "Del hueco."
32. Manrique, "Del espacio gay," 15.
33. Biographical information on www.Leticiaocharan.com; see also Cabrera López, *Una Inquietud*, 323–25.
34. Amador, "El secreto deseo," 16.
35. Ocharán, "Del hueco."
36. Pepe Zúñiga to José Zúñiga Sr., Lourdes, March 13, 1974; Strasbourg, June 26, 1974; Kotor, Montenegro, September 5, 1974, August 31, 1974; Rome, December 6, 1973; to Guadalupe Delgado, Milan, November 16, 1982; personal archive of José Zúñiga.
37. Covarrubias, "De voz y cuerpo presente," 9; Monsiváis, "Diez y va un siglo," 11–13; Blas Galindo, "Un triunfo," 19–21; Castellanos, "Del cuerpo," 27; Gargallo, "Nuestra semana," 47–50, and other essays in *Diez va un siglo.*
38. Monsiváis, "Diez va," 13.
39. Castellanos, "Del cuerpo," 27.
40. del Conde "Enrique Guzmán," 18; McCaughan, "Gender, Sexuality," 121–32.
41. Manrique, "Del espacio gay," 15.
42. Andres Henestrosa, "José Zúñiga," Exposición José Zúñiga, Galeria Estela Shapiro, ca. 1982; personal archive of José Zúñiga.
43. "Conversación con el Pintor Oaxaqueño José Zúñiga." *Carteles del sur: El Diario de Oaxaca*, July 28, 1985; personal archive of José Zúñiga.
44. Guizar, "Las marimbas."
45. On Patiño, see Debroise, "A Kitsch Dandy," 204–7.
46. Reynoso López, "La Guerrero," 128–31.
47. Reynoso López, "La Guerrero," 115–19.

Bibliography

Archives

Archivo Histórico de la Secretaría de Educacíón (AHSEP), Mexico City.
Archivo Particular de Felida Medina, Mexico City.
Archivo Particular de José "Pepe" Zúñiga, Mexico City.
Centro Nacional de Investigación, Documentación, y Información de Artes Plásticas (CENIDIAP). Instituto Nacional de Bellas Artes, Mexico City.

Interviews

Pedro Banda, Mexico City, March 19, 2009.
Juan Buendía, Mexico City, February 9, 2011.
Juan Castañeda, Aguascalientes, March 10, 2011.
Guillermo Ceniceros and Esther González, Mexico City, August 16, 2009, March 11, 2011, April 26, 2013.
Elizabeth Del Castillo Velasco González, Mexico City, March 13, 2011.
Elva Garma, Mexico City, March 8, 2011.
Epifanio López Sánchez, Mexico City, February 9, 2011.
Gloria Elvia "La Boogie" Martínez Figueroa and Jesús "Chucho" Zúñiga, Mexico City, February 9, March 14, 21, 2011.
Daniel Manrique and Emma Briseida Avila López, Mexico City, February 17, 2009.
Felida Medina, Mexico City, June 15, 2008.
Rogelio Naranjo, Mexico City, March 16, 2009.
Marta Pacheco Zúñiga, Mexico City, June 15, 2006.
Susana Pacheco Zúñiga, Mexico City, June 15, 2006.
Nicolás Ramírez Zúñiga and Pepe Zúñiga, Oaxaca, February 12–15, 2006.
Ivan Restrepo, Mexico City, August 15, 2010, August 24, 2011.

Cuauhtémoc Rodríguez and María Antonieta Fernández Moreno de Rodríguez, August 23, 2008.
Alicia Uruastegui, Mexico City, November 28, 2008.
Efrén Zúñiga, Mexico City, June 12, 2006, August 15, 2009.
Jesús "Chucho" Zúñiga, Mexico City, July 31, 2006, September 8, 2008, March 14, 2011; Oaxaca, May 9–13, 2009, December 16–18, 2011.

Published Works

Acevedo Rodrigo, Ariadna, and Paula López Caballero, eds. *Ciudadanos inesperados: Espacios de formación de la ciudadanía ayer y hoy*. Mexico City: El Colegio de México and Centro de Investigación y Estudios Avanzados, 2012.
Adorno, Theodor, and Max Horkheimer. "The Culture Industry: Enlightenment as Mass Deception." In Adorno and Horkheimer, *Dialectic of Enlightenment: Philosophical Fragments*, 120–267. London: Verso, 1979.
Agostoni, Claudia, ed. *Curar, sanar, y educar: Enfermedad y sociedad en México, siglos XIX y XX*. Mexico City: Universidad Nacional Autónoma de México, Instituto de Investigaciones Históricas / Benemérita Universidad Autónoma de Puebla, 2008.
Aguilar Camín, Hector, and Lorenzo Meyer. *In the Shadow of Revolution: Contemporary Mexican History, 1910–1989*. Austin: University of Texas Press, 1993.
Aguirre Garcín, Ramón. "Antonio Rodríguez en el IPN." In *Creadores del Siglo XX Testimonios de nuestro tiempo: Antonio Rodríguez*, ed. Heriberto M. Galindo Quiñones, 23–27. Mexico City: Instituto Politécnico Nacional, 2008.
Agustín, José. *La contracultura en México: La historia y el significado de los rebeldes sin causa, los jipitecas, los punks, y las bandas*. Mexico City: Grijalbo, 1996.
Agustín, José. *La tumba*. Mexico City: Grijalbo, 1964.
Alcubierre Moya, Beatriz. *Ciudadanos del futuro: Una historia de las publicaciones para niños en el siglo XIX mexicano*. Mexico City: El Colegio de México, Universidad Autónoma del Estado de Morelos, 2010.
Alcubierre Moya, Beatriz, and Tania Carreño. *Los niños villistas: Una mirada a la historia de la infancia en México, 1900–1914*. Mexico City: Instituto Nacional de los Estudios Históricos de la Revolución Mexicana, 1996.
Alejo Peralta Fundación. *Bolero: Clave del Corazón*. Introducción de Carlos Monsiváis. Mexico City: Ingeniero Alejo Peralta Fundación y Díaz Ceballos, 2004.
Alvárez Amaya, Jesús. "Una gira por Oaxaca en avión." In *Antonio Rodríguez, Un humanista sin fronteras*, ed. Heriberto M. Galindo Quiñones, 41–42. Mexico City: Instituto Politécnico Nacional, 2011.
Alvárez Garin, Raúl, Gilberto Guevara Niebla, Herman Bellinghausen, and Hector Aguilar Camín, eds. *Pensar '68*. Mexico City: Cal y Arena, 1988.
Amador, Julio. "El secreto deseo de seducir." *La onda*, April 15, 1979, 15–16.
Anaya, José Vicente, "*El Corno Emplumado*: Revista de los poetas que sueñan demasiado." *Alforja* 36, spring 2006, www.alforjapoesia.com/monografico/mon36.htm.
Anguiano, Raul. *Expedición a Bonampak*. Mexico City: UNAM, 1950.

Aquino Casas, Arnulfo. "El 68 en la gráfica política contemporánea: El cartel y la estampa de implicación social en México." *Aportes*, July–December 2009, http://discursovisual.net/dvweb13/aportes/apoarnulfo.htm.
Arraros, José. "Concubinage in Latin America." *Journal of Family Law* 3, no. 1 (1963): 330–39.
Arteaga, Agustín. "Byron Gálvez." In *Byron Gálvez, Obra pictórica: Semblanza de treinta años*. Museo de Palacio de Bellas Artes. CONACULTA and INBA, Mexico City, March 6–May 10, 1996.
Ayala Blanco, Jorge. "Lo mejor y lo peor de la XI Reseña Mundial." *México en la cultura, Novedades* 1030, December 15, 1968, 4–5.
Baena Solís, Federico. "Que te vaya bien." In *Gran Cancionero mexicano: Las canciones que nos han hecho amar, llorar, y recordar*, vol. 1, 1247. Mexico City: Sangorn Hermanos, 2005.
Barreiro, Juan José, and Marcela Guijosa. *Titeres mexicanos: Memoria y retrato de autómatas, fantoches, y otros artistas ambulantes*. Mexico City: Syntex, 1997.
Basurto, Carmen. *Mi patria, Libro tercero*. (1941). Mexico City: Editorial El Material Didáctico de Prof. Carlos Rodríguez, n.d.
Benítez, Fernando. *Los indios de México*. Mexico City: Biblioteca Era, 1967.
Berryhill, Michael. "Mexican Art International." *Star Telegram*, Fort Worth, TX, 1981.
Bizberg, Ilan, Lorenzo Meyer, and Francisco Alba, eds. *Historia contemporanea de México: Transformaciones y permanencias*, vol. 2. Mexico City: Océano, 2004.
Blanco Labra, Víctor. *Rockstalgia: Crónicas rocanroleras, años 50 y 60*. Mexico City: Editorial Diana, 2006.
Blas Galindo, Carlos. "Un triunfo sobre la hipocresía y sobre las tinieblas." In *Diez va un siglo: Libro conmemorativo de los diez años de la Semana Cultural Lésbica-Gay*, 19–21. Mexico City: Difusión Cultural UNAM, Museo Universitario del Chopo, Circulo Cultural Gay, FONCA, 1997.
Bliss, Katherine E. *Compromised Positions: Prostitution, Public Health and Gender Politics in Revolutionary Mexico City*. College Station: Penn State University Press, 2002.
Bliss, Katherine E. "For the Health of the Nation: Gender and the Cultural Politics of Social Hygiene in Revolutionary Mexico." In *The Eagle and the Virgin: Nation and Cultural Revolution in Mexico (1920–1940)*, ed. Mary Kay Vaughan and Stephen E. Lewis, 197–218. Durham, NC: Duke University Press, 2006.
Bliss, Katherine E. "The Science of Redemption: Syphilis, Sexual Promiscuity, and Reformism in Revolutionary Mexico City." *Hispanic American Historical Review* 79, no. 1 (1999): 1–40.
Blum, Ann. "Breaking and Making Families: Adoption and Public Welfare, Mexico City, 1938–1942." In *Sex in Revolution: Gender, Politics, and Power in Modern Mexico*, ed. Jocelyn Olcott, Mary Kay Vaughan, and Gabriela Cano, 127–46. Durham, NC: Duke University Press, 2006.
Blum, Ann. *Domestic Economies: Family, Work, and Welfare in Mexico City, 1884–1943*. Lincoln: University of Nebraska Press, 2010.

Bonifaz Nuño, Ruben. *Santos Balmori*. Mexico City: UNAM, 1983.
Bracho, Julio. "La opinión de Julio Bracho sobre Lis y Fando." *Siempre!* 808, December 18, 1968, 4.
Brown, Timothy S. "'1968' East and West: Divided Germany as a Case Study in Transnational History," *AHR* Forum, *American Historical Review* 114, no. 1 (2009): 69–96.
Buffington, Robert. *Criminal and Citizen in Modern Mexico*. Lincoln: University of Nebraska Press, 2000.
Buffington, Robert. "Toward a Modern Sacrificial Economy: Violence against Women and Male Subjectivity in Turn-of-the-Century Mexico City." In *Masculinity and Sexuality in Modern Mexico*, ed. Victor M. Macías González and Anne Rubenstein, 157–95. Albuquerque: University of New Mexico Press, 2012.
Burton, Julianne. "Don (Juanito) Duck and the Imperial Patriarchal Unconscious: Disney Studios, the Good Neighbor Policy, and the Packaging of Latin America." In *Nationalisms and Sexualities*, ed. Andrew Parker, Mary Russo, Doris Sommer, Patricia Yaeger, 21–41. New York: Routledge, 1992.
Burton, Julianne "'Surprise Package': Looking Southward with Disney." In *Disney Discourse: Producing the Magic Kingdom*, ed. Eric Smoodin, 131–47. New York: Routledge, 1994.
Cabrera López, Patricia. *Una inquietud de amanecer: Literatura y política en México, 1962–1987*. Mexico City: Plaza y Valdés Editores, 2006.
"Cachorro." "Cementerio de automóviles." *Devenir*, August 2, 1968.
Calhoun, Craig, ed. *Habermas and the Public Sphere*. Cambridge, MA: MIT Press, 1993.
Camarillo de Pereyra, María Enriqueta. *Nuevas rosas de la infancia: Lecturas para niños, libro segundo para tercer año*. (1912). Mexico City: Editorial Patria, 1958.
Canby, Vincent. "*Teorema*: The Screen: A Parable by Pasolini." *New York Times*, April 22, 1969.
Carey, Elaine. *Plaza of Sacrifices: Gender, Power, and Terror in 1968 Mexico*. Albuquerque: University of New Mexico Press, 2005.
Castellanos, Alejandro. "Del cuerpo individual al cuerpo social." In *Diez va un siglo: Libro conmemorativo de los diez años de la Semana Cultural Lésbica-Gay*, 27. Mexico City: Difusión Cultural UNAM, Museo Universitario del Chopo, Círculo Cultural Gay, FONCA, 1997.
Castro, Rosa. "Nuevos luces al muralismo mexicano." *Siempre!* 710, February 1, 1967, republished in *Homenaje a Benito Messeguer*. Mexico City: Instituto Nacional de Bellas Artes, 1983.
Ceballos, Miguel Angel. "Arturo Rivera pinta la belleza de lo terrible: Pinta la belleza de lo terrible para no traspasar el umbral de la locura." *El Universal*, May 16, 2006, F2, Sección Cultura.
Cedujo, Guadalupe. *Chiquillo: Libro de lectura oral para segundo año*. (1930). Mexico City: S. Turanzas del Valle, n.d.
Ceniceros, Guillermo. *Guillermo Ceniceros: Setenta años*. Mexico City: Ediciones La Cabra, Gobierno del Estado de Durango, Gobierno del Estado de Nuevo León, Consejo para la Cultura y las Artes de Nuevo León, 2009.

Charlton, Thomas L., Lois E. Myers, Rebecca Sharpless, eds. *History of Oral History: Foundations and Methodology*. Lanham, MD: Altamira Press, 2007.

Chassen López, Francie. *From Liberal to Revolutionary Oaxaca: The View from the South, Mexico, 1867–1911*. College Station: Pennsylvania State University Press, 2005.

Christensen, Terry, and Peter Haas. *Projecting Politics: Political Messages in American Films*. Armonk, NY: Sharpe, 2005.

Chumacero, Ali. "Introducción." In *Zúñiga*, Mexico City: Galería de Arte Misrachi, 1969.

Coffey, Mary K. *How a Revolutionary Art Became Official Culture: Murals, Museums, and the Mexican State*. Durham, NC: Duke University Press, 2012.

CONCANACO, Presidente Francisco Cano Escalante and Secretaría de Educación Pública. *Primer concurso nacional de pintura*, September 20, 1969.

Covarrubias, José María. "De voz y cuerpo presente." In *Diez va un siglo: Libro conmemorativo de los diez años de la Semana Cultural Lésbica-Gay*, 9–10. Mexico City: Difusión Cultural UNAM, Museo Universitario del Chopo, Círculo Cultural Gay, FONCA, 1997.

Covo, Milena. "La composición social de la población estudiantil de la UNAM, 1960–1985." In *Universidad Nacional y Sociedad*, ed. Ricardo Pozas Horcasitas, 28–135. Mexico City: Grupo Editorial Miguel Angel Porrua, 1990.

Crespo de la Serna, Jorge Juan. "Miscelanea de exposiciones." *Novedades*, March 20, 1969.

Crónica Urbana. February 22, 2011 (757), Alejandro Rosales/Doctora Corazón. http://conexiontotal.mx/2011/02/22/crónica-urbana-128.

Cuevas, José Luis. "The Cactus Curtain." *Evergreen Review* 2, no. 7 (1959): 11–20.

Dallal, Alberto. "José Zúñiga: La restitución del tiempo humano." *Exposición José Zúñiga*, Galeria Estela Shapiro, Mexico City, 1985.

Dallal, Alberto. "Reflejo del ritmo." In *Reflejo del ritmo: Antología de Santos Balmori*, ed. Helena Jordan de Balmori. Mexico City: Programa Editorial de la Coordinación de Humanidades 1997.

Davis, Diane. "El rumbo de la esfera pública: Influencias locales, nacionales, e internacionales en la urbanización del centro de la ciudad de México, 1910–1950." In *Actores, espacios, y debates en la historia de la esfera pública en México*, ed. Cristina Sacristán and Pablo Piccato, 233–72. Mexico City: Instituto de Investigaciones Históricas–UNAM and Instituto Mora, 2005.

Debroise, Olivier. *Arturo Rivera: El rastro del dolor*. Mexico City: Secretaría de Educación Pública, 1987.

Debroise, Olivier, ed. *La era de la discrepancia: Arte y cultura visual en México, 1968–1997/The Age of Discrepancies: Art and Visual Culture in Mexico, 1968–1997*. Mexico City: Universidad Nacional Autónoma de México, 2006.

Debroise, Olivier. "A Kitsch Dandy." In *La era de la discrepancia: Arte y cultura visual en México, 1968–1997*, ed. Olivier Debroise, 204–7. Mexico City: UNAM, 2006.

Debroise, Olivier. "Me quiero morir." In *La era de la discrepancia: Arte y cultura visual en México, 1968–1997*, ed. Olivier Debroise, 276–82. Mexico City: UNAM, 2006.

de Car, Xorje. "Teatro." *Nuevo epoca* 17, December 15, 1968.
de Certeau, Michel. *The Capture of Speech and Other Political Writings*. Translated by Tom Conley. Minneapolis/St. Paul: University of Minnesota Press, 1998.
de Certeau, Michel. *The Practice of Everyday Life*, 3rd ed. Translated by Steven Rendall. Berkeley: University of California Press, 2011.
de la Mora, Sergio. *Cinemachismo: Masculinities and Sexualities in Mexican Film*. Austin: University of Texas Press, 2006.
del Castillo Troncoso, Alberto. *Conceptos, imágenes y representaciones de la niñez en la Ciudad de México, 1880–1920*. Mexico City: El Colegio de México, Instituto Mora, 2006.
del Conde, Teresa. "Carlos Olachea." *Carlos Olachea (1940–1986): Exposición: Homenaje en memoriam*. Escuela Nacional de Artes Plásticas, Mexico City, August 20, 1986.
del Conde, Teresa. "Emilio Ortiz," *Emilio Ortiz: Arte fantástica mexicano: Oleos/pasteles*. Museo de Arte Moderno, Mexico City, July–August 1977.
del Conde, Teresa. "Notas sobre la ruptura." In *Seis décadas: La Esmeralda (1943–2003)*, ed. Lilian Stein, 27–30. Mexico City: 2003.
del Conde, Teresa. "Las pistas de Arturo Rivera." Ciudad Universitaria, 1991, Instituto de Artes Gráficas de Oaxaca Catalog Collection.
del Conde, Teresa. "Richard Rocha: In memoriam." *La jornada*, January 29, 2008, 6A, Sección Cultura.
Delgadillo, Daniel. *Adelante*, libro tercero, 29th ed. Mexico City: Herrero Hermanos, 1942.
Delgadillo, Daniel. *Poco a poco*, libro segundo, 40th ed. Mexico City: Herrero Hermanos, 1943.
Delgadillo, Daniel. *Saber leer*, libro cuarto, 14th ed. Mexico City: Herrero Hermanos, 1942.
de Maria y Campos, Armando. "*Olímpica*, de Héctor Azar, en el Teatro de la Universidad." *Novedades*, December 13, 1964.
Dickstein, Morris. *Dancing in the Dark: A Cultural History of the Great Depression*. New York: Norton, 2010.
Diez va un siglo. Libro conmemorativo de los diez años de la Semana Cultural Lésbica-Gay. Mexico City: Difusión Cultural Universidad Nacional Autónoma de México, Museo Universitario del Chopo, Circulo Cultural Gay, FONCA, 1997.
Driben, Lelia. *La generación de la ruptura y sus antecedentes*. Mexico City: Fondo de Cultura Económica, 2012.
Ebert, Roger. "*Gospel according to St. Matthew*." Review, *Chicago Sun Times*, March 14, 2004.
Eineigel, Susanne. "Distinction, Culture, and Politics in Mexico City's Middle Class, 1890–1940." PhD diss., University of Maryland–College Park, 2011.
Elias, Norbert. "Terrorism in the German Federal Republic: A Social Conflict between Generations." In *The Germans*, ed. Michael Schroter, trans. Eric Dunning, 229–98. New York: Columbia University Press, 1998.
Elizondo, Salvador. "Arturo Rivera." *Arturo Rivera, Exposición: Dibujos, Temperas, y Oleos*, Museo de Arte Moderno, Mexico City, April–May 1982.

Engel, Ilya. "Teatro." *Impacto*, no. 958, July 10, 1968.
Esparza, Manuel. *Eulogio Gillow y el poder (1887–1922).* Oaxaca: Carteles Editores, 2004.
Esperón, Manuel, and Ernesto M. Cortázar. "Yo soy mexicano." In *Gran cancionero: Las canciones que nos hecho amar, llorar y recordar*, vol. 1, 1570. Mexico City: Sanborn Hermanos, 2005.
Esperón, Manuel, and Pedro Urdimalas, "Amorcito corazón." In *Gran cancionero: Las canciones que nos hecho amar, llorar y recordar*, vol. 1, 71. Mexico City: Sanborn Hermanos, 2005.
Estrada, Julio. "Antonio Rodríguez: Liderazgo crítico." In *Antonio Rodríguez: Un humanista sin fronteras*, ed. Heriberto M. Galindo Quiñones, 63–75. Mexico City: Instituto Politécnico Nacional, 2011.
Fein, Seth. "Myths of Cultural Imperialism and Nationalism in Golden Age Mexican Cinema." In *Fragments of a Golden Age: The Politics of Culture in Mexico since 1940*, ed. Gilbert Joseph, Anne Rubenstein, and Eric Zolov, 139–98. Durham, NC: Duke University Press, 2001.
Ferguson, Harvie. *Modernity and Subjectivity: Body, Soul, Spirit.* Charlottesville: University of Virginia Press, 2000.
Fernández, Francisco. "La responsabilidad del diseño en José Zúñiga." *El gallo ilustrado, El Día*, October 13, 1977.
Fernández, Gloria. "Cinco Pintoras Abstractas Mexicanas. Una Mirada Feminista." Museo de Mujeres, A.M., Mexico City, n.d.
Fernández, Justino. *Catálogo de la exposición, Benito Messeguer*, UNAM, Ciudad Universitaria, 1963.
Fernández Aceves, María Teresa, Carmen Ramos Escandón, and Susie Porter, eds. *Orden social e identidad de género: México siglos XIX y XX*. Guadalajara: CIESAS-Universidad de Guadalajara, 2006.
Figueroa, Diego. "Julio Galán yo quiero morir ensayo." *Implosion in the Nothing*, July 15 (no year), http://implosioninthenothing.tumblr.com/post/7661897932/julio-galan-me-quiero-morir-ensayo.
Flores Rivera, Salvador (Chava Flores). *Relatos de mi barrio.* Mexico City: Ageleste, 1994.
Flores y Escalante, Jesús. *Salón México: Historia documental y gráfica del danzón en México.* Mexico City: Asociación Mexicana de Estudios Fonográficos, A.C., 2006.
Ford, Eileen. "Children of the Mexican Miracle: Childhood and Modernity in Mexico City, 1940–1968." PhD diss., University of Illinois, Champaign-Urbana, 2008.
Franco, Jean. *Decline and Fall of the Lettered City.* Cambridge, MA: Harvard University Press, 2002.
Frazier, Lessie Jo, and Deborah Cohen. "Mexico 68: Defining the Space of the Movement, Heroic Masculinity in the Prison, and Women in the Streets." *Hispanic American Historical Review* 83, no. 4 (2003): 617–60.
French, William. *A Peaceful and Working People: Manners, Morals, and Class Formation in Northern Mexico.* Albuquerque: University of New Mexico Press, 1996.
French, William. "Prostitutes and Guardian Angels: Women, Work, and the

Family in Porfirian Chihuahua." *Hispanic American Historical Review* 72, no. 4 (1992): 529–53.
Frerot, Christine. *El mercado del arte en México 1950–1976*. Mexico City: INBA, 1990.
Fromm, Eric. *Art of Loving*. New York: Harper, 1956. Spanish ed., Buenos Aires: Paidós, 1966.
Galindo Quiñones, Heriberto M., ed. *Antonio Rodríguez: Un humanista sin fronteras*. Mexico City: Instituto Politécnico Nacional, 2011.
Galván, Luz Elena. "Un encuentro con los niños a través de sus lecturas en el siglo xix." *Rostros históricos de la educación*, ed. María Esther Aguirre Lora, 221–32. Mexico City: CESU, UNAM–Fondo de Cultura Económica, 2001.
Gamboa, Fernando. *Alfredo Falfán: Lo imaginal: Exposición*. Museo del Palacio de Bellas Artes, Mexico City, February–March 1994.
García, Angélica. "Alejandro Jodorowsky: El teatro fuera del teatro." *Revista Apuntes*, Pontifica Universidad de Chile, n.d., 110–16.
García Canclini, Nestor. *Hybrid Cultures: Strategies for Entering and Leaving Modernity*. Translated by Christopher Chiappari and Silvia López. Minneapolis: University of Minnesota Press, 1995.
García Manzano, Guillermo. *Oaxaca: Espacios culturales*. Oaxaca: Carteles Editores, 2005.
García Martínez, Luz. "Forma y símbolo del arte bizantino." *Universo de el Búho*. www.reneavilesfabila.com.mx/universodeelbuho/76/76-lmartinez.pdf.
García Martínez, Luz. "Guillermo Ceniceros y la fiesta espiritual del arte." *Revista El Búho* 10, no. 109 (July 6, 2009): 123.
Gargallo, Francesca. "Nuestra semana de cada año." In *Diez va un siglo. Libro conmemorativo de los diez años de la Semana Cultural Lésbica-Gay*, 47–50. Mexico City: Difusión Cultural UNAM, Museo Universitario del Chopo, Circulo Cultural Gay, FONCA, 1997.
Gienow-Hecht, Jessica C. E., ed. *Decentering America*. Oxford: Berghahn Books, 2008.
Gilbert, James. *Men in the Middle: Searching for Masculinity in the 1950s*. Chicago: University of Chicago Press, 2005.
Giunta, Andrea. *Avant-garde, Internationalism and Politics: Argentine Art in the 1960s*. Translated by Peter Kahn. Durham, NC: Duke University Press, 2007.
Goldman, Shifra. *Dimensions of the Americas: Art and Social Change in Latin America and the United States*. Chicago: University of Chicago Press, 1994.
Goldman, Shifra. *Pintura mexicana contemporanea en tiempos de cambio*. Mexico City: IPN/Editorial Domes, 1989. Translated as *Contemporary Painting in Mexico in a Time of Change*. Albuquerque: University of New Mexico Press, 1995.
Gómez de León, José, and Cecilia Rabell, eds. *La población de México: Tendencias y perspectivas sociodemográficas hacia el siglo XXI*. Mexico City: CONAPO-Fondo de Cultura Económica, 2001.
González Casanova, Pablo. *Democracy in Mexico*. Translated by Danielle Salti. New York: Oxford University Press, 1970.
González Cosío, Arturo. *Historia estadística de la universidad, 1910–1967*. Mexico City: UNAM, Centro de Investigaciones Sociales, 1968.

González de Alba, Luis. *Los días y los años.* (1970). Mexico City: Planeta, 2008.
González Dueñas, David, ed. *Antologia pánico.* Mexico City: Joaquín Mortiz, 1996.
González Matute, Laura. "La Escuela Nacional de Pintura, Escultura y Grabado La Esmeralda: Su fundación." In *Seis décadas: La Esmeralda (1943–2003)*, ed. Lilian Stein, 13–25. Mexico City: n.p., 2003.
González Pagés, Andrés. *20 obras: Leticia Ocharán.* Villahermosa: Gobierno del Estado de Tabasco, 1980.
González Ramírez, Manuel. "La suave patria en un libro petreo." *El sol de Zacatecas*, June 19, 2007.
González y González, Luis. *Pueblo en vilo: Microhistoria de San José de Gracia.* Mexico City: El Colegio de México, 1968.
Goodman, Paul. *Growing Up Absurd: Problems of Youth in the Organized Society.* New York: Vintage, 1962.
Gran cancionero mexicano: Las canciones que nos han hecho amar, llorar y recordar. 2 vols. Mexico City: Sanborn Hermanos, 2005.
Granados Chaparro, Pavel. *XEW: 70 años en el aire.* Mexico City: Editorial Clio and Sistema Radiopolis, 2000.
Greaves, Cecilia. *Del radicalism a la unidad nacional: Una visión de la educación en el México contemporaneo, 1940–1964.* Mexico City: El Colegio de México, 2008.
Grele, Ron. "Oral History as Evidence." In *History of Oral History: Foundations and Methodology*, ed. Thomas L. Charlton, Lois E. Myers, Rebecca Sharpless, 43–99. Lanham, MD: Altamira Press, 2007.
Grever, María. "Jurame." In *Gran cancionero mexicano: Las canciones que nos han hecho amar, llorar y recordar*, vol. 1, 700. Mexico City: Sanborn Hermanos, 2005.
Gual, Enrique P. "Zúñiga, el futuro." *Excelsior*, March 18, 1969; personal archive of José Zuñiga.
Gudiño Cejudo, María Rosa. "Estado benefactor y ciudadanos obedientes: Guerra de paludismo—Cruzada heróica y erradicación de paludismo en México, tres cortometrajes para una campaña, 1955–1960." In *Ciudadanos inesperados: Espacios de formación de la ciudadanía ayer y hoy*, ed. Ariadna Acevedo Rodrigo and Paula López Caballero, 167–90. Mexico City: El Colegio de México and Centro de Investigación y Estudios Avanzados, 2012.
Guerrero, Julio. *El génesis del crimen: Un estudio de psiquiatria social.* (1901). Mexico City: Conaculta, 1996.
Guevara Niebla, Gilberto. *La democracia en la calle: Crónica del movimiento estudiantil mexicano.* Mexico: Siglo Veinte Editores, 1988.
Guizar, Eduardo. "Crónica musical en México: El caso de Chava Flores." *Studies in Latin American Popular Culture* 23 (2004): 55–69.
Gustafson, Reid. "'He Loves the Little Ones and Doesn't Beat Them': Working-Class Masculinity in Mexico City, 1917–1929." PhD diss., University of Maryland, College Park, 2014.
Guy, Donna J. "The Politics of Pan American Cooperation: Maternalist Feminism and the Child Rights Movement, 1913–60." *Gender and History* 10, no. 3 (1998): 449–69.

Habermas, Jürgen. "Further Reflections on the Public Sphere." In *Habermas and the Public Sphere*, ed. Craig Calhoun, 421–61. Cambridge, MA: MIT Press, 1993.

Habermas, Jürgen. *The Structural Transformation of the Public Sphere: An Inquiry into a Category of Bourgeois Society.* Translated by Thomas Burger. Cambridge: Polity Press, 1992.

Hall, Stuart. *Encoding and Decoding in the Television Discourse.* Birmingham, UK: Centre for Contemporary Cultural Studies, 1973.

Hansen, Miriam Bratu. "Fallen Women, Rising Stars, New Horizons: Shanghai Silent Film as Vernacular Modernism." *Film Quarterly* 54, no. 1 (2000): 10–22.

Hellman, Judith Adler. *Mexico in Crisis.* Philadelphia: Holmes and Meier, 1983.

Hershfield, Joanne. *Imagining the Chica Moderna: Women, Nation, and Visual Culture in Mexico, 1917–1950.* Durham, NC: Duke University Press, 2008.

Hershfield, Joanne. *Mexican Cinema/Mexican Women, 1940–1950.* Tucson: University of Arizona Press, 1996.

Hijar Serrano, Alberto, ed. *Frentes, coaliciones y talleres.* Mexico City: Conaculta INBA, Casa Juan Pablos, Centro Nacional de Investigación, Documentación e Información de Artes Plásticas, 2007.

Hijar Serrano, Alberto. *Leticia Ocharán: Eros y Tánatos—Lo simple y lo complejo.* Mexico City: UNAM, 1986.

Hijar Serrano, Alberto. "¡Muera el arte burgues! México en la Bienal de Paris: Agruparse o Morir." In *La era de la discrepancia*, ed. Olivier Debroise, 216–41. Mexico City: UNAM, 2006.

Hiriart, Hugo. "La revuelta antiautoraría." In *Pensar 68*, ed. Raúl Alvárez Garin, Gilberto Guevara Niebla, Herman Bellinghausen, Hector Aguilar Camín, 17–21. Mexico City: Cal y Arena, 1988.

Imágenes. "Efemérides: Enrique Guzmán (1952–1986)." *Imágenes*, Revista Electrónica del Instituto de Investigaciones Estéticas, November 9, 2006.

Instituto Nacional de Bellas Artes. *Homenaje a Benito Messeguer.* Mexico City: INBA, 1983.

Irwin, Robert McKee, Edward J. McCaughan, and Michelle Rocío Nasser, eds. *The Famous 41: Sexuality and Social Control in Mexico City, c. 1901.* New York: Palgrave Macmillan, 2003.

Jackson Albarran, Elena, "Children of the Revolution: Constructing the Mexican Citizen, 1920–1940." PhD diss., University of Arizona, 2008.

James, Daniel. *Doña María's Story: Life History, Memory, and Political Identity.* Durham, NC: Duke University Press, 2006.

Jameson, Fredric. "Periodizing the 60s." *Social Text* 9/10 (1974): 178–209.

Jardón, Raúl. *El fuego de la esperanza.* Mexico City: Siglo Veintiuno, 1998.

Jiménez, Juan Carlos. "Me quiero morir, Julio Galán." *Alharaca blogs*, February 8, 2011.

Jodorowsky, Alejandro. "Método pánico." In *Antologia pánico*, ed. David González Dueñas. (1966). Mexico City: Joaquín Mortiz, 1996.

Jodorowsky, Alejandro. *Teatro pánico.* Mexico City: Era, 1965.

Jordán de Balmori, Helena, ed. *Reflejo del ritmo: Antología de Santos Balmori.*

Mexico City: Programa Editorial de la Coordinación de Humanidades, 1997.

Joseph, Gilbert, Anne Rubenstein, and Eric Zolov, eds. *Fragments of a Golden Age: The Politics of Culture in Mexico since 1940*. Durham, NC: Duke University Press, 2001.

Kessler Harris, Alice. "Why Biography?" AHR Roundtable, Historians and Biography. *American Historical Review* 134, no. 3 (2009): 625–30.

Kram Villareal, Rachel. "Gladiolas for the Children of Sánchez: Ernesto P. Uruchurtu's Mexico City." PhD diss., University of Arizona, 2008.

Lam, Rafael. "La leyenda de Las Mulatas de Fuego." *Música cubana* (La Habana) (4), 1999; also, Unión de Escritores y Artistas de Cuba, no. 3, n.d. www.uneac.org.cu/index.php?module=publicaciones&act=publicacion_numero&id=36&idarticulo=6.

Lara, Agustín. "Señora Tentación." In *Gran cancionero mexicano: Las canciones que nos han hecho amar, llorar y recordar*, vol. 2, 1321. Mexico City: Sanborn's, 2005.

Lara Chávez, Hugo. *Una ciudad inventada por el cine*. Mexico City: Conaculta/Cineteca Nacional, 2006.

Lara Elizondo, Lupina. "Arturo Rivera (1945–)." In *Visión de México y sus artistas, Siglo XX, 1951–2000*, vol. 2, ed. Lupina Lara Elizondo, 216–19. Mexico City: Qualitas Compañía de Seguros, 2001.

Lara Elizondo, Lupina, ed. *Visión de México y sus artistas, Siglo XX, 1951–2000*, vol. 2. Mexico City: Qualitas Compañía de Seguros, 2001.

Leidenberg, Georg. "Habermas en el Zócalo: la 'transformación de la esfera pública' y la política del transporte público en la ciudad de México, 1900–1947." In *Actores, espacios, y debates en la historia de la esfera pública en México*, eds. Cristina Sacristán and Pablo Piccato, 179–98. Mexico City: Instituto de Investigaciones Históricas–UNAM and Instituto Mora, 2005.

Levi, Heather. "Masked Media: The Adventures of Lucha Libre on the Small Screen." In *Fragments of a Golden Age: The Politics of Culture in Mexico since 1940*, ed. Gilbert Joseph, Anne Rubenstein, and Eric Zolov, 330–72. Durham, NC: Duke University Press, 2001.

Lewis, Oscar. *The Children of Sánchez: Autobiography of a Mexican Family*, 50th anniversary edition. New York, Vintage, 2011. Spanish ed., Mexico City: Fondo de Cultura Económica, 1964.

Librado Luna Cárdenas, Daniel, and Paulina Martínez Figueroa. *La Academia de San Carlos en el movimiento de 1968*. Mexico City: Escuela Nacional de Artes Plásticas, 2008.

Loaeza, Guadalupe, and Pável Granados Chaparro. *Mi novia, la tristeza: El recuento biográfico más completa, informado y original que se haya escrito sobre Agustín Lara*. Mexico City: Oceano, 2009.

Loaeza, Soledad. "Gustavo Díaz Ordaz: El colapso del *Milagro Mexicano*." In *Historia contemporanea de México: Transformaciones y permanencias*, vol. 2, ed. Ilan Bizberg, Lorenzo Meyer, and Francisco Alba, 117–55. Mexico City: Oceano, 2005.

Lomnitz, Claudio. "Ritual, rumor, y corrupción en la conformación de los 'sentimientos de la nación.'" In *Vicios públicos, virtudes privadas: La corrupción en México*, ed. Claudio Lomnitz, 241–74. Mexico City: Centro de Investigaciones y Estudios Avanzados en la Antropología Social and Porrua, 2000.

MacDonald, Dwight. "Masscult and Midcult." In Dwight MacDonald, *Against the American Grain*, 1–75. New York: Da Capo, 1952.

Macías-González, Victor M. "Hombres de mundo: La masculinidad, el consumo, y los manuales de urbanidad y buenas maneras." In *Orden social e identidad de género: México siglos XIX y XX*, ed. María Teresa Fernández Aceves, Carmen Ramos Escandón, and Susie Porter, 267–97. Guadalajara: CIESAS-Universidad de Guadalajara, 2006.

Macías-González, Victor M. "The Lagartijo at the High Life: Masculine Consumption, Race, Nation, and Homosexuality in Porfirian Mexico." In *The Famous 41: Sexuality and Social Control in Mexico City, c. 1901*, ed. Robert McKee Irwin, Edward J. McCaughan, and Michelle Rocío Nasser, 227–50. New York: Palgrave Macmillan, 2003.

Macías-González, Victor M., and Anne Rubenstein, eds. *Masculinity and Sexuality in Modern Mexico*. Albuquerque: University of New Mexico Press, 2012.

MacMasters, Merry. "Pedro Banda retrata la pobreza campesina sin resignaciones: 'Tienen alegría, luchan.'" *La jornada*, May 15, 2007, 5A, Sección Cultural.

Magdaleno, Margarita. "Antonio Rodríguez: Crítico de arquitectura y urbanismo." In *Antonio Rodríguez: Un humanista sin fronteras*, ed. Heriberto M. Galindo Quiñones, 129–56. Mexico City: Instituto Politécnico Nacional, 2011.

Malanich, Nara. "Non-Normative Families, Natal Equality, and Social Citizenship in Twentieth-Century Latin America." Research proposal, September 2010.

Manrique, Daniel. *Tepito Arte Acá: Una propuesta imaginada*. Mexico City: D. R. Grupo Cultural Ente, 1995.

Manrique, Jorge Alberto. "Del espacio gay: Una decáda." In *Diez va un siglo: Libro conmemorativo de los diez años de la Semana Cultura Lésbica-Gay*, 15–16. Mexico City: Difusión Cultural UNAM, Museo Universitario del Chopo, Circulo Cultural Gay, FONCA, 1997.

Marcuse, Herbert. *One-Dimensional Man*. Boston: Beacon Press, 1964.

Margadant, Jo Burr, ed. *The New Biography: Performing Femininity in Nineteenth-Century France*. Berkeley: University of California Press, 2000.

Martínez Espinosa, Ignacio. "José Zúñiga exhibe sus pinturas." *La prensa*, April 27, 1969.

Marwick, Arthur. *The Sixties: Cultural Revolution in Britain, France, Italy and the U.S., 1958–1974*. New York: Oxford University Press, 1998.

McCaughan, Edward. *Art and Social Movements: Cultural Politics in Mexico and Aztlán*. Durham, NC: Duke University Press, 2012.

McCaughan, Edward. "Gender, Sexuality, and Nation in the Art of Mexican Social Movements." *Nepantla: Views from the South* 3, no. 1 (2002): 105–8.

Medina, Cuauhtémoc. "Recovering Panic." In *La era de la discrepancia: Arte y cultura en México, 1968–1997*, ed. Olivier Debroise, 97–111. Mexico City: Universidad Nacional Autonoma, 1996.

Mendoza, Christian. "El neomexicanismo y el arte contemporáneo." *El Blog Hotel Garage*, May 3, 2012. http://hotel-garage.com.mx/blog/2012/05/03/el-neomexicanismo-y-el-arte-contemporaneo/.

Mendoza, María Luisa. "El teatro." *El Día*, July 7, 1968.

Merleau-Ponty, Maurice. *The Structure of Behavior.* Translated by Adela Fisher. Boston: Beacon Press, 1963.

Mills, C. Wright. *The Power Elite.* Oxford: Oxford University Press, 1956.

Mondragón, Sergio. "*El Corno emplumado*: Una revista mexicana de poesia con una vocacíón latinoamericana—una historia de los sesenta." *Alforja* 36 (spring): 2006.

Monroy Nasr, Rebecca. "Antonio Rodríguez: Más de una vida a repensar." *La jornada*, December 4, 2008, Sección Opinión.

Monroy Nasr, Rebecca. "Haz la luz: La mirada de Antonio Rodríguez y el foto-periodismo contemporáneo." *Cuicuilco* 14, no. 41 (2007): 143–67.

Monroy Nasr, Rebecca. "México: En la escritura de luz." In *Antonio Rodríguez: Un humanista sin fronteras*, ed. Heriberto Galindo Quiñones, 176–82. Mexico City: Instituto Politécnico Nacional, 2011.

Monsiváis, Carlos. "Agustín Lara: El harem ilusorio." In *Amor perdido*, 61–86. Mexico City: Era, 1977.

Monsiváis, Carlos. *Aires de familia: Cultura y sociedad en América Latina*. Barcelona: Editorial Anagrama, 2000.

Monsiváis, Carlos. *Amor perdido.* Mexico City: Era, 1977.

Monsiváis, Carlos. *La cultura mexicana en el siglo XX*. Mexico City: El Colegio de México, 2010.

Monsiváis, Carlos. "Dancing: El Salón México." In *Escenas de pudor y liviandad*, 47–52. Mexico City: Delbolsillo, 2004.

Monsiváis, Carlos. "De marzo de 1970: Díos nunca muere." In *Dias de guardar*, 91–114. Mexico City: Ediciones Era, 1970.

Monsiváis, Carlos. *Días de guardar.* Mexico City: Ediciones Era, 1970.

Monsiváis, Carlos. "Diez y va un siglo: A la memoria de Francisco Galván, Marco Osorio y Victor Manuel Parra." In *Diez va un siglo. Libro conmemorativo de los diez años de la Semana Cultural Lésbica-Gay*, 11–13. Mexico City: Difusión Cultural UNAM, Museo Universitario del Chopo, Circulo Cultural Gay, FONCA, 1997.

Monsiváis, Carlos. *Escenas de pudor y liviandad.* (1981). Mexico City: Delbolsillo, 2004.

Monsiváis, Carlos. *Entrada libre. Crónicas de una sociedad que se organiza.* Mexico City: Era, 1987.

Monsiváis, Carlos. "Instituciones: Celia Montalván, 'Te brindas, voluptuosa e impudente.'" In *Escenas de pudor y liviandad*, 23–46. (1981). Mexico City: Delbolsillo, 2004.

Monsiváis, Carlos. "Los días del terremoto." In *Entrada libre: Crónicas de una sociedad que se organiza*, 17–122. Mexico City: Era.

Monsiváis, Carlos. *Pedro Infante: Las leyes del querer.* Mexico City: Aguilar, 2008.

Monsiváis, Carlos. *El 68: La tradición de la resistencia*. Mexico City: Bolsillo Era, 2008.

Monsiváis, Carlos. "South of the Border, Down Mexico's Way: El cine latinoamericano y Hollywood." In *Aires de familia: Cultura y sociedad en América Latina*, 51–78. Barcelona: Editorial Anagrama, 2000.
Moreno Rivas, Yolanda. *Historia de la música popular mexicana*. Mexico City: Alianza/Conaculta, 1979.
Moreno Villareal, Jaime. *Francisco Zúñiga: La tierra sustantiva*. Mexico City: Galeria Guerreo, 2001.
Naremore, James. *More Than Night: Film Noir in Its Contexts*. Berkeley: University of California Press, 2008.
Nasaw, David. "Introduction." AHR Roundtable, Historians and Biography, *American Historical Review* 134, no. 3 (June 2009): 573–78.
Navarrete Cortés, Alejandro. "Symbolic Production in Mexico in the 1980s." In *La era de la discrepancia*, ed. Olivier Debroise, 289–97. Mexico City: UNAM 2006.
Norma, Carmen. *Rosita y Juanito*. 9th ed. Mexico City: Ediciones Aguilas, 1953.
Ocampo, Octavio. *Yo metamórfico*. Mexico City: Fundación Miguel Alemán, 2011.
Ocharán, Leticia. "Del hueco a la superficie pictórica." *Novedades* 194 (June 29, 1984).
Olcott, Jocelyn, Mary Kay Vaughan, and Gabriela Cano, eds. *Sex in Revolution: Gender, Politics, and Power in Modern Mexico*. Durham, NC: Duke University Press, 2006.
Oles, James, and Carlos Molina. *Arte moderna de México: Colección de Andrés Blaisten*. Mexico City: UNAM, 2005.
Overmeyer-Velázquez, Mark. *Visions of the Emerald City*. Durham, NC: Duke University Press, 2006.
Pacheco, José Emilio. *Las batallas en el desierto*. Mexico City: Era, 1981.
Parker, Andrew, Mary Russo, Doris Sommer, and Patricia Yaeger, eds. *Nationalisms and Sexualities*. New York: Routledge, 1992.
Pasolini, P. P. *Teorema*. Translated by Emilio Pezzoni. Barcelona: Piados, 1987.
Paz, Octavio. *Laberinto de la soledad*. Mexico City: Fondo de Cultura Económica, 1950.
Paz, Octavio. *Posdata*. In *Obras completas: El peregrino en su patria—historia y política de México*. Mexico City: Fondo de Cultura Económica, 1993.
Pensado, Jaime. *Rebel Mexico: Student Unrest and Authoritarian Political Culture during the Long 1960s*. Palo Alto, CA: Stanford University Press, 2013.
Pérez, Rafael Alfonso. "Xavier Esqueda." *Xavier Esqueda: Metáforos*. Exposición, Secretaría de Hacienda y Crédito Público, Mexico City, July–October 2005.
Pérez Rosales, Laura. "Trayectora de la pintura en Mexico, 1951–2000." In *Vision de México y sus artistas: Siglo XX, 1951–2000*, vol. 2, ed. Lupina Lara Elizondo, 59–65. Mexico City: Quálias, Compania de Segura, n.d.
Pernet, Corinne. "'For the Genuine Culture of the Americas': Musical Folklore, Popular Arts, and the Cultural Politics of Pan Americanism, 1933–1950." In *Decentering America*, ed. Jessica C. E. Gienow-Hecht, 132–68. Oxford: Berghahn Books, 2008.

Piccato, Pablo. *City of Suspects: Crime in Mexico City, 1900–1931*. Durham, NC: Duke University Press, 2000.
Piccato, Pablo. "Honor y opinión pública en la ciudad de México, 1900–1947." In *Actores, espacios, y debates en la historia de la esfera pública en México*, ed. Cristina Sacristán and Pablo Piccato, 145–78. Mexico City: Instituto de Investigaciones Históricas-UNAM and Instituto Mora, 2005.
Piccato, Pablo. "Murders of *Nota roja*," *Past and Present*, forthcoming.
Piccato, Pablo. *The Tyranny of Opinion: Honor in the Construction of the Mexican Public Sphere*. Durham, NC: Duke University Press, 2010.
Poniatowska, Elena. *La noche de Tlatelolco*. Mexico City: Era, 1999.
Poole, Deborah. "An Image of 'Our Indian': Type Photographs and Racial Sentiments in Oaxaca (1920–1940)." *Hispanic American Historical Review* 84, no. 1 (2004): 37–82.
Portelli, Alessandro. *The Death of Luigi Trastulli and Other Stories: Form and Meaning in Oral History*. Albany: SUNY Press, 1990.
Portilla, Jorge. *Fenomenologia del relajo*. Mexico City: Fondo de Cultura Económica, 1966.
Pozas Horcasitas, Ricardo, ed. *Universidad nacional y sociedad*. Mexico City: UNAM, Centro de Investigaciones Interdisciplinarias en Humanidades y Miguel Ángel Porrúa, 1990.
Pulido Esteva, Diego. "El 'cantinismo': Culturas del alcohol en la Ciudad de México a principios del siglo XX." Coloquio internacional "Historia de género y de las mujeres en México," Colegio de México, Mexico City, 13–15, 2013.
Quilodrán Salgado, Julieta. *Un siglo de matrimonio en México*. Translated by Carolina Aguirre Quilodrán and Isabel Estèvez Denaives. Mexico City: El Colegio de México, Centro de Estudios Demográficos y de Desarrollo Urbano, 2001.
Rabell, Malkah. "La pasión en un cementerio de automóviles." *El Día*, May 22, 1968.
Ramírez, Ramón. *El movimiento estudiantil de México*. 2 vols. (1969). Mexico City: Era and Benemérita Universidad Autónoma de Puebla, 2008.
Ramírez Vázquez, Pedro. *El Museo Nacional de Antropología: Arte, arquitectura, arqueología, etnografía*. Introduction by Ignacio Bernal, 40–43. Mexico City: Tlaloc, 1968.
Ramos, Samuel. *El Perfil del hombre y la cultura en México*. (1934). Mexico City: Austral, 1965.
Randall, Margaret. "Asi nació el Corno." *Alforja* 36 (spring): 2006.
Rath, Thomas. *Myths of Demilitarization in Postrevolutionary Mexico*. Chapel Hill: University of North Carolina Press, 2013.
Read, Herbert. *Cartas a un joven pintor*. Buenos Aires: Ediciones Siglo Veinte, 1964.
Restrepo, Ivan. "Antonio Rodríguez: Maestro de su tiempo." In *Antonio Rodríguez: Un humanista sin fronteras*, ed. Heriberto Galindo Quiñones, 203–8. Mexico City: IPN, Instituto Politécnico Nacional, 2011.
Revueltas, José. *México 1968: Juventud y revolución*. Mexico City: Ediciones Era, 1978.
Reyes, Mara. "El cementerio de automóviles." *Excelsior*, May 26, 1968.

Reynoso López, Guillermo. "La Guerrero: Colonia Aguerrida." Unpublished manuscript, study undertaken for Father Abel Fernández Valencia, Parish of the Immaculate Heart of Mary. Mexico City, 1995.

Riesman, David, Nathan Glazer, and Reuel Denney. *The Lonely Crowd: A Study of the Changing American Character.* (1950). New Haven, CT: Yale University Press, 2001.

Robles, Sonia. "Shaping Mexico Lindo: Radio, Music and Gender in Greater Mexico, 1923–1946." PhD diss., Michigan State University, 2012.

Rodman, Seldon. *The Insiders: Rejection and Rediscovery of Man in the Arts of Our Time.* Baton Rouge: Louisiana University Press, 1960.

Rodríguez, Antonio. "Abró nuevas rutas en el arte mural." *Homenaje a Benito Messeguer*, Museo del Palacio de Bellas Artes, Mexico City, September–November 1983.

Rodríguez, Antonio. "Francia hoy: Revisión total en la ciudad de la luz." *Siempre!* 780 (June 5, 1968): 19, 70.

Rodríguez, Antonio. *A History of Mexican Muralism.* Translated by Marina Corby. New York: Putnam, 1969.

Rodríguez, Antonio. "José Zúñiga: Pintor de la dualidad armónica." *Excelsior*, November 24, 1984, 5.

Rodríguez, Antonio. "José Zúñiga y el juego de las antinomias." *Exposición José Zúñiga: El juego de las antinomias*, Galería Estela Shapiro, Mexico City, 1979. Personal archive of José "Pepe" Zúñiga.

Rodríguez, Antonio. "La pintura mural en su función de arte público." *Exposición Homenaje Benito Messeguer*, Obra Plástica, Galeria Metropolitana October 23–November 9, 1984.

Rodríguez, Antonio. "Presentación." Catalog, *Exposición de Pintores Jovenes de la Escuela Nacional de Pintura la Esmeralda*, Instituto Politécnico Nacional, Mexico City, March 1966. Personal archive of José "Pepe" Zúñiga.

Rodríguez, Antonio. "Presentación." *Exposición de José Zúñiga*, Galeria Chapultepec, February–April 1969. Personal archive of José "Pepe" Zúñiga.

Rodríguez, Antonio. "El refinamiento y la emotividad de José Zúñiga." Exposición, *Dos Decadas 1964–1984*, Instituto Francés de América Latina, November 14–30, 1984.

Rodríguez, Antonio. "El Sol Negro en la Obra de Zúñiga." *Excelsior*, November 12, 1980. Personal archive of José "Pepe" Zúñiga.

Rodríguez, Antonio. "Zúñiga." *Exposición de José Zúñiga: Imagen y Presencia.* Galería Estela Shapiro, Mexico City, 1983. Personal archive of José "Pepe" Zúñiga.

Rodríguez Kuri, Ariel. "Hacia Mexico 68: Pedro Ramírez Vázquez y el proyecto olímpico." *Secuencia* 56 (2003): 37–73.

Roper, Michael. "Slipping out of View: Subjectivity and Emotion in Gender History." *History Workshop Journal* 59 (spring 2005): 57–72.

Roumagnac, Carlos. *Los criminales en México.* Mexico City: Librería de la Viuda de Ch. Bouret, 1908.

Rozental, Sandra. "Mobilizing the Monolith: Patrimonio and the Production of Mexico through its Fragments." PhD diss., New York University, 2012.

Rubenstein, Anne. *Bad Language, Naked Ladies, and Other Threats to the*

Nation: A Political History of Comic Books in Mexico. Durham, NC: Duke University Press, 1998.
Rubenstein, Anne. "Bodies, Cities, Cinema: Pedro Infante's Death as Political Spectacle." In *Fragments of a Golden Age*, ed. Gilbert Joseph, Anne Rubenstein, and Eric Zolov, 199–233. Durham, NC: Duke University Press, 2001.
Rubenstein, Anne. "Theaters of Masculinity." In *Masculinity and Sexuality in Modern Mexico*, ed. Victor M. Macías González and Anne Rubenstein, 132–56. Albuquerque: University of New Mexico Press, 2012.
Rubli, Federico. *Estremécete y rueda: Loco por el rock & roll*. Mexico City: Chapa Ediciones, 2007.
Sacristán, Cristina, and Pablo Piccato, eds. *Actores, espacios, y debates en la historia de la esfera pública en México*. Mexico City: Instituto de Investigaciones Históricas-UNAM and Instituto Mora, 2005.
Sainz, Gustavo. *Compadre lobo*. Mexico City: Grijalbo, 1977.
Samperio, Guillermo. "Las cosas de Maciel." *Las cosas de los niños*, Exposición de Leonel Maciel, Polyforum Siqueiros, Mexico City, ca. 1981.
Sánchez, Alberto Ruy. "Irma Grizá y sus paisajes desdoblados." Review. Website of Irma Grizá, 1990, www.irmagriza.com/pages/reviews.htm#.
Sánchez, Oswaldo. "El cuepro de la nación: El neomexicano—la pulsión homosexual y la desnacionalización." *Curaré* 17 (January–June 2000): 138–39.
Sánchez Calleja, María Eugenia, and Delia Salazar Anaya, eds. *Los niños: Su imagen en la historia*. Mexico City: INAH, 2006.
Sánchez Puig, María de Lourdes. "La osadía Jodorowsky: Los primeros happenings latinoamericanos." Joint BA thesis in art history and communication, Universidad Iberoamericana, 1996.
Sanders, Nichole. *Gender and Welfare in México: The Consolidation of the Postrevolutionary State*. College Station: Pennsylvania State University Press, 2011.
Scardaville, Michael. "Alcohol Abuse and Tavern Reform in Late Colonial Mexico City." *Hispanic American Historical Review* 60, no. 4 (1980): 643–71.
Schwartz, Barth David. *Pasolini Requiem*. New York: Pantheon 1992.
Sedgwick, Eve Kosofsky, and Adam Frank. *Touching Feeling: Affect, Pedagogy, and Performativity*. Durham, NC: Duke University Press, 2003.
Sedgwick, Eve Kosofsky, and Adam Frank. *Shame and Its Sisters: The Silvan Thomas Reader*. Durham, NC: Duke University Press, 1995.
Silverberg, Robert. *Lost Cities and Vanished Civilizations*. Philadelphia: Chilton, 1962.
Sluis, Ageeth. "City of Spectacles: Gender Performance, Revolutionary Reform, and the Creation of Public Space in Mexico City, 1915–1939." PhD diss., University of Arizona, 2005.
Smoodin, Eric, ed. *Disney Discourse: Producing the Magic Kingdom*. New York: Routledge, 1994.
Soldatenko, Michael. "Mexico '68: Power to the Imagination!" *Latin American Perspectives* 32, no. 4 (2005): 111–32.
Soler, Gabilondo. *Cri-Cri: Canciones Completas*. Prologue by José de la Colina. Mexico City: Colección Los Trovadores, Ibcon, 1999.
Solís, Luis Martín. *Teatro para títeres*. Mexico City: El Milagro, 2004.

Sosenski, Susana. "Diversiones malsanas: El cine y la infancia en la Ciudad de México en la década de 1920." *Secuencia: Revista de historia y ciencias sociales* 66 (September–December 2006): 35–64.

Sosenski, Susana. "El niño consumidor: Una construcción publicitaria de la prensa mexicana en la década de 1950." In *Ciudadanos inesperados: Espacios de formación de la ciudadanía ayer y hoy*, ed. Aridana Acevedo Rodrigo and Paula López Caballero, 191–222. Mexico City: El Colegio de México and Centro de Investigación y Estudios Avanzados, 2012.

Sosenski, Susana. *Niños en acción: El trabajo infantil en la ciudad de México, 1920–1934*. Mexico City: El Colegio de México, 2010.

Spiegel, Gabrielle M. "Comment on a Crooked Line." *American Historical Review* 113, no. 2 (2008): 400–416.

Stein, Lilian, ed. *Seis décadas: La Esmeralda (1943–2003)*. Mexico City: n.p., 2003.

Stern, Alexandra Minna. "Responsible Mothers and Normal Children: Eugenics, Nationalism, and Welfare in Post-revolutionary Mexico." *Journal of Historical Sociology* 12, no. 4 (1999): 369–97.

Suri, Jeremi. "The Rise and Fall of an International Counterculture, 1960–1973." AHR Forum, *American Historical Review* 114, no. 1 (2009): 45–68.

Taibo, Paco Ignacio, II. *'68*. Translated by Donald Nicholson Smith. New York: Seven Stories Press, 2004.

Tamayo, Rufino. "Los colores de Alfredo Falfán." *Alfredo Falán: Lo imaginal*. Museo del Palacio de Bellas Artes, Mexico City, February–March, 1994.

Taracena, Berta. "José Francisco." *Exposición, Entre el dolor y la fiesta*, Palacio de Bellas Artes, Mexico City, 1991.

Therborn, Goran. *Between Sex and Power: Family in the World, 1900–2000*. New York: Routledge, 2004.

Thompson, Lanny. "Households and the Reproduction of Labor in Mexico, 1876–1970." PhD diss., State University of New York at Binghamton, 1989.

Tibol, Raquel. *Confrontaciones: Crónica y recuento*. Mexico City: Ediciones Samara, 1992.

Tibol, Raquel. "Introducción." In Shifra Goldman, *Pintura mexicana contemporánea en tiempos de cambio*. Mexico City: Instituto Politécnico Nacional/Editorial Domes, 1989, i–xxiii.

Tierra Adentro. "Días de radio." (December 2005–March 2006): 137–38.

Torres Bodet, Jaime. "Discurso del Dr. Jaime Torres Bodet, Secretario de Educación Pública." *Política*, October 1, 1964, 8.

Tsaseva, Jritsina, Radio Bulgaria, "Ester González: Una pintora mejicana cuativada por la iconografía eslava." Asociación de Periodistas Hispanohablantes en Bulgaria, n.d.

Tuñón, Julia. "La ciudad actriz: La imagen urbana en el cine mexicano (1940–1955)." *Historias* 27 (October 1991–March 1992): 189–97.

Tuñón, Julia. *Mujeres de luz y sombra en el cine mexicano: La construcción de una imagen, 1939–1952*. Mexico City: El Colegio de Mexico, Instituto Mexicano de Cinematografía, 1998.

Unger, Roni. *Poesia en Voz Alta in the Theater of Mexico*. Columbia: University of Missouri Press, 1981.

Valero Meré, José Luis. *100 años de Lucha Libre en México*. Mexico City: Anaya, 1978.
Vallarino, Roberto. "Byron Gálvez: Una obra que nos permite recuperar lo sagrado." *Byron Gálvez, obra pictórica: Semblanza de treinte años*. Museo de Palacio de Bellas Artes, Conaculta, INBA, Mexico City, March 6–May 10, 1996.
Vaughan, Mary Kay. *Cultural Politics in Revolution: Teachers, Peasants, and Schools in Mexico, 1930–1940*. Tucson: University of Arizona Press, 1997.
Vaughan, Mary Kay. "The Mexican Revolution and the Modernization of Patriarchy in the Countryside, 1930–1940." In *Hidden Histories of Gender and the State in Latin America*, ed. Elizabeth Dore and Maxine Molyneux, 194–214. Durham, NC: Duke University Press, 2000.
Vaughan, Mary Kay. "Primary Schools in the City of Puebla, 1820–60." *Hispanic American Historical Review* 67, no. 1 (1987): 39–46.
Vaughan, Mary Kay, and Stephen E. Lewis, eds. *The Virgin and the Eagle: Cultural Revolution in Mexico (1920–1940)*. Durham, NC: Duke University Press, 2006.
Vázquez, Josefina. *Nacionalismo y educación en México*. Mexico City: El Colegio de México, 1970.
Vázquez Mantecón, Alváro. "Los Grupos: Una reconsideración." In *La era de la discrepancia*, ed. Olivier Debroise, 194–99. Mexico City: UNAM, 2006.
Velázquez Jiménez, Javier. "Divinas palabras, entrevista con Juan Ibañez, November 2002." *El nacional*, February 19, 26, 1988. www.elpasajero.com/divinas02.html.
Voekel, Pamela. "Peeing on the Palace: Bodily Resistance to Bourbon Reforms in Mexico." *Journal of Historical Sociology* 5, no. 2 (1992): 183–208.
Volpi, Jorge. *La imaginación y el poder: Una historia intelectual de 1968*. Mexico City: Ediciones Era, 1998.
Wright Rios, Edward. *Revolutions in Catholicism: Reform and Revolution in Catholicism, 1887–1934*. Durham, NC: Duke University Press, 2009.
Zabludovsky, Jacobo. "De Fando y Lis, a Fango y Chis." *La cultura en México, Siempre!* 809 (December 25, 1968): 43, 70.
Zavala, Adriana. *Becoming Modern, Becoming Tradition: Women, Gender, and Representation in Mexican Art*. College Station: Pennsylvania State University Press, 2011.
Zavala, Adriana. "María Izquierdo." In *The Eagle and the Virgin: Nation and Cultural Revolution in Mexico, 1920–1940*, ed. Mary Kay Vaughan and Stephen E. Lewis, 67–78. Durham, NC: Duke University Press, 2006.
Zolov, Eric. "Discovering a Land—Mysterious and Obvious: The Renarrativizing of Post-revolutionary Mexico." In *Fragments of a Golden Age*, ed. Gilbert Joseph, Anne Rubenstein, and Eric Zolov, 234–72. Durham, NC: Duke University Press, 2001.
Zolov, Eric. "Expanding Our Conceptual Horizons: The Shift from an Old to a New Left in Latin America." *Contracorriente* 5, no. 2 (2008): 47–73.
Zolov, Eric. *Refried Elvis: The Rise of the Mexican Counterculture*. Berkeley: University of California Press, 1999.

Zolov, Eric. "Showcasing the 'Land of Tomorrow': Mexico and the 1968 Olympics." *Americas* 61, no. 2 (October 2004): 159–88.

Zúñiga, Francisco. "Notas autobiográficos de Francisco Zúñiga." In *Zúñiga*, introduction by Ali Chumacero. Mexico City: Galería de Arte Misrachi, 1969.

Zúñiga, José. "Entrevista con Benito Messeguer." August 5, 1981 (recorded and transcribed). Archive of José "Pepe" Zúñiga.

Index

www.ingramcontent.com/pod-product-compliance
Lightning Source LLC
LaVergne TN
LVHW020506100826
845148LV00003B/707

* 9 7 8 0 8 2 2 3 5 7 8 1 0 *